Medieval Women and War

Material Culture and the Medieval World

Series Editors:
Emma Cayley, University of Leeds, UK
Chris Briggs, University of Cambridge, UK

About the Series
This new academic series provides a medium for interdisciplinary medieval history with a strong emphasis on material culture – the physical evidence of a culture in the form of the objects it makes, from art and the built environment to items concerned with everyday life.

The study of the things people make and the ways those things inhabit and act upon the world brings new depth to existing historical narratives. Using methodologies borrowed from archaeology, art history, literary studies and anthropology, the study of material culture can provide information about aspects of social and cultural relations for which documents provide little evidence. While historians of the early Middle Ages have long used material remains to learn about the period, material culture's influence on the high and late Middle Ages is a more recent phenomenon.

This series supplements student-oriented handbooks on material culture by providing the space for sustained treatment of aspects of the Middle Ages in which material culture contributes to more nuanced interpretation. It acts as a beacon for new researchers and the best new scholarship.

New and Forthcoming:
Medieval Women and War, Sophie Harwood (2020)

Medieval Women and War

Female Roles in the Old French Tradition

Sophie Harwood

BLOOMSBURY ACADEMIC
LONDON • NEW YORK • OXFORD • NEW DELHI • SYDNEY

BLOOMSBURY ACADEMIC
Bloomsbury Publishing Plc
50 Bedford Square, London, WC1B 3DP, UK
1385 Broadway, New York, NY 10018, USA
29 Earlsfort Terrace, Dublin 2, Ireland

BLOOMSBURY, BLOOMSBURY ACADEMIC and the Diana logo are trademarks of Bloomsbury Publishing Plc

First published in Great Britain 2020
This paperback edition published in 2022

Copyright © Sophie Harwood 2020

Sophie Harwood has asserted her right under the Copyright, Designs and Patents Act, 1988, to be identified as Author of this work.

Cover images: Medieval Diamonds (© Picturenow / Universal Images Group via Getty Images), Women removing Hector's armour (1480) (© Bibliothèque nationale de France)

All rights reserved. No part of this publication may be reproduced or transmitted in any form or by any means, electronic or mechanical, including photocopying, recording, or any information storage or retrieval system, without prior permission in writing from the publishers.

Bloomsbury Publishing Plc does not have any control over, or responsibility for, any third-party websites referred to or in this book. All internet addresses given in this book were correct at the time of going to press. The author and publisher regret any inconvenience caused if addresses have changed or sites have ceased to exist, but can accept no responsibility for any such changes.

A catalogue record for this book is available from the British Library.

A catalog record for this book is available from the Library of Congress.

Library of Congress Control Number: 2020941022

ISBN: HB: 978-1-7883-1519-7
PB: 978-1-3501-9926-2
ePDF: 978-1-3501-5042-3
eBook: 978-1-3501-5040-9

Series: Material Culture and the Medieval World

Typeset by Integra Software Services Pvt. Ltd.

To find out more about our authors and books visit www.bloomsbury.com and sign up for our newsletters.

For Nina, Clare and Rio

Contents

List of figures	viii
List of tables	x
Acknowledgements	xi
Notes on the text	xiii
Abbreviations and sigils	xiv
Introduction	1
1 Reading texts through the manuscript tradition, 1150–1400	7
2 Women as reasons for war	23
3 Women as victims of war	39
4 Women as ancillaries in war	77
5 Women as warriors in war	93
6 Women as diplomats in war	119
Conclusion	141
Appendix 1: Catalogue of manuscripts	144
Appendix 2: Manuscript illustrations of women	155
Notes	164
Bibliography	192
Index	212

Figures

1	Abduction of Hesione	58
2	Abduction of Helen	58
3	Abduction of Helen	58
4	Abduction of Helen	59
5	Combat of Aeneas and Turnus as Lavine watches from a tower	59
6	Women watch a battle from Troy's walls	60
7	Diomedes and Briseide	60
8	Briseide gives her sleeve to Diomedes	61
9	Diomedes and Briseide	61
10	Mourning for Hector on the anniversary of his death	62
11	Hecuba, Andromache, Helen, Cassandra, Polyxena, other women and Trojan men mourn over Hector's dead body	62
12	Hecuba, Polyxena and Helen mourn at the anniversary of Hector's death	63
13	Execution of Polyxena and Hecuba	63
14	Sack of Troy and execution of Priam | Women given away, execution of Polyxena and execution of Hecuba	64
15	Trojan women and other treasures of Troy ready for distribution to the Greeks	65
16	Women and Master Goz gather around Hector's bedside	65
17	Briseide cares for Diomedes	66
18	Visit of the Trojan men to the Trojan women	66
19	Women remove Hector's armour | Women and Priam at the bedside of Hector	67
20	Aeneas and Evander | Venus gives armour to Aeneas's messenger	67
21	Polyxena, Helen, Hecuba and other women care for Troilus and remove his armour and weapons	68
22	Troilus's armour is removed by Trojan women	68
23	Penthesilea and the Amazons in battle	69
24	Paris greets Penthesilea upon her arrival in Troy	69
25	Penthesilea and the Amazons in battle	70
26	The Greeks throw Penthesilea's body into the River Scamander	70
27	Achilles drags the body of Troilus behind his horse | Ajax and Paris kill each other | Pyrrhus kills Penthesilea	71

28	Burning of Troy | Penthesilea's body is thrown into the river	72
29	Philemenis follows Penthesilea's (unseen) funeral cortège	72
30	Cassandra, Hecuba, Andromache and Polyxena	73
31	Cassandra mourns Cassibelan and makes her prophecies	73
32	Cassandra makes her prophecies to Priam	74
33	Andromache pleads with Hector	74
34	Andromache pleads with Hector	75
35	Andromache pleads with Hector	75
36	Hecuba plots Achilles's death with Paris	76
37	Hecuba and Priam speak about Polyxena and Achilles	76
38	Hecuba speaks with Achilles's messenger	76

Tables

1 Manuscripts of the *romans d'antiquité*   11
2 Owners and readers of the *romans* manuscripts   16

Acknowledgements

My greatest debt of gratitude is owed to Rosalind Brown-Grant and Alan V. Murray at the University of Leeds, who first supported, guided and encouraged me along this *chemin de longue étude* when I was a doctoral researcher at the Institute for Medieval Studies. Their insights, ideas, vision, patience and sense of humour made my time working with them an absolute privilege. I would also like to thank the anonymous readers for Bloomsbury Publishing, who offered just the right balance of validation and constructive criticism during the various stages of this project. And I wish to express my gratitude to Olivia Dellow, Joanna Godfrey, Anna Henderson, Rhodri Mogford and Laura Reeves at Bloomsbury for their belief in the topic and for providing the practical assistance needed to turn my ideas from a proposal into a book.

A lot of this work is based on research that I was able to undertake thanks to the financial support of a University of Leeds 110 Anniversary Scholarship. I must also thank the University of Leeds' Department of History, *Medium Ævum* and the Royal Historical Society for funding thoroughly enjoyable and productive research trips to Milan, Venice, Vatican City, London, Paris and Nottingham. Thank you as well to the staff at the British Library, Bibliothèque nationale de France, Biblioteca Nazionale Marciana and Österreichische Nationalbibliothek for going out of their way to obtain high-resolution reproductions and grant the publication rights for many of the illustrations included in this book, and for doing so at minimal (or no) cost in the interests of research and the sharing of ideas and knowledge. Images from other locations did come with some quite hefty price tags attached, and their publication and inclusion in this work was only made possible thanks to a generous award from the Scouloudi Foundation in association with the Institute of Historical Research, for which I am very grateful. I also thank Rosalind Brown-Grant and Jeff Rider for writing the statements of recommendation that supported my application to the foundation and for many other letters that they have written in support of my work over the years.

While I have been working on this book, it has been my honour to belong to a number of academic communities that have nurtured and motivated me throughout the years. Thank you to Jane Gilbert, John Gillingham, Susan Reynolds, Alexandra Sapoznik and Alice Taylor, whom I met when I was a postgraduate in London and encouraged my passion for the Middle Ages from the start. The Institute for Medieval Studies at the University of Leeds has a special place in my heart and I am particularly grateful to a kinship of women that I met within its walls and who provided support in all the forms of that word: Natalie Anderson, Sara Barker, Isabella Bolognese, Emma Chippendale, Kirsty Day, Joanna Phillips, Eleanor Warren and Vanessa Wright. I would also like to thank the numerous scholars that I met at conferences, seminars and on Twitter, who provided positivity and energy when it was most needed, particularly Kristin Bourassa, Erika Graham-Goering, Hetta Howes, Roberta Magnani, Amy Louise

Morgan, Simon Parsons and Sally Spong, as well as my fellow committee members of the Medieval Culture and War Conference, Inês Meira Araújo, Eric Bousmar, António Martins Costa, Michael Depreter, Trevor Russell Smith, Iason-Eleftherios Tzouriadis and Quentin Verreycken.

There are many others in the academic world who have helped me: I should like to mention Matthew Bennett and Katherine Weikert for sending me an advance copy of their book on medieval hostageship, George A. Kennedy for gifting me his book on the Latin *Iliad*, Elizabeth Morrison and Anne D. Hedeman for several long email exchanges about art history and manuscript illustrations, and Catherine Hanley not only for sending me an advanced preview of her book on Empress Matilda but also for pioneering so much of the work upon which much my own relies. In addition, my passion for medieval studies is constantly kept aflame thanks to the enthusiasm and liveliness of the students that it has been my pleasure to teach at the University of Leeds, University of York and Humboldt-Universität zu Berlin, and I thank them for keeping me both buoyant and grounded.

Last but not least, a special thank you to my friends and family for taking such an interest in my work and being my constant cheerleaders, to my husband for making me endless cups of much-needed tea, and to my faithful hound, Freddie, for reminding me of the importance of daily walks and treats over all else.

Notes on the text

Editions

Quotations from *Thèbes* come from *Le Roman de Thèbes*, ed. by Léopold Constans, 2 vols (Paris: Firmin Didot, 1890). Quotations from *Troie* come from Benoît de Sainte-Maure, *Le Roman de Troie*, ed. by Léopold Constans, 6 vols (Paris: Société des Anciens Textes Français, 1904–12). Quotations from *Enéas* come from *Le Roman d'Enéas*, ed. by J. J. Salverda de Grave, 2 vols (Paris: CFMA, 1925–29).

Translations

All translations of Old French and modern European languages are mine unless otherwise indicated.

Spellings

Anglicized forms of spellings for people, places and characters are used except in cases where the French form is in common usage. For example, Eleanor of Aquitaine (not Aliénor d'Aquitaine) and Helen (not Hélène), but Marie de France (not Mary of France) and Camille (not Camilla). Adjectives or possessives are used where necessary to differentiate the Old French characters from their classical counterparts, for example, 'Benoît's Cassandra' and 'the classical Cassandra,' or 'the Old French Camille' and 'Virgil's Camille.'

Abbreviations and sigils

Abbreviations

BAV   Biblioteca Apostolica Vaticana
BL   British Library
BnF   Bibliothèque nationale de France
fr.   français
ÖN   Österreichische Nationalbibliothek

Sigils

Manuscripts that contain at least one of the *romans d'antiquité* are referred to using sigils. The sigils are of my own designation and are assigned based on the first letter of the location in which the manuscript is found (e.g. P for Paris) followed by a number (if there is more than one manuscript in this location, e.g. the manuscript located in Geneva is the only one and is therefore identified as 'G', not 'G1'). The number is determined by the dating of the manuscript (e.g. P1 is the oldest Paris manuscript and P19 the latest). The full shelfmarks and their sigils are detailed in Appendix 1 (arranged by sigil) and in the bibliography (arranged by shelfmark).

Introduction

Heather J. Tanner's edited collection on medieval women presents a powerful perspective on how elite women exercised power in the Middle Ages. It convincingly demonstrates that women in positions of authority were not 'exceptional' in the sense of being unusual or breaking from the norm but that the opposite was true: powerful women were established, accepted and even customary.

> General scholarly acceptance of the quotidian nature of elite women's power is arguably the last hurdle to clear for those seeking to understand not only medieval elite women, but also the operation of medieval power structures as a whole. The underlying objective of the 'Beyond Exceptionalism' movement is the acceptance of female public agency, authority, and power as a 'non-story' in medieval society, without losing sight of the predominance of patriarchy and accepted misogyny.[1]

This theory is one that inspired this book. Traditional medieval scholarship has frequently looked upon women's participation in warfare as something either absent or 'exceptional'. Women's roles in warfare have often been overlooked so that even when their contributions, participation or achievements are there in the sources, they are excluded from the scholarship in favour of focusing on their male counterparts. In the most recent translation of one of this book's key texts, the *Roman de Troie*, the epigraph simply reads – '[t]hese men shine darkly' – suggesting that we are about to embark on an epic of purely male proportions.[2] But the *Roman de Troie*, as we will see, is one of the richest texts we have in the Old French tradition for studying the role of women in warfare. Its women shine brightly, sometimes literally in fact when we look at illuminated manuscript illustrations. If we wish to understand the operation of medieval power structures of war as a whole, then we need to look at the women.

Due in large part to the influential work of Georges Duby, the structure of medieval society was seen for many decades through the paradigm of three estates – knights, clerics and labourers – those who fight, those who pray and those who work.[3] This theory of societal structure is now considered to be 'problematic' at best, not least because women did not fit into this paradigm and were therefore almost entirely absent or marginalized;[4] Duby even defined the entire period of the Middle Ages as 'resolutely male'.[5] But as scholars such as Theodore Evergates and Amy Livingstone show, this analysis bears no weight and represents only 'the musings of a historian whose Middle Ages did not easily accommodate women'.[6] The Middle Ages that subsequent scholars have been exploring recently confirm that medieval women did play an active role in medieval society, including when it came to war: they fought; they occupied ancillary and political roles; they managed family life and responsibilities when their male kin were absent on campaigns or if armies passed through their towns and villages. Conflicts were frequent in the Middle Ages, from large-scale wars and invasions between nations, to armed pilgrimages and religious campaigns such as the crusades, to civil wars or local feuds and revolts. Such frequent and brutal activities left their traces on its society in the historical record, the archaeological record, and the cultural and literary record. It is within this latter record, specifically the cultural and literary works of the Old French tradition, that this study makes its investigation.

The Old French tradition encompasses an enormous array of texts, narratives, genres and media. French was the most prevalent vernacular literature in medieval Europe from around 1100–1400 and its corpus is vast. From *c.* 1100 (and probably earlier) texts including hagiography, political treatises, *chansons de geste*, romances, *lais*, chronicles, *fabliaux* and allegorical works begin appearing and by the mid-twelfth century the rate of literary activity is notably high. It was Jean Bodel, a late twelfth-century poet writing in Old French, who was the first to identify three distinct themes and literary cycles prevalent in this tradition: 'de France et de Bretaigne et de Rome la grant' (*of France, of Britain and of the Great Rome*).[7] In other words, these categories divide the texts into tales of Charlemagne and his retinue, stories of Arthur and his knights, or narratives from classical antiquity. Within this tradition, descriptions and depictions of conflict in all its many guises can be found: battles, sieges, crusades, invasions, single combat, feuds and tournaments permeate the texts of manuscripts and are rendered as miniatures, paintings and tapestries. It would be impossible for this book to consider the entirety of the Old French tradition within its pages, and so the principal corpus focuses on three key works: the anonymous *Roman de Thèbes* (*c.* 1150–55), the anonymous *Roman d'Enéas* (*c.* 1156), and Benoît de Sainte-Maure's *Roman de Troie* (*c.* 1160–65). These texts are known as the *romans d'antiquité* ('Romances of Antiquity') and henceforth will be collectively referred to as 'the *romans*'. References are made to other works from the Old French tradition where necessary or helpful, but the *romans* have been chosen as the core corpus because they were well-known texts during the Middle Ages and because they provide a particularly rich, complex and exhaustive portrait of warfare. It is a warfare that is recognizable as representative of a medieval style of conflict rather than a classical version.[8]

The *romans* are relatively underused as a source for studying war in medieval literature, despite the fact that they are frequently characterized as warfare narratives.[9] This is likely for the practical reason that *Troie*, by far the longest of the three texts at 30,000 lines (while the other two are around 10,000 lines each), is not available in an especially accessible edition: Léopold Constans's complete six-volume edition is over a hundred years old and only found in a few dozen libraries worldwide; Emmanuèle Baumgartner and Françoise Vielliard's more recent paperback edition contains only selections and omits roughly 60 per cent of the text including over half of the battle scenes; the publication of Glyn S. Burgess and Douglas Kelly's translation of the complete text into English last year is certainly valuable and useful for introducing and opening up the text to a much wider audience, but it still leaves anyone wanting to study the complete Old French version with no choice but to go back to Constans's edition. Work on the *romans* has therefore tended to avoid looking specifically at warfare other than a few very specific details such as tents, clothing and heraldry and focuses instead on individual episodes or characters through which courtly love, sexuality, or questions of dynasty and genealogy can be considered.[10] Nevertheless, the *romans* are becoming ever-more accessible thanks to several recent publications of new editions of the texts: during the time that this book was being prepared not only was Burgess and Kelly's translation of *Troie* released in 2017, but a new critical edition of *Thèbes* by Luca di Sabatino was published the year before in 2016, while a new edition of *Enéas* by Wilfrid Besnardeau and Francine Mora-Lebrun and new English translation of *Thèbes* by Joan M. Ferrante and Robert W. Hanning were both published the year after in 2018. This current effort to make the *romans* even more accessible can only be applauded.

Despite the lack of detailed studies of warfare in the *romans*, the field in which my study appears is certainly not an empty one and there are a number of scholars whose work has been particularly important to my research and methodology: Catherine Hanley's monograph *War and Combat, 1150–1270: The Evidence from Old French Literature* is a meticulous investigation of the depiction of warfare in Old French texts, particularly in chronicles, epics and romances; Sophie Cassagnes-Brouquet's monograph *Chevaleresses: Une Chevalerie au Féminin* definitively shows that medieval female warriors amount to much more than just Joan of Arc; Sarah Kay's study of 'the problem of women' in *chansons de geste* revealed how the real 'problem' was not actually with the texts' female characters, but in the scholarly traditions of studying these texts that had created a pervasive misrepresentation and mischaracterization of the roles and importance of women;[11] Elizabeth Morrison and Anne D. Hedeman's studies of illuminations and illustrations of *Troie* and the *Grandes Chroniques de France* showed the additional value that could be gleaned from considering texts within their manuscript traditions.[12] My work springboards from Hanley's work by using a different corpus of texts and reorienting the focus specifically onto women's roles; it sits alongside Cassagnes-Brouquet's study by considering not only the figure of the warrior, but the other roles that women occupy during war, too; it encourages a re-evaluation of the women of the *romans d'antiquité* just as Kay asked for a re-evaluation of the women of the *chansons de geste*;[13] finally, it harnesses Morrison and Hedeman by considering the manuscript and illustrative traditions of the *romans*, which means the chronological range of investigation runs from the twelfth up to the end of the fourteenth century. The illustrations are particularly important because they provide additional insights into how the texts were received, particularly in cases where the images diverge from the texts. As twelfth-century French gradually fell out of use, later users of the manuscripts doubtless relied more heavily upon the illustrations to aid their comprehension. Given this importance, I have consulted all but one of the illustrated *romans* manuscripts and am therefore able to include one of the most comprehensive surveys of the complete illustrative tradition of the *romans d'antiquité*.[14] I hope in this way that my work will provide a new perspective on women and war in the Old French tradition through this specific examination of *Troie*, *Enéas* and *Thèbes*.

The use of literary works as historical sources is not without problems and a note of caution is useful for those approaching such texts in this way. Traces of a wide range of historical issues including government, religion, sex and marriage, cultural differences and interchange, war and conflict, crusade, chivalry, and class can be found throughout Old French literature, traces that are sometimes missing from traditional historical sources, which is what makes literature so potentially rich and valuable. But, as Simon Gaunt and Sarah Kay remind us, 'overwhelmingly literary texts reflect not so much material events as people's ideas, desires, or anxieties; as a result they influence their historical environment as much as they mirror it'.[15] This is not to say that these texts do not provide reflections and replications, too: practical details in particular, such as methods of combat, weapons, clothing, and food and drink, are overwhelmingly drawn from the contemporary environments in which these texts were produced. But, when it comes to certain intellectual concepts, then these texts are better seen as participating in a debate rather than capturing one particular fixed model. Thus, details that we find within the Old French tradition may have been drawn from their historical realities, but similarly they could have been placed there to influence, inspire or educate the reader as idealized exemplars or cautionary tales: the relationship between literary representation and historical reality is best seen as a reciprocal one.

The texts and their sources

The *romans* form an unbroken narrative that begins with the Theban wars and ends with the founding of Rome. *Thèbes* relates the story of Oedipus and Jocasta and the sons of their incestuous relationship, Eteocles and Polynices. The question of who should rule Thebes after Oedipus's death leads to a civil war with the two brothers on opposing sides: Eteocles remains in Thebes while Polynices joins forces with the Argives and launches several assaults on the city. Eventually the two are killed and their uncle, Creon, takes control of Thebes. *Troie* then moves the action from Thebes to the kingdom of Peleus, the father of Achilles. It begins with the story of Jason and the Argonauts's quest for the Golden Fleece, through the first sack of Troy by Hercules and the Greeks, followed by Paris's kidnapping of Helen and the ensuing Trojan wars, which ultimately end in the complete destruction of Troy. *Enéas* then opens with a few Trojan survivors fleeing from the city's ruins in search of a new homeland, led by Aeneas. They stop in Carthage, where Aeneas has a passionate affair with Dido, which ends tragically as she kills herself when he leaves. He goes on to Italy where he challenges Turnus to the right to marry Lavine, through whom he wishes to inherit the kingdom and found his own prophesized dynasty. This he does and their descendants go on to found Rome. One of their descendants, Brutus, will also become the eventual founder of Britain.

All three are broadly defined as translations of classical Latin works: *Thèbes* is a translation of Statius's *Thebaid* (c. 45–96), *Enéas* a translation of Virgil's *Aeneid* (c. 29–19 BCE) and *Troie* a combined translation of Dares Phrygius's *Excidio Trojae historia* (c. 400–99) and Dictys Cretensis's *Ephemeridos belli Trojani* (c. 300–99). Translation needs to be understood in its medieval rather than its modern sense, meaning that they are far from word-for-word reproductions.[16] The *romans* poets make frequent diversions from their source material and are better said to have been inspired by their classical sources. They were part of the larger *translatio studii* and *translatio imperii* topos in medieval literature. In the prologue to *Troie*, its author, Benoît de Sainte-Maure, outlines the framework of *translatio* within which he is working (ll. 1–144) and directly names his source as Dares. It was Dares's purported eyewitness account of the Trojan war that was widely circulated in medieval Europe in lieu of Homer's *Iliad*, for which there was not a complete Latin translation until the fourteenth century.[17] His other source is Dictys, although Benoît only names him about four-fifths of the way into the narrative (ll. 24417–19). But Benoît clearly drew on additional sources to develop his narrative: together, Dares's and Dictys's texts amount to approximately one and a half thousand lines of Latin prose, but Benoît's work is just over thirty thousand lines of verse. The influence of Ovid in the expansion of the love scenes in particular has been well examined and Benoît may have been influenced in this respect by *Thèbes* and *Enéas*, too.[18] He also has a penchant for enlarging the battle scenes and councils. Although he is relatively faithful in following the number of battles given by Dares (*Troie* has twenty-three battles compared to Dares's eighteen), the length of description differs significantly. For example, the first battle in which the Amazon queen Penthesilea fights is described by Dares in just 4 lines (D.36) whereas Benoît turns it into 234 lines (ll. 23485–719).[19] Dictys's version gives slightly more detail than Dares's, but Penthesilea appears in only one battle (IV.2–3) as compared to three battles in *Troie* (Battles 21–23).[20] The details for Benoît's battles do not come from his Latin sources, but from the historical realities of medieval warfare and tournaments. In fact, charges of anachronism have been made against *Troie* in part because of the overt presence of twelfth-century (rather than classical) fighting techniques, equipment and ideals.[21] For example, in Dictys's account of Penthesilea's battle, the two sides use bows or throw spears with minimal hand-to-hand combat. However, in *Troie*, the battles in which she fights see the combatants using swords in duels and jousting with lances against each other. We know that the preferred weapons of the nobility from 1100 to 1400 were indeed lances and swords, so such a representation of combat would have been more recognizable to a contemporary audience.[22]

The poets of *Thèbes* and *Enéas* make little attempt to identify their sources, although this is fairly common of medieval texts.[23] However, there is no doubt that they were very familiar with their classical sources. The first two of the *Thebaid*'s twelve books are reproduced in *Thèbes* with relatively few amendments while the following ten books appear to a greater or lesser extent.[24] Dominique Battles convincingly argues that the chronicle tradition of the First Crusade was also influential to the transposition of the tone and content of *Thèbes* from a classical to a medieval milieu and that crusade stories account for the biggest changes as compared to the *Thebaid*.[25] Ferrante and Hanning also highlight various episodes in the text that are evocative of not only the First Crusade but possible references to the Second Crusade and the crusades in Spain, too.[26] However, preserving this aspect of civil war between family members in *Thèbes* was still important to retain. *Thèbes* was written between 1150 and 1155. This was not long after the struggles between William the Conqueror's three sons – Robert Curthose, William Rufus and Henry I of England – at the end of the eleventh century for the throne of England. It was also the period during which time the wars of the Anarchy (1135–54) between Stephen of England and Empress Matilda (Henry I's daughter) were coming to an end. The Anarchy, essentially a civil war with two cousins leading opposing sides, ended when Stephen agreed to recognize Matilda's son, Henry FitzEmpress, as his heir, with Henry eventually being crowned as Henry II of England in 1154. Given that Henry is one of the most likely patrons of *Thèbes*, it is not unreasonable to assume that the *Thèbes* poet would have considered civil war between members of the same family to be a pertinent topic for this *roman*'s audience.

Considerably more space is dedicated to the female characters in *Thèbes* as compared to the *Thebaid*:[27] the description of Adrastus's daughters, Argia and Deiphyle, is only five lines in the *Thebaid* (I, ll. 534–39) but fifty-one lines in *Thèbes* (ll. 1030–81);[28] the conversation between Jocasta and Eteocles in *Thèbes* in which she counsels him (ll. 3887–4108) does not have an equivalent scene in the *Thebaid*; the scene in which Jocasta and her daughters, Antigone and Ismene, travel to the Argive camp for negotiations is just under a hundred lines in the *Thebaid* (VII, ll. 474–561) but nearly four hundred lines in *Thèbes* (ll. 4109–4491); the description of Jocasta's daughters at the moment when they accompany her to the Argive camp occupies fifty-six lines in *Thèbes* (ll. 4117–73) but is only a subclause of a single line in the *Thebaid* (VII, l. 479). As with *Troie*, the increased importance of women in *Thèbes* has usually been attributed to an Ovidian influence because of the increased focus on love scenes, although this influence is not quite as strong as previously claimed.[29]

More has been written about the sources of *Enéas* than either of the other two *romans*, particularly its relationship with Virgil's *Aeneid*, Servius's glosses of the *Aeneid* and Ovidian texts (again).[30] The ways in which the *Enéas* poet adapts the *Aeneid* yield interesting comparisons, particularly with regard to its female characters. The differences between Virgil's and *Enéas*'s Dido and the classical and medieval Lavine have been well examined in previous studies so I shall not summarize or repeat them here.[31] Suffice to say that as with *Troie* and *Thèbes*, the text gives its female characters more development and attention than its classical source had done.

Thèbes, *Enéas* and *Troie* undoubtedly owe an enormous debt to Statius, Virgil, and Dares and Dictys respectively, and Ovid, crusade narratives and glossed manuscripts of classical works in general, but these sources alone do not explain adequately how the poets were able to develop their female characters so significantly. For that, we can look at the historical environment in which the poets were working as this influence has not been investigated to the same extent. The twelfth century was a period that allowed a lot of powerful women to flourish, and it is possible that some of the narratives' characters were inspired by or even intended as a form of homage to leading women of their day.[32] Equally, the figures that the poets developed may have been drawn to act as exemplars or mirrors, intended to inspire and to direct the actions of the elite women who may have been reading these texts or listening to them read at court. The *romans* pioneered a more complete and holistic representation of warfare, one that did not consist only of men on the battlefield, but that acknowledged the many roles and experiences that both men and women had during times of conflict. Looking at these texts in this way sheds new light on women's roles in the Old French tradition in general and illuminates how they are important to our understanding of the historical period in which they circulated.

1

Reading texts through the manuscript tradition, 1150–1400

Before we look at the ways in which women and war are presented in the *romans d'antiquité* in particular, we need to explore the values and uses of these texts in general. *Troie* is currently extant in thirty manuscripts, the oldest being a late twelfth-century copy produced in Venice and the most recent being a late fourteenth-century copy produced in Bologna.[1] *Enéas* can be found in nine manuscripts; the oldest is an Italian copy that was produced between 1190 and 1225, while the most recent was produced in England at the end of fourteenth century. *Thèbes* is only extant in five manuscripts, the oldest being a Parisian copy from the end of the thirteenth century while the most recent is the same late fourteenth-century copy that was produced in England and in which we also find the latest copy of *Enéas*. We must be cognizant of the fact that the reasons for which the texts were first composed in the mid-twelfth century as compared to the reasons for which later manuscript copies were commissioned at the end of the fourteenth century are unlikely to be the same. The historical landscape in which the *romans* began their journey was not the same one in which they finished, and the people with whom they came into contact were from different geographic locations, different social classes, and had different interests and political allegiances. All of these affect the ways the texts were used. By looking at the original composition of the *romans* and then tracing them through their later manuscripts and illustrations, we can gain a better understanding of how the topic of women and war was received or interpreted within their folios.

A question of patronage

Current consensus is that the *romans* poets were writing at the court of Henry II of England and Eleanor of Aquitaine, either under their patronage or with the intention of obtaining it.[2] Eleanor married Henry II in 1152, after the annulment of her fifteen-year marriage to Louis VII of France. She had been duchess of Aquitaine in her own right since 1137 (and would remain so until her death in 1204) and became queen consort of England from 1154 to 1189. Benoît addresses a '[r]iche dame de riche rei' (*powerful lady of a powerful king*, l. 13468) in *Troie* who is probably Eleanor, as the epithet of 'riche rei' is usually associated with Henry II.[3] There is also a simple lack of plausible alternatives for this 'dame': Eleanor of Castile, Joan of Sicily, Margaret of France, Marie de Champagne, Alice of Blois and Adele of Champagne have all been considered but ultimately rejected as other options.[4] Elizabeth A. R. Brown attempted to minimize Eleanor's role as a patron by suggesting that Eleanor was 'far more concerned with the realities of political life than with matters cultural and intellectual', but her study of Eleanor's political life focused on the latter half of her life (from the 1170s onwards) rather than the earlier part, during which the *romans* were composed (between 1150 and 1165).[5] Even Karen M. Broadhurst's more recent study, which sought to challenge the scholarly opinion concerning Henry and Eleanor as famed patrons of literature, conceded that the case for Eleanor is still the most appropriate.[6]

The passage containing the 'riche dame' dedication is actually omitted from eleven of the *Troie* manuscripts, and in the mid-thirteenth-century MS P3 it is even reassigned to the Virgin Mary:[7]

Riche fille de riche rei,	*Powerful daughter of a powerful king,*
De vos nasquié tote leece	*from you all joy was born the day of the*
Le jor de la Nativité:	*Nativity: you are the daughter and*
Vos fustes fille et mere Dé.	*mother of God.*
(*Troie*, ll. 13467–70)[8]	

It has been suggested that the dedication was omitted in certain manuscripts because it was 'a puzzle' to scribes.[9] However, it is equally possible that these omissions were made precisely because the 'dame' was indeed Eleanor: following the decline in her reputation after her death in 1204, and the fact that the majority of manuscripts still extant today were produced after this date in territories outside of the Plantagent realm, later copyists may simply have wanted to remove any association with her from the text.[10] This would also explain why we do not find any dedication in the prologue or epilogue, where we would usually expect to find dedications; they may have more easily been omitted by later scribes on the lookout for such dedications. In fact, the 'riche dame' allusion that is still extant in sixteen manuscripts could have slipped past scribes who would just not have expected a dedication in the middle of the text.

One explanation for why we do not have physical evidence linking Eleanor to the *romans* is because we only have one *roman* manuscript (the late twelfth-century MS M) that was produced during her lifetime. The only possible patron portrait of Eleanor that is actually in existence today is in a twelfth-century psalter (The Hague, Koninklijke Bibliotheek, MS 76.F.13).[11] If there were more extant twelfth-century manuscript copies of the *romans* then perhaps we could expect a higher chance of further patron portraits of Eleanor. A key barrier to establishing more definitive links between Eleanor and the *romans* is therefore not a lack of probability, but a lack of original documents contemporaneous with her lifetime. A manuscript of *Troie* that was produced while she was still alive, MS M, was specifically commissioned for or by Geoffrey of Villehardouin;[12] Geoffrey was a knight and chronicler who had participated in the Fourth Crusade (1202–04), and more significantly for our purposes, he was Marshal of Champagne from 1185 to 1199 at the time that Marie de Champagne, Eleanor's daughter by her first marriage, was countess consort and regent of Champagne. Although the manuscript was made in Italy, Geoffrey may have commissioned a copy of this particular text not just for its content (which no doubt was of particularly pertinent interest to a knight and chronicler) but also for its connections between its patrons and his Champenois lieges. The *romans* are sometimes linked to the court of Champagne in other manuscript exemplars when they are bound or copied together with works associated with Marie de Champagne: for example, the romances of Chrétien de Troyes, one of Marie's most well-known patroness, appear in four of the thirteenth-century French *romans* manuscripts (MSS P2, P5, P8 and P12). In MS P2, which was produced in Champagne, we find a portrait of Marie de Champagne as the manuscript's sole illustration. We therefore see the *romans* linked to Champagne in two ways: firstly, through this association of Chrétien's texts with the *romans* in at least four codices, and secondly, through MS M, which contains only *Troie* and yet was commissioned by someone deeply connected to the Champenois court. If the *romans* were indeed produced at Eleanor's court, then this link takes on a familial form that evokes the mother-daughter relationship between Eleanor and Marie, a relationship about which much has been written, and which suggests that these texts were connected not just on the basis of their narratives, but on the basis of their patrons, too.[13]

Benoît is also linked with Henry and Eleanor through his connection to Robert Wace, another poet with an undisputed position at their court: his *Roman de Brut* (c. 1150–55) was composed for Eleanor while Henry commissioned his *Roman de Rou* (c. 1160–75).[14] The *Rou* links to another of Benoît's works, the *Chronique des Ducs de Normandie* (c. 1180), as the former ends with a complaint that the completion of the narrative is to be done by 'Maistre Beneeit' (*Master Benoît*, l. 11419) and that a previously promised financial reward from a 'reis' (*king*, l. 11425) has subsequently been denied to him.[15] Benoît's *Chronique* picks up from where Wace ended the *Rou* and makes a direct allusion to Henry: 'Par le buen rei Henri' (*by the good king, Henry*, l. 32062).[16] As the *Rou* is narratively connected to the *Chronique*, so Wace's *Brut* is connected to the three *romans* as it narrates the story of Aeneas's descendant Brutus, his founding of Britain and the resulting kings of Britain. The manuscript evidence shows that they were often seen in the same tradition: five of the *romans* manuscripts also contain the *Brut*.[17] Indeed, of all the other texts with which the *romans* are collected, the *Brut* is the one that most commonly recurs. That two writers were working on such interwoven subject matters suggests that they were working under the same influence or in the same place and is indicative of shared patronage, even if a question mark must still remain over such a hypothesis. At the least we can say that Benoît must have been confident that *Troie* would come to the attention of Henry and Eleanor and it was written under so-called prospective patronage, that is the speculative dedication of a text to an influential person in the hope of attracting a future reward, commission or favour.[18] If the consequence was that Benoît was subsequently given the commission of the *Chronique* (at the expense of Wace) then this was an effective strategy.

Some evidence exists for linking Eleanor to *Thèbes*, too. In the description of Adrastus's daughters, Argia and Deiphyle, the poet writes, 'Mieus vaut lor ris et lor baisiers | Que ne fait Londres ne Peitiers' (*their smiles and kisses are worth more than either London or Poitiers*, ll. 971–72).[19] Reto Roberto Bezzola first highlighted the link between this couplet and Eleanor: 'Cette comparaison, qui réunit les deux capitales d'Aliénor dans un même vers, deux villes qui, pour d'autres que la reine d'Angleterre et comtesse de Poitiers n'avaient absolument rien de commun, ne saurait être un simple hasard' (*this comparison, that unites Eleanor's two capital cities within the same verse, two cities that for anyone other than the Queen of England and the Countess of Poitiers would have absolutely nothing in common, cannot simply be coincidence*).[20] However, this allusion appears in only one (the late thirteenth-century MS G) out of the five extant *Thèbes* manuscripts.[21] Furthermore, the quality and accuracy of MS G has been called into question by one of its editors.[22] The allusion to London and Poitiers in this copy is probably an addition by the scribe and could provide clues as to who commissioned this particular copy of *Thèbes*, the identity of whom is currently unknown. In fact, if London and Poitiers are used as a metaphor for Eleanor, then this couplet is actually an insult, for it essentially judges her as worth less than these two women. Combined with the fact that this manuscript also contains additional misogynistic passages, omits one of Priam's daughters, omits Cassandra's speeches and dates to a time when Eleanor's reputation was suffering, perhaps all we can conclude is that this particular manuscript was copied by or commissioned for someone with a rather low view of certain women.[23]

Eleanor and Henry would have been drawn to these narratives because of the authority they helped to give to the Plantagenet right to England's throne – the legitimacy of which was frequently challenged during the twelfth century. This concern for the power and rightfulness of the Plantagenet dynasty would have been important not just to Henry, but to Eleanor too. During the time of the *romans*' composition, she gave birth to six of the eight children that she would eventually have with Henry: William IX of Poitiers (*c.* 1153–56), Henry the Young King (*c.* 1155–83), Matilda of England (*c.* 1156–89), Richard I of England (*c.* 1157–99), Geoffrey II of Brittany (*c.* 1158–86) and Eleanor of England (*c.* 1161–1214). Their futures were reliant on the authority and legitimacy of their father's claim to his titles. The significance of Trojan ancestry to the Plantagenet ideology is evident not just from the *romans*, but from Benoît's *Chronique* and Wace's *Brut* and *Rou*, too. These texts established Trojan descent for the Plantagenets specifically by presenting the Trojan Antenor as the founder of the Danish race, from whom the Normans (and thence, by this period, the Plantagenets) were descended, as well as establishing Brutus of Troy (a descendant of the Trojan Aeneas) as the founder of Britain.[24] The *Chronique*, the *Brut* and the *Rou* can (and, in certain manuscripts, do) happily sit alongside *Thèbes*, *Troie* and *Enéas* as interrelated texts telling an unbroken historical narrative from the Theban wars of antiquity right up to the Norman dukes and English monarchs who were Henry II's ancestors. Their motivation for patronizing such texts would therefore seem clear.

Material value: Manuscripts, readers and visual imagery

Beyond the period of composition, the manuscript traditions and ownership patterns give us clues as to how the texts were used later and many of them have an interesting story in relation to historical women, too. From Table 1 we can see that in the thirteenth century, most manuscripts were produced in French territories while during the fourteenth century there is a shift to Italian territories. The two earliest manuscripts (the only two that are datable to the end of the twelfth century) were also produced in Italian territory, while the only manuscript produced within English territory is one of the latest of all the manuscripts, MS L4. This puts a twist on the theory that the *romans* were used for promoting Plantagenet political ambitions as it appears they rarely circulated within Anglo-Norman territories. Of course, it is not possible to draw definitive conclusions based on such selective evidence; of the six manuscripts for which the provenance has not yet been established, these may include territories not yet represented, and no doubt there were many other now–non-extant copies whose provenance are similarly mysterious.[25] However, given that, for example, there are only two extant manuscripts of Benoît's *Chronique* and both are believed to have an Anglo-Norman provenance (one from Anjou and one from either England or Normandy), it is surprising that only one of the extant manuscripts of the *romans* has a similar provenance.[26] The majority of the earlier illustrated manuscripts (those produced before 1340) were made in French territories. Elizabeth Morrison's study of illuminated manuscripts of *Troie* between 1260 and 1340 compellingly argues that the purpose of these illustrations was to promote the claim of Trojan origins for the Capetian dynasty, who saw themselves as descendants of Hector in particular.[27] She expands on Anne D. Hedeman's theory that *Troie* was used as an 'unofficial prologue' to the *Grandes Chroniques de France*, which had sought to represent the French monarchy in general as the descendants of various members of the Trojan diaspora.[28] This explains why manuscripts containing *Troie* were popular in French territories.

Table 1 Manuscripts of the *romans d'antiquité*[29]

MS	Date	Provenance	Illustrations	Contents	Ownership
M	1190–1206	Venice	17	*Troie*	Partly known
F1	1190–1225	Italy	No	*Enéas*	Unknown
L1	1200–20	Champagne	No	*Troie*	Partly known
P1	1200–25	Unknown	4	*Troie*	Unknown
N	1200–50	Unknown	No	*Troie*	Partly known
P2	1225–50	Provins/Champagne	1 (not for *Troie*)	*Troie* and other texts	Unknown
P3	1237	Unknown	No	*Troie*	Unknown
P4	1200–1300	Unknown	No	*Troie*	Unknown
P5	1235–65	N. France	1 (for *Enéas*)	*Troie*, *Enéas* and others	Partly known
P6	1264	Paris/Burgundy	38	*Troie*	Unknown
L2	1250–1300	Amiens/Arras	15	*Troie*	Partly known
P7	1285	Picardy	33 (1 for *Troie*)	*Troie* and others	Partly known
Nt	1286	Flanders/N.W. France	83 (33 for *Troie*)	*Troie* and others	Partly known
P8	1288	Paris	No	*Thèbes*, *Troie* and others	Partly known

Table 1 Manuscripts of the *romans d'antiquité* (Continued)

MS	Date	Provenance	Illustrations	Contents	Ownership
G	1275–1300	Unknown	1 (for *Troie*)	*Thèbes* and *Troie*	Partly known
P9	1275–1300	Lorraine	No	*Troie* and another text	Partly known
P10	1292	Picardy	1 (for *Enéas*)	*Enéas* and others	Unknown
P11	1285–1300	N. France	2	*Troie*	Partly known
Vt	1275–1325	C. Italy	254	*Troie*	Partly known
P12	1300	Arras/Picardy	1 (not *Enéas*)	*Enéas* and others	Partly known
P13	1300	Paris	4	*Thèbes* and *Enéas* (originally *Troie* from MS P14)	Partly known
P14	1300	Paris	27	*Troie* (originally *Thèbes* and *Enéas* from MS P13)	Partly known
Mn	1300	Paris/Picardy	25 (1 for *Enéas*; 23 for *Troie*)	*Troie*, *Enéas* and others (possibly incl. *Thèbes*)	Partly known
P15	1300–25	N. Italy	Yes[30]	*Troie* and others	Partly known
P16	1300–50	N. France	Possibly[31]	*Troie*	Unknown
P17	1330–40	Paris	53	*Thèbes*, *Troie*, *Enéas*	Partly known
V1	1330–40	Naples	422	*Troie*	Partly known
Vn	1330–40	Padua/Bologna	199	*Troie*	Unknown
F2	1344	Florence	No	*Troie* and another text	Partly known
P18	1340–50	Verona/Padua/Venice	202	*Troie*	Unknown
L3	1340–60	Italy	No	*Enéas*	Partly known
SP1	1340–60	Bologna/C. Italy	168	*Troie*	Unknown
V2	1360–69	N. Italy	2 (1 for *Troie*)	*Troie* and another text	Partly known
P19	1350–1400	Italy	No	*Troie* and another text	Unknown
L4	1375–1400	England	No	*Thèbes*, *Enéas* and others	Partly known
SP2	1380–1400	Unknown	No	*Troie*	Partly known

Numerous aristocratic families in medieval Europe claimed to be descended from the Trojans and sought to solidify this claim in written texts. The *romans* were not the first texts to have made such a link. It was Fredegar, writing in the seventh century in the first book of his Frankish *Chronicle*, who had first claimed Trojan ancestry for the Franks.[32] The ninth-century chronicle *Historia Brittonum* then gave Trojan ancestry to the Britons.[33] Next, the Anglo-Normans appropriated the legend even before the *romans* were written: Geoffrey of Monmouth recorded in his *Historia Regum Britanniae* (*c.* 1136) that Brutus had made his first foundation on the banks of the River Loire in France before settling in Britain.[34] And finally, the Trojan origin of France and its dynasty spread throughout medieval French writings so that by the end of the Middle Ages almost every member of the French nobility was claiming Trojan ancestry.[35]

The Italian manuscripts have garnered less critical attention, despite often being longer and more luxurious. Of the seven illustrated Italian manuscripts, five contain a remarkable number of images: MS SP1 has 168, MSS Vn and P18 have about 200 each, MS Vt has 254 and MS V1 has over 400. The narrative of *Troie* can almost be read from the illustrations alone, without the need to understand the text. This is reflective of a decline in the popularity and readability of twelfth-century French by the fourteenth century, particularly in non-French-speaking territories, but coupled with a continued desire to share the Trojan stories. However, MS P18's language was specifically revised into a Franco-Venetian dialect, which shows that certain audiences were still interested in the specifics of the text.[36]

There is a definite trend for illustrated copies of *Troie*, but very few of *Thèbes* or *Enéas*. MSS Mn, P10 and P13 provide a historiated initial at the start of *Enéas* and MS P13 gives a historiated initial at the start of *Thèbes*, but the lavish mid-fourteenth-century Parisian MS P17 is the only manuscript that affords a significant illustrative scheme to both of these texts. However, it is interesting to note that despite the paucity of illustrations, it tends to be two of their female characters, Dido and Jocasta, who consistently appear.[37] *Troie* disproportionately captured the imagination of commissioners and illustrators, suggesting that it must have been the individual heroes of that narrative that made it so popular. Hector and Penthesilea went on to become part of the *Neuf Preux* and *Neuf Preuses* traditions, which is a possible explanation for why texts that elaborate their particular battles and prowess continued to be popular. This *Neuf Preux* topos began in Jacques de Longuyon's *Voeux du Paon* (1312) and consisted of nine 'worthy' men who personified the ideals of chivalry: these were three pagans (Hector of Troy, Alexander the Great and Julius Caesar), three Jews (Joshua, David and Judas Maccabeus) and three Christians (King Arthur, Charlemagne and Godfrey of Bouillon). The *Neuf Preuses* then appeared in Jean Le Fèvre's *Livre de Leësce* (*c.* 1380–87) and gained widespread popularity through sculpture, tapestry and written works, particularly in Italy and France.[38] Unlike the *Preux*, the *Preuses* were neither organized into three triads of pagans, Jews and Christians, nor were its members consistent. But in contrast to Hector and Penthesilea, the heroes of *Thèbes* and *Enéas* were rather more problematic: Polynices and Eteocles were the products of incest and guilty of fratricide, while Aeneas was one of the traitors and conspirators during the Trojan wars, as well as the abandoner of Dido. Their stories were important for the narrative completeness of the lineage of the kings and queens of Western Europe, but it was not necessary to visually venerate them to the same extent.

In addition to the illustrative contents of the manuscripts, the other texts with which the *romans* are collected are important. Of the thirty-six manuscripts containing at least one *roman*, fourteen contain at least one other text. These include *matière de Bretagne*, *matière de France*, *matière de Rome*, narrative histories, crusade narratives, religious texts, hagiographies, fables, *fabliaux* and lyric poetry; almost all of these other texts also come from the Old French tradition.[39] The three *romans* were sometimes collected together, showing that they were sometimes received as a trilogy: two early fourteenth-century Parisian manuscripts, MSS P13 (containing *Thèbes* and *Enéas*) and P14 (containing *Troie*), were originally intended to form one codex; another early fourteenth-century Parisian manuscript, MS Mn, initially contained all three *romans* (along with Wace's *Brut*), although *Thèbes* has now been lost, and a mid-fourteenth-century Parisian manuscript, MS P17, contains not only all three *romans*, but also an original 'general introduction' on its first folio that acts as a prologue to the entire collection.[40] Despite the rich variety of texts with which they were collected, there is a pattern in the way in which they are grouped.

In the thirteenth century, the *romans* were generally collected together with narratives that highlighted the ancestral link to the Trojans, while simultaneously emphasizing ideas of courtliness and chivalry. Nine of the thirteenth-century manuscripts contain texts other than the *romans*: Wace's *Brut* appears in five (MSS P2, P5, P10, P12 and Mn) and his *Rou* in one (MS P8); Chrétien de Troyes's romances appear in four (MSS P2, P5, P8 and P12); the *Continuations* of the Grail narrative appear in two (MSS P2 and P5); Gautier d'Arras's *Ille et Galeron* appears in two (MSS P8 and Nt); narratives of Alexander the Great appear in two (MSS P8 and Nt). The choice of texts emphasizes the place of the Trojan narratives within a longer continuous historical narrative and the role of chivalry, courtliness and love within that narrative. MS L1 had at least one reader who was particularly taken with the representation of love for he has written into the margins the phrases 'folx est qui aime' (*whoever loves is a fool*, fol. 38ʳ) and 'amor m'a mis en grant' (*love brought me into greatness*, fol. 56ʳ). MS P5 is a good example of the way in which both narrative history and courtly and chivalric norms are put into relief. It begins with *Troie*, followed by *Enéas*, followed by the *Brut*, into which have been inserted four *romans* by Chrétien (*Erec et Enide*, *Le conte du Graal*, *Cligès* and *Yvain*) and finishes with the *Roman de Dolopathos*. *Troie*, *Enéas* and *Brut* have been ordered to tell a chronological narrative and the Chrétien romances are inserted into the middle of the *Brut* at the moment when the text tells of King Arthur so as to maintain a smooth linear narration.[41] This manuscript presents how medieval nobles explained their descent from the Trojan heroes by linking *Troie*, *Enéas* and the *Brut*, while the insertion of the Chrétien romances makes explicit the aspect of courtly love and chivalry that are expected of Christian heroes. The protagonists of *Troie* and *Enéas* are of course non-Christian, but they nevertheless embody qualities of nobility, courage and valiance. This is an effort on the part of the manuscript compiler to make the heroes of the classical epics evolve through the *Brut* until they emerge as the Christian heroes of the Arthurian romances. The *romans* themselves are written in a style that emphasizes chivalry and courtliness. Indeed, this is another of the reasons why they have sometimes been judged as anachronistic as classical translations.[42] Juxtaposing the *romans* with works such as Chrétien's romances makes this all the more evident. Battles and warfare were important, but the manner in which these wars were conducted was evidently also of interest. These thirteenth-century manuscripts present warfare not only as a heroic exploit conducted by generations of Western Europeans stretching back to classical antiquity, but as something in which ideas of honour, discipline, virtue and courtly love also played an important role.

Meanwhile, in the manuscripts of the fourteenth century, the *romans* are no longer found with any Arthurian texts and are typically on their own or with each other, rather than with other texts. The reasons for which the *romans* were valued seem to change: rather than emphasizing courtly love or romanticizing adventures in distant and fantastical worlds, they instead juxtapose texts that highlight the practical and harsher aspects of warfare. Those that appear with particular frequency include *Hector et Hercule* (c. 1300–24), which appears in three of the Italian manuscripts (MSS P15, F2 and V2); the *Histoire ancienne jusqu'à César* (c. 1210) which appears in two Italian manuscripts (MSS P15 and P19); and two crusade narratives (the *Ordène de Chevalerie* (c. 1200–50) and a *chanson de geste* on the siege of Antioche) which appear in the only English manuscript (MS L4). These accompanying texts are almost exclusively historical or classical narratives. The prominence of three manuscripts that collect *Troie* with *Hector et Hercule* is particularly noteworthy. MS P15 is even described in the 1426 inventory of the library of the dukes of Milan at Visconti Castle as a manuscript relating 'Gesta Herculis et plurium aliorum ac Troiani' (*the deeds of Hercules and many other events at Troy*).[43] The emphasis on the deeds of Hercules is curious as Hector actually defeats him in *Hector et Hercule and* he only appears briefly at the start of *Troie*. However, by the fourteenth century the legend of Hercules was of great moral value, for he was a role model for valour and wisdom: the monsters that he fought were metaphors for moral obstacles and the strength he demonstrated in defeating them was a simile for the strength needed to enter Heaven.[44] Maybe *Troie* had a similar use: it provided exemplars for honourable, wise and moral behaviour and therefore had a didactic value.

In certain circles, the *romans* were also doubtless valued purely as works to entertain and amuse. The thirteenth-century MS Nt demonstrates this most effectively. It shows signs of frequent use, suggesting that it was often taken out to be read or looked at. Along with *Troie* it contains *Ille et Galeron*, Heldris of Cornwall's *Roman de Silence*, part of the *Roman d'Alexandre*, the *Chanson d'Aspremont*, Raoul de Houdenc's *Vengeance Raguidel*, eleven *fabliaux* and fifteen lines from one of Marie de France's fables. The diversity of the texts means that there was something for everyone on every occasion. Even the accompanying illustrations suggest a certain playfulness; they are often unconnected to the texts but instead show fantastical beasts and creatures, so even those not able to read the texts could enjoy the whimsical illustrative scheme.

The commissioners and owners of the manuscripts also provide clues as to their value and use. There is selective information available about the ownership of twenty-three manuscripts, although this information is not always from the medieval period. Despite the paucity of information (and the usual uncertainty over whether those who owned the manuscripts actually read them or that those who did not own them may nevertheless have had access to them through a family library or performed readings), we can see that there is considerable variety in terms of the spread of ownership. Table 2 details the persons known to have owned (or interacted in some way with) at least one of the *roman* manuscripts, listed in approximate chronological order with the manuscript with which they are associated. Once again there is a dearth of medieval owners with Anglo-Norman sympathies. For example, the Goyon-Matignon family, who owned MS P5, was an ancient Breton family with connections to Normandy that had a fairly antagonistic relationship with the Plantagenets as there is a record of two members of the family, Guignes and Seldivin de Goyon, being taken prisoner by Henry II in 1177.[45] Similarly, Jacques II de Bourbon, who owned MSS P13 and P14, was a staunchly anti-English figure: his father, Jean de Bourbon, had been involved in battles with the English, having been captured at the Battle of Poitiers in 1356.

Jacques II led a force in support of Owain Glyndwr's invasion of England in 1403 and later supported Charles VII of France's troops during the Hundred Years War (1337–1453).[46] Meanwhile the Laval family, who originally owned MS Nt, were also known to have opposed the English during the Hundred Years War and the reason this manuscript ended up in England was because it was plundered from the Laval castle in 1428.[47] Patterns in the origins of the manuscripts combined with these details of their ownership make it appear that these texts were more popular in regions or among families that were not known allies of the Anglo-Normans. Regardless of whether legitimizing the Plantagenet dynasty had been their original purpose when commissioned, this was obviously not why they came to be valued by later owners.

Table 2 Owners and readers of the *romans* manuscripts[48]

Owner/reader	Manuscript
Geoffrey of Villehardouin (1160–1212)	MS M
Milon of Brabant (d. 1224)	MS M
'Plonbeoli de plombeolis' (thirteenth-century hand)	MS M
Béatrice de Gavre (d. 1315)	MS Nt
Bertrand Goyon Matignon (thirteenth or fourteenth century)	MS P5
'Madame de Martignie' and 'Madame Maulevrier' (fourteenth-century hand)	MS L1
Lucas Boni of Florence (fourteenth century)	MS F2
Robert of Anjou (1277–1343)	MS Vt
Guido Gonzaga (1290–1369)	MS V2
John II of France (1319–64)	MS P11
Anne de Laval (1385–1466)	MS Nt
John Talbot, earl of Shrewsbury (1384–1453)	MS Nt
Francesco I Gonzaga (1366–1407)	MS V1
Henry Despenser, bishop of Norwich (1341–1406)	MS L4
Charles V, VI or VII of France (fourteenth or fifteenth century)	MS P11
Jacques II de Bourbon, count of La Marche (1370–1438)	MSS P13 & P14
Cristoforo Moro (1390–1471)	MS L3
John Bertram of Thorp Kilton (d. 1471)	MS Nt
Jacques d'Armagnac, duke of Nemours (1433–77)	MSS P13 & P14
Charles de Croÿ, count of Chimay (1455–1527)	MS P12
Dukes of Milan (1426–89)	MS P15
Jean d'Averton, lord of Couldreau (c. 1400–99)	MS SP2
Cardinal Agostino Trivulzio (1485–1548)	MSS N & Mn
Charles V, Holy Roman emperor (c. 1500–58)	MS SP2
Gian Vincenzo Pinelli (1535–1601)	MS M
Cardinal Federico Borromeo (1564–1631)	MS M
Étienne Tabourot, lord of the Accords (1549–90)	MS P17

Owner/reader	Manuscript
Cardinal de Mazarin (1602–61)	MSS P7 & P8
Pierre Bourdelot (1610–85)	MS Vt
Philibert de la Mare (1615–87)	MS P9
Louis XIV of France (1640–1715)	MS P17
Edward Harley, earl of Oxford and Mortimer (1689–1741)	MS L2
Jean-Baptiste La Curne de Sainte-Palaye (1697–1781)	MS P8
Thomas Phillipps (1792–1872)	MS G
Maurice Johnson (1815–61)	MS L4

It is also notable that there is relative diversity in terms of gender, social status and occupation, when it comes to ownership. Although the data points to the majority of owners being men, there are several women in this list and one of them (Béatrice de Gavre) is one of the few whom we can actually identify as the original intended recipient of the manuscript, rather than a later owner. With regard to status we have monarchs and emperors such as John II of France, Robert of Anjou, Charles V, Holy Roman emperor and Louis XIV of France owning copies of these manuscripts. There are also people who are virtually untraceable in historical records; for example, MS M's 'Plonbeoli de plombeolis' has not yet been identified and nor have the Madames Martignie and Maulevrier of MS L1. Finally, we see people from the different estates of medieval social structures: one owner is a scribe (Lucas Boni); there are owners from the church (such as Cardinal Agostino Trivulzio, Cardinal Federico Borromeo and Bishop Henry Despenser of Norwich); and there are owners from the nobility and knightly echelons (such as Geoffrey of Villehardouin, Milon of Brabant and John Talbot). Just as the collections in which these texts appear suggest that they were valued in different ways, so too the variety among their owners suggests that they had no single audience.

Certain manuscripts stand out for having features that suggest a particular connection to women. As mentioned above, MS P2 contains only one historiated initial and it is of Eleanor's daughter, Marie de Champagne. Meanwhile, in addition to MS Nt having been commissioned for Béatrice de Gavre, it also contains a text that was patronized by a woman (*Ille et Galeron*, which was dedicated to Beatrice I of Burgundy) and texts that were written by women (Marie de France's *Fables*). The thirteenth-century MS N also reveals a potential female readership as it contains a version of the text in which the unfavourable descriptions of women have been purposefully omitted.[49] Folio 81 should contain the passage in which the narrator of *Troie* makes a misogynistic digression about the infidelity of women (ll. 13457–70) but it was left out of the original copying of the manuscript, as were a number of other passages, that are not necessarily specific to women. At some point, a later scribe went back and added in those missing passages into the margins of the manuscript, presumably when another codex became available from which to copy. However, when it came to the part where this misogynistic passage should also have been added, the scribe just makes a note in the margin that there is still a passage missing here. This signals that they must have had the passage available to them, but they purposefully chose not to include it. Jung speculates that the scribe thought this passage was 'trop long' (*too long*) and therefore left it out.[50] Alternatively, this scribe deliberately chose not to rectify this omission specifically because they anticipated that this particular manuscript would have a female readership who would not appreciate this passage, especially as its position in the margin would attract extra attention.

Some manuscripts contain a disproportionate number of illustrations of women compared with how often they appear in the text. There are only two manuscripts containing illustrations of *Thèbes* (MSS P13 and P17, both made in fourteenth-century Paris) and yet the only character to be illustrated in both is Jocasta. Similarly, there are only four manuscripts of *Enéas* with any illustrations (MSS P5, P10, P17 and Mn) and yet the only character (other than Aeneas) to be illustrated in all four is Dido. Women also appear with disproportionate frequency in manuscripts of *Troie*. For example, the extensively illustrated Italian MS Vt contains 254 illustrations, of which 53 (roughly 20 per cent) include women. In comparison, of the thirty thousand lines of text, approximately four thousand lines (roughly 13 per cent) relate to descriptions of women or the actions of women. And of the 163 named characters in *Troie*, only 19 (about 10 per cent) are women. Women therefore appear more frequently in illustrations than they do in the text. In one manuscript, MS P17, a later reader has even added a large sketch (approximately thirty-by-forty centimetres in size) of a woman onto the flyleaf of the manuscript (fol. i^v). Whether this is a reader's own interpretation of one of the characters from the text or simply a sketch of a contemporary woman is not known. But it does suggest that at least one person handling this manuscript was so interested in images of women that they even added one of their own.

Illustrations of women appear to have been the focus of specific attentions from users of the manuscripts: in the heavily illustrated MS Vt, Helen and Paris's first meeting (fol. 33^r), their ride to Troy (fol. 36^v) and Andromache's attempts to prevent Hector from returning to battle (fol. 118^v) have been rubbed, touched or potentially the manuscript left open with these folios exposed in such a way that a lot of their colour is missing; in MS Nt (the thirteenth-century manuscript that was commissioned for Béatrice de Gavre), Penthesilea's arrival in Troy has been damaged (fol. 121^v); in the early fourteenth-century French MS Mn, Penthesilea's arrival to Troy has been obscured (fol. 106^v), while the only illustration to accompany *Enéas* in this manuscript, of Dido watching Aeneas sail away from Carthage, has also been spoiled (fol. 148^r); in MS P17 (the manuscript with the large sketch of an unidentified woman added to the flyleaf), the abduction of Helen has been damaged (Figure 4) with very particular attention paid to erasing Helen's face, as has the image of Lavine in her tower (Figure 5); in another of the extensively illustrated Italian manuscripts, MS V1, Medea and Jason's amorous activities in bed show signs of wear and tear (fol. 10^v), while in another lavishly Italian manuscript, MS Vn, the illustration of this scene has been very forcibly erased (fol. 11^r). Jung speculates that the damage to the illustration of Penthesilea in MS Mn was caused by someone 'qui n'avait pas de tendresse pour les Amazones' (*who had no fondness for the Amazons*), but the opposite could be true.[51] A study of British Library devotional manuscripts reveals how damage to certain images was caused by rubbing and kissing as a form of iconophilia and that these images are actually the ones most passionately venerated by readers.[52] While iconophilia has so far been almost exclusively linked to devotional and religious materials, there must exist the possibility that such behaviour could manifest itself in relation to secular texts or tales, too. It is not possible to ascertain definitively whether this damage was the action of users who were either particularly fond of an image or particularly averse to such an image. All we can say is that the illustrations outlined above provoked some kind of physical reaction from their audience, and at the least, it shows that users of these manuscripts were engaging with the female characters, often more so than the male figures.

In spite of medieval audiences' apparent interest in illustrations of women, there has been rather less enthusiasm in recent scholarship: images of women in the *Troie* manuscripts have sometimes been overlooked or even misidentified as illustrations of men. For example, a historiated initial of Penthesilea's dead body was (until very recently) labelled by the British Library as 'the body of a dead king', despite the fact that there are three ways to identify her as Penthesilea (Figure 26):[53] the illustration appears at the point in the narrative immediately following Penthesilea's death; it shows a dead warrior being placed into a river and Penthesilea is the only warrior in *Troie* to receive such a fate; it depicts the warrior with long flowing hair coming down from a crown and such hair is a sign of a virgin woman (which Penthesilea was).[54] Jung agrees that it is 'probablement' (*probably*) Penthesilea's body but he is not confident in this.[55] He later states that 'femmes n'apparaissent pas' (*women do not appear*) in this manuscript, despite the fact that, as well as this illustration of Penthesilea, there is also a historiated initial of Hecuba, Polyxena and Helen mourning at Hector's bier (Figure 12).[56] Jung concedes that there are women in this scene but dismisses them because 'les figures féminines ne sont pas individualisées' (*the female figures are not distinctly individualized*).[57] However, this is typical of MS L2's style and instead the text that this historiated initial accompanies makes it clear who is pictured: it is the initial 'Q' from the 'Quant' at the start of line 17489. From lines 17511 to 17515 we are told that Hecuba, Polyxena and Helen were by Hector's bier, which is doubtless exactly who these three women are intended to represent. Therefore, while it is true that women do not dominate the illustrative scheme, and nor would we expect them to, it is also not true to say that they 'n'apparaissent pas'. Similarly, the miniature of Penthesilea and the Amazons in battle from the thirteenth-century MS P6 was discounted by two researchers because it was claimed that it was 'impossible to determine the sex of the combatants' despite the fact that they have long blonde hair visible under their helmets and Penthesilea's white caparison and shield are specifically described by the text as a way to identify her (Figure 23).[58] Additionally, an illustration in the same manuscript that shows Penthesilea's death is mislabelled by Jung as showing Troilus's death (Figure 27).[59] In fact, Jung writes of this manuscript:

L'*ambiente* est encore purement guerrier. Les femmes – Medea, Briseide, Polixena – sont absentes. La reine Ecuba cependant apparaît trois fois [...]. Andromacha est aussi représentée, avec son fils [...]. Mais il n'y a pas de scènes d'amour.[60]	*The ambience is purely martial. The women – Medea, Briseide, Polyxena – are absent. Queen Hecuba, however, appears three times [...]. Andromache is also represented, with her son. But there are no love scenes.*

However, Polyxena does appear in at least two of the miniatures (mourning the death of Hector alongside other Trojan women on fol. 102ʳ and at her execution on fol. 155ʳ). Indeed, of this manuscript's thirty-eight miniatures, women appear in nine of them.[61] As it was unfair to say that women 'n'apparaissent pas' in MS L2, so too it is not accurate to describe women as 'absentes' from MS P6 simply because there are no love scenes. If anything, it shows us that the illustrator of this manuscript found the non-love scenes in which women appear to be of greater importance.

Finally, some manuscripts have either omitted or erased women to a certain degree or alternatively, the scribes add in their own commentaries to their actions. Four thirteenth-century French manuscripts, MSS Mn, P8, P14 and L2, are all missing the description of the Amazons' kingdom and the way in which they govern, procreate and train for battle.[62] Of these four, MSS Mn, P14 and L2 have been linked to the same miniatures' workshop, yet MS Mn's single illustration of Penthesilea is significantly damaged, while the corresponding image in MS P14 was completely left out from the illustrative scheme.[63] When it comes to omitting warrior women it should also be noted that there are no illustrations of Camille in any *Enéas* manuscripts, even those that contain illustrations of male warriors. Similarly, MS P16 (whose illustrations were never completed but whose rubrics indicate the intended illustrative scheme) appears to have had no plans to include illustrations of Penthesilea. There is nothing to indicate her arrival, her battles, her death or her funeral. There are spaces left on fol. 143ʳ and fol. 146ʳ with rubrics that suggest these were left for depictions of battles twenty-one and twenty-two (in which she and the Amazons participated), but she is not named, nor are the Amazons, and indeed the description for battle twenty-one (the first in which she appears) actually reads 'Ci est la xxie bataille du noble Roy priant' (*here is the twenty-first battle of the noble King Priam*). Meanwhile, MS G reduces the number of Priam's daughters from three to two, omits Cassandra's prophecies, and adds in over sixty unique and original lines that Jung rightly describes as 'un passage misogyne' (*a misogynistic passage*), which attacks Briseide's character.[64] Whereas the damaged illustrations can be interpreted in different ways as to the damagers' attitudes to the illustrations' subjects, these omissions and edits are much less ambiguous.

Conclusion

The *romans*' poets most likely had a place at the court of Henry II and Eleanor of Aquitaine and these specific works would have been welcomed not just for bringing classical texts into the vernacular, but for the way they linked to vernacular histories and made genealogical connections between the Plantagenets and their heroic Trojan ancestors. Later manuscript copies suggest that audiences were not only interested in a simple succession of events but wanted to explore the manner in which these events had taken place and the chivalric worthiness of those who had participated in them, which is why we see the *romans* appearing with romances such as Chrétien's works or chivalric poems such as the *Ordène de chevalerie*. The provenance of the manuscripts shows a shift in the thirteenth and fourteenth centuries away from Anglo-Norman territories and into France and Italy. Evidence from the owners and readers of these manuscripts is diverse and shows the many ways in which these texts were repurposed. There is relatively sparse information on the original commissioners or patrons of these manuscripts, but what little there is often tells powerful stories. The shared ownership of MS M by two knights of the Fourth Crusade, Geoffrey of Villehardouin and Milon of Brabant, underlines *Troie*'s value as a narrative of conquest but also a narrative of camaraderie where soldiers are lauded for the strength of their bonds. Manuscripts such as MS Nt and MS L1 also show that *Troie* attracted a female readership. In fact, the *romans* manuscripts suggest that the texts had a complex and varying relationship to women. Some manuscripts promote and celebrate their female characters by including elaborate illustrations or omitting passages that have a misogynistic undertone. Other manuscripts do the opposite and omit women from the illustrative scheme, reduce the amount of text dedicated to their descriptions and add extra misogynistic passages. Beyond the intentions of the original manuscript architects, later readers have left their mark in their interactions with the female characters: illustrations of women attract particular attention as compared to illustrations of men and are more likely to be damaged. Whether this damage is a sign of fondness or disgust cannot be deduced, but it does show that they were provoking reaction and that those characters were clearly of interest for hundreds of years after their original creation.

2

Women as reasons for war

In 1405, the prominent political thinker and court writer during the reign of Charles VI of France, Christine de Pizan (c. 1364–1430), wrote her *Livre des Trois Vertus* – a mirror for princesses that was dedicated to Margaret of Nevers (c. 1393–1442). In her chapter on advice for women during times of conflict, she explains that 'grans maulx et dommages au royaulme' (*great harm and much damage to a whole kingdom*) can occur merely due to the quarrel of a 'bien petit baron ou chevalier' (*a very unimportant baron or knight*).[1] She goes on to give several other examples of disputes between individual men that ultimately escalated into largescale destructive wars that brought great suffering to the entire kingdom of France. But is this view, that wars are caused by the quarrels of a few individual men, representative of a wider consensus on the causes of war? The *romans* contribute to this debate in their exploration of the Theban, Trojan and Latin wars. This includes the extent to which women are represented as factors in the outbreak of hostilities or whether masculinized ideas of vengeance, feuding, martial glory, chivalric honour, dynastic power, territorial supremacy and the construction of masculinity itself have a greater responsibility.

Reasons for violence: Feminine figures

The *romans* present several ways in which women are blamed or portrayed as the reason or motivation for violence: they are abducted or wronged and must be rescued or avenged; they are offered up as a prize or reward to the victor in battle; knights wish to display their martial prowess to watching women; and women themselves take up arms or implore men to fight on their behalf. The *romans* are far from unique in this sense. For example, the figure of the abducted woman appears dishearteningly frequently across the Old French tradition: Chrétien de Troye's *Lancelot, ou le Chevalier de la Charrette* (c. 1175–81), a text also found in MSS P2 and P5, is narratively driven by Meleagant's abduction of Guinevere and Lancelot's quest to rescue her; in Wace's *Brut*, which is also found in MSS Mn, P2, P5, P10 and P12, Arthur is lauded for slaying a giant from Mont St Michel who abducts women from the nearby town; in the *Roman d'Alexandre* and the *Histoire Ancienne jusqu'à César*, narratives also found in MSS Nt and P8 and MSS P15 and P19 respectively, Alexander rescues Candaculus's wife who has been abducted by the king of the Belices. This trope is one of the most thoroughly explored in *Troie*, through the figures of Helen and Hesione. Helen is the more well-known of the two and has been cited as the reason for the Trojan wars throughout the centuries. There are several reasons why Hesione has not been remembered to the same extent as Helen. Her character is underdeveloped in comparison to Helen's, she has no direct speech and is generally only referred to rather than being present in any scenes. She rarely appears in illustrations and when she does it is only at the point of her abduction. Essentially, she is portrayed as more of an object than a person. In classical versions (such as Apollodorus of Athens's *Chronicle*, Homer's *Iliad* and Ovid's *Metamorphoses*) there is a prologue to her abduction that does not appear in *Troie* in which we are told that she was actually rescued rather than abducted by Hercules after Laomedon tried to execute her as a human sacrifice. Her fate in those texts is therefore more of a blessing in order to escape the murderous intentions of her brother. But in *Troie* we are not told this, and her abduction is a straightforward wrong. In contrast, Helen's abduction is more ambiguous (as will be discussed) and therefore more divisive. Also, while Hesione's abduction triggers Antenor's diplomatic envoy to Greece, it is only Helen's abduction that triggers actual battles; essentially, had Hesione's abduction prompted the Trojans to sack the city in which she was being held (rather than to send a polite group of diplomats) it would have attracted more attention. Indeed, in Emmanuèle Baumgartner and Françoise Vielliard's edition of extracts from *Troie* they completely omit the abduction of Hesione altogether, but do include that of Helen.

At first glance, the medieval texts and their classical sources suggest that Helen's abduction is the primary reason for the war. In Dictys's account, Helen is abducted by Paris, provoking Menelaus and the Greeks to sail to Troy and demand her return. Priam gives her the choice to return to Greece but she states that she prefers to remain in Troy:

Tunc Priamus inter regulos medius adstans facto silentio optionem Helenae, quae ob id in conspectum popularium venerat, offert, si ei videretur domum ad suos regredi. Quam ferunt dixisse neque se invitam navigasse, neque sibi cum Menelai matrimonio convenire. (Dictys, I.10)	*Then Priam, standing in the midst of the princes and calling for silence, said that Helen (who had come into public view for this purpose) should have the right to decide. When he asked her; 'Do you want to go home?' her answer, so they reported, was 'No'. She had not sailed, she said, unwillingly, for her marriage to Menelaus did not suit her.*

Helen seems complicit in her abduction, choosing to leave and wishing to stay with Paris rather than return to Menelaus. Benoît picks up on this in *Troie* and suggests that Helen was a willing participant, having fallen in love with Paris. When the Trojans attack the temple to take her away, the narrator tells us that '[n]e se fist mie trop leidir, | Bien fist senblant del consentir' (*she did not rend herself too much and even made it appear as if she were consenting*, ll. 4505–06). This apparent complicity makes the term 'abducted' problematic although the word 'senblant' (*appear*) does allow the spectre of doubt to haunt the scene. However, to a medieval sensibility it would not have been problematic and this was a straightforward abduction. Helen's legitimate marriage to Menelaus meant that her rightful place was by his side and her departure with Paris, even willingly, automatically made him her abductor and she an abductee. For example, in 1285, a man 'abducted' a Benedictine nun from her religious house and was sentenced to imprisonment despite her apparent consent and indeed desire to run away with him.[2] Abduction to a medieval mindset only indicated 'taking away' and was unconcerned with the giving or withholding of consent.[3] In this context, therefore, we can speak about Helen's abduction without necessarily needing to discuss her acquiescence.

Helen's abduction is illustrated in six manuscripts (MSS P6, P17, Vt, V1, Vn and P18). Had the illustrations of MS P16 been completed it is highly likely to have featured within its folios, too, as there is space left for a miniature on fol. 26^v accompanied by this rubric: 'Comment li roys prianz son navie en grece et comment paris son filz ravie heleine pourquoy troi fu destruite secondement' (*how Priam's fleet went to Greece and how his son Paris abducted Helen, which is why Troy was destroyed a second time*). The rubric itself is pretty blunt in its summary that Helen's abduction was the reason for the Trojan war. Given that *Troie*'s text does not seem particularly concerned over the question of her consent, the miniatures disagree over her complicity. MS P17 includes two renditions of her abduction; one is included as part of the frontispiece and another at the point in the text where her abduction is described. In the frontispiece (fol. 42^r) we see her forcibly manhandled by men in armour who pick her up and carry her into a boat. Her body is limp and her arms hang loosely, showing her powerlessness against the flurry of activity produced by the soldiers carrying her away. Similarly, in the later (damaged) miniature (Figure 4) she is picked up off the ground, though this time by a single male figure (presumably Paris). This miniature is one of those that has been subject to certain attentions from a user of the manuscript and is heavily obscured and damaged over Helen's upper half. Paris's face is featureless, presumably due to the attentions of the same user rather than the miniaturist having intentially left it blank as there is no sign that any of the other illustrations in this manuscript were unfinished. The indication in this manuscript is that Helen was forcibly, violently and unwillingly taken from her home and this has produced a strong reaction in at least one later user.

In contrast, the Italian manuscripts give a more ambiguous rendering of this scene. In MS Vn we see the violence around the abduction as soldiers attack various Greek men and take others prisoner (Figure 3). But in the centre of the frame, Helen and Paris have a serene appearance. Paris holds his hand out to Helen indicating that he is speaking to her rather than just picking her up and carrying her off, while Helen has her hands folded gently and looks directly at Paris. The soldier behind her, with his sword drawn, reminds us that there is an element of coercion, but similarly it is also possible to interpret this scene as Helen going willingly, even if her countrymen put up a fight. It actually looks more like a rescue scene than an abduction. Similarly, in the Italian MS Vt, the figures of Helen and Paris are drawn so closely together that they overlap (Figure 2). Their heads incline towards one another, suggesting an intimate relationship. To the sides of the scene we see looting and violence, but this does not affect Helen as she walks calmly out of the scene accompanied by Paris. He is no longer shown as a violent abductor, but as a saviour – quite literally a knight in shining armour.

Regardless of the circumstances of Helen's abduction, *Troie* and its sources make its disastrous consequences clear. Dares gives us Panthus's warning to Priam that if Paris takes Helen from Greece, Troy is destined to fall (*Dares*, D.8). Benoît reproduces Panthus's prophecies (ll. 4077–118) and adds Cassandra's prophecies to them: '[s]e de Grece a femme Paris, | Destruit iert Troie e li païs' (*if Paris has a wife from Greece, Troy and its lands will be destroyed*, ll. 4147–48). Helen is cited as the reason for war, but Paris is implicated alongside her. However, as the war progresses, Paris's responsibility diminishes, while Helen's increases. We see this first in Achilles's speech to the Greek chiefs as he attempts to persuade them to make peace and argues that the reason for which they initially went to war is not a good enough reason to continue:

Trop fol plait avons entrepris,	*We foolishly committed ourselves*
Qui pour l'acheison d'une femme	*to a distant quarrel; all for the*
Avons guerpi tant riche regne,	*sake of a woman we have left our*
Tant reiaume, tant bon païs.	*rich lands, our kingdoms and our*
[...]	*good territories. [...]*
Mout est mauvaise l'acheison	*The reason for our terrible*
De nostre grant destrucion.	*suffering is a very bad one.*
(*Troie*, ll. 18174–77, 18189–90)	

We then see this later in the narrative, when Helen's own words during her lament for Paris invoke her responsibility, making it almost a confession:

Ja plus terre ne me sostienge	*This land can no longer support*
Ne ja mais par femme ne vienge	*me for never has a woman*
Si grant damage com par mei!	*brought such much damage as I*
Tant riche duc e tant bon rei	*have! So many great dukes and*
E tant riche amiraut preisié	*so many great kings and so many*
En sont ocis e detrenchié!	*worthy chiefs have been killed*
[...]	*and hacked to pieces! [...]*
Mil mui de sanc de cors vassaus	*A thousand measures of blood*
De chevaliers proz e leiaus	*from the bodies of worthy and*
Sont espandu par m'acheison.	*loyal knights have been spilled*
[...]	*for my sake. [...]*
Que ne m'ocit le rei Priant,	*King Priam should kill me, for it*
Qui par mei est vis confonduz.	*is through me that his life has*
(*Troie*, ll. 22927–32, 22957–59, 22962–63)	*become desolate.*

Her whole speech is nearly one hundred lines long and all of it is a variation on the theme of how she is solely to blame for all the death and destruction that the war has brought and her wish to die as atonement. This is a considerable departure from Benoît's classical source: in Dares we are told only that Helen took part 'magno ululatu' (*with loud lamentations*, D.35). Dictys presents an even starker difference for not only is the scene in which Helen laments Paris's death entirely absent, but a woman named Oenone, his wife before Helen's abduction, is present at his funeral and her grief is so great that she dies on the spot and is buried with him (*Dictys*, IV.21).

Whether Helen truly believes that she is the cause and deserves such punishment is debatable; this could also be a strategy to stay on the good side of Priam and Hecuba, who are now her only chance for safety as she is more vulnerable following Paris's death. Such laments certainly do not do her any harm, for the narrator tells us:

Tel l'i a dame Heleine fait	*Helen displayed such [grief]*
E tant i a crïé e brait	*and cried and lamented so*
Que Prianz e sis parentez	*much that Priam and his*
L'en sorent puis merveillos grez:	*relatives were very grateful. She*
Mout en fu puis de toz amee	*was very much loved by them*
E mout l'en ont tuit honoree.	*all and was very much*
(*Troie*, ll. 23073–78)	*honoured.*

In any case, nobody disagrees with her and in accepting responsibility she makes herself a sympathetic figure who wins the court's love, respect and protection. Paris's death seems to absolve him of responsibility and there is no mention of the fact that he had abducted her in the first place. As the figure who has been 'left behind', Helen has no choice but to accept the blame and throw herself at the mercy of the Trojan court.

But Helen's abduction was not the first to take place in *Troie*. The first destruction of Troy by the Greeks, led by Hercules, results in the abduction of Hesione. Philippe Logié argues that this abduction is actually the most important factor in determining the causes of the war, for it is this event that sets in motion the 'jeu du *tort* et du *droit*' (*game of right and wrong*) that plays out for the rest of *Troie*.[4] Paris's initial expedition to Greece is to recover Hesione. However, he abducts Helen instead. It is at this point that Priam suffers what Logié calls his 'fatal aveuglement' (*fatal blindness*): 'Priam voit dans Hélène la monnaie d'échange qui lui permettra de retrouver Hésione, mais, par une contradiction étrange et inexpliquée, il autorise son fils à l'épouser' (*Priam sees in Helen the means of exchange that would allow him to reclaim Hesione, but, for by some strange an unexplained contradiction, he instead allows his son to marry her*).[5] In these terms, the abduction of Helen was 'justifiable' in retaliation for the abduction of Hesione. Achilles makes this clear:

Ja en menerent Greu s'antain,	*The Greeks previously abducted*
Soror son pere, Esionain,	*[Paris's] aunt, the sister of his*
Que mout fu quise e demandee:	*father, Hesione, whom they came*
Se cist en ra ceste menee,	*to reclaim many times. If [Paris],*
Quel tort, quel honte e quel damage	*in return, abducted [Helen],*
I peut aveir nostre lignage	*where is the wrong, the shame or*
Ne nos meïsmes, qui ci somes?	*the harm in that to our lineage or*
(*Troie*, ll. 18201–07)	*to us who are here?*

However, Priam's refusal to return her in exchange for Hesione, places him in the wrong. Priam essentially approves the abduction of Helen and abandons Hesione, which tips the scales of right and wrong in favour of the Greek, a fact that they can then exploit. The question of causality is complex: the Greeks lay the foundation for the war by abducting Hesione; Paris's abduction of Helen is retribution to avenge this earlier abduction; however, Priam's failure to exploit this opportunity for rebalance by exchanging Helen for Hesione ultimately leads to the outbreak of the first battle.

This view of Paris simply as a 'rebalancer' of justice is also rather generous. Not only are abductors rarely the heroes of their stories, but in determining his motivations for abducting Helen it was clear that he always had the intention of claiming Helen for himself, regardless of Hesione's position. This is thanks to an earlier promise that had been made to him during the 'Judgement of Paris'. This episode recounted how Paris was asked by three goddesses to judge which of them was the most beautiful and in return they would give him a gift: Juno promises to make him a powerful king, Minerva offers wisdom and skill in war and Venus promises the most beautiful woman in the world (Helen). He had chosen Venus and therefore feels he is 'due' his reward. He tells this story to the council of Trojans before they set out to Greece while explaining that this is why he is eager to go (ll. 3846–928). Justifying Paris's abduction of Helen as vengeance for the Greek's abduction of Hesione is rather a retrospective attempt to excuse his actions; essentially, he simply felt entitled to Helen and was willing to act violently to realize this entitlement.

Another way that women are presented as the origin of violence is when they are offered up as prizes to whomever is successful in battle. Again, this role is not uncommon in the Old French tradition.[6] In Chrétien's *Erec et Enide,* which is also found in three of the thirteenth-century French manuscripts, MSS P2, P5 and P8, Erec defeats Yder in a tournament in order to win a prize hawk that he presents to Enide and subsequently secures her hand in marriage. In another of his romances, *Yvain, ou Le Chevalier au Lion*, which is also found in four of the thirteenth-century manuscripts, MSS P2, P5, P7 and P12, Yvain is offered the reward of a lord's daughter's hand in marriage if he can defeat two demons that are threatening the town. In Marie de France's *Chaitivel* (*c.* 1160–80), four knights compete in a fierce tournament in hopes of winning their lady, but three are killed and the fourth is invalided to his bed for the rest of his life. So in *Enéas*, we find Lavine, the daughter of King Latinus, has been promised to Turnus, the king of the Rutuli, but the gods have promised Aeneas that he will inherit the Latin lands and found the Roman dynasty through his union with Lavine. The Latin wars are therefore a battle between Turnus and Aeneas to decide who will win the right to marry her. She first actively appears in the narrative in conversation with her mother. The queen attempts to persuade her to love Turnus, but she is resistant:

'Or sui en pais et a repos,	'Now I am at peace and repose,
Ne m'i metrai, car ge n'en os,	I will not, for I do not dare, put
En tel destreit dont ge n'ai cure;	myself in such distress for which I
Forz est li mals a desmesure.	have no care; [love] is an evil of
Ge n'enprendrai oan amor,	very great strength. I will not
Dont cuit aveir mal ne dolor.'	involve myself in love, from
Molt est salvage la meschine.	which I believe only to have
(*Enéas*, ll. 8015–21)	pain.' The maiden was very stubborn.

The vocabulary links love with war. Lavine uses 'pais' (*peace*) and 'repos' (*repose*) to describe her emotional state when not in love and the words 'destreit' (*distress*), 'mals' (*evil*) and 'dolor' (*pain*) to describe the state of being in love: she gives the impression that love is violent and painful. Her analysis is prescient, for when she eventually succumbs to love it is described in similarly aggressive terms:

> Amors l'a de son dart ferue;
> Ainz qu'el se fust d'iluee meüe,
> I a changié cent feiz color.
> Or est chaeite es laz d'amor,
> Voillë o non, amer l'estuet.
> Quant veit que eschiuer nel puet,
> Vers Eneas a atorné
> Tot son cörage et son pensé;
> Por lui l'a molt Amors navree;
> La saiete li est colee
> Des i qu'el cuer soz la mamele.
> (*Enéas*, ll. 8057–67)
>
> *Love hit her with his arrow; before she left that place, she changed colour a hundred times. Now she has fallen into Love's trap, and whether she wants to or not, she must love him [Aeneas]. When she saw that she could not escape, she turned all her heart and thoughts to Aeneas; Love had wounded her deeply for him; the arrow plunged into her right to her heart under her breast.*

The line '[v]oillë o non' (*whether she wants to or not*) is the most powerful as it shows Lavine's complete lack of agency. The description of her injuries as a result of love continues in similarly violent terms, with words such as 'colp mortal' (*mortal blow*), 'tressuer' (*to sweat*), 'trenbler' (*to tremble*), 'tressalt' (*she shivers*), 'senglot' (*she sobs*), 'fremist' (*she shudders*), 'crië' (*she wails*), 'plore' (*she cries*), 'gient' (*she groans*) and 'brait' (*she screams*). It is not shown as a pleasant experience. Of course, this amount of suffering was one of the tropes of *fin amors* and courtly love, a concept that was emerging contemporaneously with the *romans*.[7] The link here between the language of love with military images (arrows, traps, escapes, mortal blows) frames Lavine's suffering as a form of battle. It is therefore not just Lavine who causes Aeneas to fight, but in return Aeneas causes Lavine to fight, although the former's fight is a physical battle while the latter's is an emotional one. However, while Aeneas wins his battles, Lavine loses hers and the narrative ends with their marriage and the prophesied founding of Rome.

Women are also given as the reason for violence because of the *fin amors* concept: the interaction between love and martial prowess was a key aspect of this emerging topos. Courtly love was an important concept not just to the *romans d'antiquité*, but to a vast swathe of the Old French tradition: romances linked war and conflict to courtly love through a chivalric paradigm and so we see knights inspired to great prowess out of love for a lady or indeed a lady falling in love with a knight because of said prowess. The author of the *History of William Marshal* (1220–29) approved of women's presence as spectators at tournaments and even believed that their support was a factor in victory for the knights 'became better men as a result of the ladies's arrival'.[8] Helen J. Nicholson's study of medieval warfare posits that one of the (many) reasons for waging war was the aim of individuals to 'attract the attention of desirable partners, so increasing the possibility of marriage and having children to carry on their line' as part of an individual's concern for dynastic legacy.[9] Thus, during several battles in *Thèbes*, we see women standing where they can watch the fighting, either on the city walls or hillsides purely to spectate. In one such battle, Parthenopeus kills a knight, and sends the knight's horse as a token of triumph and love to Antigone, which she gratefully receives:

> Ço sache bien que por cest don
> Li cuit rendre gent guerredon;
> Ço sache bien senz nule dote
> Que il a mei et m'amor tote.
> (*Thèbes*, ll. 4395–98)
>
> *Know that in exchange for this gift I will offer him a noble recompense. He should know without a doubt that I am his with all my love.*

There is something rather coquettish about this mysterious 'gent guerredon' (*noble recompense*) that she will offer him. When Parthenopeus is later killed, the narrator describes how his companion Dorceus fans his dying body with a large ermine sleeve that Antigone had given to him 'par druerie' (*through tender love*, l. 9375). However, his dying speech to Dorceus is rather strange:

> A ma mére tot dreit iras,
> Freit message li porteras.
> Quant ele parlera o tei,
> Se tu li dis come est de mei,
> Elle morra sempres, ço crei:
> Di que navrez fui al tornei,
> Et por iço a lé t'envei:
> Pré lé que ne meint duel por mei.
> (*Thèbes*, ll. 9301–08)
>
> *Go straight to my mother, bring her this sad message. When she speaks with you, and you tell her what has happened to me, she will soon die, I believe; tell her that I was wounded in battle and it is for this that I have sent you to her: beseech her not to suffer for me.*

He does not mention Antigone as we may have expected. She has inspired him to do great deeds on the battlefield, but once fallen he thinks only of his mother. While Parthenopeus is keen for Antigone to share in his triumph as demonstrated in the gift-horse, he does not want her to share in his failure. Through the ermine sleeve the narrator invokes her image by his side as he dies, but Parthenopeus himself does not mention her. If masculinity is partially constructed by military prowess and success in battle, then his fall would be seen as emasculating and not something that he wishes to share with her.

Troie also contains a scene in which a horse is sent from a knight to his lady as a token of affection and conquest. Diomedes sends a horse to Briseide, which he has won in battle from Troilus, her former lover:

> Diomedès est alez joindre
> O Troïlus por la danzele:
> Jus le trebuche de la sele.
> Le destrier prent par le noël.
>
> *Diomedes went to engage with Troilus for [the sake of] the maiden: He knocked him from the saddle. He took the horse by the bridle.*

Un suen vaslet, un dameisel,	*He called his vassel, a young man,*
A apelé e si li tent:	*and gave it to him:*
'Va tost,' fait il, 'isnelement	*'Go now', he said, 'quickly*
A la tente Calcas de Troie	*to the tent of Calcas of Troy*
E di a sa fille la bloie	*and say to the blonde girl*
Que jo li envei cest destrier:	*that I am sending her this horse:*
Guaaignié l'ai d'un chevalier	*I won it from a knight*
Qui mout par se fait bien de li.'	*who really wants to do well for her.'*
(*Troie*, ll. 14286–97)	

His token is initially rejected by Briseide who does not appreciate him speaking ill of Troilus. However, eventually he wins her over and she gives him a token of her reciprocated affection:

La destre manche de son braz	*She gave him the right sleeve*
Neuve e fresche d'un ciglaton	*from her arm, which was*
Li baille en lieu de confanon.	*made of new and fresh silk for*
[...]	*him to use in place of a*
Dès or puet saveir Troïlus	*banner. [...] From now on Troilus knew*
Que mar s'atendra a li plus.	*that it was futile to expect more from her.*
(*Troie*, ll. 15176–78, 15183–84)	

These scenes are featured in some of the manuscript illustrations. In the fourteenth-century Neapolitan MS V1, we see Diomedes's squire delivering the horse to Briseide in her tent while the battle rages in close proximity (fol. 112^r). However, the later action of her gift of her sleeve is not illustrated and we only see them speaking in her tent (fol. 116^v); her reciprocation of love is indicated through their joined hands, but there is no sign of the sleeve. MS Vn is also missing the scene of the sleeve. It includes the scene in which Troilus is unhorsed by Diomedes and we see the squire taking hold of the horse (fol. 84^r), but the moment when it is delivered to Briseide is not shown. We later see Diomedes and Briseide talking in her tent, with Troilus's horse next to her, but we see neither the sleeve donation nor do they join hands (Figure 7). However, a slightly later direct copy of MS Vn, MS P18, does include the sleeve scene. As before, we have the illustration of Diomedes unhorsing Troilus and giving the horse to his squire to deliver to Briseide. In the corresponding scene for their later meeting in the tent, we now see the moment at which she gives her sleeve to him (Figure 8). It is possible that the earlier illustrator of MS Vn had accidently omitted this sleeve from his rendition of this scene, as there certainly is space for it to be drawn, which could explain the distance between the two. Regardless of why it was not included in MS Vn, the illustrator of MS P18, copying MS Vn, clearly noticed the mistake and thought it important to rectify it. If we look at the Italian MS Vt, we see another variation in the illustrative scheme of these scenes. There are separate illustrations for Diomedes's unhorsing of Troilus (fol. 109) and the squire giving the horse to Briseide (fol. 110) followed by the scene in which the two are reunited in the Greek camp (Figure 9). In this image we see Troilus's horse tied up outside the tent, while the two figures do not appear to be speaking as Diomedes has his arms folded across his body. However, rather than a scene of conversation, this is in fact the moment at which Briseide detaches her sleeve in order to give it to Diomedes: we see her right arm raised as her left hand appears to reach for the right sleeve in order to detach it, just as the text relates. Despite the variations in these manuscripts, the constant across all four is to show some combination of Diomedes's unhorsing of Troilus, the transfer of the horse to Briseide and the subsequent union of the two lovers: Diomedes's actions on the battlefield certainly seem to be influenced by his desire for Briseide.

The manuscript illustrations in MSS P17, V1 and Vt also show images of women watching the battles from the city walls. For example, one of the very few illustrations of Lavine that we have (one of only two) is of her watching from a tower as Turnus and Aeneas do battle (Figure 5). Similarly, MSS V1 and Vt have numerous instances of unidentified women watching the battles from the windows or walls of Troy (Figure 6 provides just one example and Appendix 2 details the other instances). The text tells us that the 'dames furent sor les murs […] | Por esguarder le grant tornei' (*ladies were up on the walls […] to watch the great tournament*, ll. 8081, 8084). It is difficult to translate the word 'tornei' here as it usually indicates a tournament in the specific context of a jousting tournament and is rarely used to indicate a battle in the context of warfare. Glyn S. Burgess and Douglas Kelly translate it as 'battle' in their translation of *Troie* but this misses some of the nuance of the word. The way in which *Troie* presents the battles is very much as a chivalric spectacle that can be compared to a tournament and the way in which women view and participate in this event is also comparable to the historical realities. David Crouch's study of tournaments shows that in the twelfth century, stands for the spectators were built and these were principally for women.[10] He explains that the role of spectator was not a passive one and that women were often involved in judging the winners of the events.[11] Moreover, E. Jane Burns's study of clothes in medieval French culture discusses the way in which a lady's sleeve functioned as a love token in combat and that it served 'as a surrogate for her inspiring presence, propelling the knight who loves her to accomplish feats of extaordinary prowess'.[12] Therefore, if we combine the scenes of the ladies watching the battles (or *torneis*) with Briseide's gift of her sleeve to Diomedes, we are immersed in a milieu that owes just as much to pageantry and tournaments as it does to warfare.

The final way that women are shown as inspiring violence is directly through taking up arms themselves. The figure of the woman warrior is the focus of a later chapter, but the women discussed here are different because they are not formally trained warriors or knights; they are accidental or reluctant fighters. One such group are the Argive women who march to Thebes to reclaim the bodies of their loved ones after the final battle in *Thèbes*: the narrator describes them as a 'grant host' (*great army*, l. 9815). The new king of Thebes, Creon, refuses to allow them to recover the bodies and so they implore the duke of Athens, Theseus, to assist them. The Argive women and the Athenian forces then launch an assault on Thebes:

Donc veïssez femnes ramper,	*So you should see the women*
O mauz d'acier les murs fausser;	*clamber, to damage the walls with*
Le mortier gratent trop fortment,[13]	*steel mallets; they scratch the stones*

Pertus i firent plus de cent;	*fiercely, they make more*
Ne lor chaleit quis oceïst,	*than a hundred openings there;*
Ne qui onques mal lor feïst:	*it was of little importance to*
Mout se combateient fortment.	*them who died or who caused*
Grant pitié en aveient gent:	*them harm: they fought with*
Por les femnes fortment ploroent.	*great strength. The people had*
(*Thèbes*, ll. 10077-85)	*great pity on them: they cried a*
	lot for the women.

This description is powerful in showing that women will join in the fight if required and will do so with great courage and strength. There are numerous stories in historical sources to show that such eventualities did occur, especially during sieges when the towns or soldiers needed reinforcements. For example, the *Histoire de Guillaume le Maréchal* (*c*. 1220) tells of the women of Drincourt helping to defend the town by attacking the invaders with axes, sticks, swords and clubs (ll. 1087-90) while the *Chanson de la Croisade Albigeoise* (*c*. 1213-28) describes women helping to defend various towns on numerous occasions.[14] The tears of the Theban people reflect the sorrow that the *Thèbes*-poet anticipates his audience will also feel upon encountering this scene. A situation in which women must take up arms is clearly not a desirable state of affairs and it creates a contrast to the episodes discussed previously in this section. In those scenes, men's efforts on the battlefield demonstrated ideals of masculinity and strength to those watching, who were portrayed as enthralled or even seduced by such viewing. But the violent behaviour of the women in this episode only results in the watchers feeling sadness and pity for them. Both sexes participate in fighting, but the responses of those around them to their actions reveal their gendering.

Having looked at these examples we can see the ways in which women are used as reasons for war. Many of the knights who take part in violence do so to impress the women who watch from the walls. The Trojan wars are provoked first by the abduction of Hesione and then the abduction of Helen and are continued by an unwillingness on the part of Priam to make peace when given the opportunity to do so. The Latin wars begin as Aeneas seeks to win Lavine from Turnus, fuelled by his desire to fulfil the prophecy of founding a great dynasty. However, this rather crude over-simplification of the reasons for these wars certainly does not give the whole picture and we need to look at other causes for the outbreak and continuation of hostilities.

Reasons for violence: Masculine ideas

Gratian's *Concordantia Discordantium Canonum*, commonly known as the *Decretum*, appeared ten to thirty years before the *romans*, in *c*. 1140, and was a particularly well-known text for students of canon law. It outlines three circumstances in which war is permissible: to recover stolen goods, to avenge injuries and in self-defence. The Trojan wars found their legitimacy using the first two circumstances, if we label

Hesione and Helen rather crudely as 'stolen goods', and consider the inhospitalities that the Greeks and Trojans mutually inflict upon one another as 'injuries'. However, it is more difficult to justify the Theban and Latin wars within Gratian's framework, unless we stretch the definition of 'injuries'. But instead of Gratian, it is better to look at the emergence of the medieval chivalric code. Maurice Keen argues that we see the chivalric age emerging as early as 1100, with the first systematic treatment of chivalry appearing with Etienne de Fougères's *Livre des Manières* (c. 1174–78).[15] Richard W. Kaeuper's work is rather more cautious in discussing the development of chivalry: he describes a 'thick European mist' obscuring its origins and warns that close investigation is difficult.[16] Instead, we need to think of these values and practices emerging gradually over a considerable period of time, while recognising that chivalry in the earlier Middle Ages could not anticipate the chivalry of the later Middle Ages; essentially, we can speak about chivalric practices in the early twelfth century and we can speak about them in the late fifteenth century, but we would not be talking about the same thing. The period in which the *romans* were first written was exactly this time of burgeoning ideas, and manuscript copies were being made at the same time that chivalry came to be more formally codified in later works such as the anonymous *Ordène de Chevalerie*, Ramon Lull's *Libre del Ordre de Cavayleria* (c. 1250–1300) and Geoffrey de Charny's *Livre de Chevalerie* (c. 1340–59). Although these works were only written down after the date of the *romans*'s composition, they essentially formalized what had been developing and percolating since the early twelfth century. Indeed, the *romans* engage with the emergence of chivalric ideas as they too explore ideas of what the ideal chivalric hero looks like. The *Ordène* provides four commandments that a knight must follow: he must not consent to any false judgement or be party to treason; he must honour women and be ready to aid them to the limit of his power; he must hear a mass every day; he must fast every Friday. Ramon's work offers a more theological account of chivalry and suggests that the primary duty of the knight was to defend the Church against unbelievers, as well as prizing honour above all else and eschewing falsehood, treachery, greed and idleness. Finally, Geoffrey's text reinforces the advice of the *Ordène* and Ramon, but extends it to all soldiers, not just knights. He goes against traditional Augustinian doctrine to suggest that earthly goods were significant and that soldiers should be materially rewarded for chivalrous action. However, despite the apparent ennobling and virtuosity that chivalry entailed, it also had negative consequences. Kaeuper has urged a reassessment of chivalric warfare that takes into consideration not only the virtues of the chivalric warrior, but also recognizes the realities of greed, deception and violence.[17] Meanwhile Craig Taylor's analysis of chivalric ideals similarly acknowledges that there was a 'negative note' to the actions of these knights, many of whom were more interested in fighting and earning profit than they were in the ideals or nobility of war.[18] The rules and regulations as to what justified a fair fight were therefore still fluid and debatable in theory as well as practice.

At one stage of the conflict, the Greek hero Achilles's actually desires to make peace rather than fight, and argues that Helen's abduction was not sufficient justification for the outbreak of hostilities. However, Thoas and Menestheus rebuke him and reveal the real reasons why the Greeks started to fight and will continue to do so:

Ne somes pas en ceste peine	*We are not in this struggle*
Por Menelaus ne por Heleine,	*for Menelaus or for Helen,*
Qui por aveir honor e pris.	*but to have honour and glory.*
Puis que si bien l'avez empris,	*Since you have begun so well,*
Ja n'en partirons senz victoire,	*we shall never leave without*
Si que de nos iert fait memoire.	*victory, and without what we*
(*Troie*, ll. 18329–34)	*have done being made memorable.*

In MSS P7, P9, P17 and Vt, the line 'Puis que si bien l'avez empris' (*since you have begun so well*) actually appears as 'Si com orent nostre ancessor' (*as our ancestors had*) and links to the previous line about having honour and glory. The fact that this breaks the rhyming couplet structure would have made it stand out and highlights how important certain scribes obviously felt about emphasising that honour and glory was part of an ancestral tradition, linking them back to their forefathers, just as the *romans* themselves sought to link medieval heroes back to their Trojan ancestors. Menestheus reinforces Thoas's sentiments:

Tant riche rei, tant amiraut,	*There are such powerful kings,*
Tant duc preisié e tant baron	*such military leaders, such*
A ci a ceste asembleison,	*renowned dukes and such barons*
Qui mieus voudraient estre pris,	*in this assembly, who would*
Mort e detrenchié e ocis,	*rather be taken prisoner, die and*
Qu'ensi s'en fussent repairié.	*be beheaded and killed, than to*
[...]	*retreat like this. [...]*
Proz d'ome ne deit doter mort	*A worthy man must not fear*
Contre si faite deshonor.	*death in the face of this kind of*
(*Troie*, ll. 18372–77, 18382–83)	*dishonour.*

In response, all the assembled Greeks reply '[b]ien dit! bien dit! ço est li mieuz!' (*well said! well said! that is the best!*, l. 18399), showing that Achilles is very much an outsider in his opinions. The overwhelming consensus is that continuing with the war is the best policy, even facing almost certain death, or actually relishing the idea of death it brings honour. This unity on the part of all the other Greeks to sacrifice whatever it takes, even their lives, to win glory and everlasting renown can be linked to ideas of masculinity and leads us back to the reasons for war. Current scholarship on war and gender suggests that masculinity is central to the ways in which war gains its meaning and legitimacy in society.[19] Recent analysis posits that masculinity is a significant explanatory variable in violence, though scholars differ on whether the relationship between war and masculinity is constitutive or causal: Nancy C. M. Hartsock's work suggests that masculinity is the key underlying cause of war, while Joshua S. Goldstein's work argues that it is the occurrence of war in the first place that demands the construction of such masculinities.[20] Masculinity is itself a near-impossible concept to define as it differs across cultures, time, location, social status, religion and politics; Ruth Mazo Karras suggests that it would be more appropriate to speak of 'masculinities' in the plural rather than the singular but that regardless, within a chivalric paradigm 'violence [is] the mode of masculine expression.'[21] It therefore follows that if violence is required for the construction of a masculine identity, then men must seek out opportunities for violence. Without war they risk losing their homosocial bonds, which were of critical importance to social structuring and their sense of gender identity. Rescuing an abducted woman or fighting to win the love of a woman were convenient and entertaining explanations to justify their violence, but the underlying motivation is more essential: war is necessary for the continuation of gender identity and gender distinctions. Women were largely excluded from the battlefield and homosocial networks and therefore allowed a clear gendered hierarchy to be maintained and perpetuated. If this were to falter, the threat to traditional patriarchal structures would be strong indeed. Karras argues that the shared experiences of hardship and violence created homosocial bonds between knights;[22] if those experiences were taken away, then the bonds that they produce would similarly disappear.

Eventually, Achilles's infatuation with Polyxena does result in him temporarily withdrawing from battle:

> Qui tres bien est d'amor espris,   Whomever is truly taken by
> Il n'a en sei sen ne reison.   love, no longer has any sense or
> Ensi par iceste acheison   reason. So, for this reason
> Laissa armes danz Achillès.   Achilles gave up his arms.
>   (*Troie*, ll. 18458–61)

Achilles's renunciation of combat actually comes at the request of Hecuba, as a way of proving his devotion to Polyxena. But, as we've seen, this decision to give up battle is not met without derision. Thoas declares:

> Sire Achillès, vos dites mal.   Lord Achilles, you speak badly.
> Tant par estes pro e vassal   You are so worthy and valiant
> Que ne devez pas consentir   that you must not accept or
> N'uevre loër a maintenir   recommend such action [as this]
> Ou point aiez de deshonor.   that would bring you dishonour.
>   (*Troie*, ll. 18257–61)

The adverse reaction of his comrades reflects their disgust not just at his renunciation of war, but the underlying indication that there is a renunciation of masculinity. Kimberly Hutchings's analysis of masculinity and war shows that at any given place or time, 'aggression, rationality or physical courage are identified both as an essential component of war and also of masculinity.'[23] While there is not a causal or constitutive relation between the two, they are linked because masculinity provides a framework through which war can apparently be rendered both intelligible and acceptable.[24] If the properties of masculinity are removed, as with Achilles's renunciation of aggression and physical courage, then the framework for war is similarly lost. This episode is therefore one of the most important scenes of *Troie* and would no doubt have been viewed as such by medieval audiences, too. Two of the illustrated manuscripts make a point of showing the impact of Achilles's absence from the conflict. In MS Vt, we see Achilles and one of his knights playing chess in their tent while beside them several soldiers are bloodied on the battlefield (fol. 145^v). In MS V1, he is shown in a similar style, playing chess next to a raging battle, not just once but in three separate illustrations over three folios (fols. 149^r, 149^v and 163^r). The other manuscript illustrations tend to show him in his tent speaking with other Greek knights at this point. MSS Vt and V1 stand out for this sharp juxtaposition of leisure activities such as chess whilst in the midst of war. It almost seems that the dangers that women present in inspiring conflict pale in comparison to the dangers that women present in encouraging men to renounce it.

Origins of peace: A woman's role

If war can find its origins in masculinity, then can peace find its origins in femininity? Women may be invoked as the origins of violence but they are often involved in bringing about the eventual peace, too. If we look at Christine de Pizan's *Livre des Trois Vertus* (c. 1405), she counsels noblewomen that it is their duty to prevent the outbreak of war or hostilities and to urge their husbands and sons to find non-violent alternatives to conflict.[25] In the *Thebaid*, it is actually Argia who urges Argos to declare war against Thebes (III, ll. 678–721), but the *Thèbes*-poet omits this from his version as the example of a woman urging conflict was evidently not one to be lauded or perpetuated. *Troie* is full of scenes in which women bring about a cessation in fighting or attempt to do so. For example, as we saw above, it was Hecuba's suggestion to Achilles that he gave up his arms as a way to prove his love for Polyxena that eventually swayed him into withdrawing from battle.

But we can see an anxiety in the treatment of women who actively attempt to dissuade men from waging war. After the second battle of *Troie*, Cassandra tries to convince the Trojans to make peace by predicting that they will all be killed and Troy destroyed if not (ll. 10417–48). However, before she can say more, she is locked up by her family; her prophecies are referred to on subsequent occasions, but she does not physically reappear until after the fall of Troy, when she is given to Agamemnon as one of the spoils of war. In addition, Andromache tries to dissuade Hector from returning to battle following a prophetic vision she has immediately prior to battle ten; she pleads with him and when rebuffed she hides his arms, persuades Hecuba and Priam to join her in dissuading Hector and places his baby son in front of him, begging him not to render the child fatherless. However, it is to no avail and it causes a permanent rift between the two:

Cele que ço li a basti.	*She who fought him on this*
Lui e s'amor e son cuer pert;	*lost his love and his heart.*
Quant el cel plait a descovert	*When she said this and he*
Sor son devié, sor sa manace,	*discovered her trickery and her*
Ja mais n'iert jorz qu'il ne l'en hace,	*threat, there was never again a*
E por un poi qu'il ne la fiert.	*day that he did not hate her; and*
(*Troie*, ll. 15404–09)	*he very nearly struck her.*

This is the only glimpse of the potential for domestic violence within the courtly chivalric setting of *Troie*, which makes it all the more shocking and memorable.

If we look at the illustrative tradition of *Troie* manuscripts, we see that this episode is often chosen for the miniatures. Andromache pleading with Hector is illustrated five times, while Priam's attempt is illustrated four times.[26] Taken together, this makes it the most illustrated episode out of the entire narrative, while the second most illustrated episode is the anniversary service for Hector's death.[27] For a text that contains twenty-three battles and has traditionally been lauded as a great narrative of warfare, it is significant that the illustrative tradition privileges scenes in which attempts are made to prevent the hero from going to battle and the scene in which the hero is dead. The discourse of the heroes leads us to believe that renunciation of battle is dishonourable, but the power with which the scenes are rendered both in text and image suggests that nonparticipation in battle was not a simple case, but a complex problem fraught with anxiety.

Conclusion

Whilst women are sometimes represented as the reasons or causes for violence, the texts indicate that they are merely the channels through which the true motivation for violence is concealed. The rescue of Helen and Hesione is a case of vengeance and feuding that could just as easily have taken place over another 'object'. Aeneas's desire for Lavine is not so much motivated by love (no matter how much of an Ovidian atmosphere the *Enéas*-poet creates) but by a dynastic desire for political power. Most importantly, the narratives take place within a martial milieu that is concerned with constructions of gender identity and in particular the construction of masculinity through violence. If such a vision of masculinity is the primary basis for cultural violence in society, then that societal violence is doomed to continue. It is not really surprising that in the twelfth century there was little desire to challenge such constructions of masculinity, certainly among the clerks, clerics, monastics and other men who were involved in much of the production of the medieval literary canon. Challenging masculinity in any way would have been a radically dangerous threat to the fabric of ordered and civilized society. War was a way to ensure that traditional patriarchal structures were maintained, and women were evoked as mere excuses through which the masculine desire for warfare could manifest itself.

3

Women as victims of war

There is surprisingly little scholarship on women as victims of war in the Middle Ages. This chapter seeks to contribute to this lacuna by examining women who die during the general *melée* of the sack of a city, are executed, take their own lives, are forced from their homes, are given away as spoils of war, are sexually assaulted or lose their loved ones, homes and other resources. The Augustinian tradition of Just War doctrine did not necessarily make exceptions for women and the best that women could 'hope' for was enslavement instead of execution.[1] The fact that the eleventh- and twelfth-century movements of the Peace and Truce of God attempted to make provisions for the protection of women shows that this was by no means an accepted norm at the time.[2] The Peace of God movement comes as close as possible to defining a noncombatant or civilian in the Middle Ages without being anachronistic. Much has been published about the problems of defining noncombatants in the Middle Ages since medieval systems of military organization did not make clear distinctions between soldiers and civilians.[3] But the Peace of God movement stated that 'certain classes of people and property [were immune] from the depredations of war. Immune classes included clergy and pilgrims, peasants and the poor, merchants, orphans and women'.[4] Even then, *chansons de geste*, for example, were known to portray their protagonists occasionally mistreating noncombatants, including women: *Girart de Vienne* and the *Chanson de Floovant* both include episodes in which the apparent heroes of the texts abuse or assault certain female characters from the enemy's side with little negative judgement cast on them for doing so.[5] It goes without saying that those who play at war do not always respect the rules.

Death and dying

The city of Troy is sacked twice during the course of *Troie*. Benoît gives us this account of its first destruction:

> Mainte dame, mainte pucele,
> Mainte borgeise riche e bele
> Veïst om foïr par les rues,
> Paoroses e esperdues:
> En lor braz portent lor enfanz.

> *One could see many ladies,*
> *many maidens and many rich*
> *and beautiful bourgeois women*
> *flee from the men through the*
> *streets, terrified and lost: they*

Tant par i esteit li dueus granz,	carried their children in their
Onques ne fu en nul lieu maire.	arms. There was such great
(*Troie*, ll. 2765-71)	lamenting there, never in any other
	place was there such great [suffering].

The description goes on to detail how the Greeks plunder the city of its valuable possessions (silks, silver, gold, precious stones, rings, horses, goshawks and cloth) before destroying its fortresses, towers, houses, walls, temples, palaces and manors (ll. 2757-88). It outlines how the Greeks raped many of the Trojan women and took others away with them. The account of the second sack of Troy gives more detail:

N'i remest povre n'orfelin,	Neither poor people nor orphans
Jovne ne vieil, cui il ataignent.	nor the young nor the old could
De l'ocise li palais teignent;	escape. The palaces were stained
Tuit decorent li pavement:	by the dead and the flagstones
De sanc sunt moillié e sanglent;	were similarly decorated: they are
N'i a rue, n'i a sentier	bloody and drenched in blood.
Ou n'ataigne jusqu'al braier.	There is not a road nor a path
Par les palais, par les veneles,	where [the blood] does not come
Par les sales riches e beles,	up to the thighs of the men. In the
Par les maisons de marbre bis,	palaces, in the alleys, in the
Muerent dames as cors gentis [...]	beautiful and rich rooms, in the
Li portal furent bien guardé	houses of dark marble, the noble
Qu'uns n'en eissist ne eschapast,	ladies died [...] The gates were
Qu'om n'oceïst e detrenchast.	well guarded so that nobody was
Es braz as meres alaitanz	able to get out or escape or one
Ont detrenchiez les beaus enfanz;	would be killed and decapitated. In
Après funt d'eles autretal.	the arms of breast-feeding mothers
(*Troie*, ll. 26064-74, 26078-83)	their beautiful children are beheaded; and
	they [their mothers] then die afterwards.

The description is savage in its conveyance of the goriness of the city's fall. It is reminiscent of other reports of another city's fall, that of Jerusalem in 1099, approximately sixty years before *Troie* was written. Raymond of Aguilers's *Historia Francorum qui ceperunt Iherusalem* (c. 1100-01) records the following scene as the crusaders took the city:

In temple et in portico Salomonis	*In the temple and porch of*
equitabatur in sanguine usque ad	*Solomon, men rode in blood up*
genua, et usque ad frenos equorum.	*to their knees and bridle reins.*
Justo nimirum judicio, ut locus	*Indeed, it was a just and*
idem euorum sanguinem exciperet,	*splendid judgment of God that*
quorum blasphemias in Deum tam	*this place should be filled with*
longo tempore pertulerat. Repleta	*the blood of the unbelievers,*
itaque cadaveribus et sanguine	*since it had suffered so long*
civitate.	*from their blasphemies. The city*
(*Historia Francorum*, XX, D-E)[6]	*was filled with corpses and blood.*

The tone is quite different from that of *Troie*. There is something almost celebratory about this horror as Raymond describes it as 'just and splendid'. Fulcher also tells this story in his *Historia Hierosolymitana* (*c.* 1101–28):

In quo etiam templo decem millia fere decollati sunt. Quod si inibi essetis, pedes vestri sanguine peremptorum usque ad bases tinguerentur. Quid narrabo? Nullus ex eis vitæ est reservatus. Sed neque feminis neque parvulis eorum pepercerunt. (*Historia Hierosolymitana*, XXVII, D)[7]	*In this temple almost ten thousand were beheaded. If you had been there your feet would have been stained up to the ankles with the blood of the slain. But what more shall I tell? Not one of them was allowed to live. They did not spare the women and children.*

Meanwhile the anonymous *Gesta Francorum* (*c.* 1100–01) adds these details:

Mane autem facto ascenderunt nostri caute supra tectum templi, et inuaserent Saracenos masculos et feminas, decollantes eos nudis ensibus.[8] (*Gesta Francorum*, X.xxxviii)	*In the morning, some of our men cautiously ascended to the roof of the temple and attacked the Saracens, both the men and the women, beheading them with naked swords.*

Two details are striking about these descriptions that link them with the description from *Troie*. First, the depth of blood: Fulcher describes it reaching 'ad bases' (*up to the ankles*) of the feet, while Raymond has it running 'ad genua' (*up to the knees*) of the pilgrims and 'ad frenos' (*up to the reins*) of their horses. Benoît's description of the blood of the Trojans running 'al braier' (*up to the thighs*) of the Greeks captures this same awfulness. Second is the method of slaughter: Fulcher describes the Jerusalemites as being 'decollati' (*beheaded*) while the *Gesta* author eschews the passive voice for the active 'decollantes' in describing the same action. Benoît also uses this detail in his description of the slaughter of Trojan citizens. He uses the words 'detrenchast' (*decapitated*) and 'detrenchiez' (*beheaded*) within the space of three lines. These details are not in Dares's or Dictys's accounts of the sack of Troy. Whether Benoît read such chronicles is not known but it is not too great a stretch of the imagination to speculate that he would have had access to or been familiar with them. As discussed in the introduction, Dominique Battles makes a strong case for the *Thèbes* poet using First Crusade chronicles as a source, so there is no reason to think that Benoît did not do the same.[9] The graphic scenes of slaughter as Troy falls may purposefully resemble the capture of Jerusalem to make it more vivid and recognizable to its medieval audience.

Additionally, it owes its style to a biblical topos that influenced the crusade chroniclers themselves. The description of the blood coming up to the horses' bridles is drawn from the book of Revelation: 'and the wine press was trodden outside the city and blood flowed from the wine press, as high as a horse's bridle'.[10] By using these sources, Benoît constructed his destruction of Troy to resemble horrors that were familiar to members of his audience who had biblical knowledge, as well as to those with involvement in the crusades. In this way, he makes *Troie* a text that can sit alongside both crusade chronicles and the Bible, as indeed it does in MSS P9 and L4.

The fact that women were vulnerable to slaughter, alongside men and children, during the sack of a city is something attested to in *Troie* and the historical sources. But women are vulnerable to death in another way in *Troie*, one that is not so prevalent in historical sources: ritual execution. This is graphically illustrated as the Greeks are apportioning the spoils of war. Dares and Dictys only briefly mention that Polyxena is executed by Pyrrhus in an act of revenge for Achilles's death (*Dictys*, V.13 and *Dares*, D.43). Benoît expands this scene from one line in the Latin to over one hundred lines in *Troie*. The moment of execution is relatively concise (four lines), but he adds two elements. First, he describes the Greek forces mourning the decision to execute Polyxena and expressing their reluctance to see such an action carried out:

> Quant li pueples sot la novele,
> Qu'ocire vuelent la pucele,
> Tuit i corent, nus n'i remaint;
> Chascuns la plore e crie e plaint.
> [...]
> S'el poüst estre rachatee,
> Li comuns toz de l'ost Grezeis
> La raensist d'or set cenz peis.
> (*Troie*, ll. 26441–44, 26540–42)
>
> *When the people learned the news that they wanted to kill the maiden, all without exception ran there; each one cried and lamented and wailed. [...] If they had been able to buy her [back], all the common people of the Greek army would have paid a ransom of seven hundred pieces of gold.*

Second, he gives Polyxena a long speech in which she admonishes the Greeks and offers herself up 'willingly', preferring to die a virgin than to live as a Greek's concubine:

> 'Seignor,' fait ele, 'vil concire
> Avez tenu de mei ocire.
> Onc ne fu mais venjance faite
> Que en si grant mal fust retraite.
> Haut home estes e riche rei
> A faire tel chose de mei?
> N'ai mort ne peine deservie.
> [...]
> D'ocire e d'espandre cerveles
> E d'estre en sanc e en boëles
> Deüsseiz estre tuit saol.
> [...]
> Que c'est merveille quos avez
> De ma mort faim ne desirier.
> [...]
> Ço sachiez bien,
>
> *'Lords', she said, 'it is a wicked decision you have made to kill me. Such an act of vengeance will be harshly judged. Are you not too noble as lords and too powerful as kings to do such a thing to me? I deserve neither death nor punishment. [...] Surely you must already be satiated with killing and splattering brains and being covered in blood and entrails. [...] It is a marvel that you still have appetite to kill me. [...] But know this: that I no longer wish to live after*

Que jo ne vueil por nule rien	all this pain.
Vivre après si faite dolor.	[...] Come death! I do not refuse it,
[...]	because I no longer wish to live
Vienge la mort, ne la refus,	and so [it is to death] that I
Quar n'ai talent de vivre plus.	pledge my virginity. Neither
Mon pucelage li otrei:	count nor king will ever have
Onc si bel n'ot ne cuens ne rei.	this beautiful thing.
(*Troie*, ll. 26475–81, 26491–93, 26501–02, 26512–14, 26521–24)	

In adding these features to Polyxena's execution, Benoît introduces complexity to the scene. The sadness of the 'comuns' (*common people*) compared to the resolution of the 'seignor' (*lords*) creates a class tension over military strategy and morality that is rarely seen in the *romans* or other Old French texts; indeed, it is rare to have scenes in which the 'comuns' are referenced at all, let alone for them to disagree with their lords. Polyxena's speech also calls into question the ethical expectations that one would have of someone who is 'haut' (*noble*) and 'riche' (*powerful*), implying that truly noble men do not execute young innocent women. She suggests that men cannot perpetrate violence indefinitely, for at some point they must be 'saol' (*satiated*). Her speech gives her a degree of agency over her death that she does not have in the classical sources. This is not to suggest that she is suicidal or would otherwise choose to die, but the language with which Benoît frames her embracing of death and dedication of her virginity to death is reminiscent of virgin martyrs and saints. For example, the earliest surviving Old French hagiographic text, the *Cantilène de Sainte Eulalie* (c. 880), recounts the life and execution of a virgin martyr:

Melz sostendreiet les empedementz	*But she would endure*
Qu'elle perdesse sa virginitet;	*impediments Rather than lose*
Poros furet morte a grand honestet	*her virginity; Thus she would*
Enz enl fou lo getterent, com arde tost;	*die in great honesty.*
Elle colpes non avret, poro nos coist.	*They threw her into the fire,*
A czo nos voldret concreidre li rex pagiens.	*that burned fiercely. She*
Ad une spede li roveret tolir lo chief.	*had no sins, so she did not*
La domnizelle celle kose non contredist.	*burn. The pagan king did not*
(*Cantilène de Sainte Eulalie*, ll. 16–23)[11]	*want to believe that. He ordered*
	her to be beheaded with a sword.
	The maiden did not oppose this.

Just as Eulalie has no 'colpes' (*sins*), so too Polyxena is 'senz malice' (*without evil*); just as Eulalie wishes to guard her 'virginitet' (*virginity*), so too Polyxena treasures her 'pucelage' (*virginity*); just as Eulalie does not oppose the order to execute her, nor does Polyxena refuse it, and just as Eulalie is beheaded, so too Polyxena is eventually 'detrenchiee' (*beheaded*). Benoît's reworking of this scene transforms Polyxena's fate from one of passive, silent and sacrificial lamb in the classical sources to one of a martyr-like figure who would not be out of place in a hagiographic text. In this way she serves a double purpose as she not only exposes the suffering of women in war but provides an example of how such suffering can become a devotional act.

But while Polyxena's fate is almost inspirational (within the hagiographic paradigm), the fate of her mother illustrates a less ennobling alternative. Upon seeing her daughter beheaded, Hecuba is filled with rage and lashes out against the Greeks. The men 'ne la porent sofrir' (*were not able to endure this*, l. 26565) and so they stone her to death, which Benoît explains 'fu damage e grant dolor, | Qu'el morut a tel deshonor' (*was a point of shame and very sad for she died in such dishonour*, ll. 26585–86). She is not given the opportunity to make a speech or to die with dignity, but is stoned in the street as a 'fole' (*mad woman*, l. 26579). It is worth noting, however, that Benoît actually softens the harshness of her fate compared to Dictys, whose version recounts that her tomb 'statuitur appellatum Cynossema ob linguae protervam impudentemque petulantiam' (*was called The Tomb of the Bitch because of her mad and shameless barking*, V.16). The method of execution is significant: beheading with a sword as Polyxena was, was considered a privileged method of execution for royalty, the aristocracy and knights.[12] But stoning was a baser form of punishment, frequently occurring in the Old Testament as the form of execution for sinners.[13] By juxtaposing Polyxena's and Hecuba's death in this way, Benoît provides two models of death by execution: one that is dignified and saintly and one that is humiliating and ignoble. These were not just examples that resonated with women but could speak to both sexes within an audience.

Illustrations of this episode typically combine Polyxena's and Hecuba's deaths in a single frame. MS Vt shows Polyxena's execution in the centre of the frame with Hecuba's protests to the left and Hecuba's death by stoning to the right (fol. 203ʳ). MSS Vn and P18 show her execution in the centre, while Hecuba is clubbed (rather than stoned) to the side (Figure 13).[14] These three are faithful to the text in showing the executions taking place at the tomb of Achilles, above which was an effigy of Polyxena herself. This composition of the serene statue of Polyxena looking down on the bloodied and dying body of the actual Polyxena makes for a cruel and striking contrast. MS V1 does not include the statue of Polyxena on Achilles's tomb, but it does include more individual illustrations to relate the sequence of events: one illustration for the execution of Polyxena (fol. 206ᵛ), one for Hecuba's protestations (fol. 207ʳ) and one for her stoning (fol. 207ʳ). The mid-thirteenth-century MS P6 is the earliest manuscript to have a full illustrative scheme and is the only one of the French manuscripts to illustrate this scene, which it includes as part of a full-page miniature (Figure 14). The top register shows the slaughter of Trojans by the Greeks (including the execution of Priam by Pyrrhus) while the bottom register shows three events each contained by an archway: the distribution of women as booty, the execution of Polyxena and the execution of Hecuba, who is actually shown here being beheaded rather than stoned. All five manuscripts, whether through the composition of the scenes or through the number of miniatures, create strong visualizations of violence against women.

Polyxena's embracing of her death is a contrast to Dido's suicide. Devastated at Aeneas's departure, Dido kills herself with Aeneas's sword and is burnt on a funeral pyre. The narrator is clear that her actions are far from honourable. He describes her suicide as an act of 'desverie' (*madness* or *devilishness*, l. 2027) and on her tomb is the (eternal and public) inscription that she died because she loved 'trop folement' (*too madly* or *too stupidly*, l. 2143): hardly an ennobling epitaph. This tomb is the invention of the *Enéas* poet, for it does not appear in the *Aeneid* and the judgement is entirely of the poet's making. The way that he has reworked this episode from his source suggests that he was more interested in highlighting the foolishness of her actions than in the tragedy of her predicament. As Aeneas says to her when they meet again in the underworld:

> Ge vos sui acheisons de mort,   *I am the reason for your death,*
> Mais ge n'i ai colpes ne tort.   *but I did nothing wrong.*
> [...]   *[...]*
> Quant ge de vos me departi,   *When I left you, I did not believe*
> Ne cuidai pas que fust ainsi,   *that it would be so, that you would*
> Ne trovesiez alcun confort   *not find any comfort that would*
> Ki vos pleüst mielz que la mort.   *please you better than death.*
> (*Enéas*, ll. 2633–34, 2047–50)

Dido does not reply but flees into a wood to join her husband. Again, the *Enéas* poet has reworked this scene to cast a harsher judgement on Dido than does Virgil. In the *Aeneid*, Dido's husband then 'respondet curis aequatque [...] amorem' (*answered her grief with grief and her love with love*, VI, l. 474) and the classical Aeneas 'casu percussus iniquo prosequitur lacrimis longe et miseratur euntem' (*was no less stricken by the injustice of her fate and long did he gaze after her, pitying her as she went*, VI, l. 475).[15] In *Enéas*, however, when Dido reaches her husband's side there is no tender comfort:

> Ne s'osot pas vers lui torner,   *She did not dare to turn toward*
> Ne ne l'osot dreit esguarder,   *him, nor did she dare to look*
> Ne prezsx de lui ne s'aprismot: *right at him, nor to approach*
> Por son forfait se vergondot.   *him too closely: for she was*
> (*Enéas*, ll. 2659–62)   *ashamed of her transgression.*

Meanwhile the detail in which Virgil's Aeneas gazes after her in sympathy is completely omitted and the poet moves straight on to describing Aeneas's journey. The *Enéas* poet makes it clear that Dido's actions are dishonourable and casts her as a suicidal hysterical woman, who in her final scene is denied even a single word or the comfort of her husband. Dido's reputation was later salvaged by Christine de Pizan in the *Cité des Dames* (*c.* 1405). Christine dedicates a whole text to Dido in Part I (text 46), in which the name Aeneas is not even mentioned and instead the entire focus is on her good sense and cleverness in the way that she founded and ruled Carthage. But in *Enéas* there is no such redemption. Juanita Feros Ruys's work on suicide in the Middle Ages concludes that suicide was not necessarily an unthinkable concept but it was one that remained largely unspoken.[16] The *Enéas* poet has no choice but to speak about Dido's suicide because of its narrative centrality, but he uses it as an opportunity to judge and condemn her. Unlike Polyxena who is honoured for embracing death, Dido is dishonoured for choosing suicide rather than displaying cardinal virtues such as prudence and temperance. Despite the dishonour associated with suicide, two images of Dido's death are found in the admittedly sparse tradition of illustrations accompanying *Enéas*. There is a historiated initial of her suicide at the start of the text in MS P13 (fol. 70ʳ) and it forms the final scene in the frontispiece to the text in MS P17 (fol. 148ʳ). Flames from her funeral pyre feature in both and make them particularly dramatic. We can imagine that at the time these manuscripts were produced, when burning at the stake was still a possible form of execution and something that readers of this manuscript may even have seen in real life, it would have provoked particularly strong reactions.[17]

Hostageship, abduction and rape

Hostageship is also being given considerably increased attention in current scholarship.[18] Defining a hostage is no simple task: Adam J. Kosto's work explains that 'medieval hostageship is best understood as a guarantee […]. Hostageship is rarely, however, simply a guarantee and in that fact lies the institution's political power and utility'.[19] Work on hostageship shows that both men and women were subject to capture for ransom. However, Yvonne Friedman points to a gender imbalance and states that if 'there is one part of crusader history in which women seem numerically dominant [it is] the sphere of captivity. Women were often the first and sometimes the only ones taken captive on both the Muslim and the Christian sides' and 'their experience of captivity and the need for their ransom would seem to be central to the history of warfare in the Latin East'.[20] Meanwhile John Gillingham argues that the treatment of prisoners in warfare undergoes a shift between 'phase one' warfare during the early medieval centuries and the 'second, more chivalrous phase' of warfare, with this transition between phases occurring in the twelfth century – the time when the *romans* were being composed.[21] In the first phase, women were the intended victims, whereas in the second phase women became collateral damage rather than the specific targets.[22] While women suffer in both phase one and two warfare, there is a shift in the reception of this behaviour. The capture of women in phase one warfare was not seen as shameful, but actually a source of pride, whereas violence against women in phase two warfare was regarded as reprehensible.[23]

We have examples of both female and male hostages in *Troie*, though the particular case of Briseide does not really help to clarify the definition of a hostage. She is the daughter of Calcas, a Trojan soothsayer who deserts Troy to join the Greeks. He leaves Briseide in Troy, at which point she becomes a de facto hostage, owing to the fact that her father is now a traitor on the Greek side. Priam states that the only reason she is not 'arse e desmenbree' (*burnt and dismembered*, l. 13113) is because she is 'franche e proz e saige e bele' (*young and noble and wise and beautiful*, l. 13112). Calcas asks the Greeks to petition Priam for her return. This they do and after some debate. However, when Briseide learns this, she collapses in distress for she has no desire to rejoin her father and when she arrives in the Greek camp she admonishes him for having brought her out of Troy. We therefore have a rather curious example of hostageship, for she has no desire to be freed. It also appears that she is released without anything being received in exchange. The sole reason for clemency on Priam's part is the fact that she is noble and beautiful.

However, if we compare the return of Briseide with another instance of hostage-release that occurs directly before the episode in which she is returned, we find a different story, and one that helps to explain Briseide's. The Greek king Thoas is captured in battle four and the Trojans hold a council to discuss his fate (ll. 11764–844). At first, Priam only wants advice on the method of execution that is the most fitting. However, Aeneas reasons that if they execute him they will provoke the ire of the Greeks for he has many allies. Hector supports Aeneas and adds that if they keep him they have the chance for a 'raençon' (*ransom*, l. 11823). Priam is convinced and agrees not to execute Thoas. Their counsel turns out to have been wise, for in the following battle, the Greeks capture Antenor:

Por Antenor sont deshaitié,	[The Trojans] were worried
E mout s'en fait Prianz irié:	about Antenor and it made
Trop ont en lui grant perte faite,	Priam very angry; he was a
Mais ço les conforte e rehaite,	great loss to them. But the only
Qu'il ne li feront se bien non	comfort and consolation that
Por Thoas, qu'il ont en prison.	they could take was that they
[...]	still held Thoas in prison. [...]
Polidamas fu mout pensis	Polydamas was thinking a lot
Por son pere, que Greu ont pris;	about his father, whom the
Mais ço comence a porpenser,	Greeks had taken. He began to
Se demain vuelent assembler,	wonder if the Greeks wanted to
Mout lor voudra chier s'ire vendre	battle the next day because he
E tel rei d'eus ocire o prendre,	wanted to vent his anger by
Par quei sis pere iert ostagiez.	killing or taking one of their
(*Troie*, ll. 12633–38,	kings because they held
12675–81)	his father as hostage.

The earliest recorded use of the word 'ostagiez' (*hostage*) before *Troie* was in the *Chanson de Roland* (c. 1040–1115), just a few decades earlier.[24] Forms of the word are used at other points throughout *Troie*. For example, when Hector suggests to Achilles that they end the war through single combat, part of his terms is that both sides will return their 'ostages' (*hostages*, l. 13174). Neither Dares nor Dictys includes hostages in their texts and it is worth remembering that Briseide's character is entirely of Benoît's own invention. The inclusion of hostages is therefore not an issue that Benoît found in his classical sources, but another example of the discussions of warfare around him, and one that he clearly thought valuable to include in his own telling of a warfare narrative. Antenor and Thoas are eventually exchanged and the value of hostages and of treating them well is clear. It is no coincidence then that the very next scene is that of Calcas's request to have his daughter returned to him. Although the return of Briseide is treated more briefly and there is no mention of her being exchanged, the fact that it is placed in such close proximity to the episode of Antenor and Thoas allows us to imagine that similar negotiations and discussions occurred. Priam, having seen the benefits that noble conduct towards a hostage had, was probably keen to continue such conduct; the Greeks' request for the return of

Briseide allows him to show this prudence and magnanimity. It also represents a development in his character as compared to the earlier refusal to return Helen in exchange for Hesione.

However, while the Antenor and Thoas episode illustrates the reasons why captors would take care of their captives, those who find themselves given away (with no expectation of return) may not be so fortunate. After the fall of Troy, the Greeks discuss how to divide the 'aveir' (*goods* or *riches*, l. 26276), which include the few noblewomen who escaped the city's sack. Cassandra is given to Agamemnon, Climena to Demophon, Aethra to Acamas, and Andromache and her two sons are given to Pyrrhus, along with the only remaining son of Priam, Helenus.[25] It goes without saying that these women are given no choice as to their fates. Nor is there any suggestion that they are being given to the Greeks for the purposes of marriage by way of a 'peace agreement', as were some historical women.[26] But Troy has been razed to the ground and its people slaughtered, so there is no need to make a peace agreement in the face of such total destruction. We are left to infer that they are given away as slaves or concubines. The distribution of women as 'booty' is illustrated in three of the manuscripts containing extensive illustrations: the mid-thirteenth-century French MS P6 (Figure 14), the mid-fourteenth-century Neapolitan MS V1 (fol. 200^v) and most interestingly the late-thirteenth- or early-fourteenth-century Italian MS Vt (Figure 15). In this illustration, we see 'le grant tresor de Troie' (*the great treasure of Troy*), as the rubric reads, piled up in a room being looked over by four Greek soldiers ahead of its distribution. This includes gold, silks, chests, goblets and (trying to hide behind a pillar) three women. The scene gives the impression that these women are treated in just the same way as a gold bowl would be: assessed for their value and distributed like treasure.

The reality of the medieval post-conflict landscape in which all the men are killed and the women and children taken captive is a formula that is used in descriptions of warfare in both Christian and Muslim chronicles from the twelfth century.[27] However, the capture and distribution of women has overt sexual implications. When Imād ad-Din al-Isfahani, the secretary and chronicler to Sultan Saladin of Egypt, Syria, Yemen and Palestine, describes the women taken captive in Jerusalem in 1187, he is thrilled at the prospect of such prisoners:

> Women and children together came to 8,000 and were quickly divided up among us, bringing a smile to Muslim faces at their lamentations. How many well-guarded women were profaned, how many queens were ruled and nubile girls married and noblewomen given away and miserly women forced to yield themselves and women who had been kept hidden stripped of their modesty and serious women made ridiculous and women kept in private now set in public and free women occupied and precious ones used for hard work and pretty things put to the test and virgins dishonoured and proud women deflowered and lovely women prostrated and untamed ones tamed and happy ones made to weep! How many noblemen took them as concubines, how many ardent men blazed for one of them and celibates were satisfied by them and thirsty men sated by them and turbulent men able to give vent to their passion.[28]

His glee and pleasure at capturing, sexually assaulting and enslaving so many women is clear to hear and no doubt reflects a general satisfaction with conquest and victory on a wider scale. These women's bodies become a trophy representing the victors' triumphs. And although more attention has generally been paid by historians to enslavement by Muslims than to enslavement by Christians, this is certainly not because Christians also did not engage in enslavement. Not only did the Europeans of the First Crusade have a slave-owning polity in their Latin Kingdom of Jerusalem, but even as late as the Third Crusade there is evidence that some crusaders saw it as a profitable line of business.[29] This means that it was practised by Christians at the time that *Troie* was composed, copied and read. The scene in which the Trojan women are shared out among the victors of war was perhaps not a completely unfamiliar one to some. We can also think of *Aucassin et Nicolette* (c. 1175–1215), a *chantefable* in which the female protagonist is a Saracen maiden (later revealed to be a princess) who had previously been sold to the Viscount of Beaucaire.[30] Women, including noblewomen, being sold and exchanged as the spoils of war were certainly not unfamiliar in the Old French tradition.

The implication that captive or enslaved were also sexually assaulted brings us to a final concern: abduction and rape. Much has been written in recent years about abduction and rape in the Middle Ages.[31] These two are linked within a medieval context because of the lexicon of medieval discourse. The word *raptus* in medieval legal terms included both abduction as well as forcible coitus.[32] Added to which, *raptus* cases were often elopements of a woman with a partner of whom her parents disapproved rather than a woman being taken as an unwilling captive.[33] Indeed, in some *raptus* cases the alleged abductor had a pre-existing relationship with the abductee and actually the abductee was asserting her freedom of choice (against her father or guardian) in choosing her future lover or husband.[34] As was discussed in the previous chapter, cases of abduction can therefore be difficult to interpret:[35] are they abductions (with no sexual connotations) in the sense of taking someone away from their home or family (either willingly or unwillingly) or are they cases of sexual assault and rape in terms of forced coitus? The ambiguity of the language means that we must look elsewhere for clues.

We will turn here to the case of Hesione. Having described the first destruction of Troy, Benoît gives the following details:

Des femmes firent lor voleir:	*They did as they wished with the*
Assez i ot des vergondees,	*women: they dishonoured many*
Sin ont des plus beles menees.	*of them and abducted the most*
La fille al rei, Esiona,	*beautiful. The daughter of the*
Ja mais plus bele ne naistra,	*king, Hesione, was the most*
Ne plus franche ne plus corteise,	*beautiful woman ever born; never*
Grant ire en ai e mout m'en peise,	*was there another woman so pure*
Cele en a Telamon menee:	*and courtly. I am very angry and*
Danz Herculès li a donee,	*it weighs on me that Telamon*
Por ço qu'en Troie entra premier.	*abducted her. Hercules gave her*
N'en ot mie mauvais loier,	*to [Telamon] because he had*

> E s'il a femme l'esposast,
> Ja guaires donc ne m'en pesast;
> Mais puis la tint en soignantage,
> Ço fu grant duel e grant damage.
> (*Troie*, ll. 2790–804)
>
> *entered Troy first. He did not have a bad reward! And if he had married her and made her his wife, I think it would not weigh on me [so much]. But afterwards he kept her as his concubine, and that was very sad and very shameful.*

Benoît cannot stop himself from inserting his own authorial judgement on the Greeks to condemn their actions and highlight their double sin: first in abducting Hesione and secondly in keeping her as a concubine. Not only is she done this dishonour, but Priam later laments her fate: 'esteit menee en servage' (*she was abducted into slavery*, l. 2876). This detail of 'servage' (*slavery*) is Benoît's own invention. Dictys does not mention the abduction of Hesione at all, while Dares only says the following:

> Telamon primus Ilium oppidum introiit, cui Hercules virtutis causa Hesionam Laomedontis regis filiam dono dedit [...]. Inde domum proficisci decreverent, Telamon Hesionam secum convexit.
> (Dares, D.3)
>
> *Telamon proved his prowess by being the first to enter Troy. Therefore, Hercules gave him the prize of King Laomedon's daughter Hesione [...]. Then they decided to set out for home. Telamon took Hesione with him.*

Hesione is mentioned on various occasions after this, but never is it stated that she is a concubine or a slave. However, evidence from multiple sources suggests that the sexual abuse of female captives was more or less taken for granted and women were routinely sexually assaulted during the conquest of a city.[36] Even when protections against such atrocities were promoted they tended to be limited to noblewomen, and there was similarly an assumption that men did nevertheless inflict violent sexual aggression upon women of all statuses during times of war.[37] Perhaps Benoît was writing what everyone would have been thinking: women would have been raped during the sack of the city and those abducted would in all likelihood have been subject to further sexual assault by their abductor.

Hesione's abduction is not illustrated in any of the French manuscripts but does appear in four of the Italian manuscripts (MSS Vt, V1, Vn and P18). Unlike scenes of Helen's abduction where she is often pictured with Paris, her *ami* and eventual husband, Hesione is always taken by unidentified soldiers. She is shown being seized by the arms or wrists and her head is always cast down looking at the floor (for example, as in Figure 1). Diane Wolfthal's work shows that such a posture is an indicator of rape.[38] The demureness of her posture may even mean that she is considered equally responsible for the occurrence of any subsequent sexual assault. Kenneth Varty's study of sexual consent in twelfth-century France finds evidence in both customary laws and sermons that women must 'cry out' and 'bite, scratch and struggle with all [their] might' or else they are at fault.[39] He cites a story from the Bible:

If a girl who is engaged is seduced within the walls of a city, both she and the man who seduced her shall be taken outside the gates and stoned to death – the girl because she did not scream for help and the man because he has violated the virginity of another man's fiancée […]. But if the deed takes place out in the country, only the man shall die. The girl is as innocent as a murder victim; for it must be assumed that she screamed, but there was no one to rescue her out in the field.[40]

The final line of this last quotation, that the raped woman of the story is innocent because there was 'no one to rescue her', brings us to the question of abduction and rape and its place within the chivalric tradition or, rather, within the chivalric literary tradition. Kathryn Gravdal's work on medieval French literature and law argues that 'rape (either attempted rape or the defeat of a rapist) constitutes one of the episodic units used in the construction of romance […]. It is a genre that by its definition must *create* the threat of rape'.[41] The abduction of both Hesione and Helen fit within Gravdal's paradigm. Gravdal uses Chrétien de Troyes's romances as her primary source and identifies five 'functions' of rape: a chivalric test, an ethical test, a social marker, patriotism and a marker of physical beauty.[42] This same structure can be seen in *Troie*. The abduction of Hesione and Helen functions as chivalric tests, for they result in both the Trojan forces and the Greek forces setting out on a mission to rescue them. The abduction of Helen also provides an ethical test, as towards the end of the narrative the Trojans beg Priam to return her to Menelaus to bring an end to the war, which he refuses, for he believes that it is now his duty to protect her within Troy, regardless of the consequences. The choice of Hesione and Helen functions as a social marker and their abduction denotes their nobility; those who are not of the aristocracy are either slain or omitted from the narrative. Their abduction encodes a patriotic message because it provokes a test of the military strength of their homeland in provoking the forces of each to set out on a rescue mission. Finally, Helen's abduction is used as a testimony to her physical beauty; indeed Venus had unequivocally labelled her as the most beautiful woman in the world during the Judgement of Paris episode. Benoît's rhetorical reasons behind expanding the attention given to women who are abducted or distributed as plunder are clear. He does not describe the sexual assault, as for example both the thirteenth- and fifteenth-century versions of *La Fille du Comte de Ponthieu* do in graphic detail, but he allows the threat of sexual violence to pervade multiple scenes throughout the narrative and therefore includes the threat of rape as an episodic unit of his *roman*.[43] Many women in the audience would also have been all too aware of this particular menace. Even Eleanor of Aquitaine herself was subject to at least two violent abduction attempts in 1152 alone: once by the future Count Theobald V of Blois and once by Henry II's younger brother, Geoffrey of Anjou.[44] When the *romans* poets were developing this aspect of their texts, they knew they were dealing with a threat that was very real.

Collateral suffering

Women who are not physically assaulted, but who still suffer as a consequence of warfare's occurrence, include those who suffer when the men to whom they are connected through familiar or romantic ties are killed or taken hostage. Thousands of men die in the *romans*, which corresponds to thousands of women suffering as a result of their loss. This chapter cannot look at each individual case of a grieving woman, so it takes two cases that are representative of two categories: mothers and *amies*. For mothers, we look at Hecuba. Her suffering is shown on multiple occasions: she makes a great speech of lamentation following the death of her first son, Hector (ll. 16425–58); as her third son, Deiphobus, lies dying on the battlefield during battle twelve, Paris evokes her in his lament, saying that she is a 'mere chaitive' (*wretched or unfortunate mother*, l. 18728) and subject to 'grant haschiee' (*great tortures*, l. 18729); when Achilles kills her fifth son, Troilus, she reaches breaking point and takes matters into her own hands:

Un jor comença a penser	*One day she began to think*
Com sereient si fil vengié	*about how her sons would be*
Del traïtor, del reneié	*avenged on the traitor, on the*
Qui les li a morz e toleiz.	*renegade who had killed them*
Pensé i a par maintes feiz:	*and taken them from her. She*
S'ele engigne par traïson	*thought about it many times:*
Sa mort e sa destrucion,	*she devised his death and*
Come de lui se puisse vengier,	*destruction through betrayal,*
Ne s'en deit nus hom merveillier	*for that was how she could have*
N'a mal ne a blasme atorner.	*vengeance and no person*
(*Troie*, ll. 21844–53)	*should be surprised by this or condemn or blame her.*

She engineers the plot in which Achilles is lured to the Temple of Apollo to be ambushed and murdered by Paris. However, her joy at the death of Achilles is short-lived, for not long afterwards the city falls to the Greeks. She attempts to escape with Polyxena and encounters Aeneas, whom she castigates for betraying the city while entreating him to protect Polyxena by way of atonement:

'Coilverz, traïtre, reneiez,	'*Scoundrel, traitor, renegade!*
Quant de mei ne vos prent pitiez	*Even if you do not take pity on me*
Ne de Troie, que si decline,	*or on Troy, which has now fallen,*
Guardez seveaus ceste meschine,	*at least protect this maiden, so*
Si que Grezeis n'en seit saisiz.	*that the Greeks cannot take her.*
Ja mar de mei avront merciz.'	*They will never have mercy on*
(*Troie*, ll. 26181–86)	*me.*'

However, as we saw at the beginning of this chapter, Hecuba's desperate attempt to save Polyxena is doomed to failure, while Hecuba herself is eventually stoned to death. The intensity of suffering that Hecuba endures as she watches her children either slaughtered on the battlefield or executed by soldiers is severe.

And it is not just mothers who are shown in grief; there are also scenes of paternal suffering, which yield an interesting comparison when juxtaposed with material suffering. At the news of his son's death, King Evander of *Enéas* has a strong physical reaction:

Ses crins, qu'il ot blans et chenuz,	*He pulled out his old white hair*
A ses deus mains a derompuz,	*with his own two hands and*
Sa barbe arachë a ses deiz,	*plucked out his beard with his*
Il s'eest pasmez plus de vint feiz,	*fingers. He fainted more than*
Hurte son chief, debat sa chiere,	*twenty times, hit his head,*
Plorant en vait contre la biere.	*smacked his face, while crying*
(Enéas, ll. 6253-58)	*and approaching the coffin.*

This violent picture of self-harming as a reaction to bereavement is something we see in Chrétien's *Yvain*, too. After Laudine's husband is killed, Yvain sees her grieving and describes how she 'romper et trenchier' (*tears and pulls*) at her hair, 'bleche' (*scratches*) at her face, 'detort' (*wrings*) her hands, and 'fiert' (*strikes*) her breast (ll. 1461-91). Hecuba's, Evander's and Laudine's reactions to bereavement seem to be typical of the Old French tradition's style of representing grief and there is no particular difference in their sufferings as part of this trope. But if we follow the lamentations of Evander, we see an important caveat for his grief:

Ki maintendra or mon païs,	*Who now will maintain my country,*
Mon realme, tote m'enor,	*my kingdom and my honour,*
Dont tu fusses eirs alcun jor?	*of which one day you [Pallas]*
N'ai mais enfant ki mon regne ait	*would have inherited? I have no*
Ne nul baron ki me manait,	*other child to take my realm or any*
Car tuit sevent bien mon poeir,	*baron to help me, because they all*
Et vielz oem sui, si n'ai nul eir;	*know well my fear: that I am an old*
N'avront mais rei de mon lignage	*man without an heir. There is now*
Ki sire seit par eritage.	*no king of my lineage who can*
(Enéas, ll. 6304-12)	*inherit and become the lord.*

Evander's sadness at the death of his son is not the simple mourning of a parent grieving for their child, but the mourning of the end of his biological line and his kingdom. His lamentation is therefore political as well as emotional and provides a contrast to the representation of female grieving, which makes no such mention of dynastic concerns.

The other category of grievers is *amies*. Within this category we can include Andromache, Helen and Polyxena from *Troie*, and Antigone, Argia, Deiphyle, Galatea and Ismene from *Thèbes*, the last of whom we will use as our case study. In Statius's *Thebaid*, the last scene in which we see Ismene is as she mourns at the side of Atys's dead body (Book VIII). However, while the mourning scene is retained in *Thèbes*, an overtly Christian scene is added:

Ysmeine chiet as piez le rei,	*Ismene threw herself at the feet of*
Mais il l'en drece tost vers sei.	*the king and then got up and went*
Demanda lé: 'Que vueus tu, suer?'	*towards him. He asked her: 'What*
[...]	*do you want, sister? [...]*
'Frére,' fait ele, 'n'en vueil mie,	*'Brother', she replied, 'there is*
Mais jo vueil mais changier ma vie:	*nothing I want, but I do want to*

None serrai, vivrai soz régle,	*change my life. I will be a nun and I*
Car n'ai mais cure d'icest ségle;	*will live under an order, because*
De tes rentes sol tant me livre	*there is nothing left in this world*
Que cent femnes en puéssent vivre.	*that my heart wants. Give me from*
Ates t'ama mout en sa vie,	*your wealth enough money to*
Fai ci por lui une abeïe.	*support one hundred women. Atys*
(*Thèbes*, ll. 6471–73,	*loved you a lot when he was*
6477–84)	*alive, so found an abbey for him'.*

As there is (of course) no classical source for this scene, we can look at contemporary historical examples that may have provided the *Thèbes* poet with inspiration. Fontevraud Abbey, where Eleanor of Aquitaine and Henry II were eventually buried, provides some interesting examples: Bertrade of Montfort became a nun there after the death of her husband, King Philip I of France, in 1108;[45] Matilda of Anjou, following the death of her husband William the Atheling in the White Ship disaster of 1120, never remarried but took her vows as a nun at Fontevraud in 1128 and later became its abbess.[46] Eleanor herself, a supporter of the abbey throughout her lifetime, semi-retired there in 1194, although she remained politically active (including playing a key role in the succession of her son, John, to the English throne in 1199) until her death in 1204.[47] Away from Fontevraud, the Benedictine nunnery of La Pommeraie was founded by Matilda of Carinthia in 1152, almost immediately after the death of her husband, Thibaut IV of Blois, and exactly at the time the *Thèbes* was being composed.[48] Ismene's story was therefore probably inspired by the actions of historical widows of which the *Thèbes* poet had heard tell, and in recreating it in this narrative he was then able to create a timeless example imbued with narrative authority for later women to follow if their husbands (or indeed any kin upon whom they were dependent) were lost to them.

Scenes of women grieving are frequently included in the illustrative schemes of manuscripts. In manuscripts with limited illustrations, it is often the only place that we find women. We see women grieving in MSS M, P6, L2, Vt, P14, Mn, P17, V1, Vn and P18. We can imagine that the illustrations of MS P16 also planned to show scenes of grieving women. For example, there is a space left for a miniature on fol. 97[r] above which the rubric reads: 'Ci parle de la grant douleur qui fu a troie quant hector fu ochis et comment il fu plainz et regretez' (*Here one speaks of the great suffering that was felt in Troy when Hector was killed and how he was mourned and missed*). Some illustrators choose to depict this grieving in a restrained manner. For example, in the French MS Mn, the historiated initial shows a woman standing by the body of Hector, which has been discreetly covered with sheeting, with her hands clasped together in prayer (Figure 10). The two attendants either side of her look down with their hands to their faces as if wiping away tears but the overall effect of the scene is calm and peaceful. In contrast, the illustrator of the Italian MS Vt adds in energy and drama (Figure 11). We see Hecuba bending over the body of Hector, which is dripping bright red blood, and clasping him around the shoulders; Priam is fainting into the arms of his attendants; Andromache throws her hands into the air in a wild gesture of grief, as does Cassandra; Helen and Paris clasp at their breasts while Polyxena pulls at her hair. The scene is crowded with people, not all of whom are named, and contains a cacophony of colour: reds, blues, greens, yellows, greys, browns and pinks. The overall effect is one of noise and chaos. It contrasts sharply with the scene seen in MS Mn. However, though both are very different, they still each convey the sense of mourning: MS Mn's is a more contemplative and reflective mourning, while MS Vt's is a raw and visceral reaction to grief.

We can also look at the relatives of hostages. For example, the case of Darius the Red in *Thèbes*: Darius is allied to Eteocles, but his son has been taken prisoner by Polynices, which causes much distress. Polynices agrees to free his son in return for control of Darius's tower, which will give him a strategic advantage over Eteocles. Darius does not wish to betray Eteocles and so he asks him whether he will agree to this exchange. Eteocles refuses and so Darius secretly hands over the tower to Polynices. Eteocles convenes a trial to decide how to punish Darius, but Jocasta and Antigone engineer a solution whereby Eteocles can marry Darius's daughter, Salamander, in exchange for leniency. Darius therefore suffers not only through his trial (during which he is beaten) but also by being placed in an ethical, patriotic and familial conundrum. And Salamander, like the women given away as prizes or booty, is essentially given away as a reward for leniency. Although the text says that Salamander eventually comes to love Eteocles, at the start it is made clear that she does not wish to be with him, for we learn that he has already propositioned her and been rejected on previous occasions:

Chiére morne vait humblement	*Her face was very sad as she*
Et plora mout avenantment;	*walked humbly and she cried very*
De plorer ot moillié le vis.	*gracefully. Her face was covered in*
[...]	*tears. [...] The king [Eteocles]*
Li reis l'amot et senz mesure,	*loved her without limit, but she*
Mais ele ert vers le rei trop dure;	*was very harsh to the king. He*
Il l'aime plus que rien que vive,	*loved her more than anything in*
Mais ele est vers lui trop eschive.	*life, but she wanted to avoid*
[...]	*being too close to him. [...]*
Jocaste sozrist vers le rei:	*Jocasta smiled to the king: 'Son'*
'Fiz,' fait ele, 'n'as dreit en tei,	*she said, 'you have no respect for*
Nen as dreit en chevalrie,	*yourself, and no right to be a*
Se d'icesté ne fais t'amie.'	*knight, if you do not take her as*
[...]	*your amie.' [...] The king*
Vers sa seror li reis se torne,	*turned to his sister, who was full*
Que est por l'autre triste et morne:	*of sadness for [Salamander]:*
'Suer,' fait il, 'ja savez vos ben	*'Sister', he said, 'you know very*
Que toz jorz l'ai preice en ven;	*well that I have begged her many*
De lé merci aveir ne dei,	*times on many occasions always in*
Car el ne l'ot onques de mei.'	*vain; I should therefore not have to*
Cele dist: 'Ore estes desus,	*have mercy toward her because she*
Ore ne l'enchauciez ja plus.'	*never had it for me.' Antigone*
(*Thèbes*, ll. 8451–53, 8459–62,	*replied: 'Now you are above her,*
8469–72, 8485–92)	*you no longer have to pursue her.'*

There is something disturbing about the way that Jocasta and Antigone are complicit in orchestrating and encouraging this exchange. Again, this is an episode that the *Thèbes* poet has added himself with no classical basis for it in the *Thebaid*, but evidently thinking that such a scene would be valuable and important for contemporary medieval audiences. We do not have to stretch our imaginations too far to conclude that the question of hostages, ransoms and upon whom the burden of responsibility lay were all topics that would have been debated at the court at which the *Thèbes* poet was writing. Yves Gravelle's work on prisoners during the crusades shows that the responsibility for liberating a prisoner was often with his family, including the daughters, wives and mothers.[49] Salamander, willingly or not, must play a role in her brother's liberation.

Finally, we see women who suffer through the destruction of their homes. We have already seen the case of the Trojan citizens during the sack of the city who, if they are lucky enough to escape the slaughter, are nevertheless faced with a world in which their homes have been razed to the ground or where they are handed over as plunder. This case focuses on one particularly poignant story from *Enéas*, involving a woman named Sylvia. Her experience mirrors what was probably the experience of many women during times of war. Her story is told in the *Aeneid* (Book VII): she has a tame stag and, thanks to the machinations of the gods, the Trojans hunt it down and shoot it though it does not die. This provokes a battle between the Trojans and the Latins and from this point on, the war between the Latins and the Trojans commences. However, the *Enéas* poet reworks this episode with details that increase its tragedy. Firstly, the gods are not involved at all: the decision by the Trojans to hunt the stag is made entirely of their free will. Secondly, while the shooting of the stag does provoke a battle, the *Enéas* poet gives us details not just of the fighting but also of the devastation brought to the surrounding lands and the pillaging of the homes. Finally, and most emotively, there is a brutal description (not in Virgil) of the fate of the stag:

Et puis fu li cers escorchiez.	*And then they flayed the stag.*
Ascaniüs a son chien pris,	*Ascanius took his dog that had*
Ki en une chanbre esteit mis:	*been hidden in a room by Sylvia,*
La pucele l'i ot mucié	*tied up with her belt and gave it*
Et de sa ceinture lié;	*the stag's hide [to eat]. They*
Li dameisels le deslia,	*chopped up the stag and*
De la cuirie li dona.	*distributed its pieces: a young*
Le cerf ont defait et chargié,	*man took its antlers and another*
Uns dameisels prist le forchié,	*took its head. They conquered it*
Et uns altres porta la teste:	*through great power.*
Conquis l'orent par grant poeste.	
(*Enéas*, ll. 3760–70)	

So many details about this added scene enhance its emotiveness: there is the detail that Sylvia has attempted to hide Ascanius's dog from him, but has not hurt it, perhaps as a way to negotiate with him later through some form of animal hostage exchange; there is the fact that the most trophy-like parts of the stag, the antlers and the head, are not taken as valued prizes by noble knights but by unnamed 'dameisels' (*young men*); finally, the way that the poet uses the word '[c]onquis' (*conquered*) to describe their victory over the stag creates an obvious connection to the fact that the Trojans are in Latium to conquer it. The implication is that they will be just as ruthless with the lands and its citizens as they were with Sylvia's stag. We never hear of Sylvia again and are left to imagine her sitting alone in her pillaged home, with her dead kinsmen around her and the skinned and headless carcass of her beloved stag abandoned in the courtyard. We can see it as a microcosm for the experience of war as suffered by the general noncombatant population. Matthew Strickland's study of the conduct of medieval warfare with regard to the targeting of noncombatants exposes the suffering and devastation that occured and he notes that other medieval writers (roughly contemporaneous with the *romans* authors) such as Orderic Vitalis (*c.* 1075–1142) and the author of the *Gesta Stephani* (*c.* 1148–53) were also moved by the misery that warfare in general and raiding in particular caused.[50] The *Enéas* poet's rendering of Sylvia's story paints a vivid picture of the distress that a passing military force could inflict upon a local population: again, something that may have been familiar to its audience.

Conclusion

Women are often shown in the role of victim and to some extent this is a feminized role. A lot of female suffering does have a male equivalent: both men and women are shown being killed, grieving and suffering. However, there are certain forms of victimization that are specifically restricted to women: ritual execution, suicide, abduction and sexual assault. This gendering of victimization means that women are shown as more vulnerable to a wider range of suffering. The overall structuring of the texts' descriptions suggests that the poets were interested in reflecting the realities of noncombatant suffering, too, even if that was not their central focus. Women are more likely to be shown experiencing grief and suffering in manuscript illustrations. For example, those gathered around the bedside of an injured or dying male warrior are usually women, and women occupy the prime spots closest to the body. In illustrations of the sack of the city there is usually priority given to the slaughter of women and children, rather than including male citizens of the city, too. Indeed, anyone browsing the illustrative cycles of these manuscripts would be forgiven for assuming that if men avoided the battlefield during times of war then they would be relatively safe, whereas there are no safe spaces for women: the violent ramifications of war were inescapable anywhere and everywhere.

Figure 1 Abduction of Hesione. *Troie*. MS P18, fol. 20ʳ © 2019 Bibliothèque nationale de France. Reproduced with the kind permission of the BnF.

Figure 2 Abduction of Helen. *Troie*. MS Vt, fol. 34ʳ © 2019 Biblioteca Apostolica Vaticana. Reproduced by permission of Biblioteca Apostolica Vaticana, with all rights reserved.

Figure 3 Abduction of Helen. *Troie*. MS Vn, fol. 29ʳ © 2019 Österreichische Nationalbibliothek. Reproduced with the kind permission of the ÖN.

Women as Victims of War 59

Figure 4 Abduction of Helen. *Troie*. MS P17, fol. 59ʳ © 2019 Bibliothèque nationale de France. Reproduced with the kind permission of the BnF.

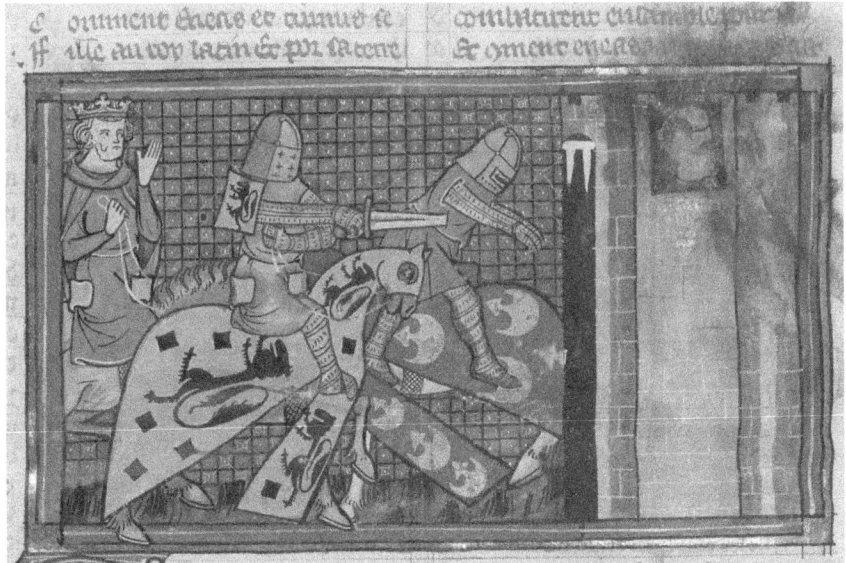

Figure 5 Combat of Aeneas and Turnus as Lavine watches from a tower. *Enéas*. MS P17, fol. 182ᵛ © 2019 Bibliothèque nationale de France. Reproduced with the kind permission of the BnF.

Figure 6 Women watch a battle from Troy's walls. *Troie*. MS Vt, fol. 108^r © 2019 Biblioteca Apostolica Vaticana. Reproduced by permission of Biblioteca Apostolica Vaticana, with all rights reserved.

Figure 7 Diomedes and Briseide. *Troie*. MS Vn, fol. 89^r © 2019 Österreichische Nationalbibliothek. Reproduced with the kind permission of the ÖN.

Figure 8 Briseide gives her sleeve to Diomedes. *Troie*. MS P18, fol. 99ʳ © 2019 Bibliothèque nationale de France. Reproduced with the kind permission of the BnF.

Figure 9 Diomedes and Briseide. *Troie*. MS Vt, fol. 115ᵛ © 2019 Biblioteca Apostolica Vaticana. Reproduced by permission of Biblioteca Apostolica Vaticana, with all rights reserved.

Figure 10 Mourning for Hector on the anniversary of his death. *Troie.* MS Mn, fol. 80ʳ © 2019 Bibliothèque Interuniversitaire de Montepellier. Reproduced by permission of the Bibliothèque Interuniversitaire de Montepellier, with all rights reserved.

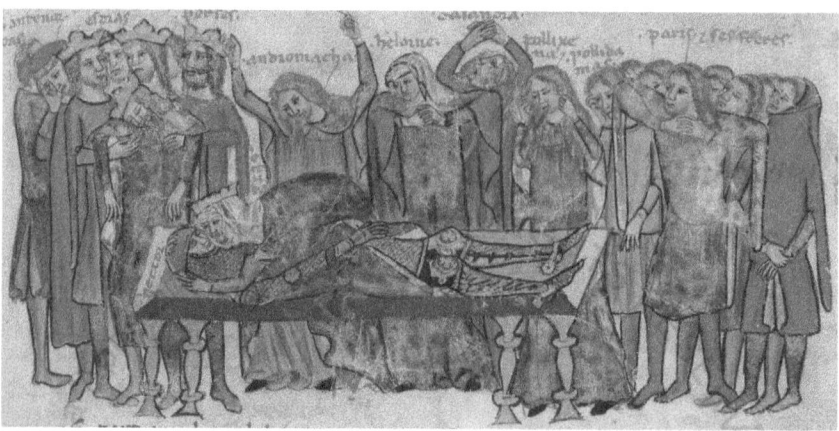

Figure 11 Hecuba, Andromache, Helen, Cassandra, Polyxena, other women and Trojan men mourn over Hector's dead body. *Troie.* MS Vt, fol. 126ʳ © 2019 Biblioteca Apostolica Vaticana. Reproduced by permission of Biblioteca Apostolica Vaticana, with all rights reserved.

Figure 12 Hecuba, Polyxena and Helen mourn at the anniversary of Hector's death. *Troie*. MS L2, fol. 109ʳ © 2019 The British Library Board. Reproduced by permission of the British Library, with all rights reserved.

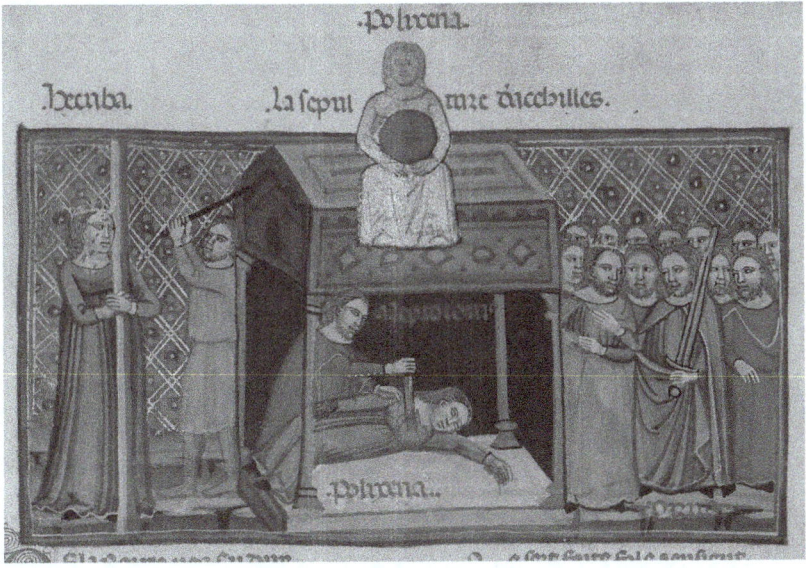

Figure 13 Execution of Polyxena and Hecuba. *Troie*. MS P18, fol. 180ʳ © 2019 Bibliothèque nationale de France. Reproduced with the kind permission of the BnF.

Figure 14 Sack of Troy and execution of Priam | Women given away, execution of Polyxena and execution of Hecuba. *Troie*. MS P6, fol. 155ʳ © 2019 Bibliothèque nationale de France. Reproduced with the kind permission of the BnF.

Figure 15 Trojan women and other treasures of Troy ready for distribution to the Greeks. *Troie.* MS Vt, fol. 200ᵛ © 2019 Biblioteca Apostolica Vaticana. Reproduced by permission of Biblioteca Apostolica Vaticana, with all rights reserved.

Figure 16 Women and Master Goz gather around Hector's bedside. *Troie.* MS P18, fol. 96ᵛ © 2019 Bibliothèque nationale de France. Reproduced with the kind permission of the BnF.

Figure 17 Briseide cares for Diomedes. *Troie*. MS P18, fol. 136ʳ © 2019 Bibliothèque nationale de France. Reproduced with the kind permission of the BnF.

Figure 18 Visit of the Trojan men to the Trojan women. *Troie*. MS V1, fol. 90ᵛ © 2019 Biblioteca Nazionale Marciana. Reproduced by permission of the Ministry of Cultural Heritage and Activities – Biblioteca Nazionale Marciana, with all rights reserved.

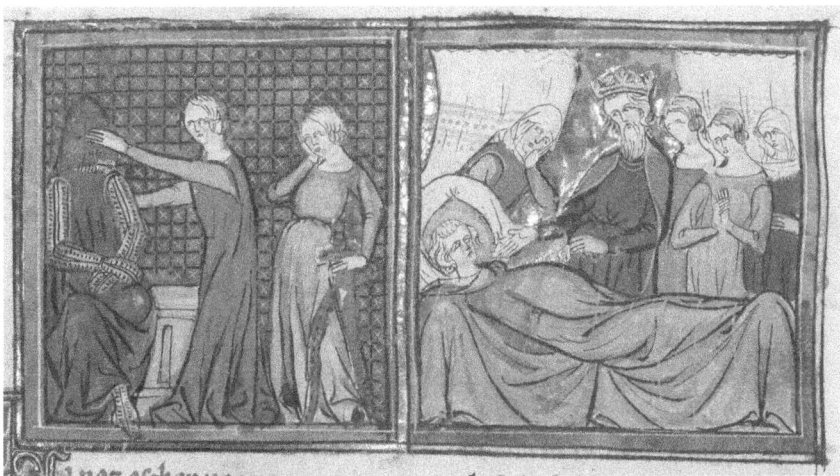

Figure 19 Women remove Hector's armour | Women and Priam at the bedside of Hector. *Troie*. MS P17, fol. 79ʳ © 2019 Bibliothèque nationale de France. Reproduced with the kind permission of the BnF.

Figure 20 Aeneas and Evander | Venus gives armour to Aeneas's messenger. *Enéas*. MS P17, fol. 165ʳ © 2019 Bibliothèque nationale de France. Reproduced with the kind permission of the BnF.

Figure 21 Polyxena, Helen, Hecuba and other women care for Troilus and remove his armour and weapons. *Troie*. MS Vt, fol. 157ᵛ © 2019 Biblioteca Apostolica Vaticana. Reproduced by permission of Biblioteca Apostolica Vaticana, with all rights reserved.

Figure 22 Troilus's armour is removed by Trojan women. *Troie*. MS V1, fol. 161ᵛ © 2019 Biblioteca Nazionale Marciana. Reproduced by permission of the Ministry of Cultural Heritage and Activities – Biblioteca Nazionale Marciana, with all rights reserved.

Figure 23 Penthesilea and the Amazons in battle. *Troie*. MS P6, fol. 138ʳ © 2019 Bibliothèque nationale de France. Reproduced with the kind permission of the BnF.

Figure 24 Paris greets Penthesilea upon her arrival in Troy. *Troie*. MS Vt, fol. 178ᵛ © 2019 Biblioteca Apostolica Vaticana. Reproduced by permission of Biblioteca Apostolica Vaticana, with all rights reserved.

Figure 25 Penthesilea and the Amazons in battle. *Troie*. MS P18, fol. 159ʳ © 2019 Bibliothèque nationale de France. Reproduced with the kind permission of the BnF.

Figure 26 The Greeks throw Penthesilea's body into the River Scamander. *Troie*. MS L2, fol. 151ʳ © 2019 The British Library Board. Reproduced by permission of the British Library, with all rights reserved.

Figure 27 Achilles drags the body of Troilus behind his horse | Ajax and Paris kill each other | Pyrrhus kills Penthesilea. *Troie*. MS P6, fol. 154ᵛ © 2019 Bibliothèque nationale de France. Reproduced with the kind permission of the BnF.

Figure 28 Burning of Troy | Penthesilea's body is thrown into the river. *Troie*. MS P17, fol. 126ʳ © 2019 Bibliothèque nationale de France. Reproduced with the kind permission of the BnF.

Figure 29 Philemenis follows Penthesilea's (unseen) funeral cortège. *Troie*. MS Vn, fol. 161ʳ © 2019 Österreichische Nationalbibliothek. Reproduced with the kind permission of the ÖN.

Women as Victims of War 73

Figure 30 Cassandra, Hecuba, Andromache and Polyxena. *Troie*. MS Vt, fol. 42ʳ © 2019 Biblioteca Apostolica Vaticana. Reproduced by permission of Biblioteca Apostolica Vaticana, with all rights reserved.

Figure 31 Cassandra mourns Cassibelan and makes her prophecies. *Troie*. MS P18, fol. 67ʳ © 2019 Bibliothèque nationale de France. Reproduced with the kind permission of the BnF.

Figure 32 Cassandra makes her prophecies to Priam. *Troie*. MS V1, fol. 26ᵛ © 2019 Biblioteca Nazionale Marciana. Reproduced by permission of the Ministry of Cultural Heritage and Activities – Biblioteca Nazionale Marciana, with all rights reserved.

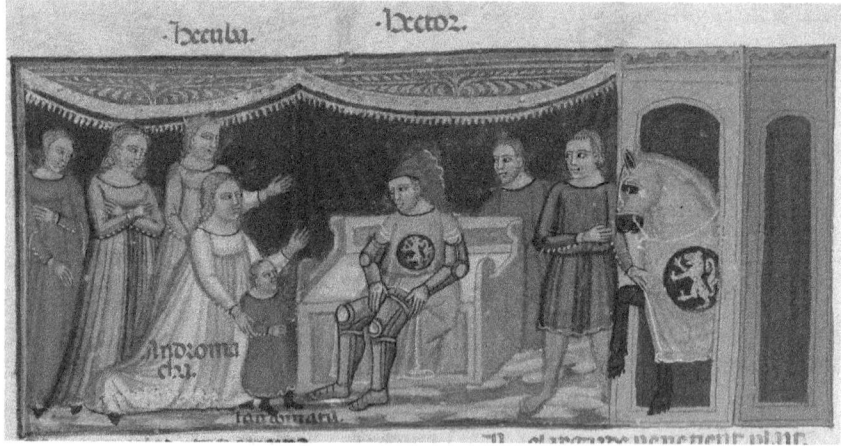

Figure 33 Andromache pleads with Hector. *Troie*. MS P18, fol. 101ʳ © 2019 Bibliothèque nationale de France. Reproduced with the kind permission of the BnF.

Figure 34 Andromache pleads with Hector. *Troie*. MS P6, fol. 90ʳ © 2019 Bibliothèque nationale de France. Reproduced with the kind permission of the BnF.

Figure 35 Andromache pleads with Hector. *Troie*. MS P17, fol. 94ʳ © 2019 Bibliothèque nationale de France. Reproduced with the kind permission of the BnF.

Figure 36 Hecuba plots Achilles's death with Paris. *Troie*. MS Vn, fol. 134ʳ © 2019 Österreichische Nationalbibliothek. Reproduced with the kind permission of the ÖN.

Figure 37 Hecuba and Priam speak about Polyxena and Achilles. *Troie*. MS Vt, fol. 136ᵛ © 2019 Biblioteca Apostolica Vaticana. Reproduced by permission of Biblioteca Apostolica Vaticana, with all rights reserved.

Figure 38 Hecuba speaks with Achilles's messenger. *Troie*. MS P18, fol. 119ʳ © 2019 Bibliothèque nationale de France. Reproduced with the kind permission of the BnF.

4

Women as ancillaries in war

Women's contributions to both the first and second world wars are now well known thanks to the work of numerous recent historians and their frequent representation in popular culture such as television series and films, but the case for medieval women has not been made as strongly or as prominently. However, research shows that medieval women certainly performed important ancillary functions to support crusading and military projects in numerous logistical, practical and organizational ways.[1] Sieges in particular were the form of warfare most likely to involve women and both *Troie* and *Thèbes* involve long sieges so we can well expect to find women there as we investigate how the *romans* represent women's involvement as ancillary forces during times of war.[2]

Basic but essential: Food, water and cleanliness

Food, water and cleanliness are essential considerations for the logistical success of warfare but there is relatively little exploration of these aspects in the texts. However, the earliest of the *romans*, *Thèbes*, does include several episodes in which the soldiers must seek out food and water sources, many of which are reminiscent of similar events in chronicles of the First Crusade.[3] When the marching Argive army is faced with a severe drought, they deviate from their route to a nearby castle where a noble lady by the name of Hipsipyle is able to provide them freshwater. Her importance is shown in the only manuscript to contain a significant illustrative scheme for *Thèbes*, the fourteenth-century Parisian MS P17, as one of its fourteen miniatures is of Hipsipyle (fol. 11ᵛ). Given that the only other female character from *Thèbes* to be illustrated is Jocasta, this makes her and her actions stand out, even if the episode in which she appears is relatively small. But this is the only episode across the three *romans* in which any connection between women and the provision of water is made at all. This is surprising given that chronicle accounts of warfare include many accounts of women bringing water to the soldiers during battle. For example, Guibert of Nogent's chronicle of the First Crusade recounts how women brought water to the soldiers in battle.[4] Similarly, the *Gesta Francorum* describes women bringing water to men on the battlefield during the Battle of Dorylaeum in 1097 (Book III, Chapter 9); the *Chanson d'Antioche* (c. 1180) describes the same event (laisse 99); Susan B. Edgington and Carol Sweetenham note that women bringing water for the soldiers occurs 'with tedious frequency' throughout the *Antioche* and such women also appear in the *Chanson de Jérusalem* (c. 1180) again 'armed with the inevitable waterbottles';[5] William of Tyre's *Historia rerum in partibus Transmarinis Gestarum* (c. 1170–84) gives an account of women bringing water to the fighters on the battlefield during the siege of Jerusalem in 1099 (Book VIII, Chapter 16),[6] and Oliver of Paderborn recounts in the *Historia Damiatina* (c. 1219–23) how women brought water to the soldiers during the siege of Damietta in 1218.[7] As Sarah Lambert observes, women bringing water to men on the battlefield is 'so commonplace as to be regarded as a topos in crusading literature'.[8] Yet the *romans* do not make use of it at all. Instead, they adapt this practice and convert it into one that is more suitable for a genre seeking to distinguish itself from a chronicle: a noble lady revealing a source of water to knights is rather more poetic and fitting for romance.

We see women's close relationship to water occurring in other ways throughout the Old French tradition: the sirens of the classical tradition are bird-women hybrids but become fish-women hybrids (mermaids) in the texts and illustrations of the medieval translations and adaptions of these tales (as indeed they are in *Troie*); Laudine is known as the Lady of the Fountain in Chrétien de Troyes's *Yvain* because of her intrinsic connection to the magical fountain in her lands; Lancelot in Chrétien's *Lancelot* is known as *Lancelot du lac* ('Lancelot of the Lake') because he was cared for in his infancy by a lady of a lake and indeed this lady of the lake figure is well known in various forms throughout the Arthurian tradition; the Demoiselle d'Escalot of the *Mort Artu* (c. 1237) dies of unrequited love for Lancelot and is found drifting on a river; Cyane dissolves into water in the *Ovide moralisé* (c. 1309–20); the eponymous protagonist of Jean d'Arras's *Roman de Mélusine* (c. 1382–94) transforms into a woman-serpent hybrid when she takes a bath, and in the next chapter we will see that Penthesilea is the only warrior to be given a watery burial, perhaps because of her sex, as her body is discarded into a river. Women in the chronicles are connected to water in a logistical and practical way, but in the Old French tradition we find that connection is still strong, although transposed into something rather more symbolic, poetic or even fantastical.

Food is a relatively small part of the *romans* in general and women are not presented with an active role in this aspect of essential supplies. A study of provisioning of the First Crusade outlines four ways an army accessed food: taking it from the outset, purchasing en route, pillaging or stealing, or provisioning by a local ally.[9] In *Thèbes*, when the Argive army runs out of the food, the knights ride out on dangerous mission to find new supplies and must fight off numerous opponents to claim and secure their supplies.[10] There are no descriptions of food-gathering or preparation in *Troie*: the word 'vitaille' (*foodstuffs*) appears only nine times (in just over 30,000 lines) and there is no mention of drinking water at all. *Troie* does not treat food and water in its narrative in the practical way that *Thèbes* does, but perhaps Benoît was more consciously differentiating his *roman* from narratives such as chronicles that had come before him by eliminating such logistical details.

It is worth making a brief note on cleanliness, for it is to be remembered that washerwomen were the only group of women to receive authorization to join the crusades.[11] They were supposed to be 'old and physically unattractive' to discourage fraternization between the sexes.[12] In addition to the basic expectations of a laundress (washing clothes and bandages), they also picked lice and fleas from men's bodies.[13]

But it is unsurprising that we do not find laundresses in the *romans,* for unnamed non-aristocratic characters appear infrequently. However, if we consider cleanliness as an aspect of health care, then we will find women in this next category.

Health care for the living and burying the dead

After battle four of *Troie*, Hector returns to his chambers where he is met by his mother, sisters, wife and other noblewomen:

Sa merel prist entre ses braz,	*His mother took him in her arms,*
E ses sorors ostent les laz;	*while his sisters (who loved him*
Del chief li ont son heaume osté	*with all their heart) undid the*
Del sanc de lui ensanglenté;	*laces of his helmet, which was all*
L'auberc li traient de son dos;	*covered in blood and lifted it from*
La nuit n'ot guaires de repos;	*his head. They also lifted away the*
Ses genoillieres li esterent	*hauberk [that covered] his back;*
Celes qui de bon cuer l'amerent.	*that night he had hardly any rest.*
Remés est en un auqueton	*And those women who loved him*
Porpoint d'un vermeil ciclaton:	*removed his knee-protectors. The*
Li sans de lui glaciez e pers	*only thing remaining was his*
Le li ot si al dos aers	*embroidered tunic, made of a*
Qu'a granz peines li ont osté.	*very precious silk. His blood,*
La ot mout tendrement ploré.	*now dried and black, was so*
(*Troie*, ll. 10219–32)	*stuck to his back that it was difficult*
	to remove [this tunic]. There was
	much piteous crying.

Despite the blood and suffering, this is a tender and intimate scene. Although the Trojan royal family certainly had servants in attendance at the palace, the task of removing Hector's bloodied clothes falls to his female relations. It raises the idea that care for wounded and bloodied bodies was not only a practical and dirty task, but one that created a bond between wounded and the carer. This bond may not be intimate or familial in all cases, but it is a moment of interaction and shared space between men and women. Such scenes are occasionally chosen for illustration and appear in MSS Vt, P17 and V1. In MS P17 we have a miniature that has been split into two registers (Figure 19): the left register shows a woman removing Hector's helmet while another woman looks on with a concerned expression; the right register shows Hector (now without armour), tucked into bed, with the women (and Priam) standing by his bedside. The split miniature shows the 'before' and 'after' and explicitly makes clear the role that the women had in creating these two scenes. Similarly, in MS V1 we see a group of women tending to Hector: one removes his helmet while another kneels to remove his knee pads and a third embraces him (fol. 75ᵛ). Despite the domesticity of the setting and the lack of narrative criticality these scenes have, they were important enough to be included in illustrations, showing that they must have been valued.

These scenes already give glimpses of physical care in the *romans*. However, there are also more direct examples of 'official' physicians in all three texts: an unnamed Armenian doctor in *Thèbes*, Goz of Puglia in *Troie* and Iapus in *Enéas*. The summoning of the Armenian doctor in *Thèbes* occurs after a scene that is reminiscent of the *Troie* scene described above. Tydeus arrives at Adrastus's court having been attacked by Theban knights:

Entre ses braz soéf l'a pris,	*[Adrastus] took [Tydeus] gently in*
Sanglenz en fu sis manteaus gris;	*his arms; his fur coat was all*
Tot soavet et bèlement,	*bloodied. With great care and*
Le descendié el pavement;	*gentleness he lay him down on the*
Il meïsmes l'auberc li trait,	*floor. He himself removed [Tydeus's]*
Et as plaies demande entrait.	*hauberk and requested a treatment*
Sor le pez ot une grant plaie:	*for the injuries. There was a great*
Quant il la vit, mout s'en esmaie;	*wound on his chest. When the king*
Quant vit la cobe de la lance,	*saw it he was greatly dismayed.*
En sa vie nen ot fiance.	*When [Adrastus] saw the injury*
[...]	*made by the lance he despaired of*
Li reis fait mander un hermine,	*[Tydeus's] chances of staying alive.*
Qui mout saveit de medicine:	*[...] The king had an Armenian*
Tant i pena et seir et main	*summoned who knew much about*
A chief d'un meis le rendi sain.	*medicine. [This doctor]*
(*Thèbes*, ll. 1825–34, 1845–48)	*dedicated himself to [treating] the pain*
	both night and day and after a month
	Tydeus was healed.

What is interesting in this scene is what happens between Adrastus's initial treatment of Tydeus and the eventual summoning of the doctor:

Sa femne, eschevelee et pale,	*[Adrastus's] wife, dishevelled and*
Vint acorant par mé la sale:	*pale, came running into the middle*
Par mé la sale, eschevelee,	*of the room; in the middle of the*
Acort come femne desvee.	*room, dishevelled, she ran*
(*Thèbes*, ll. 1837–40)	*like a mad woman.*

The claustrophobic repetition of the words 'eschevelee' (*dischevelled*), 'par mé la sale' (*into the middle of the room*) and 'femne' (*woman*) in just four lines gives this short passage its own sense of intense madness. There is no indication that Adrastus's wife is able to provide the tender loving care that we saw from Hecuba and Andromache. It is not surprising that Adrastus chooses to summon a doctor rather than entrust the care of Tydeus to this particular woman.

Physical care in *Troie* is somewhat more equitably split, though the association specifically with 'mires' (*doctor*) or 'mecines' (*medicine*) is still the exclusive domain of men. Having been cared for by his female relatives after battle four, Hector is attended to by a doctor:

Li bons mires Goz li senez,	*The good doctor Goz the wise, who*
Qui devers Oriënt fu nez,	*was born in the East and was just*
Qui plus preisiez fu en son tens	*as valued in his time as*
Que Ypocras ne Galiëns,	*Hippocrates or Galen, examined*
Li a ses plaies reguardees	*[Hector's] wounds and cleaned and*
E afaitiees e lavees.	*washed them. He made him drink a*
Beivre li fist une poison	*potion that soon healed him.*
Que tost le traist a guarison.	
(*Troie*, ll. 10245–52)	

When Hector is more seriously injured after battle eight, Goz reappears:[14]

Broz [Goz] li Puilleis, li plus senez	*Goz of Apulia, the most*
Qui de mecines fust usez,	*knowledgeable of men,*
Ne d'oignement freis ne d'enplastre,	*practised medicine using fresh*
Dedenz la Chambre de Labastre,	*ointments and plaster, treated*
Tailla Hector si gentement	*Hector while in the Chamber of*
Que mal ne trait, dolor ne sent.	*Alabaster so carefully that he*
Totes les dames, les puceles,	*did not feel any pain. All the*
Totes les riches dameiseles	*ladies, maidens and rich young*
Sunt davant lui e nuit e jor.	*women were there before him*
(*Troie*, ll. 14605–13)	*both night and day.*

Once again, we see the combination of men and women in the care of Hector. Illustrations of these scenes are faithful in their inclusion of women alongside the doctor. In MS P18, we see Goz seated on Hector's right side, holding his hand, and we see four women on the left side of his bed, with one of them also holding his hand (Figure 16). We also see women standing at the head of his bed. The other men in the scene stand at the edges and do not have any actual contact with Hector or the bed. Goz has the prime position, but women occupy the second, third, fourth, fifth and even sixth most prominent spots in the room. Similarly, this scene is indicated in MS Vt by the fact that it is one of only two full-page illustrations (fol. 112^v) and it shows signs of having been touched or exposed frequently. Once again, the prominence of the women is shown in the composition of the scene: Goz stands closest to Hector, but the figures who are then closest to him are Hecuba, Helen, Cassandra and Polyxena. Only after the women do Priam, Hector's brothers and other attendants appear. The women may not have the official training of Goz to qualify them as *mires*, but nevertheless their presence is clearly valued and there is no indication that it is unwelcome or inappropriate.

There are suggestions in the historical record that women tended to the wounded and sick during warfare albeit it in an unofficial capacity. Certainly we know that female medical practitioners did not only concern themselves with women (nor male medical practitioners only with men) and women are found throughout the medical record in general as physicians, surgeons, apothecaries and healers.[15] This means that women were very plausibly involved in treating the sick or wounded in battle even if this is not explicitly stated.[16] For example, there is a suggestion of this occurring during the

Fifth Crusade while John of Joinville relates how a Parisian 'bourjoise' woman treats Louis IX of France when he is afflicted with dysentery during the Seventh Crusade.[17] But this 'unofficial' capacity is important. Monica H. Green argues that the definition of a medical practitioner needs to be broad if we are to capture more than a handful of women within our research net.[18] The women in *Troie* do not administer ointments or potions like Goz, but they do provide care and attention. A nurse is defined as a person who cares for the sick, injured or infirm, and according to the Oxford English Dictionary its first recorded use in English was in the early seventeenth century, even though the concept of the role was certainly recognized many centuries earlier. It would be problematic to apply this terminology retrospectively to these women, but it is important to acknowledge that images of what we would now call nursing are apparent in such twelfth-century texts, even if the vocabulary was not there to capture it. There are also instances of this medical care being performed by women for injured men throughout the Old French tradition although it is often similarly associated with magic and the supernatural. April Harper's study of female healers in medieval literature shows that the majority of texts that include feminine healing was produced in the twelfth and thirteenth centuries and was often from within the Old French tradition.[19] She cites examples such as Iseult of Ireland who heals Tristan in Béroul's *Le Roman de Tristan* (c. 1150–70), Enide, Morgan le Fay and Guivret's sisters from Chrétien's *Erec et Enide* who all tend to Erec at some point and Nicolette from *Aucassin et Nicolette* who comforts Aucassin as he languishes in a cell. We can also add the Lady of Noroison from *Yvain*, who heals Yvain's ailments with an ointment that was a gift from this same Morgan le Fay. Of course, the figure of the female healer was a very important one not just in the Old French tradition, but throughout medieval history and culture, where it was (and is) much debated, although most of these studies look at the practice in general rather than in the specific context of warfare.[20] These figures in *Troie* give us some of the first literary precursors to a character that would become increasingly present in the later Middle Ages.

In *Enéas* we find yet another different situation. Aeneas is injured during the final battle and is taken into a pavilion on the battlefield while the doctor is summoned:

Uns molt buens mires Iapis	*A very good doctor, Iapus, came; he*
I est venuz et vit la plaie,	*saw the wound, felt the iron tip and*
Senti le fer, molt i essaie,	*tried to see if he could extract it; but he*
Saveir se traire l'en porreit;	*was unable to remove it in any way,*
Nel pot aveir en nul endreit	*even with forceps or tongs and Aeneas*
A tenailles n'a ferrement,	*cried out loudly. The doctor went to*
Et Eneas crie forment.	*his bag and took a box, from which*
A sa male li mires vait,	*he took some dittany, soaked it and*
Prent une boiste, si'n a trait	*then made Aeneas drink it. When he*
Del ditan, si l'a destrempé,	*had done so, the arrowhead*
Beivre li fist; quant l'ot passé,	*came out [of the wound] and the*
La saiete s'en est vollee	*shoulder was quickly healed.*
Et la plaie sempres sanee.	
(*Enéas*, ll. 9552–64)	

Here the healing episode appears to be an entirely male-dominated episode, which is not surprising given that it takes place in the encampments of the itinerant Trojans and next to the battlefield, rather than in a domestic setting such as Hector's chambers. However, the actions and emotions of Ascanius and the barons are similar to those of the women in *Troie*: while Hector is being treated for his wounds Andromache 'mout tendrement ploré' (*very tenderly cried*, l. 10232) as do the other ladies, and while Aeneas is being treated for his wounds Ascanius and the barons 'plorent forment' (*cry a lot*, l. 9599). The narrator therefore creates a setting that is similar to the domestic space that we have seen elsewhere.

Another care process in which women are involved is care for the dead. It goes without saying that the *romans*, with their combined fifty thousand lines and thirty-three battles, rack up quite a tally of dead. It is not possible to calculate how many people actually die across all three (not least because the reporting is inaccurate and used predominantly for poetic effect), but we can assume that it is in the thousands. Of the named characters who are killed, a not insubstantial amount of space is often dedicated to describing their tombs, funerals and commemoration ceremonies. Hector and Achilles in *Troie* and Pallas and Camille in *Enéas* are afforded particularly impressive tombs, having already had elaborate mourning ceremonies before their funerals.[21] But it is *Thèbes* that affords the most interesting insight into the treatment of the dead. The first we see of this is after Tydeus has killed fifty knights and the women of Thebes learn of their deaths:

Trestuit ensemble en vont al rei,	*All together [the women] went to find*
Demandent lui par grant esfrei	*the king [Eteocles] and asked him*
Que il a fait de lor amis,	*with great distress what he had done*
Ou les querront, en qual païs.	*with their loved ones, where they*
Li reis lor enseigna le val	*would find them, in what land.*
Ou geseient mort li vassal;	*The king indicated the valley where*
Et cil i vont o granz dolors.	*they would find the dead soldiers and*
[…]	*they went there with great sadness.*
Quant il orent assez ploré,	*[…] When they had cried a lot and*
Et de lor amis dementé,	*lamented their loved ones, they*
Enterrent les, car contre mort,	*buried them, for against death they*
Ço sévent bien, n'a nul resort.	*knew that there is no solution.*
(*Thèbes*, ll. 1955-60, 1967-70)	

Burial of the dead is not an easy task; it is very physically demanding.[22] Nevertheless, the location, repatriation and burial of their deceased menfolk are clearly a task that falls to the women and nobody challenges their suitability for this task. At the end of *Thèbes*, the lengths to which the women will go to fulfil this duty are even more extreme. They walk from Argos to Thebes to retrieve the bodies:

Les piez ont nuz, a duel sont mises.	*The feet [of the women] were bare,*
Par les monz et par les valees,	*and this caused them suffering.*
En vont dolentes, esguarrees.	*Through mountains and valleys*

Treis jorz aveient ja erré.	*they travelled, sad and dejected.*
[...]	*They walked for three days [...].*
A grant esforz a Thèbes vont,	*They are going to Thebes, which is*
Por eus veeir et enterrer,	*very painful, to find them [their*
Pur sevelir et conreer,	*fallen men] and bury them, to shroud and*
Que ne les manjucent oisel,	*care for them, so that neither birds, nor*
Chien ne leon, leu ne corbel.	*dogs, nor lions, nor ravens can eat them.*
(*Thèbes*, ll. 9818–21, 9982–86)	

This episode, in which the ladies walk barefooted for days to Thebes, is the denouement of the entire narrative. Having described the sadness and lamenting of the women, the narrator ends with: '[d]e tal guise fina la guerre' (*in such a way the war ended*, l. 10215) followed by a few final lines as a warning about the evils that can come about through warring and vengeance. This bleak ending is rendered slightly differently depending on the manuscript of *Thèbes* being consulted, but certainly this version is the darkest and 'makes the audience aware of the irreparable damage done to societies by warfare' than the versions found in some other codices.[23]

Neither historical nor archaeological records provide a lot of details to confirm whether this representation of women taking responsibility for the burial of the dead after battle is something drawn from the realities of the contemporary environment. It is certainly not from the classical sources, for while the *Thebaid* does recount the women seeking out their dead, their recourse is to cremate them on great funeral pyres rather than burying them in this Christian fashion. The fate of what happened to the dead after medieval battles is rarely mentioned in contemporary chronicles or accounts of the time and despite many studies and investigations there is relatively little historical or archaeological scholarship. A common assumption is that the bodies were collected, stripped for their armour or valuables and buried in mass graves on or close to the battle sites.[24] The fourteenth-century chronicler Froissart records that Edward III of England declared a truce for three days after the Battle of Crécy (1346) so that the battlefield could be cleared of bodies and burials made while Monstrelet's account of the Battle of Agincourt (1415) claims that there were four days after the battle during which fallen lords and princes were reclaimed, washed and returned for burial in their homelands.[25] There is no indication, however, as to who was responsible for this clearing or collecting. The return of bodies to their homes was something that only those of high social status might expect: either they were put in a lead coffin with herbs and spices to try to slow putrefaction and temper the smell of decomposition, they were excarnated (the bodies were boiled to remove the flesh so that the bones alone could be transported) or they were eviscerated (the entrails are removed and the rest of the body transported).[26] Another possibility, rather than the logistically challenging task of being returned to one's home, was to be moved to nearby churches. This could happen directly after a battle but even years later: Tim Sutherland and Simon Richardson's research at the battle site of Towton suggests that bodies were initially buried where they fell but were then moved to consecrated ground many years later.[27] Evidence from the battlefields at Bosworth (1485) and

Aljubarrota (1385) also suggest that bodies were initially buried where they fell and then later exhumed and reburied in consecrated ground.[28] But for some of the unluckiest bodies, they were simply left to rot where they lay. Contemporary accounts following the Battle of Poitiers (1356) suggest that the bodies were left on the field for weeks or even months after the battle.[29] The question of whether the dead of the victorious and those of the defeated were treated the same is also one that remains particularly problematic. Anne Curry and Glenn Foard contend that there is no reason to believe the winning side would have 'behaved badly' to the dead of the losing side for, regardless of political hostilities, the Christian right to burial was still taken very seriously.[30] However, when forces from different religious backgrounds (as during the crusades) clashed, these rights may not have been observed. Typically, each side was responsible for its own dead and if there were no participants available or remaining from the defeated side then their fallen would have been left to scavengers, animals and the elements. Benoît has several such scenes of clearing the dead in between battles in *Troie*. Between battles two and three, there is a truce of two months specifically for this purpose:

Le champ ou la bataille fu,	*They ordered a search of the*
Ou tant chiés ot sevrez de bu,	*battlefield on which so many*
Ou tant ot morz e detrenchiez,	*beheaded men lay, alongside many*
Ont comandé qu'il seit cerchiez.	*dead and mutilated men. Many*
D'ambedous parz i ot grant gent:	*people[31] from both sides joined in the*
Chaschuns i cerche son parent	*search, each one looking for a*
O son ami o son seignor;	*relative or a loved one or a lord.*
La ot assez lermes e plors.	*Many tears were shed there and*
As morz donerent sepouture.	*there was much weeping. They*
Si come il ert leis e dreiture.	*buried the dead in accordance with*
(*Troie*, ll. 10321–30)	*their rites and as was proper and just.*

After battle seven, Benoît describes a particularly horrific and vivid scene of the dead:

I ot des morz si grant merveille	*There were such an amazing number*
Que tote la terre vermeille:	*of dead there that all the land was*
Les eves e li flueve grant	*bright red: the waterways and the*
Corent de san trestuit sanglant;	*great river flowed filled with blood;*
Des charoignes ist la flairor	*a terrible smell came from the rotting*
E li airs est pleins de puör	*bodies and the air was filled with the*
Des cors qui sont, piece a, ocis,	*smell from the bodies that had been*
Qui ne son tars n'en terre mis;	*killed long ago but had neither been*
E por l'olor, que si est male,	*cremated nor buried. Due to the*
En gisent mil envers e pale,	*smell, which was so bad, thousands*
Gros e enflé. Chascuns engrote:	*[of people] lay down all pale,*
Por poi la gent n'en perist tote.	*swollen and bloated. Everyone was*
(*Troie*, ll. 12805–16)	*retching: the people were close to dying [from the smell].*

A truce is granted again so that the dead can be cleared and Benoît goes on to describe that the kings and dukes are given elaborate tombs, while great pyres are built for the other thousands of bodies; he even includes rather gruesome details such as the sound of crackling human bones in the fires (l. 13038). He makes it clear that this responsibility for clearing the dead is one that falls to both 'cil dedenz e cil defors' (l. 13044, *those from both within and without [the city]*); that is both the Greeks and the Trojans occupy themselves with their own fallen. So, if the Argives have been completely defeated, it is possible that the Argive women would indeed have taken it upon themselves to make the journey to Thebes to ensure their kin were afforded the proper funeral rites. Given the current dearth of sources for historians looking into the question of battlefield dead, *Troie* and *Thèbes* could be useful sources for detailing some of the possibilities of the practicalities of clearing the battlefield dead.

Companionship and the question of prostitution

According to certain crusade chroniclers, the two 'stereotypical female roles' for women were that of washerwoman or prostitute.[32] The tired old maxim that 'wherever there are soldiers, there are prostitutes' has been trotted out on too many occasions and in too many sources over too many centuries to attempt to list here. But clarification is needed on the word 'prostitute', as women characterized as prostitutes in the Middle Ages probably do not correspond to sex workers by today's definitions. A medieval prostitute was defined by sex outside the bonds of matrimony or the number of partners she had rather than an exchange of money; sex work in today's sense doubtless took place, but it also applied to any illicit or extramarital sexual activity.[33] Similarly, all of the principal crusade chroniclers mention female participants, many of whom would have been especially vulnerable at certain times and given the high death rates of men (their husbands, fathers or brothers), they often had little choice but to form attachments to other men who helped in providing protection; they then would have been identified as prostitutes in the chronicles due to a general clerical stigmatization of unmarried women.[34] There is no such labelling or stigmatization in the *romans*, but we do instead have numerous scenes of both romantic and platonic love and companionship, in which the company or affections of a woman are shown to have beneficial effects.

The platonic support often comes from family. For example, between battles four and five, three Trojan men, Aeneas, Polidamas and Troilus, go to visit the Trojan ladies (ll. 11845–11944). The narrator does not tell us their intentions for this visit, but it appears that they are there for a break from the horrors of the battlefield and some comfort. Hecuba obliges by making a speech about how grateful they (the ladies) are to them (the men) for fighting and defending their city and how important their actions are. Helen gives them all gifts, though it is not specified what these gifts are. Polyxena kisses Troilus. The illustrations that sometimes accompany this scene show these intimate moments of support and closeness between the men and women. In MS Vt (fol. 91ᵛ) we see Helen in the process of giving a gift to Polidamas in the centre, while next to them Polyxena embraces Troilus.[35] MS V1 illustrates this scene by showing the men gathered on one side of the room and the women on the other, with the only point of contact being the moment at which one of the ladies (probably Helen) gives a gift to one of the men (Figure 18). It is not clear what the gift is, but it looks like a length of fabric from the way that it hangs and may represent a sleeve intended to be worn as a favour. Intriguingly, it looks as though the scribe had left the space for the miniature but written the name 'Doroscaluz' in the bottom centre of the folio underneath the gap, with pen flourishes around it. Doroscalu was one of Priam's illegitimate sons who had been killed in battle four and his burial is described following this visit of the men to the women. This looks like an example of where the scribe and the illustrator have disagreed over the illustrative scheme: the scribe has written in Doroscalu's name to indicate that an image of his burial should appear here, but the illustrator has chosen to illustrate the meeting of the men and women instead. Doroscalu's burial is actually never illustrated in this manuscript. Clearly the illustrator thought that the meeting between the men and women was of greater importance.

We also find numerous romantic scenes as a source of support and comfort. The relationship between Briseide and Diomedes is a good example, as are its accompanying illustrations. After Diomedes is injured in battle fourteen, Briseide finally reciprocates his feelings and gives her love to him. The scene is illustrated in both MSS Vn and P18 and shows Briseide sitting by Diomedes's bedside, holding his hand (Figure 17).[36] The composition of the figures is almost identical to the scene earlier in which the doctor attended Hector at his bedside (Figure 16). This gives the effect of showing Briseide's love as being comparable to the attentions of a medical practitioner; in essence, her love is as powerful to Diomedes in restoring him to health capacity as had he been attended by a doctor. This scene demonstrates that the effect of a woman's love can have positive consequences not just in sexual or emotional terms but in physical terms, too: were it not for Briseide's affections, Diomedes might not have regained his strength to return to the battlefield.

It is harder to find evidence of this kind of behaviour in the historical record because these kinds of interactions are unlikely to have been recorded by chroniclers, which is another instance of how literary sources can help to fill in the gap. Nevertheless, we find a few hints that this kind of familial or marital support was similarly valued and appreciated from the sheer number of wives who partnered with their husbands to go on crusade. For example, Robert the Monk's chronicle of the First Crusade relates the great distress experienced by the wife of Philip I of France's constable when he is killed and she has to be restrained by other women to stop her from hurting herself.[37] Meanwhile, in Albert of Aachen's chronicle of the First Crusade we hear of a noblewoman of great beauty who is killed while playing dice with a clerk at the siege of Antioch, highlighting the shared enjoyment that men and women took from engaging in such enjoyable pastimes together (while simultaneously acting as a moral judgement on the part of Albert that such a fate was not undeserved for partaking in such a questionable activity).[38] Eleanor of Aquitaine had also travelled with her first husband, Louis VII of France, on the Second Crusade, although the extent to which their presence was a comfort or a strain to each other is uncertain to say the least: apparently relations between the two had deteriorated so drastically by the end of their sojourn that when they stopped in Rome on their return to France the Pope was compelled to attempt to mediate their problems and reconcile them.[39] Benoît, unsurprisingly, opts for a rather more idealized view of how a lover's presence can be a comfort and a support.

Military clothing and equipment

The manufacture and provision of medieval military equipment appears to have been a predominantly male domain.[40] However, as Green argued that the definition of medical practitioner should be broad, so too it is fruitful to adopt a similar strategy in defining providers of military equipment. Shulamith Shahar has shown evidence for women sharpening tools and making scabbards for swords and knives while P. J. P. Goldberg has shown that women were involved in the manufacturing of certain arms, particularly coats of mail, bows and arrows.[41] While scabbards, mail and archery accoutrements can easily be categorized as military equipment, there are other items that could similarly be placed in such a category. For example, there are chronicle accounts of women providing stones to soldiers to be used as missiles and projectiles: Oliver of Paderborn provides this detail during his description of the capture of Damietta in 1249, while in the *Chanson d'Antioche* they even resort to throwing the stones themselves;[42] Fulcher of Chartres's chronicle of the First Crusade describes women bringing stones to the defenders of Joppa during its siege in 1123;[43] Jordan Fantosme's *Chronique de la Guerre entre les Anglais et les Écossais en 1173 et 1174* (c. 1174) describes women of the town carrying stones to the barricades during the siege of Dunwich (ll. 869–70);[44] the *Chanson de la Croisade Albigeoise* tells us that women also carried stones to help build defences during the siege of Toulouse and even suggests that Simon de Montfort himself was killed by a stone from a mangonel that was operated by a woman.[45] Women also helped in the maintenance of military equipment: during the siege of Jerusalem in 1099, Albert of Aachen describes how girls and women helped to transport materials to weave the panels of a siege engine, an activity at which they would also doubtless have been skilled.[46] Additionally, they helped optimize the conditions in which military technology operated: for example, in Ambroise's account of the siege of Acre they helped to clear rubble and fill in ditches so that the siege machines could be brought as close to the city walls as possible.[47] In one particularly committed scene, a woman is shot by a Saracen while filling a ditch and uses her dying words to beseech those around her to use her dead body as further filling for the ditch.[48]

Finally, though not a piece of physical equipment, most strategists would agree that intelligence is an essentially military tool and there is historical evidence of women acting as intelligence gatherers and spies. By the time of the Hundred Years War, the role of women in espionage was apparently so well known that certain military commanders issued ordinances to remind men not to reveal any sensitive information to local women.[49] Similarly, Anne Curry has argued that there is 'ample evidence' to show that women were used as spies by both the English and the French.[50] For example, she highlights the stories of two women who were well paid to go to Chartres, Gallardon and Senonches to gather information from male prisoners about the disposition of troops, as well as a woman sent to spy on enemy actions between

Nogent and Chartres.⁵¹ The fact that there is 'ample' evidence of female spies in the sources suggests that this role was even more prevalent than the sources let on; for surely the truly deftest of spies would not have ended up recorded within the folios of chronicles but would have remained an undetected anonymous figures in the shadows, allowing us only to speculate over their actions and identities.

The *romans*, as with the section on food and water, do not directly feature the tropes that are found in the contemporary historical literature: the women do not provide stones to soldiers, fill in ditches or assist with the maintenance of equipment. Nevertheless, they do give examples of the ways in which women provide items for men that are of use to them in battle. For example, in *Enéas*, Venus makes a deal with Vulcan, her estranged husband and the god of the forge and metalworking, whereby he will manufacture a hauberk, helmet, shield, breeches, lance and sword for Aeneas.⁵² The items that he produces are (unsurprisingly) unparalleled:

N'i mist mie Vulcans deus meis,	*It did not even take Vulcan two months*
Que les armes a aprestees,	*to complete the arms and to give*
A sa femme les a donnees;	*them to his wife [to give to Aeneas].*
Buenes furent, el mont n'ot tels,	*They were excellent, no man ever*
Nes peüst pas faire oem mortels.	*had the same, nor could any mortal*
(*Enéas*, ll. 4408–12)	*man have made [such arms].*

An illustration of this episode does not show Vulcan producing the equipment, but it does show Venus giving the armour to Aeneas's messenger (Figure 20). The miniature has been split into two registers: Aeneas is in conversation with Evander about the war in the left register and Venus handing the armour to the messenger is in the right register. The construction of these two registers shows why armour will be needed (on the left) and the provision of that armour (on the right). Here we have a woman taking responsibility for providing a knight with equipment and tools for his upcoming battles, and the male god who produced that equipment is left entirely out of the illustration.

We find a similar episode in Chrétien's *Lancelot*, when the wife of Meleagant's seneschal is responsible for obtaining armour for Lancelot so that he can participate in an upcoming tournament (ll. 5494–5512) and in Renaut de Beaujeu's *Le Bel Inconnu* the protagonist's armour is also given to him by his mother (ll. 4973–74). This is not to suggest that the gifting of armour was something only women did; indeed, the Old French tradition has numerous examples in which men gift armour or other forms of clothing to each other and the ritual and symbolism behind such gifting are often highly significant.⁵³ When the gift or provision comes from a woman there is no suggestion that this makes it less valuable, but it may change the significance behind the gift. Gifts of clothing or armour have previously been categorized into four expressions: to show the largess of the giver, restorative gifts, identificatory gifts or love gifts.⁵⁴ The seneschal's wife's gift to Lancelot in *Lancelot* was a love gift; Blanches Mains's gift to Giglain in *Le Bel Inconnu* was an identificatory gift; but Venus's gift to Aeneas does not really fall into any of these categories. It creates its own category, that of a mother's desperation to protect her child, in this case by gifting a set of armour that makes Aeneas practically invincible. Of course, Venus is a pagan goddess, but this is not how she necessarily would have been received by contemporary audiences; she was part of the euhemeristic tradition and would therefore have been seen as a historical figure. Renate Blumenfeld-Kosinski has argued that there is actually an absence of euhemerism in the *romans* and instead the gods are simply removed from their divine spaces and reoriented as didactic mouthpieces, which is why the quarrels and pastimes that occupied the gods in the classical versions are excised from the *romans*.[55] However, it is possible to accept both the traditional euhemeristic explanation and Blumenfeld-Kosinski's 'reorientation' theory when considering the role of the gods in the *romans*. When the *Enéas* poet has to reconcile the fact that Aeneas, the purported ancestor of medieval kings and queens, is also the son of a pagan goddess, he can do so by carefully selecting and editing the scenes in which Venus features so that the overall impression is not one of a supernatural goddess, but of a (mortal) mother of a future king. There is a parallel here again with Arras's *Mélusine*. In one version of this narrative, we learn that Jean de Berry inherits the Lusignan territories from Mélusine, a supernatural woman who turns into a hybrid woman-snake once a week. This has been referred to as 'magical politics' whereby Jean d'Arras entirely redefines the relationship between motherhood and dynastic inheritance.[56] Can we apply the same theory to *Enéas*? If Venus becomes a figure legitimately connected to the dynasties of the medieval aristocracy, then we can interpret the episode of her provisioning of arms to Aeneas as similarly legitimate and something that would have been seen as perfectly realistic rather than supernatural.

The *romans* manuscripts also include several illustrations of women taking responsibility for handling military equipment. In MS Vt we see Troilus's return from battle and his reunion with the women: one holds his sword, another his shield, two carry his mantel, one has his helmet, another his hauberk and another his coif (Figure 21). There is a similar scene in MS V1 after Hector returns from battle: one lady holds his sword, another his helmet and a third removes his knee pads (fol. 90ᵛ). Later in the manuscript Troilus receives the same treatment: two ladies carry away his helmet and hauberk (Figure 22). There is no indication that these women are passing the armour and weapons on to another party; indeed in Figure 22 it is clear that they are carrying them out of the room, presumably to replace them in storage. Later in the narrative, Andromache is even able to hide Hector's armour from him, showing that she had more control over it than he or any of his attendants (*Troie*, ll. 15410–12). They are performing duties that a squire would more commonly have been expected to fulfil. However, there is no indication either in the text or the illustrations that it was inappropriate for these women to take responsibility for these items. The illustrations suggest that women were involved in the care and upkeep of armour and military equipment, just as much as they were involved in the care and upkeep of clothing or physical health. In this sense, there is no gendering of care in terms of what that care encompasses: women are cast in this role of carer, but that care can also be for traditionally masculine items such as hauberks or swords.

Conclusion

The ways in which the *romans* poets present women's ancillary roles are very different from other contemporary sources such as chronicles. Accounts of the crusades and sieges often describe women with responsibilities such as providing water to soldiers on the battlefield or gathering stones to be used as projectiles. Such scenes do not appear in the *romans*. However, that is not to say that women are absent from this role. *Thèbes* adapts the trope of women providing water on the battlefield to one in which a noble woman helps to lead the Argive army to water. *Enéas* describes how Venus is responsible for Aeneas's fantastic armour and weaponry. *Troie* has multiple examples of the ways in which women can support the warriors: undressing the men after battle and ensuring that the bodies of these men are taken care of as well as ensuring that the armour and weaponry is removed and returned to their rightful places. There are actually more illustrations of women handling the weapons and armour of the Trojan heroes than there are of these heroes' squires doing the same thing. They also support the doctors in tending to the injured warriors. In the case of Diomedes, where there is no doctor available, the illustrations of Briseide at his bedside in MSS P18 and Vn position her at his bedside in the exact same way as Goz had been positioned at Hector's bedside. And finally, they provide emotional support and love to help keep them psychologically strong. The visit of the Trojan men to the women was so important to MS V1's illustrator that he ignored the instruction to include an image of Doroscalu's funeral so as to have the space to illustrate this visit instead. The *romans* do show women performing ancillary functions during times of warfare, even if those ancillary functions are different to those that we find in other sources. That is not to say that they are less valuable or less likely to be reflective of the contemporary realities at the time. Instead, we can say that the *romans* are once again contributing to the contemporary debate on medieval women by showing the many ways in which they supported the war efforts.

5

Women as warriors in war

The *Enéas* poet composed the following original scene in which the Trojan warrior Tarchon meets the Volscian queen, Camille, on the battlefield. Tarchon suggests:

> Femme ne se deit pas combatre.   A woman must not fight.
> [...]   [...]
> Metez jus l'escu et la lance,   Put down the shield and the lance and
> Et le halberc, ki trop vos blece.   the hauberk that is so bad for you.
> [...]   [...]
> Ce nen est pas vostre mestier,   This is not your calling, which is
> Mais filer, cosdrë et taillier.   really to spin, to sew or snip [fabric].
> (*Enéas*, ll. 7076, 7082–83, 7085–86)

Camille responds by killing him on the spot, thereby rather undermining his argument that she is not suited to battle. There were numerous historical and literary precedents of women warriors and warrior-queens that the *romans* poets undoubtedly knew about and who have inspired the development of their female figures from the minimal outlines that their classical sources gave them. Within the Old French tradition specifically, women warriors were rather thin on the ground before *Troie* and *Enéas*. After their appearance, we start to see more interest in the figure of the female warrior. In 1190, Huon d'Oisy wrote the *Tournoiement des Dames* (Tournament of the Ladies), a *lai* in which around thirty noble ladies from the north of France compete in a tournament.[1] This inspired at least four other similar works during the thirteenth and early fourteenth centuries and the 'Tournament of Ladies' topos has even been classified as its own literary genre.[2] The first half of the thirteenth century also saw the composition of a text with one of the most complex and fascinating of medieval women warriors as its protagonist, Heldris of Cornwall's *Le Roman de Silence*. The only extant copy of this text is found alongside *Troie* in MS Nt (the thirteenth-century manuscript that was commissioned for Béatrice de Gavre and which was discussed in Chapter 1 as having a particular connection to female patrons and a female readership). Silence is born a girl, but raised as a boy, where she excels in all manner of chivalric activities. She becomes a celebrated knight (in disguise as a man) and the romance recounts her adventures and exploits in France and England. Eventually her true sex is revealed by Merlin at the narrative's end and she is stripped of her knightly guise and 'converted' back into a woman before marrying the king. A vast amount has been written about the question of gender in *Silence*, which I shall not attempt to reproduce or summarize here, but no chapter on women warriors would be complete without mentioning her name.³ The fourteenth century also saw the appearance of the *Neuf Preuses* in Jean Le Fèvre's *Livre de Leësce*, a *topos* that became a popular subject for medieval sculpture, tapestry and written works, particularly in Italy and France.⁴ And in 1405, Christine de Pizan's allegorical *Cité des Dames* was filled with inspirational and influential women, including numerous warrior-queens like Penthesilea, Camille, Semiramis, Zenobia, Menalippe and Hippolyta. However, before the *Tournoiements des Dames*, the *Roman de Silence*, the *Neuf Preuses* or Christine and even before the *romans d'antiquité*, the figures of women warriors had already been debated in philosophical, historical and literary texts for hundreds of years.

Philosophical debates from antiquity to the Middle Ages

Plato began exploring the idea of women's participation in warfare long before the *romans*. In his *Republic* (c. 380 BCE), women's roles in the Ideal State are discussed and it is suggested that they could be educated and trained with men for physical combat.⁵ This is not to suggest that Plato was a proto-feminist of women's advocate by any stretch of the imagination. Although Plato argued for women's inclusion in his ideal polity, this was for pragmatic reasons only and he was frequently sexist and misogynistic in other aspects of his work.⁶ When his mentee, Aristotle (c. 384–22 BCE), wrote his *Politics*, he restricted women to the domestic sphere in subservience to men and declared that 'the male is by nature superior and the female inferior, the male ruler and the female subject'.⁷ It was Aristotle's *Politics*, rather than Plato's *Republic*, that was first translated into Latin and was widely studied by medieval thinkers.⁸ Early medieval chroniclers, who would probably not have read Plato or Aristotle as they were not translated into Latin until the thirteenth century, often documented the exploits of warrior women without particular comment.⁹ The Abbot of Cluny, Peter the Venerable (c. 1092–1156), wrote that 'it is not altogether exceptional among mortals for women to be in command of men, nor entirely unprecedented for them even to take up arms and accompany men to battle'.¹⁰ The Bishop of Rennes, Marbod (c. 1035–1133), praised the biblical Judith for beheading Holofernes and taking up arms against her enemies.¹¹ Yet from the thirteenth century onwards, roughly contemporaneous with the translation and circulation of Aristotle and Plato, chroniclers and clerks began to express increasing levels of surprise and outrage at women who participate in military activities.¹² Albert the Great (c. 1206–80) believed that women were not capable of military activity because of their natural 'timiditatem' (*timidity*);¹³ Ptolemy of Lucca (c. 1236–1327) and Giles of Rome (c. 1243–1316) used Aristotle's theories on the purported mental and physical weaknesses of women to support their political treatises in which they categorically rejected the idea of female participation in warfare.¹⁴ Ptolemy argued that, even if women were physically capable of fighting, their minds were still 'unsuitable'.¹⁵ Indeed, so corrupting did Ptolemy view the influence of women that he considered a complete ban on contact between soldiers and women and only conceded to allow interaction as he believed it could 'prevent homosexuality'.¹⁶

Meanwhile canon lawyers argued over the validity of a woman's crusader vow, the relationship between the vow and combat, and whether she needed her husband's consent to take the vow in the first place.[17] Taking the vow was generally accepted for the First and Second Crusades on the condition that combat was not involved, but later twelfth-century regulations aimed to prevent unarmed pilgrims (of either sex) accompanying the military expeditions.[18] Nevertheless, Muslim chroniclers of the twelfth-century crusades, such as Imad al-Din (1125–1208), Ibn al-Athir (1160–1233) and Baha al-Din (1145–1234), wrote numerous accounts of battles in which large numbers of Christian women from Western Europe participated in the fighting.[19] However, from the thirteenth century onwards the number of women in fighting roles somewhat dwindles, even if the presence of women on crusade campaigns is still evident well into the fourteenth century.[20] Furthermore, from the late twelfth and thirteenth centuries we even see debates and resolutions that led to women being accepted into military orders such as the Knights Hospitaller, the Knights Templar and the Teutonic Order and into chivalric orders such as the Order of the Garter and the Order of the Ermine.[21] Writers, thinkers and lawyers were clearly just as engaged in debating the relative merits and demerits of women warriors in the Middle Ages as were writers and thinkers from centuries before them.

Historical and literary precedents

The narrative role of these women came from classical sources but the way in which their characters are developed and their roles expanded cannot be attributed to these sources alone and must have had other influences. There were certainly numerous historical women who could have been influential or inspirational in this sense and summarizing such a list is a challenge. In the interests of brevity, I shall outline five such women here, all of whom would have been well-known figures to the members of the elite circles in which the *romans* manuscripts were circling and whose reputations would also have been familiar to the *romans* poets. We begin with Matilda of Canossa (1046–1115): she led armies into battle during the Investiture Controversy and defeated the Holy Roman Emperor Henry IV. Matilda had actually wanted to take the veil and enter a convent before taking up her military leadership, but it was Pope Gregory VII's suggestion that she serve God by supporting him in war that changed her mind.[22] She had advanced knowledge of military intelligence, manoeuvring and surprise and used it in her strategizing.[23] Although she did not lead the charges herself, this was due to political and strategic constraints rather than a lack of willingness or ability. Her reputation and successes were so great that later biographers 'embarked upon a wild goose chase to find the men they were certain must be found to explain her military successes'.[24] But of course they were not successful in this search. Although she eventually defeated Henry IV, she ultimately made his son, the Holy Roman Emperor Henry V, her heir.

This Henry V was the first husband of Empress Matilda of England (1102–67), the daughter of Henry I of England and Matilda of Scotland, granddaughter of William the Conqueror and Matilda of Flanders, and Henry I's chosen heir to the

English throne. Her claim was unpopular and the crown was seized instead by her cousin, Stephen. The civil war that followed is known as the Anarchy. Matilda played an active role both politically and militarily in England for the first twelve years of the war, and although she eventually returned to Normandy in 1147, she did not give up her claim entirely.[25] Although she was ultimately unsuccessful in claiming her rights through her battlefield exploits, she was successful in claiming them through negotiations for her son; when Stephen died in 1154, his son was bypassed in favour of Matilda's son, who was crowned Henry II of England. Given that the earliest of the *romans*, *Thèbes*, was composed sometime between 1150 and 1155, it would be almost impossible that its poet would have been unaware of Matilda's military role in the conflict as well as her political role in negotiating the terms of Henry's inherited kingship. Matilda lived until 1167, during which time she continued to be politically active in diplomatic negotiations in Normandy.[26] It was during this period that the other two *romans* were completed. She had continued to be a formidable force throughout this period of her life with her preferred style in charters being 'empress, daughter of the king', with a clear sense that the title of empress was superior to that of queen or duchess anyway.[27] If the *romans* poets wanted to develop the role of powerful warrior-queens found in their classical source material, they would not have had far to look.

On the other side of the Anarchy was a third Matilda: Matilda of Boulogne (1105–52), the queen consort of England through her marriage to Stephen. She also commanded military units and strategic negotiations during the Anarchy.[28] She used her authority to support her husband and his position as king, which attracted the favourable comment of chroniclers as society had an expectation that women would further the agendas of their husbands by counselling them or acting as proxies.[29] This expectation of playing a political (and, when necessary, a military) role means that women who acted as such were not exceptions, but a reflection of the ideal.[30] In fact it was women who did not use their authority to support their husbands or sons who were the anomalies, and the *romans* poets would no doubt have been keen to represent this ideal in their own works.

If we move to Flanders, we meet Sibylla of Anjou (c. 1112–65), sister of Geoffrey Plantagenet and therefore Henry II's paternal aunt. She governed Flanders while her husband was on a pilgrimage to the Holy Lands from 1138–39 and again from 1147–49 when he participated in the Second Crusade. During this second absence, Baldwin IV of Hainaut attempted to seize control of Flanders, but Sibylla, heavily pregnant at the time, raised an army and resisted the attack. The chronicler Lambert de Wattrelos describes her attacking Baldwin with a 'virile heart' while her son wrote a letter in which he described his mother as governing with 'an iron fist'.[31] She is described burning villages and towns until Baldwin was forced to retreat. Her reputation was certainly well known and well regarded.

Finally, we return to Eleanor of Aquitaine. The extent of her participation in military activities is speculative at best due to a lack of reliable primary sources.[32] There was a myth associated with Eleanor that she and her ladies dressed as Amazons while on the Second Crusade, which came from a thirteenth-century Byzantine chronicle:

Females were numbered among them, riding horseback in the manner of men, not on coverlets sidesaddle but unashamedly astride and bearing lances and weapons as men do; dressed in masculine garb, they conveyed a wholly martial appearance, more mannish than the Amazons. One stood out from the rest as another Penthesilea and from the embroidered gold which ran around the hem and fringes of her garment was called Goldfoot.[33]

However, the once-popular trend of identifying Eleanor as this 'other Penthesilea' has subsequently been dispelled.[34] Later chroniclers were generally more interested in portraying her as 'scandalous' rather than in an accurate fashion.[35] John of Salisbury and William of Tyre claimed that she engaged in an adulterous and incestuous affair with her uncle, Raymond of Poitiers, while the Minstrel of Reims transformed these stories into an elaborate tale of her affair with Sultan Saladin himself.[36] Despite the dearth of reliable sources for Eleanor's actions on crusade, there is significant evidence to show that she exercised political and military command through her vassalage of crusading knights, in particular that of the sojourn of the French army in Antioch in 1148.[37] Surely the *romans* poets, writing only a few years later, could not have failed to have her in their minds when writing the characters of their powerful warrior-queens, especially given the possibility that they were writing under her patronage or at her court.

Alongside this impressive array of historical women, there were literary influences to consider, too: classical warrior women, holy warrior women and poetic warrior women. The classical sources include not just Virgil, Dares and Dictys but Aethicus Hieronymus's *Cosmographia* (c. 600–700), Isidore of Seville's *Etymologiae* (c. 600–36) and Ovid's *Metamorphoses* (c. 8). Ovid's Callisto is even described in similar terms as those quoted at the start of this chapter in reference to *Enéas*'s Camille regarding a dislike for so-called women's tasks or pastimes: 'non erat huius opus lanam mollire trahendo | nec positu uariare comas' (*it was not her task to soften wool by drawing it out nor to vary her hairstyle*).[38] Biblical warrior women such as Judith and Deborah could also have played a part in encouraging the *romans* poets to develop their female warriors more fully. Deborah leads ten thousand Israelite troops alongside their general, Barak, who only agrees to go into battle if Deborah is with them (Judges 4). Meanwhile Judith takes up a sword and beheads the Assyrian general, Holofernes, before instructing the Israelites on the strategy for the subsequent battle, from which they emerge victorious (Judith 13–15). The figure of Judith was particularly and increasingly popular throughout the Middle Ages. For example, she is the protagonist of the Old English poem *Judith* (c. 700–1025); she appears in the *Vita* of Christina of Markygate (c. 1096–1155) as a 'favourite' of the Virgin Mary; she is included in the twelfth-century *Speculum Virginis* (a guide for nuns) as the figure of Humility; she is carved into the stone archivolt of Chartres Cathedral (est. 1184–1220); she is referred to in at least four of Geoffrey Chaucer's *Canterbury Tales* (c. 1387–1400), including *The Merchant's Tale*, *The Tale of Melibee*, *The Monk's Tale* and *The Man of Law's Tale*; she is also admitted into Christine de Pizan's *Cité des Dames* and is evoked in her *Ditié de Jeanne d'Arc* (c. 1429).[39] The importance of the women-warrior tradition combined with the newly emerging ideas of chivalry means that the female warriors of the *romans* had a huge potential to be some of the greatest dramatic characters and heroic exemplars.

Knightly virtues of the chivalric hero: *Courtoisie, prouesse* and *loyauté*

The question of what distinguished a savage brute (immorally and unethically slaughtering those around them) from a courtly chivalric knight (with a code of honour whose actions are legitimized as worthy and righteous) was important to the medieval mind.[40] The *romans* were written at a time when the idea of chivalry was becoming increasingly discussed and conceptualized; numerous other sources (textual, artistic and material) attest to this exploration but as was outlined in Chapter 2, it is not really possible to speak of an established code of chivalry in the mid-twelfth century. Courtly romances such as Chrétien de Troyes's works also had a part to play in the construction of the chivalric model. Maurice Keen highlights several chivalric qualities that are overwhelmingly present in Chrétien's texts including 'prouesse' (*prowess*), 'loyauté' (*loyalty*) and 'courtoisie' (*courtliness*).[41] From the moment that Penthesilea is introduced in *Troie* and Camille in *Enéas*, there is little doubt as to their knightly virtues as the poets use the same chivalric vocabulary with which they had previously used to describe the male heroes. The following description of Hector is given in *Troie*:

> Sol pröece li remaneit
> E li frans cuers, quil somoneit
> De toz jorz faire come ber.
> Puis qu'il n'aveit a armes per,
> Ne n'eüst nul de sa largece,
> De tant valeit mieuz sa pröece.
> De corteisie par fu teus
> Que cil de Troie e l'oz des Greus
> Envers lui furent dreit vilain:
> Onc plus corteis ne manja pain.
> De sen e de bele mesure
> Sormontot tote creature.
> (*Troie*, ll. 5347–58)

> *Prowess alone was always with him*
> *and his noble heart summoned him all*
> *the time to act like a baron [should].*
> *Nobody could equal his arms or*
> *match his largesse, so*
> *that his prowess was all the more*
> *praiseworthy. His courtesy was such*
> *that those of Troy and from the Greek*
> *army were like peasants next to him.*
> *No one more courtly ever broke bread.*
> *In wisdom and in good judgement*
> *he was above all others in the world.*

We can compare this to the introductory description of Penthesilea:

> La reïne Panthesilee,
> Proz e hardie e bele e sage,
> De grant valor, de grant parage,
> Mout ert preisiee e honoree;
> De li esteit grant renomee.
> Por Hector, que voleit veeir
> E por pris conquerre e aveir,
> S'esmut a venir al socors.
> Mout furent riches ses ators,

> *Queen Penthesilea,*
> *worthy and hardy and beautiful and*
> *wise, of great valour and of high*
> *nobility; she was very much prized and*
> *honoured, and had a great reputation.*
> *She wanted to see Hector*
> *and to win and achieve great glory,*
> *which is why she had come to his aid.*
> *Her equipment was very grand,*

Mout amena riche compaigne,	and she led a noble company,
E fiere e hardie e grifaigne.	who were proud and hardy and fierce.
(*Troie*, ll. 23360-70)	

Both descriptions mention *prouesse* and *courtoisie*. They are both 'hardi' (*hardy*) and have 'riche' (*grand*) equipment; she is 'sage' (*wise*) and he has good 'sen' (*sense*); she has 'grant valor' (*great valour*) and he has great 'pröesce' (*prowess*); she is of 'grant parage' (*high nobility*) and he excels in 'corteisie' (*courtliness*). The way in which Penthesilea's army is introduced is also interesting. Emmanuèle Baumgartner and Françoise Vielliard's modern French edition translates 'compaigne' as 'guerrières' (*female warriors*) but my translation (*army*) retains the gender ambiguity of the original text. The feminine forms of 'fiere' (*proud*), 'hardie' (*hardy*) and 'grifaigne' (*fierce*) in the extract relate to the fact that the word 'compaigne' is feminine, rather than necessarily suggesting that this company is made up exclusively of women. Although Benoît goes on to explain that Penthesilea's army does consist of female warriors only, at this earlier point there is a deliberate strategy of ambiguity to keep the audience or reader guessing as to whether Penthesilea was commanding an army of men. The words *fiere*, *hardie* and *grifaigne* have all been previously applied in this same combination to all-male companies (cf. ll. 6886, 7412 and 10632) and certainly she has been introduced as a leader with the qualities needed to hold such a position.

Camille is introduced in equivalent terms:

A grant merveille par fu bele	She was of an extraordinary beauty,
Et molt esteit de grant poeir;	and had very great abilities;
Ne fu femme de son saveir.	no other woman had her knowledge.
Molt ert sage, proz et corteise	She was very courteous, worthy and
Et molt demenot grant richeise;[42]	wise and she demonstrated a lot of
A merveille teneit bien terre	greatness; she governed her land
Et fu toz tens norrie en guerre,	very well and was brought up
Et molt ama chevalerie.	in constant wars, and she really loved
(*Enéas*, ll. 3962-69)	chevalerie.[43]

There is also a similar initial ambiguity as to the sex of Camille's followers:

A l'ost et amena grant gent:	She led an army of many people:
Bien ot o sei de chevaliers	for she led at least four
Des i que a quatre milliers.	thousand knights with her.
(*Enéas*, ll. 4173-75)	

From the masculine 'chevaliers' (*knights*) in this extract and 'barnage' (*barons*) in the previous description, we could infer that her army is just made up of men. A later instance describing her army also suggests that she is commanding men: 'Bien o treis milie chevaliers | Toz conreez sor lor destriers (*She had three thousand knights all armed on their war horses*, ll. 6909-10). Again, we have the masculine 'chevaliers', so is her army made up only of male knights? After all, we know that the feminine forms of the word – either *chevaleresse* or *chevalière* – did exist in the Middle Ages and could be used to denote a female knight, specifically one who fought on horseback or was a member of a chivalric order.[44] If the poet does not use this feminine form of the word, then is he speaking about male knights only? We need to look at the next scene:

Camille issi fors al tornei,	*Camille went forth to the tourney,*
Cent puceles mena o sei,	*taking a hundred maidens with her,*
Bien armees de covertures,	*all well defensively armed,*
Tot de diverses armeüres;	*all with different equipment:*
Molt par i ot bele compaigne.	*they were a beautiful company*
Quant els furent fors en la plaigne.	*when they took to the field.*
Li Troïen les esguarderent,	*The Trojans saw them,*
A grant merveille les doterent;	*and were very afraid of this*
Quant poigneient a els damesses,	*marvel. When the women*
Cuidoent que fussent deesses.	*galloped to them, they believed*
(*Enéas*, ll. 6979–88)	*they were goddesses.*

This is the first time the narrator has mentioned Camille being accompanied by anyone other than *chevaliers*, yet suddenly we are faced with a hundred 'puceles' (*maidens*) riding into battle. Subsequent descriptions of Camille in battle only mention her fighting alongside women. So, are the thousands of *chevaliers* she is described as leading in earlier descriptions actually all women? The specific spelling of *chevaliers* is used in all extant manuscripts of *Enéas* for these passages so it is unlikely to be the case of a single scribe making a copying error and mistaking *chevalières* for *chevaliers*. Or was Camille leading thousands of men, among whom happened to be one hundred warrior women? The problem is that while *chevaleresse* and *chevalière* did come to mean a female knight, when these texts were composed in the mid-twelfth century this was not their meaning: *chevalière* or *chevaleresse* was only used to signify the wife of a knight.[45] There was no feminine equivalent at this exact time, even if one started to be used at a later point.[46] *Chevalier* was not a rigid or fixed term at this point and could denote anyone involved in military activities from king to vavasour.[47] Could it be the case that it is also fluid in terms of gender at this precise point? This uncertainty would give us the possibility that *chevaliers* is actually being used to describe a group of both men and women (as would be the standard grammatical structure since there is no way of differentiating whether the plural masculine form denotes exclusively male objects or a mixture of male and female) or purely a group of women. The copyists of the later manuscripts also appear to make no attempt to correct *chevaliers* for *chevalières* or *chevaleresses*. This is significant for other texts from a similar period if we throw out the assumption that *chevalier* necessarily denotes only a male knight: the *Enéas* poet shows us how it could be used interchangeably for both male and female warriors at this time. Similarly, he describes Camille as a 'reis' (l. 3977, *king*) when there was unequivocally the vocabulary in the twelfth century to speak of a queen had he wanted to use the feminine version. It seems to be a stylistic choice of the *Enéas* poet that he occasionally uses what we traditionally think of as masculine terminology for women who embodied the virtues of or performed a traditionally 'male' role.

Unlike in *Troie*, where there are numerous other portraits of the narrative's heroes against which we can make a comparison, there are relatively few opportunities to compare Camille's introduction in *Enéas*. The descriptions of Aeneas are only ever a few lines long and limit themselves to his physical features and clothing. Similarly, among the Latin troops, there is little description. Turnus is introduced almost in passing with just three lines during the council of Latinus with Aeneas and his allies are given sparse one- or two-line introductions at best (see ll. 3897–3958): Mesapus is even introduced with fewer lines of description than the description given to his horses (ll. 3931–48). In contrast, the description of Camille occupies 148 lines (ll. 3959–4106). This elaborate description has been somewhat exhaustively and quite unflatteringly compared to Virgil's version by Erich Auerbach.[48] Essentially the *Enéas* poet gives more details of her beauty, her clothing and equipment, the splendour of her horse, and the wonder and admiration that she inspires in all those who see her. Jessie Crosland is similarly disparaging and suggests that Camille is transformed into a kind of tasteless 'Lady Godiva'.[49] However, although a great deal of attention is given to Camille's physical appearance, both Auerbach and Crosland ignore the density of vocabulary that establishes her not just as a beautiful lady but simultaneously as a figure from the realm of hitherto masculine *chevalerie*: 'poeir' (*power*, l. 3963), 'sage, proz et corteise' (*wise, worthy and courteous*, l. 3965), 'norrie en guerre' (*brought up with war*, l. 3968), 'ama chevalerie' (*loved chevalerie*, l. 3969), 'prisot armes a porter, | A tourneier et a joster, | Ferir d'espeë o de lance' (*loved to bear arms, to tourney and joust with an iron sword or lance*, ll. 3973–75), 'vaillance' (*valiance*, l. 3976), 'ert reis' (*she was a king*, l. 3977), 'sagement' (*wisely*, l. 3982), 'richement' (*richly*, l. 4085), 'l'ost et amena' (*she led an army*, l. 4086), 'proz' (*worthy*, l. 4094), 'ele se deüst onkes combatre, | Joster ne chevalier abatre' (*she had to fight, to joust and to battle against knights*, ll. 4097–98). All of these terms can be (and are) equally applied to the male warriors of the narrative. The *Enéas* poet does go to great lengths to illustrate that she is a beautiful woman, but he goes to similar lengths to illustrate that she is a warrior; he obviously did not see the two as mutually exclusive.

Penthesilea's and Camille's introductions establish them as exemplars of *courtoisie* through their noble birth, rich apparel and wisdom. The poets go on to provide examples of the chivalric virtues of *prouesse* and *loyauté* that they display on the battlefield. From Penthesilea's first battle, we are left in no doubt as to her martial prowess. She uses swords and lances to engage the enemy in the *melée* until the ground is 'de sanc vermeil destenpree' (*soaked with red blood*, l. 23647). She fights with Greek heroes in one-to-one combat: she 'josta' (*jousted*, l. 23625) with Menelaus and unhorsed him and 'josterent' (*jousted*, l. 23629) with Diomedes until he retreated. Telamon attempts to attack her by surprise, but her comrades help her and she overcomes him and takes him prisoner. By the end of the battle, the Trojans agree that she '[a]veit le pris de cel jornal' (*should have the prize for that day*, l. 23715) for nobody else 'fet tant d'esforz, | Ne tant des lor ocis e morz' (*made such a show of force nor killed as many people*, ll. 23717–18). Priam is convinced that his people will be 'rescos' (*rescued*, l. 23724) because of her. Benoît's enthusiasm for recounting Penthesilea's martial accomplishments continues throughout battles twenty-two and twenty-three. His version is substantially longer and more detailed than Dares or Dictys. In Dares, Penthesilea's battles are described in a single sentence: '[o]ccurrit Penthesilea et fortiter in proelio versatur, utrique per aliquot dies acriter pugnaverunt, multosque occiderunt' (*Penthesilea, having entered the fray, proved her prowess again and again. For several days they fought fiercely and many were killed*, D.36). In Dictys, she fights in one battle and he only describes her exploits as equalling but not exceeding those of one of the Greek warriors: '[c]adunt sagittis reginae plurimi neque ab Teucro secus bellatum' (*the queen slaughtered many, using her bow; as did Teucer for us [the Greeks]*, IV.2). Despite the fact that Benoît reiterates during one of her battles that he is retelling everything exactly 'cum l'estoire me retret' (*as the history [his source] tells him*, l. 24252) in fact he is substantially elaborating to show in unambiguous detail that she is a warrior of great prowess and the martial equivalent of (or indeed superior to) any male warriors.

Ten manuscripts include illustrations of Penthesilea, making up thirty illustrations in total and these most commonly show her in battle.[50] Eighteen of these thirty show her on the battlefield. Of these eighteen, thirteen show her in the midst of combat and often at the point of victory: for example, with her spear or sword penetrating the body of her opponent. The remaining five illustrations show the moment at which she is killed. She wears armour that has no discernible difference from the armour of men; she rides astride (not side-saddle) and she often has a helmet that covers her face. However, even when her face is covered, the illustrators still ensure that she is always identifiable. For example, in the French MS P6 she carries a white shield and her horse has a white caparison (as described by the text) as well as having a long blonde plait visible under her helmet and a crest shaped as a crown (Figure 23); in the Italian MS Vt she carries a shield that is heraldically styled *azure, a queen's head argent, crowned or* (Figure 24) and she carries this shield in subsequent battle scenes; in the Neapolitan MS V1 her helmet has a crest shaped as a crown and she wears her veil as a lambrequin (fol. 186ʳ); in the Italian MS Vn she is styled with a distinctive heraldic pattern of *azure semé of marguerites* (fol. 143ʳ); and in MS P18 (the copy of MS Vn) she is similarly styled with a distinctive heraldic pattern as well as a plait showing under her helmet and a rubricated caption added above the illustration's frame (Figure 25). Clearly all the illustrators were keen that she should be distinctive on the battlefield.[51]

One of the earliest illustrated *Troie* manuscripts, MS P6, contains eight full-page miniatures (each divided into two or three registers). Penthesilea is included in one of these full-page miniatures (Figure 27): the top register shows Achilles dragging the body of the recently deceased Troilus behind his horse; the middle register shows Ajax and Paris killing each other; the bottom register shows Pyrrhus killing Penthesilea. Although this miniature illustrates her death rather than her success on the battlefield, she is given the same treatment as one of Hector's brothers, positioning her as equal to Paris and Troilus and figuratively (if not literally) as part of Hector's family. This manuscript had already illustrated an example of her triumphing on the battlefield (Figure 23) just as it had done for Paris and Troilus. This illustration of her eventual defeat does not therefore show weakness or failure but quite the opposite; it places her as the knightly equal of Troilus and Paris. They fell not because of inadequacy, but because of the apparent perfidious and cowardly Greeks;[52] the same could now be said of Penthesilea.

The *Enéas* poet also elaborates on Camille's prowess in battle and carefully engineers the scene between Tarchon and Camille (quoted at the beginning of this chapter) in which her martial skills are directly questioned, only for her to prove conclusively that such questioning is unfounded. This scene is different from its equivalent in the *Aeneid*. In Virgil's version, Tarchon's disparaging comments are not directed at Camille but are addressed to the Tuscans as a way to motivate them into battle:

Femina palantis agit atque haec agmina vertit: quo ferrum quidve haec gerimus tela inrita dextris? at non in Venerem segnes nocturnaque bella, aut ubi curva choros indixit tibia Bacchi. (*Aeneid*, XI, 734–37)	*And can a woman drive you off and smash your ranks? Then what good is the sword? Why bother brandishing these useless weapons? Yet when it comes to love and night-time battles or when the curving flute proclaims the dances of Bacchus, then you are not lazy.*

The phrase 'nocturnaque bella' (*night-time battles*) is particularly important here, because the *Enéas* poet takes this idea and re-contextualizes it into a sexual innuendo so that instead of being used to motivate troops, it is used by Tarchon to antagonize and attempt to humiliate Camille:

Femme ne se deit pas combatre, Se par nuit non tot en gisant, La puet faire home recreant. (*Enéas*, ll. 7076–78)	*A woman should not fight except at night when she is lying down, there she can make a man surrender.*

Virgil's 'nocturnaque bella' becomes the *Enéas* poet's 'combatre | Se par nuit' (*fight only at night*) but rather than motivating a group of men to fight against a woman, it motivates a woman to fight (and kill) a man. The last we see of Virgil's Tarchon is his triumph on the battlefield before the poet's gaze turns to another section of the fighting. But the last we see of the *Enéas* poet's Tarchon is his death at the hands of Camille. *Enéas* revises the *Aeneid* to show that not only do his narrative's women warriors demonstrate great prowess, but those who doubt or criticize it will end unhappily.

Both poets show that Camille and Penthesilea demonstrate *loyauté* to their companions and are treated loyally in return. This is not loyalty only between women, but loyalty across the sexes. It is loyalty that finds its common ground in military comradeship. Penthesilea shows loyalty to Hector, a man whom she has never met, but to whom she is devoted out of respect for his reputation and legacy. Benoît makes it clear that her motivation for fighting the Greeks is to avenge Hector: '[s]a mort lur farai comparer: | Ja ne s'en savront si garder' (*I will make them pay for his death: nothing will protect them*, ll. 23415–16). Again, Benoît is departing from his source material here. Dares does not propose any particular impetus for Penthesilea's participation in the war while Dictys's Penthesilea is motivated either by 'pretio an bellandi cupidine' (*money or love of war*, III.15). Penthesilea's loyalty to Hector is of Benoît's own invention and another part of his strategy of placing her into a chivalric mould.

Penthesilea's arrival at Troy is a commonly chosen scene for illustration and appears in six manuscripts (MSS Nt, Vt, Mn, V1, Vn and P18). There are fewer total illustrations of her arrival than of her on the battlefield (six versus eighteen respectively), but her arrival scene appears in a greater number of manuscripts (six instead of five). In four illustrations she is greeted by Priam, often accompanied by a form of embrace (their arms entwined in greeting as they reach out across their mounts) and in MS Vt she is welcomed by Paris (Figure 24). The only illustration that shows her arriving without being greeted is in the early fourteenth-century Parisian MS Mn, in which she is simply shown riding towards Troy (fol. 106ᵛ), and which is one of the illustrations that was discussed in Chapter 1 as being damaged or defaced (something that has happened to none of the other illustrations in this manuscript). The illustrative scheme of MS Mn has been linked to MS P14, another early fourteenth-century manuscript from Paris, and which is one of the manuscripts that does not include any illustrations of Penthesilea at all. It has also been linked to the slightly earlier thirteenth-century MS L2, which only illustrates her dead body.[53] As mentioned in Chapter 1, these three manuscripts (MSS Mn, P14 and L2) also omit the descriptions of the Amazonian kingdom that Benoît includes as an introduction to Penthesilea's entry into the narrative (ll. 23302–56). It appears that the producers of these three manuscripts (and at least one later user) were not particularly interested in the Amazons.

We see bonds of loyalty between Penthesilea and her troops: for example, when she is killed by Pyrrhus, her soldiers are spurred to exact swift revenge on the Greeks:

E des danzeles que dirons?	*And of her maidens, what can we say?*
Veient que lor dame ont perdue.	*They saw that they had lost their lady.*
[...]	*[...]*
Fors de lor sen e pleines d'ire,	*Out of their minds and filled with*
Se vuelent totes faire ocire.	*rage. They all wanted to die.*
[...]	*[...]*
Tuit se vuelent a mort livrer:	*All wanted to give themselves to*
Mesle pesle s'entrefereient,	*death. They fought pell-mell and*
E si a fais s'entrocïeient	*killed so many that the living were*
Que sor les morz erent li vif.	*walking on the [bodies of the] dead.*
(*Troie*, ll. 24334–35, 24337–38, 24344–47)	

Again, this passionate devotion is of Benoît's invention and is used to highlight how well Penthesilea fits within a chivalric mould. In Dictys and Dares, her followers simply flee the battlefield after they see her fall (*Dictys*, IV.3 and *Dares*, D.36). We also see a bond between Penthesilea and Philemenis. The former comes to the aid of the latter during battle twenty-two and recovers him from the clutches of the Greeks:

La reïne de Femenie	*The queen of Femenie rallied*
Ra ajosté sa compaignie:	*her troops. Quickly she helped*

Hastivement refait monter	*Philemenis of Outremer back*
Philemenis d'outre la mer:	*into his saddle: he was very grateful*
Grant gré l'en sot, mout l'en mercie;	*and very thankful to her and said*
Dit qu'el li a rendu la vie.	*that she had given him back his life.*
(*Troie*, ll. 24169-74)	

It comes as no surprise then that when Penthesilea's body is recovered from the river into which it had been thrown after her death, it is Philemenis who determines that she should be returned to Femenie and volunteers to accompany her body (ll. 25279-83 and ll. 25767-808). The return of Penthesilea's body to Femenie is not part of Dares or Dictys. We can surmise that not only did Benoît want to show Penthesilea as a loyal warrior, but how she earned the loyalty of others. It is this reciprocity that also places her within the chivalric structure.

The bonds of loyalty between Camille and Turnus, as well as Camille and her troops, are also something that the *Enéas* poet explores in detail. The first interaction between the two presents not just a military bonding but almost a playful friendship. Camille and her army are awaiting Turnus and when he arrives, the narrator recounts the following scene:

Turnus la vit, cele part vait,	*Turnus saw her and went to where*
La meschine vers lui se trait,	*she was, the maiden went towards*
Parla a lui en sozriant:	*him, too and spoke to him while*
'Vos nos alez trop demorant;	*smiling: 'You have lost too much time*
La fors sont ja li correor	*in getting here; the scouts are already*
Et nos demoron tote jor.'	*on their routes, and we have been*
(*Enéas*, ll. 6935-40)	*waiting all day.'*

Were it not for the 'en sozriant' (*while smiling*), her greeting and admonishment of his tardiness might have seemed directly critical. But the 'en sozriant' communicates that friendly bond; this gentle mockery is as close to boisterous camaraderie as we get in *Enéas*. The two discuss their strategy for facing Aeneas's army, which includes Camille setting an ambush for Aeneas. During this ambush and the ensuing battle, Camille is set upon by two Trojans, but one of her ladies comes to her aid and they kill the two men (ll. 7126-38). This episode is not in the *Aeneid* and was invented by the *Enéas* poet to create a scene in which Camille is shown with loyal followers. Following Camille's death in the *Aeneid*, she is avenged by the goddess Diana but the *Enéas* poet changes this, too, so that in his version she is avenged by one of her ladies:

Une pucele l'a veü	*A maiden saw him [Camille's*
El point a lui, si l'a feru	*killer] and followed him and*
Que mort l'abat, puis li a dit:	*struck him so hard that he died,*
'Ceste joie a duré petit:	*and she said to him: 'His joy*
De ma dame ai pris la venjance.'	*was brief: I have avenged my lady.'*
(*Enéas*, ll. 7207-11)	

Turnus's reaction to her death is extreme and it helps determine the next stage of development in the plot, as will be discussed later in this chapter. Suffice to say here that he is devastated at her loss. Penthesilea and Camille are therefore paragons of *courtoisie*, *prouesse* and *loyauté* in much the same way that male heroes are, and they display the requisite virtues that allow them to participate in the chivalric tradition. Where the classical sources lack examples to demonstrate these virtues, the poets can be seen inventing new scenarios and scenes in which to prove these attributes. Clearly, the poets had a strategy and a desire to show their female warriors actively participating in the heroic structure. Penthesilea did later became one of the *Neuf Preuses* just as Hector was one of the *Neuf Preux*, confirming that she was seen as much a part of the chivalric tradition as was Hector. However, Penthesilea, Camille and their followers possess another virtue that their male equivalents do not and which is not a virtue typically discussed or included in later manuals of chivalry or in many later *romans*: the virtue of virginity.

Knightly virtues of the gendered hero: Virginity and chastity

Although romances are sometimes dismissed as historical sources for chivalric models, they contain important details that are often lost or excluded from non-literary sources. This is the case when it comes to looking at the gendered virtue of virginity, which the *romans*' female knights exemplify, but that is largely absent both from medieval and modern analyses of chivalry. This virtue has probably been overlooked precisely because it is associated with what I am terming 'feminine chivalry'. However, there are echoes of it in other medieval romances in which it is exemplified by both male and female warriors. The fact that virginity does not consistently appear as a chivalric virtue in later medieval texts seems like a strategy to make it possible for men to enter into the chivalric tradition. After all, aside from a few Grail knights, most male knightly protagonists were current or future rulers who needed heirs in order to continue their line. Virginity and chastity were therefore dynastically not appropriate, which is an idea we will explore.

Penthesilea, Camille and their followers are all virgin warriors, yet the poets never specifically use the word 'vierge' (*virgin*) or its derivatives. In fact, this word is almost entirely lacking from both narratives; it is never used in *Enéas* and it only appears once in *Troie* as Polyxena proclaims her willingness to be executed: 'O ma virginité morrai' (*I will die with my virginity*, l. 26511). *Vierge* is a loaded term as it is connected to a specifically Christian concept of virginity and it was a word intrinsically associated with the Virgin Mary;[54] however, the Amazons, the Volscians, the Greeks and the Trojans were not Christian. Instead, the poets prefer the word 'pucelle' (*maiden*) when referring to virginal women: Benoît uses *pucelle* at least eighty times and the *Enéas* poet uses it at least thirty times (roughly the same proportion given the comparative length of their two texts). *Pucelle* was ambiguous as it was used as a synonym for a girl or young woman without any necessary implication as to the status of her virginity.[55] However, there are clear indications that the *romans* poets used it as a synonym for *vierge*, maybe because they simply wanted to avoid the Christian connotations with which the word *vierge* was associated. Firstly, they never use it to denote a woman who is married (and, presumably, sexually active): Helen and Andromache are almost exclusively described as *dames* (ladies) or *femmes* (women). For comparison, Camille is only referred to as *Dame* once and this is by Tarchon during his attempted defamation of her character. Secondly, they use a derivative of *pucelle* to describe the loss of virginity: when Jason goes to bed with Medea the narrator tells us 'la despucela' (*he [Jason] deflowered her/ took her virginity*, l. 1648) and when explaining the ways and traditions of the Amazons, Benoît explains that 'ja n'erent despucelees' (*they were never deflowered/never lost their virginities*, l. 23350). The other terms used for Camille, Penthesilea and their followers are *meschine* and *damoisele*, though not with as great frequency and often for the purposes of rhyme within the couplet structure of both texts: both these words were used to denote young women, with *meschine* often being used for particularly young women or girls and *damoisele* primarily being used as a method of address. Both had the implication of virginity (because of the implication of youth and an unmarried status) though they were slightly more ambiguous than *pucelle* in this sense.[56]

Both poets give descriptions of the sexual practices (or absence of such practices) of their women warriors:

D'eles i a mout grant partie	*A large section of them [the*
Que ja a nul jor de lor vie	*Amazons] never made [sexual]*
Ne seront d'omes adesees	*approaches to men for even a single*
Ne ja n'ierent despucelees.	*day of their lives and they never lost*
Armes portent: mout sont vaillanz.	*their virginities. They [the virgin*
(*Troie*, ll. 23347–51)	*Amazons] bore arms and were very valiant.*

The state of virginity is exactly what enables them to be warriors in the first place for *Troie*'s description of Femenie explains that Amazonian women are divided into two: those who procreate and those who fight (ll. 23302–56). It is not possible to do both. Meanwhile the *Enéas* poet is almost coy in his description of Camille's sexual activities: 'Ne la nuit nuls oem n'i entrast | Dedenz la chambre o ele esteit' (*At night no man may enter there into the room where she was*, ll. 3980–81). The use of enjambment here rather makes the second line redundant, although without it the first line would be quite crude.

This virginal state and desire to remain chaste set them apart from the male warriors. In *Troie*, the principal heroes such as Jason, Hercules, Hector, Paris, Troilus, Ulysses, Ajax, Diomedes, Achilles, Agamemnon and Menelaus all have (or have had) wives or *amies* with whom they engage in sexual activity. In *Enéas*, Aeneas begins the narrative having just lost his wife during the sack of Troy, then has his affair with Dido and finally marries Lavine. Turnus is promised to Lavine and while there is no indication that they have consummated their relationship, there is certainly no indication that he would remain celibate once married. In contrast, the women warriors are completely devoted to the maintenance of their virginity. When Tarchon suggests to Camille that she should prostitute herself to the Trojans, she feels 'honte et molt grant ire' (*shame and much great anger*, l. 7107). The word *honte* shows that her abstention from sexual activity is something of which she is proud.

Virginity allows them to be taken seriously by the men around them as they transcend the alleged female vice of lust that was of such concern to male medieval thinkers. It was a frequent assertion of misogynist writers that 'women were naturally more lustful and voracious in their sexual appetites than men and that they could easily exhaust and destroy their husbands' health with their importunacies'.[57] Isidore of Seville suggested that 'a woman is called "female" [*femina*] through the Greek etymology for "burning force" [φως] because of the intensity of her desire. For females [*feminas*] are more lustful than males, among women as much as among animals'.[58] When Joan of Arc (who was also frequently referred to as *la pucelle*, just like Camille and Penthesilea) appeared in the fifteenth century, one of the reasons people believed she was capable of leading an army was because she ('miraculously') elicited no sexual arousal from her soldiers.[59] Being devoted virgins meant that Penthesilea, Camille and their ladies escaped accusations of lustfulness or desire only for sexual gratification when operating within a male-dominated sphere.

Furthermore, their virginity and celibacy make it possible that they were intended as moral exemplars for women. Virginity was the greatest virtue to which a medieval woman could aspire. For women for whom virginity was not a viable option, because of the expectation or requirement to procreate, it was still spiritually attainable through chastity, which created a kind of 'reformed' or 'honorary' virginity.[60] In fact, it has been argued that there was no singular understanding of virginity in the Middle Ages and that there were 'numerous different virginities', each conceptualized in varying and variable ways depending on gender, status, age, region and time.[61] Penthesilea and Camilla are examples of 'traditional virginity' but they are also examples of chastity, something to which anyone could aspire. If we look at female warriors in later medieval literature, they are either virgin maidens who subsequently marry (like Silence in the *Roman de Silence*) or 'reformed virgins' through their practice of chastity after childbearing (like Zenobia in Christine de Pizan's *Cité des Dames*). In fact, Semiramis (another of the *Neuf Preuses*) is the single example of a female warrior who was sexually active at the time of carrying out her martial action.[62] Sexual purity is apparently a prerequisite for women wanting to hold the title of *chevalier*. To a modern reader this might sound restrictive but to a medieval reader, especially a female reader, this could have been quite liberating. Virgin and chaste women were often represented as cut off from the rest of the world in a convent or cell, with their bodies 'placed within the custody of their own internalized vigilance, decorum and shame and within the physical enclosure of veiling and claustration'.[63] But as Jocelyn Wogan-Browne has argued, female chastity is not merely a case of 'textual oppression and misogyny, of the containment of women and their absence from history' but requires that attention is given specifically to women's readings of different texts.[64] Women reading *Troie* or *Enéas* found particularly powerful exemplars in Penthesilea and Camille: they were chaste and virginal but they were certainly not cloistered or isolated from society. On the contrary, their status as virgins allowed them to defy patriarchal structures and claim their place in even one of the most traditionally masculine of roles on one of the most public stages: the battlefield.

Heroic virginity in the tradition of the classical romances distinguishes itself from virginity in other branches of the Old French tradition, such as hagiography or non-classical romances. In hagiography, virginity is often central to the narrative as it is the focus of an attack, a test or a defence.[65] The body of the virgin is threatened, abused, tortured, mutilated and eventually killed in such horrific ways that there are several proponents of this type of hagiography being a form of 'rape-pornography' where the tortured virgin is used as a passive object intended for the reader's enjoyment.[66] Other readings suggest that many virgin martyrs set up their own battles and actively defied patriarchal figures or heteronormative ideals to such an extent that these figures were read, rewritten and re-enacted by numerous influential contemporary female writers and thinkers, such as Clemence of Barking, Bridget of Sweden, Julian of Norwich and Christine de Pizan.[67] In non-classical romances, virginity and chastity are often used as tests of marital fidelity instead; there is an idea that being unchaste is synonymous with being unfaithful, rather than necessarily not abstaining from sex. Such chastity tests are a particularly popular motif in Arthurian literature. For example, Robert Biket's *Lai du Cor* (*c.* 1100–25) describes a magical horn that can only be drunk from by a knight if his lady is faithful to him; in the anonymous *Lai du Cort Mantel* (*c.* 1180–1220) a magical cloak reveals the infidelities of its wearers by changing size to reveal the areas of the body that have engaged in adulterous activities. Variations of these chastity tests appear in the *Livre de Caradoc* (*c.* 1180–1200), in the *Roman de Renart le Contrefait* (*c.* 1399–22) and in the prose *Tristan* (*c.* 1230). In hagiography and Arthurian romance, virginity or chastity appears as something to be tested and often leads to the physical abuse or emotional humiliation of the woman. In *Silence*, the question is complicated further by the fact that Silence is in disguise as a man, yet she too must fiercely defend her sexual purity, even when the person seeking to claim it is another woman (who believes Silence is a man at this point). Silence rejects the sexual advances of this woman, but it is ultimately this episode which leads to her final public exposure as a woman and means that she loses her cherished position as a knight. There is also the implication that she must give up her virginity, too, for the narrative ends with her marriage to the king. But in the classical-romance tradition, the virginities of the female warriors are not questioned, doubted, tested or taken away from them. Virginity is not used as a way to define them as women, even if it is used to differentiate them from men.

While none of the male warriors in the *romans* are virgins or practise chastity, and while virginity appears to be a virtue only associated with 'feminine chivalry', it is important to a small subsection of later medieval male knights: the Grail knights. The Grail narrative first appears in the twelfth century in Chrétien de Troyes's *Perceval, ou le Conte du Graal* (*c.* 1180–91) but it gains the most popularity in the thirteenth century with appearance of the four *Continuations* to Chrétien's text as well as the prose Vulgate Cycle and the later post-Vulgate Cycle. Grail narratives (Chrétien's work and the *Continuations*) appear in two of the thirteenth-century French manuscripts, MSS P2 and P5, showing that they were occasionally seen as companions to the *romans* in the manuscript context. During the quest for the Holy Grail in Thomas Malory's *Morte d'Arthur* (*c.* 1460–70), only three knights are successful in reaching it: Percival, Galahad and Bors. All three are chaste. Percival and Galahad are virgins, while Bors 'would be if virginity could be born again', for he is essentially a 'reformed virgin' having begotten a child but subsequently practised chastity and prioritized his knightly duties to defend women's virginities.[68] The virtue of virginity for medieval men is sometimes complicated by the fact that there is some confusion (in the medieval sources) over how to distinguish between male virginity and male chastity.[69] It was a particularly emotive topic in the twelfth century at the time that the *romans* were being written as the issue of clerical celibacy and male virginity was at the centre of the monastic reform movement, led by Bernard of Clairvaux and others. Some argued that spiritual perfection could only be achieved through virginity and the cloistered life, while others wanted to reposition or reclassify it within an ecclesiastical hierarchy of values.[70] Male knights may not typically remain virginal or chaste, but the Grail story shows that when they do, they achieve the greatest of rewards. Malory refers on occasion to Galahad and Percival as 'maydyns' (*maidens*) while Galahad is referred to as a 'pusyll' (*pucelle* or *maiden*).[71] This reinforces the idea that the concept of virgin warriors was still gendered, hence these male knights being referred to with feminine nouns.

Virginity (whether technical or honorary) is a virtue that is embodied by the *romans*' female knights and is seen in later courtly chivalric narratives such as Malory's *Morte* to be exemplified by male knights. Malory's language implies that the image of the virgin warrior never lost the association of being a feminine trait, despite the great deeds and achievements to which it could lead. When the men who wrote the great treatises and manuals of chivalry were gathering their source material, they may have excluded virginity or chastity as a virtue partly because of this association with femininity, as well as the associated problems for kings or lords who needed to have heirs for the security and continuation of their dynasty. Indeed Arthur, one of the *Neuf Preux* and apparently a paragon of chivalric virtue, had no children, but there is no indication this is due to virginity or chastity on his part; instead it is often used as another way to cast negative judgement and highlight another apparent failing on the part of his queen, Guinevere.[72] Childless marriages were often seen as the fault of the woman and in the cases of queens could be used as a way to mock their husbands' sexual performance or back up accusations of incest or adultery.[73] This strategy of gendering warriors is not just something we see in the definition of their virtues, but something we can also see in the death of the warriors.

The death of the warrior

Ancient Greek models of male warrior friendships used death as 'the seal' of the friendship and allowed for expressions of love and devotion.[74] A number of *chansons de geste* derive their impetus from the relationships between two men.[75] Ideals of homosocial bonding were of central importance to these earlier texts and the death of a man in one of these pairs is obviously important. So what happens when we find that one of the knights is female? Can we still see aspects of the homosocial despite the differences in their sex? This depends to a certain extent on how their roles as warriors are gendered and requires a closer examination of the texts. We have already seen that the virtues of virginity and chastity make their roles as warriors fit into a feminine form of chivalry. Do their deaths similarly differentiate them from their male equivalents in any way?

When warriors die, they are mourned by their companions, compatriots and allies and this outpouring of grief is usually public. For example, Hector and Penthesilea are mourned not just by their armies but by all the citizens of Troy, too. Firstly, for Hector:

> Quant en la vile fu entrez,
> Oc nel vit nus sor piez estast,
> Ne de dolor ne se pasmast.
> Braient femmes, braient enfant,
> Toz li pueples, petit e grant.
> (*Troie*, ll. 16320–24)

> *When they entered the city, there*
> *was not a single inhabitant who,*
> *upon seeing [Hector's body],*
> *could stay standing and stop*
> *themselves fainting from sadness.*
> *Women, children, all the people,*
> *all cried together.*

And this is the scene of mourning following Penthesilea's death:

> En la cité ot grant dolor,
> Grant plaint, grant esmai e grant plor.
> Nule rien n'i prent heitement:
> Ne veient mes com faitement
> Il aient socors ne aïe.
> La reïne de Femenie
> Fu plainte mout e regretee
> (*Troie*, ll. 24425–31)

> *There was much sadness in the*
> *city, great loss, much dismay and*
> *many tears. Nobody was able to*
> *find any comfort. They could not*
> *see from where any aid would*
> *now come. The Queen of Femenie*
> *was deeply mourned and regretted.*

So far, so similar. But what is different is the response of their armies in the moments immediately following their deaths: when the male warriors die it evokes such deep shock that their men lay down their arms and faint or retreat. In contrast, when the female warriors die, it evokes a desire to seek violent revenge. For example, this is the immediate reaction to Hector's death:

> Gietent lances, gietent escuz:
> La mort Hector les a vencuz
> Et si en sont descoragieé,
> Si angoissos e si irié
> Que li plusor, estre lor gré,
> Se sont en mi le champ pasmé.
> (*Troie*, ll. 16239–44)

> *They threw down their lances*
> *and shields, for the death of*
> *Hector had vanquished them.*
> *They were so tired, so helpless*
> *and so angry, that many of*
> *them fainted on the battlefield.*

It is a similar scene when Paris is killed:

> Mout en furent descoragié,
> Desconforté e esmaié;
> Tel duel en ont qu'onc puis le jor
> Ne tindrent place ne estor.
> (*Troie*, ll. 22843–46)

> *They were so discouraged,*
> *so upset and troubled,*
> *their sadness was such that*
> *they refused to stay on the*
> *battlefield any longer that day.*

But the reaction to Penthesilea's and Camille's deaths is quite different. As already discussed above, both Penthesilea and Camille are avenged by their followers who enact swift vengeance on their leaders' assailants. The death of a male warrior elicits such strength of sadness that it causes his troops to abandon the battle, whereas the death of a female warrior incites her troops to fight all the more fiercely.

The impact that their deaths have on the development of the narratives offers the starkest contrast between male and female deaths: *Enéas* contains four large-scale pitched battles and Camille dies in the fourth; *Troie* contains twenty-three battles and Penthesilea dies in the twenty-third. Essentially, after the deaths of the leading female warriors, the wars stop. This is not to suggest that their deaths are the sole causal factors behind ending the wars, but they do seem to be contributing reasons. After Penthesilea's death, the Greeks persuade Priam into negotiating a peace treaty by pointing out that Troy has nobody left to defend it:

N'avez mais qui por vos contende	*You have nobody left to fight for*
Ne qui vostre cité desfende.	*you nor anybody who defends*
De vostre gent est mort la flor.	*the city. The flower of your*
(*Troie*, ll. 24531–33)	*people is dead.*

The word 'flor' (*flower*) could represent one of the male warriors such as Hector or Troilus, who at various other points in the text had been referred to as the 'flor de chevalerie' (*flower of chivalry*), but it might also represent Penthesilea: after all, Hector had died in battle ten and Troilus in battle nineteen and yet the Trojans had found a way to continue fighting after those losses. Indeed, with *flor*'s feminine form and occurring in the scene directly proceeding Penthesilea's death, it is a possibility that it was intended to represent her. It is only at this point, when the final *flor* of Troy has gone, that Priam agrees to surrender.

Similarly, when Camille dies it provokes Turnus into a pessimistic analysis of his chances of eventual success as he has nobody left to support him:

Ne sai par cui seie rescos.	*I do not know who would be able*
Vos estïez a mon besoing	*to save me, for you [Camille] were*
Preste toz tens, fust pres o loing.	*always ready to help, whether*
(*Enéas*, ll. 7396–98)	*from near or far.*

And the use of *flor* appears again:

D'altres femmes estïez flors:	*You [Camille] were the flower of*
Onkes nature, ce me senble,	*all other women, for Nature could*
En un cors n'ajosta ensenble	*never again combine such*
Si grant proece o grant belté.	*[martial] prowess with such*
(*Enéas*, ll. 7400–03)	*beauty again in one body.*

Camille's funeral and the decision of the Latin king to negotiate a peace settlement are put in direct juxtaposition in just a few dozen words:

Quant Camille fu entonbee,	*Once Camille was put in her*
L'uiserie fu estopee,	*tomb, the entrance was sealed,*
Toz les aleors en desfont	*and all the means of access*
Ki esteient lai sus amont,	*leading to where Camille had*
Par o Camile i fu portee.	*been carried were destroyed; the*
La sepolture ont delivree.	*sepulchre was emptied. During*
Endementiers que ce fu fait,	*this time, the Latin king wanted*
Li reis Latins volt faire plait	*to negotiate with the Trojans to*
As Troïens d'acorder sei.	*agree terms of a peace.*
(*Enéas*, ll. 7719–27)	

Turnus persuades him to propose a deal whereby he and Aeneas will face each other in one-to-one combat and whoever wins the duel will win the war: he wants to end the large-scale slaughter of the battles. The power of a single death is evident: one of their deaths will truly end the war, but it is Camille's death that inspires such a solution to be conceived in the first place.

Why do the deaths of Camille and Penthesilea have such a profound effect? There must be another reason other than the fact that they are simply the last ones standing and therefore the war must end. I suggest that their status, not just as female warriors but again as virgin warriors, is relevant. After all, virgins can be seen as a threat to patriarchal structure, for essentially, they are defined by their refusal to have sex with men. Despite entering the conflicts in order to support and avenge male characters, Penthesilea and Camille are doubly threatening with their virginity and their roles as warriors. They were accepted during the wars themselves, but these were exceptional circumstances and drastic measures had to be taken; only at the moment of their deaths are the male characters reminded that such extraordinary events are not desirable and should not be normalized. Additionally, their deaths transform them into pseudo-martyrs, echoing the martyred virgins of hagiographic texts, for 'it is only *in death* that [a woman's] virginal status is confirmed and [her] role as martyr fixed'.[76] The images of Camille's and Penthesilea's deaths as virgin warriors have echoes with the images of other virgins from the hagiographic branch of Old French – who had similarly been forced to fight – even if the latter's battles were in defence of their virginity and spiritual purity rather than in defence of a city or a country. Once they have been 'martyred' for their causes, it would only have been right to end the fighting out of recognition of their sacrifice.

Illustrations of Penthesilea's dead body are common: eight out of the ten manuscripts show either the moment of her death on the battlefield or her body being thrown into the river (or both). If we combine the number of manuscripts that show the moment of her death with the number of manuscripts that show her being thrown into the river, it would actually exceed the number of manuscripts that show her arrival into Troy, which was previously cited as the most widely illustrated scene. MSS M, L2 and P17 are the only three to show her dead without having shown her previously in battle (as MSS P6, Vt, V1, Vn and P18 do), thereby disassociating her from her triumphs on the battlefield and choosing only to focus on her downfall. The lavish French MS P17 is a particularly interesting copy. This is the only manuscript that contains an illustrated copy of *Enéas* and so the only opportunity we would have to find an image of Camille. However, while there are illustrations of Pallas's death and his funeral, there are no illustrations of Camille's death or her funeral; this is despite the fact that both of their deaths are critical to the development of the narrative and that both of their tombs are described in elaborate detail. The illustrator seems to have excluded her deliberately, for this manuscript's illustrations of *Troie* with regard to women warriors are also notable: it only shows Penthesilea once and this is when her dead body is thrown into the river (Figure 28). Not only is this a rather ignoble scene to choose out of all the possible scenes in which Penthesilea features, but she is not even afforded the entirety of a double-column frame: it has been broken into two registers and she is in one half. All of the thirty-one illustrations accompanying *Troie* in MS P17 occupy the width of two columns and only eight are split into two registers like this. It would appear that this manuscript's illustrator was not enthusiastic about visualizing women warriors as successful and therefore either omitted them or showed them dead in a small register. Instead, this illustrator places a greater emphasis on love scenes than do earlier illustrated manuscripts;[77] perhaps its patron was more comfortable with women only being objects of love rather than instruments of war.

This is true of the majority of the illustrated *Troie* manuscripts that were produced in France. Of these, only the earliest, MS P6, shows her in battle. The others only show either her arriving (MSS Nt and Mn) or dead (MSS L2 and P17). In contrast, the illustrated Italian manuscripts give a much more complete version of her exploits: they show her arrival (MSS Vt, V1, Vn and P18), at least two of her in battle (MSS Vt, V1, Vn and P18), her death (MSS M, Vn and P18) and her funeral (MS V1). Part of this is no doubt due to the fact that the Italian manuscripts have a richer illustrative tradition, so it is not surprising that Penthesilea would appear more frequently. Nevertheless, there could be a historical explanation for this pattern. Whereas Italy had had women such as Matilda of Canossa providing a powerful example of the advantages that were achieved when a woman ruled and led armies, France was rather more reluctant to accept women in such powerful positions. The fifth-century legal code known as the Salic Law excluded women from dynastic succession in France, and the validity and legitimacy of this code was coming under increasing scrutiny throughout the period that the *romans* were being written, copied and commissioned.[78] As Craig Taylor explains, the 'supposed inability of women to hold public office was clearly contradicted by contemporary reality: there were queens in other kingdoms, such as Portugal, Castile, Sicily, Hungary, Poland, Sweden, Denmark and even Naples', which meant the 'familiar repertoire of misogynist arguments against female rulership and succession was clearly problematic'.[79] Although no queens reigned in their own right in France, they did play prominent roles in public affairs and successfully wielded power as consorts, regents or guardians. Some even made direct challenges to Salic Law.[80] By the fifteenth century, political lawmakers and constitutional theorists in France 'slowly abandoned the more misogynist arguments [...] in favour of a new authority that did not require them to assert the inferiority of women': that authority was a careful manipulation of Salic Law to dispassionately and judicially exclude women from the right to the highest position of power in the country.[81] The threat of women who might take up arms to achieve their political objectives may therefore have made certain patrons nervous of depicting female warriors. Removing the illustrations and leaving only the text as a way to access these women meant that casual handlers of the manuscript could not just stumble across images of warrior women. Sophie Cassagnes-Brouquet raises the possibility that descriptions of women warriors in literature and chronicles inspired noblewomen to adopt these cultural models and even to take up arms themselves.[82] Whether or not this was the case, at least in this case, this strategy of excluding visual depictions of women warriors might instead have encouraged female readers only to extrapolate and imitate the moral and allegorical levels of the text but avoided glamourizing the physical state of being a warrior itself.

Only four manuscripts show Penthesilea's retrieval from the river or her subsequent funeral and return to Femenie. Most of the manuscripts make a point of showing the mourning around the bedsides, bodies or funeral monuments of the male heroes; the anniversary of Hector's death is one of the most illustrated scenes in the entire *Troie* tradition.[83] While MSS M (fol. 156ʳ) and V1 (fol. 200ᵛ) specifically show the dead body of Penthesilea with weeping mourners nearby, MSS Vn and P18 do not show her body at all; instead, they show Priam weeping within Troy while Philemenis and his followers ride away (Figure 29).[84] In a catalogue of the illustrations of MS Vn, this scene is described as follows: 'die Verbündeten der Trojaner ziehen fort, um an dem bevorstehenden Abschluß des Friedensvertrages nicht teilnehmen zu müssen. Am Stadttor bleibt Priamus mit dem Ausdruck der Trauer' (*the allies of the Trojans leave so that they do not have to participate in the conclusions of the peace treaty. Priam stands at the city gates with an expression of sadness*).[85] However, we can be confident that these illustrations actually represent Penthesilea's funeral cortège, despite the absence of her body in the frame. The illustrations appear at the point in the text in which Penthesilea's funeral cortège is described:

Vait s'en li reis Philemenis	*King Philemenis departed with*
Moût angoissos e moût pensis:	*great anguish and in deep thought:*
De dous mil chevaliers de pris	*out of two thousand valued*
N'en meine que nuef cenz e dis.	*knights he took (only) nine*
Cist en conduit Panthesilee,	*hundred and ten with him. These*
Que tant fu proz e honoree	*knights bore Penthesilea, who was*
(*Troie*, ll. 25767–72)	*so worthy and honourable.*

The description explains that Philemenis accompanies Penthesilea's body back to Femenie (ll. 25777–808). We know that the mounted king in Figure 29 is Philemenis because of the rubricated caption found in the corresponding illustration in MS P18. The text gives no indication that Priam wept over the forthcoming peace treaty, but there is a description of him weeping over Penthesilea's death. Furthermore, the illustration shows two foot soldiers walking ahead of Philemenis on his horse, which is an unusual placement of figures: all the other illustrations in these two manuscripts show kings with their followers literally following behind them. These two soldiers are therefore not actually *in front* of Philemenis, but are following *behind* Penthesilea's cortège. The decision to omit Penthesila is strange; after all, she had previously been illustrated arriving in Troy, fighting on the battlefield, killed by Pyrrhus and thrown into the river, so it is not that the illustrators were uncertain of how to draw her. They are also not unaware of how to represent dead bodies: they show numerous other deathbed scenes. However, in the case of Penthesilea, they have chosen to remove her from the scene of her own funeral procession and instead to focus the viewer's attention onto a king who is accompanying her body (Philemenis) and a king who is mourning her loss (Priam). It is as if the (male) mourners are more important than the (female) mourned.

The deaths of these two women, so valued in life as valiant warriors, are physical reminders that something is dangerously amiss in their societies to have come to such a point: not only to be at war, but to be in a situation where having women on the battlefield is considered normal and even desirable. The men must therefore eliminate the circumstances that allow such a situation to arise; that is, they must eliminate the state of war and return to a state of peace, where social structures and boundaries can be more easily contained. This is a potential explanation for why the deaths of Camille and Penthesilea bring about the ends of their respective wars and why their deaths are especially significant.

Conclusion

The *romans* provide evidence that, at the time ideas and concepts around chivalry were emerging and being codified, there were two complementary strands: a masculine chivalric code and a feminine chivalric code. The only way in which the latter differed from the former was that it demanded the virtue of virginity be upheld, whereas this virtue was optional in the former in cases where it would have impeded the ability of the hero to procreate and ensure a stable line of inheritance. The development of the *Neuf Preuses* alongside the *Neuf Preux* also demonstrates that there was a parallel idea of both masculine and feminine chivalry in the Middle Ages, even if modern studies of chivalry tend to prioritize the men alone. Medieval knights themselves even occasionally enjoyed playing with gender when it came to the presenting their skills at tournaments: a renowned tournament champion, Ulrich von Lichtenstein (1200–75), frequently dressed as the goddess Venus when competing, while at Henry II of Jerusalem's coronation in 1286 a great tournament was held in which one side dressed as Knights of the Round Table while the other side dressed as Amazons.[86] The gendering of warriors is further seen in their deaths: in both *Troie* and *Enéas*, the wars end after the battle in which the principal female warrior has been killed. This reflects their importance to the narrative structures of the texts and their value to the male warriors. The death of women on the battlefield is dramatic enough to highlight just how dangerous the state of war was not only in terms of death and destruction, but in allowing a set of circumstances to arise in which it was considered acceptable to have women acting as warriors. By returning to a state of peace, social structures and boundaries can be rebuilt and women are no longer required as warriors. Historically, women were probably not an everyday sight as warriors, but there is evidence that they appeared with greater frequency than some scholarship would have us believe.

The fact that early manifestations of what would later become a chivalric code show signs of making provisions for both male and female warriors suggests that women as warriors was not an entirely unthinkable suggestion: a form of feminine chivalry was being explored alongside masculine chivalry so that (if required) women could be warriors without needing to be 'manly'. Of course, in an ideal world there would be no such requirement. But the Middle Ages, as now, was not an ideal world and given that there may be such a requirement, it would have been sensible to make provisions for such an eventuality. By the time Joan of Arc appeared on the scene in 1429, such a presence on the battlefield had already been pioneered by dozens if not hundreds of such *chevaleresses*, both historically and culturally. What was actually more surprising about Joan's military leadership was not her gender, but the fact that she had little to no formal education or training and had a low social status rather than being from the noble estate of knights and ladies. Penthesilea, Camille, the *Neuf Preuses* and numerous historical women had already helped to establish that a woman could be a perfect chivalric hero.

6

Women as diplomats in war

In the period during which the *romans* were produced, historical women were playing a powerful role in politics and diplomacy, and this was not a role for which the *romans* poets could find any great precedent in their classical sources. Not only did women hold powerful positions as queens, empresses or duchesses in their own right, but they also provided counsel to kings, emperors, dukes and barons and other members of the ruling elite through their positions as consorts, regents, guardians or members of council meetings.[1] This role as counsel-giver and political advisor is one of the most powerful, which is why it has been chosen as the final role for consideration. It is also the role that has the most historical precedent and for which hundreds of sources and documents exist. In terms of the historical record, the five women discussed in the previous chapter (Matilda of Canossa, Matilda of Boulogne, Empress Matilda, Sibylla of Anjou and Eleanor of Aquitaine) certainly have a place in this chapter, too. It almost goes without saying that those who have a warrior role naturally have a political role, even if those with a political role do not necessarily have a warrior role. But there are an additional five whom I would like to outline in this chapter and who also would likely have been well known to the societies in which the *romans* manuscripts were circulating. We start with Matilda of Flanders (1031–83), the wife of William the Conqueror and great-grandmother of Henry II. She held an active political role throughout her tenure as duchess of Normandy and Queen Consort of England: while William was in England in 1066, she remained in Normandy and acted as a senior magnate and regent for her son Robert; in 1075, she was present at the restoration of Gisors to Rouen Cathedral by Count Simon of the Vexin; from 1077–78 she supported the revolt of her son, Robert Curthose, against her husband, William the Conqueror;[2] in 1080, she was authorized to preside over a land plea at Cherbourg and on other occasions she acted directly in partnership with William.[3] In fact, she was the first duchess of Normandy to be crowned queen of the English (in 1068) and this was done at the behest of William himself.[4] Like William, she had authority in both Normandy and England, which she evidently put to use, as there are records of her attestations of royal diplomas in Winchester, Windsor, London, Bury St Edmonds, Salisbury and Downton between 1069 and 1082.[5]

Secondly, there is Adela of Normandy (1067–1137), Countess of Blois, Chartres and Meaux, the daughter of Matilda of Flanders and mother of Stephen I of England. She acted as regent while her husband was on the First Crusade and then again after his death in 1102 and was eventually canonized as Saint Adela. Her actions while her husband was on crusade helped to consolidate comital authority over her own domains, as well as to support her brother, Henry I of England, in his attempts to ensure that Normandy and England were under joint rulership.[6] From 1108 to 1120, her skills as a negotiator and diplomatic presence with the princes of northern France, the king of France and the king of England, helped alleviate the conflicts that arose over the status of Normandy during this time.[7] Thirdly, we come to Matilda (or Edith) of Scotland (1080–1118), queen of England, wife of Henry I of England and mother of Empress Matilda. Matilda was an active partner in administering Henry's lands in both England and Normandy. She was present at the councils where policy decisions were made, passed judgements and issued charters.[8] Moreover, none of the sources that write about her involvement in such matters express any shock or annoyance that this was the case; indeed it was expected that the queen would be involved in this way.[9] She played a key role in the English Investiture Controversy that took place between 1102 and 1107 between the papacy and Henry, acting as an intercessor between Archbishop Anselm and her husband by writing letters and mediating their interactions.[10]

The final two women take us away from Normandy and across to *Outremer*, although they still have familial connections to the Anglo-Norman world. Women rulers were relatively frequent in the Latin Kingdom of Jerusalem and one such woman was Queen Melisende of Jerusalem (*c.* 1109–61) who was crowned (with her husband, Fulk of Anjou) in 1131.[11] She ruled alongside her husband until his death in 1143 and then as regent until her son, Baldwin III, came of age in 1145. There ensued a period when the kingdom was divided between her and Baldwin, before a civil war that ultimately reunited the kingdom but led to Melisende's exclusion from its government.[12] The chronicler William of Tyre was enthusiastic about Melisende's political acumen. He described her as 'a most prudent woman with much experience in almost all secular matters' and stated that 'she ruled the kingdom with such diligence and [...] wisdom that she could be said to have equalled her [male] ancestors in these respects'.[13] He clears her of blame in the civil war, accusing Baldwin's advisors instead.[14] William's chronicle was written between 1170 and 1183, approximately ten to thirty years after the *romans*. However, we can speculate that stories of Queen Melisende would have reached the Anglo-Norman court well before this time and were even transmitted by Eleanor of Aquitaine or Henry II themselves: Melisende's husband, Fulk of Anjou, was Henry's grandfather, while Eleanor had visited Melisende's Jerusalem herself during the Second Crusade.

The second woman from *Outremer* was one of Melisende's sisters, Alice of Antioch. She married Bohemond II of Antioch in 1126 and when he died she tried to keep control of the city rather than let it return to the control of her father or brother-in-law. She made several attempts to maintain power but was ultimately unsuccessful and died not long after. Whereas William of Tyre had been enthusiastically supportive of Melisende, he made strong objections to Alice. He described her as 'wicked', 'tyrannical', and 'guided by an evil spirit'.[15] However, more recent scholarship on Alice concludes that the reality was quite the opposite and that Alice was just as powerful a force as Melisende.[16] So what do the queens and women of the *romans* look like in comparison to this impressive record? Are they good advisors, skilled negotiators or do they act unilaterally to intervene and take matters into their own hands? The texts and illustrations provide a number of answers.

Advisors

The length of time for which advice-giving has been debated makes it clear that it has always been an important aspect of political and diplomatic relations. The Old Testament's Book of Proverbs makes frequent reference to the value of seeking counsel: '[w]here there is no guidance the people fall, but in abundance of counsellors there is victory' (Proverbs 11:14); 'a wise man is he who listens to counsel' (Proverbs 12:15); '[t]hrough insolence comes nothing but strife, but wisdom is with those who receive counsel' (Proverbs 13:10); '[l]isten to counsel and accept discipline (Proverbs 19:20); '[p]repare plans by consultation and make war by wise guidance' (Proverbs 20:18); 'by wise guidance you will wage war and in abundance of counsellors there is victory' (Proverbs 24:6). It also warns against poor counsel: '[t]he thoughts of the righteous are just, but the counsels of the wicked are deceitful' (Proverbs 12:5). Proverbs even personifies wisdom and counsel as a woman:

> Wisdom shouts in the street, she lifts her voice: '[...] I will make my words known to you. Because I called and you refused, I stretched out my hand and no one paid attention; and you neglected all my counsel and did not want my reproof; I will also laugh at your calamity; I will mock when your dread comes, when your dread comes like a storm and your calamity comes like a whirlwind, when distress and anguish come upon you [...]. So they shall eat of the fruit of their own way and be satiated with their own devices. For the waywardness of the naive will kill them and the complacency of fools will destroy them.
> (Proverbs 1:20–32)

The value of seeking and following wise advice and the pitfalls of ignoring advice or trusting in bad counsellors was a topic of importance in scripture, just as it had been in the classical texts that preceded it, and given the value of both scripture and classical works to medieval society it is therefore not surprising that this was also important in contemporary writings.

Sally Burch North outlines the most common sources of counsel in the twelfth century: a person's own judgement, the family group, close *amis* (not necessarily romantic *amis*, but in the sense of close companions), the Church and feudal vassals.[17] This last category has received particular attention in relation to its role in feudalism and kingship more generally.[18] However, it is the category of family and *amis* that concern us as this is where we tend to find women in the Old French tradition. For example, Catherine Hanley has highlighted several key episodes in various *chansons de geste*, including the *Chanson de Guillaume* (c. 1140), *Garin le Loherenc* (c. 1130–60), *Girart de Vienne* (c. 1180) and *Aymeri de Narbonne* (c. 1205–25) in which women act as advisors to their male kin on strategy during times of conflict.[19] Often their advice is related to vengeance or resisting attacks and therefore takes the form of strategies for exacting swift and efficient violence.

This is quite a contrast to the scenes of women as advisors in the *romans d'antiquité*. In the oldest of the three, *Thèbes*, we have numerous instances in which Jocasta tries to advise her sons to end their conflict and make peace. Indeed Jocasta is described by Karen Pratt as the epitome of 'queen as peace-maker, while her sons and the other men are vengeful, war-mongering, hot-headed males'.[20] For example, when Eteocles is advised by his barons to seek a peace agreement with his brother, it is Jocasta who is given the final speech in the council to urge him to accept their proposal:

'Crei ces barons que tu veis ci;	'Have faith in the barons that you see
Fai ço que il te loeront:	here. Do what they advise you: I agree
Ja ne te forsconseilleront.'	with the advice that they are giving you.'
(*Thèbes*, ll. 3576–78)	

Jocasta plays an important role in summarizing the advice that the barons have given and then providing her own judgement as to the validity of that advice and whether the king should follow it or not. Eteocles rejects the advice and has an angry tantrum, at which point the narrator makes it clear that such behaviour is unacceptable and states that '[n]us hon ne deit honor tenir, | Se il ne puet auques sofrir' (*no man deserves to govern if he is not capable of patience*, ll. 3639–40).

Cassandra's attempts to provide advice to her male kin meet similarly frustrating ends. In classical versions of the Trojan legend, Cassandra has the gift of prophecy but is cursed never to be believed.[21] She foretells the fall of Troy but is ignored by the Trojans due to this curse. In Dictys, there is almost no mention of her ability to foretell the future; only in one case does she make a prediction but it comes late in the narrative and is related to the death of Agamemnon and the destruction of the Greeks following their sack of Troy (*Dictys*, V.16). Dares includes two occasions on which she predicts the fall of Troy but they are very succinct. The first is one line and appears as the Trojans are chopping wood to build ships for their mission to Greece: 'Cassandra postquam audivit patris consilium, dicere coepit quae Troianis ratura essent, si Priamus perseveraret classem in Graeciam mittere' (*when Cassandra heard of her father's intentions, she told what the Trojans were going to suffer if Priam should send a fleet into Greece*, D.8). The next line relates that preparations were soon finished and the Trojan forces ready to depart, so we can assume that her words had no impact. The second occasion is when she sees Paris bringing Helen to Troy:

Quam ut aspicit Cassandra,	*When Cassandra saw [Helen], she*
vaticinari coepit memorans	*began to prophesy, repeating what*
ea quae ante praedixerat.	*she had already said. Then Priam*
Quam Priamus abstrahi et	*ordered her carried away and*
includi iussit.	*locked up.*
(*Dares*, D.11)	

Benoît recreates both these scenes in *Troie*, but he does so with amendments that frame Cassandra's words as advice that has been ignored, rather than as a prophecy that has not been believed. For the first scene, Benoît provides more detail in her prophecy on the manner in which Troy will be destroyed and includes the response of the Trojans:

Bien lor anonçot chose veire:
Cui chaut? qu'il ne la voustrent
   creire.
Se Cassandra e Helenus
En fussent creü e Panthus,
Ancor n'eüst Troie nul mal.
   (*Troie*, ll. 4159–63)
	*She told them all the things that were
	to come: but who was interested?
	They did not want to believe her. If
	Cassandra, Helenus and Panthus had
	been believed, then Troy would not
	have had any suffering.*

Benoît states that the Trojans did not 'voustrent' (*want*) to believe her; there is no suggestion that she has been cursed to be disbelieved and that they are unable to believe her through no fault of their own. Benoît's Trojans make a conscious decision to ignore her advice because it is not to their liking. An implicit judgement is made of this rejection of valid advice. A later reader of this text picks up on this and goes as far as to write a note into the margin of the thirteenth-century MS P3 to highlight this fact: the words '[r]esponsa non credentes divina nec formidantes hec omnia sunt in causa destructionis troiana' (*they did not believe her prophecy because of fear and so everything was lost in the [subsequent] destruction of Troy*) on fol. 25ʳ just after this scene. Benoît also mentions Helenus and Panthus, two other Trojan advisors and foretellers who have similarly attempted to dissuade Priam from the mission to Greece. By grouping Cassandra with Helenus and Panthus, who in turn had been grouped together with Paris, Troilus and Hector as advisors to Priam, Benoît places her counsel on the same plane and gives her the same status as the other (male) advisors, rather than isolating her as a lone voice of dissent.

Benoît also expands the second scene from Dares, in which Cassandra is locked up. Dares's version is two lines long but Benoît's stretches to fifty-two lines (ll. 4883–4934). Benoît specifically describes all those to whom she directs her advice and this time she does not address the men, but the women: she addresses her mother, the ladies and the young maidens and implores them to flee the city. Cassandra has learnt that her advice will go unheeded by the male Trojans and her change of tactic to address only the Trojan women shows a strategic acumen as well as casting a judgement once again on the men, who were too stubborn to listen to her previously and upon whom she therefore wastes no more effort. It also suggests that Priam's decision to have her locked away is a direct reaction not just to her words, but her potential to incite other women to form a resistance, too.

Benoît then creates an original scene showing Cassandra's prophecies between battles two and three. Whereas the first scene used her prophecies to advise the men (not to go to Greece) and the second scene used her prophecies to advise the women (to flee from Troy before it was too late), this third scene uses her prophecies to express despair at the now inevitable fate of Troy. Her speech is positioned more as a lament rather than as advice. Benoît tells us that this time she is speaking before 'la gent' (*the people*, l. 10448), with no distinction as to whether they are male or female. Once again, she is locked away and this time she does not reappear until the sack of Troy. However, while her physical presence is missed, the memory of her words still pervades the text. At the end of battle nine, the narrator invokes her predictions:

Ne cuit que nus hom oie mais	*I believe nobody has ever heard of*
Si grant dolor, si grant damage.	*such great suffering, such great loss.*
Ço que dist Cassandra la sage	*Everything the wise Cassandra said*
Avendra tot dès ore mais.	*will soon happen from this point on.*
(*Troie*, ll. 15250–53)	

And when the ladies are mourning Paris's death, they also name Cassandra:

Ha! Cassandra, les voz pramesses	*Ah! Cassandra, all your predictions*
Sont bien veires e d'Eleni.	*are coming true and those of Helenus.*
Maleüré, dolent, chaiti!	*Those unhappy, sad, wretched [two]!*
S'en eüssent esté creeit,	*If they had been believed,*
Ne nos fust pas si meschaeit.	*We would not be so doomed.*
(*Troie*, ll. 16418–22)	

The reminders of Cassandra's attempts to advise them to act otherwise are scattered throughout the narrative to remind audiences that this tragedy was avoidable if advice had been followed.

Cassandra is not the only advisor who has counselled against the war – so do Panthus and Helenus. However, the image of the female counsellor was of more interest to medieval illustrators, as the manuscript illustrations accompanying *Troie* depict a rather edited version of events. Four of the illustrated *Troie* manuscripts include Cassandra's prophecies. MS V1 illustrates the first scene in which Cassandra attempts to dissuade Priam from authorizing the expedition to Greece (Figure 32). It is a large illustration occupying the bottom third of the page. On one side, workers are shown constructing wooden ships. On the other side, Cassandra stands before Priam. She is pointing to the palm of one hand with the finger of her other hand, as if enumerating a list of reasons. The juxtaposition of the construction of the Trojan navy alongside Cassandra speaking to Priam creates both a sense of urgency to the scene (willing Cassandra to convince Priam of the error of his ways before the fleet is complete) and a sense of futility (the decision has already been made). There is a deliberate decision to isolate Cassandra as a figure of interest. The recto of the folio has another illustration of Priam's council with numerous men giving him advice, but it is not clear who these men are as there are no accompanying captions: it could depict Hector, Paris, Troilus, Panthus and Helenus but it might also represent the whole council chamber without particular emphasis on individuals. In contrast, the illustration of Cassandra leaves no doubt as to her identity; not only is she the only woman in the scene, but a caption has been added above her figure identifying her as Cassandra. The handwriting of the caption is found on a few other folios in the manuscript, but quite sporadically and infrequently. It does not appear to be the hand of the manuscript's illustrators or scribes and is most likely an annotation by a later reader. Not only was Cassandra considered important enough by the illustrator to have her own scene, but she was of such interest to a later reader that she had her own caption.

MSS Vn and P18 also illustrate Cassandra's prophecies, but they choose a different scene, the third scene, which is original to Benoît, in which Cassandra makes her final prophecies as to the ineluctability of destruction (Figure 31).[22] Both illustrations are found at the bottom of the folios and stretch across both columns. As with the construction of the boats and the council chamber in MS V1, these illustrations depict two scenes within one frame. On the left, Cassandra stands under an arch in Troy, with one arm reaching towards the other side of the frame. On this other side, a group of mourners is shown around the dead body of Cassibelan, one of Priam's illegitimate sons who was slain in battle two. The mourner closest to Cassandra's side has an arm outstretched, reaching back towards her, and while all the other mourners are looking at Cassibelan, this mourner has his gaze fixed on Cassandra. The enclosed arch represents the locked place in which she is put as punishment for her speech, yet the two outstretched arms suggest both a sadness on her part that she was unable to prevent the tragedy now unfolding and an equal regret on the side of the Trojan mourner that they had not listened. The visual representation of the consequences of disregarding sage advice is unambiguous. The Italian MS Vt has a unique way of figuring Cassandra's prophecies in its illustrative scheme. She does not actually appear at the point in the text when her prophecies are given. Her first appearance is after Helen and Paris have entered Troy. She stands alongside Hecuba, Andromache and Polyxena (Figure 30). One of her hands is pressed to her forehead, indicating distress. In her other hand she holds a scroll that is partially unfurled and upon which we can read the words: 'se Paris a de Grece ce feme destruit sera cest regne' (*if Paris takes a wife from Greece then this kingdom will be destroyed*). Rather than illustrating the point at which she first delivers her prophecies, this miniature acts as a reminder. The scenes before it have shown the happiness between Helen and Paris as they marry and the celebrations of the people of Troy as they are welcomed home. But this appearance of Cassandra and her scroll means that her warnings cannot be forgotten.

Another woman from *Troie* whose advice is disregarded with terrible consequences is Andromache, Hector's wife. On the eve of battle ten, she has a vision that he will be killed if he fights the next day and she attempts to persuade him to stay within Troy. Benoît uses several words to characterize the vision itself. The gods send her 'signes' (*signs*, l. 15285), 'visïons' (*visions*, l. 15285) and 'interpretatïons' (*premonitions*, l. 15286), while Andromache describes it as a 'merveille' (*marvel*, l. 15302). All of these words imply something supernatural or divine. Only Hector uses the simpler word *songe* (l. 15334), which merely indicates a dream. Hector's failure to recognize that her vision is of prophetic importance leads to his downfall. Prophetic visions often carried authority and importance in medieval society and were not necessarily to be dismissed: the gospel of Matthew relates that Mary and Joseph were warned of Herod's plan to kill the babies in a dream vision; Joan of Arc was guided by prophetic visions, which were used as a sign of her divine authority; Pope Innocent III endorsed St Francis of Assisi's order (the future Franciscans) after a prophetic dream. There are numerous studies on the importance of visions and prophetic dreams in the Middle Ages.[23] Hector is angered by Andromache's attempts to dissuade him from battle and so she asks Priam to intervene. He does not want to forbid Hector from fighting as he relies on him to lead the Trojan forces. However, he is also reluctant to ignore Andromache:

Se il n'i vait, la perte iert lor:	*If he [Hector] alone does not go to battle,*
Sor eus revertira le jor.	*they [the Trojans] will have a great loss,*
Ensorquetot n'ose müer	*things will turn on them that day. But*
Qu'il nel retienge de l'aler:	*he [Priam] does not dare to do anything*
La dame set de grant saveir:	*but prevent him from going: for he*
Ne deit om mie desvoleir	*knows that the lady [Andromache] is*
Ço que por bien dit e enseigne.	*very wise. He must not refuse what she*
(*Troie*, ll. 15367–73)	*says and counsels for the good.*

The fact that Priam places Andromache's request to forbid Hector from battle above his own desire to send Hector to battle shows how deeply he respects her counsel. Priam attempts to dissuade Hector from fighting but is also rejected. Hecuba, Helen and Polyxena also attempt to stop him from going and he likewise rejects them, too. Andromache accosts him as he is putting on his armour and makes a final attempt to stop him by placing their infant son at his feet and making a desperate speech:

Hui iert ta mort, hui iert ta fin;	*Today will be your death, today will be*
De tei remandra orfelin.	*your last; he [your son] will be an orphan*
Crüel de cuer, lou enragié,	*because of you. Cruel heart, enraged*
A que ne vos en prent pitié?	*wolf, why do you not have any pity?*
Por que volez si tost morir?	*Why do you want to die so soon?*
Por que volez si tost guerpir	*Why do you want to abandon me and*
E mei e lui e vostre pere	*[your son] and your father and your*
E voz freres e vostre mere?	*brothers and your mother? Why are you*
Por quei vos laissereiz perir?	*leaving us to perish? How would we be*
Com porrons nos senz vos guarir?	*able to survive without you? Alas!*
Lasse, com faite destinee!	*What a fate is before us!*
(*Troie*, ll. 15475–85)	

This speech is entirely of Benoît's own invention and its effect is powerful. The use of anaphora and parallelism in phrasing the rhetorical questions creates an intensity that would have been hard to miss, especially if heard read aloud. In creating this moment for Andromache, Benoît intends to highlight her plight and make Hector's eventual rejection of her advice seem even starker and more foolish in response to such a powerful entreaty. The emotive reference to their son becoming an orphan, while said son is physically in front of him, is also powerful. The implication that by following one duty (to battle) he would be abandoning another duty (to his family) highlights what was no doubt a pressing concern not just for Hector but for many members of the *Troie* audience. The conclusion of the speech with exclamatory remarks gives it a dramatic ending. The narrator then tells us that she fell to the ground with her face in the dirt and has to be helped back up by Helen. Hector makes it clear that he is sceptical about following the advice of 'une fole, une desvee' (*a mad woman, a crazy woman*, l. 15584). He rejoins the battle and is killed, just as foretold.

The decision to reject Andromache's advice is not really commented on by the *Troie* narrator. When Hector's body is brought back to Troy, there are lamentations that

Cassandra's advice was not followed, but no mention of Andromache's advice. However, the illustrative tradition that accompanies this scene, as well as evidence from later texts that provide a commentary on these actions, suggests that it was an important episode for medieval audiences. It appears in six of the illustrated *Troie* manuscripts (MSS P6, P17, Vt, P18, Vn and V1). In the earliest illustrated manuscript, MS P6, Hector stands in the middle of the frame with his arms raised in speech, with Priam and Hecuba kneeling on one side with their hands in the prayer position, while Andromache kneels on the other side with her son in her arms (Figure 34). Hector has his face turned away from Andromache and looks only at Priam. This illustration appears out of sequence in the manuscript as it is found before the start of battle nine, whereas this scene actually occurs on the eve of battle ten. The reason for this image appearing 'out of place' is because there was no space left for an illustration at the appropriate point in the text. The illustrator was therefore faced with the choice of either omitting this scene altogether or of putting it somewhere else. At this point in the manuscript the illustrator had already drawn six battle scenes (and would go on to include a further ten) so must have decided it was more important to show this scene than yet another battle.

The mid-fourteenth-century Parisian MS P17 has thirty-seven miniatures accompanying *Troie*, of which sixteen have an illuminated background in gold (as opposed to painted in colour) and are therefore particularly prominent.[24] The scene of Andromache's attempt to dissuade Hector from battle is one of these sixteen. It shows Hector and a companion riding from the gates of Troy with a lance in one hand and a sword in the other, while Andromache stands in front of them with her son in her arms and surrounded by four other women (Figure 35). Unlike the illustration in MS P6, there is no indication of any discussion and no sign of Priam. The fact that Hector is mounted and armed (contrary to the description in the text) indicates that his mind is made up and he is virtually in battle already; Andromache's demure posture and gentle presentation of their son show she is already doomed to failure.

The miniature of this scene in MS Vt makes an effort to show the desperation of Andromache's plight (fol. 118ᵛ).[25] Her hair is loose and cascading over her shoulders. This is a stark contrast with how she has been visualized in previous illustrations, where her hair has been styled to hang neatly just below her chin. She is without a crown, which again she has worn in all previous illustrations; her position as a princess of Troy is secondary to her status simply as a mother and wife. On the left of the illustration she kneels before Hector, holding their son. She appears smaller than the other women and smaller than Hector, suggesting already a certain impotence. Hector's squire is in the process of attaching his knee protectors, implying again that Hector is on the verge of departure. On the right side of the illustration she speaks with Priam to beg him to intervene, while she tears at her clothes (or her heart). The miniature shows more wear than other miniatures in the manuscript, indicating that this scene attracted particular attention from later readers or that the manuscript was sometimes left open at this point. Again, we can infer its importance not just to its illustrator, but to later users of the manuscript, too.

In the Italian manuscripts MS P18 (Figure 33) and MS Vn, Hector is seated while two squires hold his horse; Andromache kneels before him with their son in front of her and Hecuba, Helen and Polyxena behind her.[26] Hecuba's and Andromache's arms are outstretched (in MS Vn only Hecuba's arm is outstretched), indicating their speech, while Hector's hands are placed on his armoured thighs, showing his reticence. Nevertheless, unlike in the French manuscripts MS P6 and MS P17, the scene does not suggest that the situation is a *fait accompli*. There is some hope as Hector is prudently sitting and listening to counsel: unlike in MS P6, he faces Andromache, and unlike in MS P17, he is not already mounted. The texts show that Hector did not afford much respect to Andromache's counsel, but the illustrators diverge from the text and depict a different version. The Neapolitan MS V1 provides the fullest illustrated version of this scene as it includes nine frames in order to detail each aspect of the text: Andromache recounts her vision to Hector (fol. 118^v), Priam attempts to persuade Hector to stay (fol. 119^r), Andromache asks Priam and Hecuba to intervene (fol. 119^v), Hector rebuffs Hecuba as Andromache faints (fol. 119^v), Andromache presents her son to Hector (fol. 120^r), Hector's squire brings him his horse as Andromache returns to Priam (fol. 120^v), Priam speaks to Hector on the road (fol. 121^r) and Priam brings Hector back to Troy (fol. 121^r).

Despite the differences between all five manuscripts, they all choose the moment where Andromache presents their son in her arms. The framing of the scene around her changes, but this is a constant. This may be another clue as to why this scene was so popular, for the imagery in all five is reminiscent of images of the Virgin Mary holding the baby Jesus, an image that had become iconic (in every sense of the word) throughout medieval European art by the twelfth century.[27] The fact that many of the illustrations show her with her hair loose creates a parallel with Mary, as loose long hair was usually an indication of a virgin (which of course Mary was, but Andromache was not).[28] This gives Andromache another source of authority for she is able to harness the power of this iconography. She is not represented as 'une folle', but as a dignified mother deserving respect and veneration.

Evidence from other literary sources on the reception of this scene show that Andromache was judged as a wise woman and that Hector was a fool for ignoring her. Christine de Pizan's *Epistre Othea* (*c*. 1400), a popular text that is still extant in over thirty manuscripts, discusses this scene. The *Epistre* is a series of one-hundred-verse texts based around mythological figures accompanied by prose moral glosses. Andromache is one of the figures featured in this work and Christine's gloss gives us an insight into how Hector's rejection of his wife's advice was judged by later audiences:

Andromacha a tout grans souspirs	*Andromache, with many great sighs*
et pleurs fist son pouoir que il	*and tears, used her power so that he*
n'alast en la bataille; mais Hector	*[Hector] would not go to battle, but Hector*
ne l'en volt croire et il y fu occis.	*did not want to believe her and there*
Pour ce dit que le bon chevalier ne	*he was slain. Therefore, a good*
doit du tout desprisier les avisions	*knight should not entirely undervalue*
sa femme, se elle est sage et bien	*the prophetic dreams of his wife,*
condicionnee, et mesmement	*if she is wise and well conditioned,*
d'autres femmes sages.	*and also those of other wise women.*
(*Epistre Othea*, LXXXVIII, ll. 10–16)[29]	

Christine also uses the example of Cassandra in the *Epistre* to make a similar point:

> Quant parler lui couvenoit ja
> ne desit chose qui veritable ne
> fust, ne en mençonge onques
> ne fu trouvee. Moult fu de
> grant savoir Cassandra, pour
> ce dit au bon chevalier que a
> celle doit ressembler.
>   (*Epistre*, XXXII, ll. 10–14)
>
> *When she felt it appropriate to*
> *speak she only said things which*
> *were true, she was never found*
> *lying. Cassandra was full of*
> *great knowledge, therefore it*
> *indicates to the good knight that*
> *he should resemble her.*

Christine was writing nearly 250 years after the *romans* were written and cannot be used as definitive evidence as to the ways in which the texts were received at their time of composition or by their earliest audiences. However, manuscripts of *Troie* were still being produced throughout the centuries leading up to Christine's composition of the *Epistre* and we can imagine that Hector's actions were still a topic of scrutiny. Indeed, the whole narrative framework of the *Epistre* takes the form of a letter to Hector, providing him with guidance on the moral and chivalric values of a good knight. The illustrations of *Troie* manuscripts show that the scenes of Andromache's advice to Hector were important to medieval audiences, not just in the twelfth century but into the fifteenth century, while Christine's text suggests that it was valued as a lesson in the indispensability of heeding good counsel, even (or especially) if it came from a woman.

In contrast, Medea's advice is taken by Jason. *Troie* opens with the story of Jason and the quest for the Golden Fleece, which was a departure from Dares and Dictys. Dictys makes no reference to the story of the Golden Fleece at all, while Dares's account is only thirty-four lines long; Benoît's version is almost two thousand lines in length. Medea does not even appear in Dares's account, but she is a major figure in Benoît's. *Troie* introduces her as a beautiful wise woman who has mastered the arts of magic and enchantment. She falls in love with Jason and attempts to dissuade him from his quest for the Golden Fleece because of the risk. He insists that he will continue. She therefore proposes to help him if he agrees to marry her. She tells him that '[f]or mei, ne t'en puet riens aider | Ne avancier ne conseiller' (*except for me, nobody is able to help, support or counsel you*, ll. 1417–18). The verb 'conseiller' (*to counsel*) particularly stands out. He agrees to the arrangement and they spend the night together before he departs. She gives him five gifts to help on his quest: a magic figurine that will protect him, an ointment that can heal wounds, a ring that makes him invisible, a parchment with a magic enchantment and a potion to pour in the face of the bulls to render them harmless. In addition, she gives him advice on exactly how and in what order to face the dangers that guard the Golden Fleece. In essence, she makes it almost impossible for him to fail if he follows her guidance.

The illustrators did not fail to pick up on Medea's importance. She appears in five of the illustrated *Troie* manuscripts: MSS P17, V1, Vt, Vn and P18. In MS P17 (the mid-fourteenth-century manuscript containing all three of the *roman* together), she only appears once and the scene illustrated is her introduction to Jason and Hercules (fol. 47^r). However, the other manuscripts make more of her story. In the extensively illustrated MS Vt she appears six times: entering Jason's bedchamber (fol. 11^r), with Jason in the Temple of Jupiter (fol. 12^r), in bed with Jason (fol. 12^r), giving gifts to Jason (fol. 12^v), watching Jason sail away (fol. 13^v) and watching him return (fol. 15^r). In the mid-fourteenth-century Italian MS Vn she appears eight times: her introduction to Jason and Hercules (fol. 8ʳ), her standing in court (fol. 8ᵛ), her engagement to Jason (fol. 9ʳ), her lying in bed with Jason standing next to the bed (fol. 10ʳ), her giving the parchment to Jason (fol. 11ʳ), she and Jason embracing (fol. 11ʳ), she and Jason in bed together (fol. 11ʳ) and finally her watching Jason sail away (fol. 12ʳ). MS P18, the copy of MS Vn, has the same illustrations. But it is the fourteenth-century Neapolitan MS V1 that gives the most thorough rendering of her story as it shows ten scenes: her first meeting with Jason (fol. 8ᵛ), talking to Jason (fol. 9ʳ), alone in her bedchamber (fol. 9ᵛ), standing next to her bed speaking with a maidservant (fol. 10ʳ), in bed with Jason standing next to her (fol. 10ʳ), giving the magic figurine to Jason (fol. 10ᵛ), in bed with Jason (fol. 10ᵛ), giving the parchment to Jason (fol. 11ʳ), she and Jason embracing (fol. 11ʳ) and finally watching Jason sail away (fol. 11ᵛ). Not only are the scenes in which Medea physically appears important, but her presence can still be detected in later illustrations that show Jason's exploits. For example, when we see Jason facing the dragon and the bull on fol. 12ʳ he is reading from the same parchment seen in the earlier illustration (on fol. 11ᵛ). The illustrators were keen to show not just how important Medea was as an advisor, but how beneficial it was that Jason followed that advice.

Negotiators

Alongside advisors, the *romans* also give us female negotiators. Negotiators are distinguished from advisors in that they speak not just with those on their own side, but those from the opposing side, too. The two most striking examples of this role are Jocasta from *Thèbes* and Hecuba from *Troie*. The former volunteers to be part of a negotiation party and travels to the besiegers' camp in order to conduct talks, while the latter is deliberately sought out by the enemy and conducts negotiations from within her own walls. Both women are reliable negotiators but their success is limited. This may in part be due to the fact that they are predominantly message-bearers, rather than being able to act unilaterally. Nevertheless, even as message-bearers they still hold an important role in diplomatic relations between the two sides.

Jocasta is a powerful negotiator and her strategy is three-fold. Firstly, there is the physical impressiveness of her diplomatic delegation. In Statius's *Thebaid*, her envoy is described as follows:

Ecce truces oculos sordentibus obsita canis exsangues Iocasta genas et bracchia planctu nigra […]. Hinc atque hinc natae, melior iam sexus.	*Lo! Jocasta, wild-eyed, with hoary unkempt hair falling about her haggard face, her bosom bruised and livid and in her hand a branch of olive […]. On this side and on that her daughters, now the better sex.*
(*Thebaid*, VII, ll. 474–79)	

The women are shown to be the 'melior sexus' (*better sex*) in contrast to the men who refuse to negotiate, but they are not described in particularly dignified terms. In contrast, the *Thèbes* poet begins by stating that Jocasta is 'bien vestue et bien conree' (*well dressed and well prepared*, l. 4112) and then devotes the next sixty-six lines (ll. 4113–79) to describing the beautiful clothes, horses and attire of her and her two daughters. They are transformed from haggard women carrying sticks to noble ladies adorned with jewels and furs. These are not the actions of desperate lowly women, but part of a spectacle of ceremonial importance.

Secondly, her mission in *Thèbes* is different from that in the Statius. In the *Thebaid*, Jocasta's mission was to convince Polynices to abandon his siege of Thebes and respect the original terms of the agreement (whereby he and Eteocles took it in turns to rule the kingdom). However, in *Thèbes*, the barons devise different terms of negotiation and propose that the kingdom should be divided in two, with each son having dominion over his own part. Eteocles initially opposes the suggestion, but with the counsel of his barons and mother he acquiesces. The barons then argue as to who should deliver the terms of the agreement to Polynices as they fear that the messenger will be slain. The concept of diplomatic immunity for messengers was not one that was known either in the classical period or the twelfth century when the *romans* were written; indeed for most of the Middle Ages, negotiators found themselves at risk and their missions were not easy.[30] However, Jocasta volunteers because she believes her status as Polynices's mother will give the messenger the immunity that he needs:

Ço dist Jocaste: 'Jo irai,	*Jocasta said this: I will go,*
Que le message conduirai:	*I will accompany the messenger:*
Que mis fiz puésse, pas ne cuit	*for I do not believe that my son is able*
Que hon seit pris en mon conduit;	*to seize him if I accompany him;*
Polinicès bien guardera	*Polynices will ensure that*
Que on nul mal ne li fera.'	*nothing bad happens to him.*
(*Thèbes*, ll. 3767–72)	

This demonstrates one of the advantages of having a close relative, particularly a female relative, as part of the negotiating team. Their status as wife, mother, sister or daughter means that they are perceived as less threatening (than a man) as well as a more sympathetic figure. The act of having Jocasta accompany the messenger is already the first step in the negotiation, reminding the two adversaries of their common link and potentially facilitating a more open dialogue than had a male knight been sent instead.

Thirdly, the role that Jocasta's daughters play is changed. In the *Thebaid* they are there to support her in a physical sense; they hold her arms on either side to enable her to walk. But in *Thèbes*, they play a role in the negotiations and build relations between the two sides. When Parthenopeus, one of Polynices's knights, sees Antigone, he falls in love with her and she with him. He asks Jocasta for her blessing to marry Antigone and she consents:

Bien otreie le mariage;	*She happily agreed to the marriage;*
Mout volentiers la li dorra,	*very willingly she gave her [Antigone]*
Mais o son fil en parlera.	*to him [Parthenopeus], but only after she*
(*Thèbes*, ll. 3958–60)	*had spoken to her son.*

This marriage of a princess from one side to a baron of the opposing side serves two functions: firstly, it allows another opportunity for the *Thèbes* poet to introduce the theme of courtly love. Secondly, it is a form of diplomatic manoeuvring in itself and part of the peace negotiations between the two sides. In the historical context of the Middle Ages, marriage was one possible strategy for seeking and sealing peace negotiations or as part of wider political machinations to create and reinforce alliances between families.[31] The placement of Antigone and Parthenopeus's betrothal during the negotiation envoy of Jocasta frames it as politically serendipitous in cementing peace negotiations. Up to this point, it appears that having an envoy of women as negotiators is nothing but beneficial.

However, despite the positive start, the talks are unsuccessful and the *Thèbes* poet makes a change to his source material to show that this breakdown is not Jocasta's fault, but rather the fault of the men with whom she is attempting to negotiate. Just as Hector and the Trojans are condemned for failing to follow good advice, so the Argives are judged for failing to respond appropriately to negotiations. In both *Thèbes* and the *Thebaid* the terms of her peace treaty are rejected after Polynices takes advice from his barons. In the *Thebaid*, this scene is followed by an episode in which a group of Argive warriors hunts down two tame Theban tigresses.[32] The killing of the tigresses prompts an outbreak of violence between the two sides and Jocasta and her daughters flee the negotiations. In *Thèbes*, after Polynices rejects the terms, the narrator announces that '[n]e dei amer par legerie | Dont l'on puésse dire folie' (*on that day the foolishness started for no good reason*, ll. 3925–26). He goes on to give his version of the story of the tigresses. However, depending on which manuscript of *Thèbes* we use, he changes the story in different ways. In MS P8 (a late-thirteenth-century Parisian manuscript) and MS G (another late-thirteenth-century manuscript of unknown provenance) we have a single tigress and she is described using the vocabulary associated with courtly ladies:[33] she drinks wine, plays games, is beautiful and even displays the heraldic device of a carbuncle. The narrator describes how upon hearing the noise of the Argives outside the walls of Thebes, '[d]e la cité vers l'ost eissi' (*she went from the city towards the army*, l. 4304), mirroring the scene in which Jocasta has left the city to go towards the Argive army. The tigress is killed by the Argives, prompting the outbreak of the first battle, and there is no mention of Jocasta at all. Unlike in the *Thebaid* where she is described fleeing back to Thebes, in *Thèbes* her movements are completely omitted. It is as if the image of the dead tigress is enough to signify that the aspirations of feminine peacefulness have been killed and replaced by the *folie* of warring men.

In three fourteenth-century manuscripts, MSS P13, P17 and L4, the story of the tigress is almost identical to that in the thirteenth-century MSS P8 and G, but with one crucial difference: the tigress is no longer a tigress but 'une guivre' (*a serpentine dragon*, l. 4604).[34] It is difficult to give an exact translation of *guivre* as this term was relatively new in the twelfth century and its meaning varied across texts.[35] It generally takes the form of snake or viper, often winged and with two to four legs, with the potential to be venomous or breathe fire. Petit argues that the late-fourteenth-century MS L4, although the most recent of the *Thèbes* manuscripts and produced in England, actually contains the oldest version of *Thèbes*;[36] if true, then the appearance of the tigress in the later versions of MSS P8 and G indicates later scribes attempting to revise the original text to bring it closer to Statius's *Thebaid*, rather than reproducing the

Thèbes poet's transformed version. The paleographical forms of *guivre* and *tigre* are sufficiently distinct (the former beginning with a descender and the latter beginning with an ascender and with a descender in the middle of the word) that we can rule out simple scribal accidental misinterpretation to explain the differences and conclude that the change must have been deliberate. The original version, with a tame serpentine-dragon, not only represents a radical departure from the tigresses of Statius's *Thebaid* but makes for a more dramatic scene when it is described and killed. This *guivre* is also female and is described in the same terms as the tigress (beautiful, fond of wine, playful and displaying the carbuncle). With the image of the serpentine-dragon it is even more inevitable that she will be killed by the Argive knights, for the topos of men slaying dragons was already well established in the twelfth century.

What is particularly interesting is the feminization of the *guivre*, an image that became popular in later medieval Francophone culture through legends such as Jean d'Arras's *Mélusine* (1382–94), but which was relatively unusual in the twelfth century. What is even more interesting is that this deliberate decision to include a *guivre* rather than a tiger may lead us back to Eleanor of Aquitaine, for in the thirteenth century there was a growing tradition of associating Eleanor with a demonic she-devil that often took the form of a serpentine-dragon, much like a *guivre*.[37] Given the information we have about the three manuscripts in which the *guivre* appears, we could also speculate that their owners or commissioners would have found it quite amusing to have a version containing a creature that was associated with damaging the reputability of Eleanor or indeed queens and women in general: the earliest ownership information for MS P13 connects it to Jacques II de Bourbon (1370–1438), a fiercely militant figure who fought in the Hundred Years War against the dynasty that Eleanor had helped to found, just as his father, Jean de Bourbon (1344–93), had done before him. MS P17 also belonged to members of the French aristocracy (at one point it was part of Louis XIV's royal collection) and is the manuscript that was discussed in previous chapters as having a questionable relationship to women: it omits illustrations of Camille despite having a rich illustrative scheme, it only shows Penthesilea once she's dead in a split-register miniature (Figure 28) unlike the male warriors who are depicted in combat in full registers, and the illustrations of Helen and Lavine have been damaged or defaced in some way (Figures 2 and 3). Meanwhile MS L4, although produced in England, was commissioned for Henry Despenser (*c.* 1341–1406), a man whose grandfather and great-grandfather (Hugh Despenser the Younger and Hugh le Despenser) had both been executed on the orders of another queen of England, Isabella of France. It is fair to say that looking at the particular ownership of these manuscripts, there may have been some appreciation for a version that contained a monstrous feminine serpentine-dragon, a figure which by this time had become something of a topos for representing the demonic natures of women. In any case, regardless of whether the scene preceding that of the breakdown of negotiations depicts the killing of a tigress or a *guivre*, the overall effect is the same: the slaughter of this beautiful but dangerous feminine creature mirrors the image of the failure of Jocasta's diplomatic mission to Polynices and both result in the outbreak of the war. The peacefulness and beauty of neither Jocasta and her daughters, nor the tigress or *guivre*, are able to triumph over the *folie* of men unwilling to compromise and determined to fight.

The female negotiator of *Troie* is Hecuba. Achilles contacts her because he wishes to negotiate for the hand of Polyxena, with whom he has fallen in love. He offers to withdraw his troops from the war in exchange for Polyxena's hand in marriage. The decision to go to Hecuba (rather than Priam) is not commented upon by either the messenger or the narrator. This course of action, to negotiate firstly with the mother, must have seemed normal. This scene appears in Dares, while in Dictys, the chosen negotiator is Hector rather than Hecuba. Notwithstanding the narrative problem that at this stage in Benoît's narrative Hector is already dead, Benoît nevertheless clearly felt that given the choice between Hecuba or one of Hecuba's sons as negotiator (he could have substituted Paris or Troilus, for example), Hecuba was the better choice. However, as soon as the messenger delivers his message, we see that while Hecuba is the primary point of contact, she occupies the more limited role of message-bearer. She wants to accept the terms but cannot do so without the consent of her husband and son:

Por quant jol voudrai volentiers,	*I would willingly [accept these*
Se jol puis trover vers le rei.	*terms] if I am able to obtain [the*
[...]	*consent] of the king. [...]*
D'ui en tierz jor a mei revien:	*Return in three days: then*
De ço que jo avrai apris	*I will have spoken with my*
A mon seignor e a Paris.	*lord [Priam] and with Paris.*
(*Troie*, ll. 17838–39, 17852–54)	

Hecuba can receive envoys of negotiation but cannot accept or decline them. She makes a compelling case to Priam for accepting Achilles's proposal. She lays out the difficult situation they are in militarily due to the loss of forces and the death of Hector (ll. 17888–901), she explains that Achilles has proposed a peace accord that would make Polyxena a powerful queen (ll. 17902–08) and end the siege (ll. 17909–15), and she reminds him of the suffering endured by the people of Troy (ll. 17916–28). Priam does not give his consent to Achilles's proposal, for he states that Achilles's withdrawal alone from the war would be insufficient to end it. Instead, he asks Hecuba to propose new terms, stating that Achilles may only have Polyxena's hand if he persuades all of the Greeks to cease hostilities. Achilles is unsuccessful in this task (as discussed in Chapter 2). He refrains from fighting in battles twelve to fifteen, but eventually rejoins the fray in battle sixteen. When Priam learns of this he vows that Achilles will never wed Polyxena. Any hopes for a peace deal are quashed.

Despite the fact that Hecuba's role in these negotiations is limited and that they are ultimately unsuccessful in brokering a peace deal, the illustrated manuscripts of *Troie* nevertheless attest to the fact that these scenes were of interest as they appear in four of the Italian manuscripts: MSS V1, Vt, Vn and P18. It was also probably intended to be included in the illustrations of MS P16 as there is space left for a miniature on fol. 107^r above which is written the rubric: 'Comment Achilles envoia un message al la fame au roy priant' (*how Achilles sent a messenger to the wife of King Priam*). MS V1 has eight illustrations to accompany this part of the narrative, appearing with such frequency that the text is almost redundant given the pictorial rendering of almost every stage of the negotiation. We see Achilles speaking to his messenger (fol. 139^r); the messenger walking from the Greek camp to Troy and speaking to Hecuba (fol. 139^v); the messenger leaving Hecuba, walking back to the Greek camp and speaking with Achilles (fol. 140^r); Hecuba speaking with Priam (fol. 140^v); the messenger speaking with Hecuba and Polyxena (fol. 141^r); the messenger walking between Troy and the Greek camp (fol. 141^v); and the messenger speaking with Achilles (fol. 142^r). The almost exhausting repetitiveness of the images gives a graphic representation of the many stages involved in the negotiation process. Hecuba's appearance four times (as compared with Priam being shown only twice) confirms her role as Achilles's primary contact in the negotiations and her centrality to this episode. MS Vt provides three illustrations: Hecuba and Achilles's messenger speaking alone (fol. 135^v), Hecuba speaking with Priam (Figure 37) and Hecuba speaking with Achilles's messenger again, while Polyxena stands to the side (fol. 137^r). In all three, Hecuba is shown with one hand raised, indicating her speech. The messenger is always shown with his arms folded (showing his silence) while Priam rests his head on one of hands (showing that he is listening). Hecuba has the agency in all three as she is shown leading the discussions. MSS Vn and P18 similarly dedicate a series of illustrations to representing the full extent of the negotiations: Achilles speaking with the messenger (MS Vn, fol. 105^v and MS P18, fol. 117^v), the messenger speaking with Hecuba (MS Vn, fol. 107^r and MS P18, fol. 118^r), Hecuba speaking with Priam (MS Vn, fol. 107^v and MS P18, fol. 108^r), Hecuba speaking again with the messenger (MS Vn, fol. 108^r and Figure 38) and the messenger back with Achilles (MS Vn, fol. 108^v and MS P18, fol. 120^r). Once again, Hecuba dominates these illustrations as compared to Priam (appearing in three out of the five, while Priam is in only one). Irrespective of the success of these negotiations, the fact that Hecuba is central to their unfolding was of importance. As with Jocasta, the breakdown of these negotiations for peace is not shown to be the fault of the queen attempting to broker peace, but rather the fault of the men with whom she is negotiating and who are unwilling to put aside violence.

Intervenors

Intervenors do not offer advice and they do not attempt to negotiate. Instead, they take unilateral action entirely of their own devising. In Hecuba we have an example of the way in which she becomes an intervenor and takes action that affects the development of the war. The incident that drives Hecuba to become an intervenor is the death of Troilus at the hands of Achilles in battle nineteen. Following this event, she devises a plot to have Achilles assassinated. Dares casts a negative judgement over Hecuba's decision to undertake such a course of action: 'Hecuba maesta [...] consilium muliebre temerarium iniit ad ulciscendum dolorem' (*mournful Hecuba devised, like the woman she was, a treacherous vengeance*, D.34). The word 'muliebre' (*like the woman she was*) is used with a decidedly negative connotation to suggest that her actions are dishonourable. However, Benoît is more sympathetic.

> Com de lui se puisse vengier,
> Ne s'en deit nus hom merveillier
> N'a mal ne a blasme atorner.
>   (*Troie*, ll. 21851–53)
>
> *In this way she is able to be avenged on him [Achilles] and nobody should be surprised nor put any blame on her.*

Her plan is to send a messenger to Achilles telling him to meet her at the Temple of Apollo where she will give him Polyxena in marriage. In fact, she convinces Paris (against his better judgement) to lay an ambush in the temple and kill Achilles. There is no suggestion that Achilles is suspicious of receiving such a message from Hecuba, implying that her power to undertake such action was not in question and her reputation as an honest diplomat was similarly intact.

The scene in which Achilles is assassinated in the Temple of Apollo is frequently illustrated. It appears in seven manuscripts (MSS P6, Nt, P17, Vt, Vn, P18 and V1). Five of these also include the preceding scene showing Hecuba giving her instructions to Paris (MSS P6, Vt, Vn, P18 and V1). There was also a plan for it to appear in MS P16 as there is space left for a miniature on fol. 133^v above which is written the rubric: 'Comment la reine ecuba manda a achilles qu'il venist parler a lui et comment paris l'ochist' (*how Queen Hecuba asked Achilles to come to speak to her and how Paris killed him*). So in the majority of cases, the scene of Achilles's death, the death of one of the greatest warriors of the Trojan legend, is not separated from a visual representation of the instigator of his death: Hecuba. Paris holds the sword, but it is Hecuba who has given the order. There is also a difference in visual representations of Hecuba when she switches from negotiator to intervenor. In the illustrations of her speaking with Achilles's messenger and Priam as discussed in the section above, she is shown in several different postures: seated with the messenger kneeling before her, seated with the messenger standing, standing with the messenger standing, seated next to Priam (who is also seated) or standing in discussion with Priam (who is also standing). All of these take place in public rooms as several of them also have other (unnamed) figures in the background or she is seated on a throne. When it comes to the moment in which she gives her instructions to Paris, the scene always contrasts with the negotiation scene. For example, in three of the Italian manuscripts, MSS Vn, P18 and V1, she is shown lying in her bed (Figure 36). The corresponding scenes in MSS V1 and P18 are shown on fols. 172^r and 148^r, respectively. Granted in MS P6 she is shown standing speaking to a standing Paris, but this manuscript is not one of the ones that has illustrated the negotiation scene and so there is nothing with which to compare. This is a clear visual distinction: when she was a negotiator she was standing or seated, but when she is an intervenor she is lying in her bed. This is not to suggest that the bedchamber is a private or informal location. Indeed, quite the opposite is often true. There were many uses for beds as a form of ceremony and they were often placed in public spaces from which a monarch was able to conduct formal proceedings.[38] The change of representation of Hecuba from one chamber to the bedchamber is therefore not necessarily an implication of a move from public to private or implicit of either an increase or decrease of importance, but a visual way of signifying a change in role. Anyone browsing the manuscript could see that a shift has taken place.

Conclusion

The historical record suggests that women were likely to play a political and diplomatic role during times of war though the exact nature of their responsibilities varied considerably. The *romans* demonstrate ways in which women wielded agency in diplomatic roles such as advisors, negotiators and intervenors during times of war. This is reflected not just in the text but in the illustrations, too: Andromache's attempts to stop Hector from going back into battle and Hecuba's role in brokering the promise of a peace deal with Achilles and in plotting his assassination all stand out across the illustrated manuscripts in *Troie* as pivotal scenes. When seen advising or negotiating there is an implication that they are wise advisors and peace-seeking negotiators, but that their counsel falls on deaf ears. That Cassandra is locked up despite her accurate predictions for the future shows the foolishness of the male characters in removing counsellors who give advice that does not accord with their own views. Indeed, any negative criticism is placed on those who fail to listen, rather than those who fail to be heard. Later medieval writers' reception of the Trojan narrative (such as Christine de Pizan) suggests that those who fail to listen to their advisors were judged negatively. Hector's failure to heed Andromache's advice not only led to his death, but to his later reputation being tarnished as a man who ignored wise counsel. Similarly, Achilles's failure to adhere to the terms of his negotiation with Hecuba causes his death and Polynices and Eteocles's failure to conduct a peace negotiation, even in the presence of their mother, eventually results in their deaths.

The female characters in the *romans* are almost exclusively preoccupied with making peace, which contrasts to many of the female advisors in the *chansons de geste*. Whether or not this reflected a historical reality is hard to say as peacemaking (in comparison to warfare) has received relatively little attention among medieval scholars. A few chapters and a single monograph on this topic have appeared, but there is still a dearth of material in comparison to the amount published on war and battles.[39] And if there is limited work on medieval peacemaking, there is even less on women's role in this process. In fact, the reason for which there is more on warfare than on peace is a gendering of these fields of research themselves. War has traditionally been thought of as the domain of men and peace that of women; given that medieval historiography has traditionally been more heavily weighted to studying men, perhaps it is unsurprising that there is therefore relatively little research on peace so far. What work there is on peacemaking does not uncover a particular role for women in the process. A survey of peacemaking during Henry II's reign uncovered numerous records of peace negotiations, but all the named participants and intermediaries are male and include a high number of bishops and clerks.[40] This probably should not surprise us and still does not exclude the possibility that women had a role behind the scenes, in spaces to which the chroniclers did not have access. This is where literature can play a part, in revealing what is otherwise concealed. However, it is most likely that the *romans* are projecting an idealized version of women's roles. Their rather neatly gendered version shows that women only get involved politically when it relates to the 'feminine' business of peace, rather than the 'masculine' business of war itself. This was a similarly idealized view championed by Christine de Pizan in the *Livre de Trois Vertus*:

Laquelle chose est le droit office de sage et bonne royne et princepce d'estre moyenne de paix et de concorde, et de travailler que guerre soit eschivee pour les inconveniens qui avenir en peuent. Et ad ce doivent aviser principaulment les dames, car les hommes sont par nature plus courageux et plus chaulx, et le grant desir que ilz ont d'eulx vengier ne leur laisse aviser les perilz ne les maulx qui avenir en peuent. (Book I, Chapter 9)[41]	*The proper role of a wise and good queen or princess is to be the means of peace and harmony and to work to avoid wars and the disasters that accompany them. And women should principally concern themselves with peace as men are naturally more foolhardy and rash and their great desire to avenge themselves means they cannot see the possible dangers or evils that may follow.*

But the dramatic licence of the *romans* means that they do not have to be quite so restrictive. Hecuba's switch from negotiator to intervenor shows how women can initiate violence, too. Indeed, the fact that her switch results in the death of one of the greatest heroes of the narrative shows just how potent the effect can be if women do turn their inclinations from peace to violence.

Women in the *chansons de geste* and other epic Old French narratives can also be found counselling their male kin to take up arms rather than to lay them down. For example, in the *Chanson de Guillaume* (c. 1140) it is William's wife Guiborc who drags him out of his despair after his loss at Archamp and tells him to continue fighting (ll. 1325–89) while in *Garin le Loherenc* there are numerous examples of women advising their male kin on the best strategies for attack or revenge.[42] The historical women who may have inspired or been inspired by these texts are also varied in their political objectives when it comes to conflict and can be found counselling for action rather than peace. Adela of Blois was the one to persuade her husband, Stephen, to take up arms again to join the minor crusade of 1101, where he was killed during the Second Battle of Ramla in 1102.[43] Alice de Montmorency (d. 1220) was much lauded in contemporary chronicles for the counsel and support that she gave to her husband during the Albigensian Crusade, where there are accounts of her participating in the councils of barons.[44] The *Chanson de la Croisade Albigeoise* (c. 1210–25), which recounts selected deeds of this crusade, places women in an important position and in particular makes numerous references to the influence of Alice herself, even suggesting that she also had a place on the battlefield (though it is possible that these were fantastical episodes intended just to enhance her fearsome political reputation).[45] In Jordan Fantosme's *Chronique de la Guerre entre les Anglais et les Écossais en 1173 et 1174* he similarly describes a council of war at which the Countess of Leicester is described encouraging her husband to take action (ll. 974–83) and there is no suggestion on the part of the chronicler that this was unacceptable or unsolicited advice.[46] If we look back to the historical women at the start of this chapter, we see examples of women using their political power in pursuit of warring activities just as we see them using it for peace or indeed for 'peacetime activities' such as patronage of arts, education or religious institutions. Outside of hagiography or allegory (such as Christine's *Livre des Trois Vertus*) it is difficult to find women in the Old French tradition directly advocating for peace – we just as often find them petitioning a knight to take up arms on their behalf – as for example happens on more than one occasion in the Arthurian tradition in particular. Despite certain attempts to present them into this ideal mould of peacemaker, the historical and cultural record shows that women with political roles or influence decided on their own courses of actions and positions, be they peaceful or otherwise.

Conclusion

War is a multifaceted phenomenon through which to raise and explore questions around women, gendering and gender roles. The *romans*' self-presentation as vernacular translations of classical texts meant that they were not necessarily seen as overtly political or social treatises. Their explorations of the boundaries of gender roles could therefore avoid any potential accusations of subversiveness by appearing only within the confines of their faithful 'translations'. However, by transposing the narratives into a recognizably medieval milieu they were still able to pass such commentary and engage in contemporary debates on the place of women within medieval society. One important caveat to this is to remember that the *romans* were produced, enjoyed and circulated within a decidedly elite context, and therefore their focus is predominantly (and unsurprisingly) on the role and representation of elite women in war. This is certainly true when it comes to considering women as reasons for the outbreak of hostilities, or powerful martial and political roles such as warriors or diplomats. These areas were almost exclusively reserved for the nobility, although as Joan of Arc came to prove, even those boundaries could be challenged at the right time and under the right circumstances. Nevertheless, despite the focus on the nobility, women of all classes and social backgrounds do still make brief appearances in the texts, either as long-suffering victims of warfare or as essential ancillary forces. In particular, the role of women in health care during and the burial of the dead after battle seems especially important and worthy of further investigation. While elite women may be the dominant figures, the occasional glimpses that we have of non-elite women are of great value in moving this research towards a more inclusive and encompassing field of investigation.

As Chapter 1 explored, the manuscript contexts for the narratives suggest that most patrons valued the *romans* for their political, historical or social significance. Furthermore, certain ownership patterns, marginalia and damage to illustrations of women, indicate that users of these manuscripts were often interested in the female characters. Similarly, there is ample evidence to show that the poets used their contemporary environments to develop their narratives, and this includes the evolution of their female characters. To some extent, the wars featured in these texts do create and reinforce gender restrictions between masculine and feminine: Chapter 2 revealed how the male characters speak at length about the honour and glory that is associated with being a fierce and brave warrior on the battlefield and actively seek out opportunities to establish their martial prowess and courage, while women are more concerned with peace. Similarly, Chapters 3 and 6 demonstrated that the gendering of suffering and peacemaking meant that women were on occasion seen in more passive or pacifist roles or simply as victims. However, the texts simultaneously challenge these limitations and ask us to re-examine the ways these positions are defined. So as Chapters 4 to 6 explained, we find women taking active ancillary roles in tasks such as handling weaponry and armour and tending to the wounded or dead after battle; we have female warriors who excel at martial exploits on the battlefield just as the male warriors do, and we see female political actors who occupy central roles in advising, negotiating and intervening in the actions of men. *Troie* and *Enéas* even present us with a specific idea of feminine chivalry as distinct from (but not inferior to) masculine chivalry. This feminine chivalry incorporates many of the traits associated with masculine chivalry, including *courtoisie*, *prouesse* and *loyauté*, but also demands the additional virtue of virginity. This is particularly important for it shows that during the twelfth century, a period when chivalry was being discussed in multiple fora and had yet to emerge into a more formalized code of conduct, early ideas did not exclude women but explored a parallel code through which they too could participate. It is also interesting to consider the extent to which the establishment of parallel male and female monastic communities influenced writers and theorists into devising structures that accommodated both sexes in the systemization of another of the medieval estates – male and female knights as well as male and female monastics.[1] Eventually both medieval writers and modern scholars alike come to treat female warriors as exceptions, rarities or aberrations, but at least at the time of the *romans*' composition we would do well to consider the gendering of chivalry and women's place within it more fully.

War may essentially have been structured as a patriarchal system in which women were fated to suffer, but the *romans* took the opportunity to explore ways for women to exert some agency and authority within that structure. This is not to suggest that women threatened this structure or attempted to overthrow it, but simply that the poets and illustrators aimed to provide exemplars for women on how they could be virtuous, valuable and powerful within that system, as well as showing men the value of such empowered women. Understanding the *romans* poets' motivation in this way helps us to understand later contemporary attitudes to women's role in warfare, too. The fact that these texts continued to be valued for centuries after their composition meant that some of these ideas or representations or characters must have had an enduring popularity. Indeed, Deiphyle and Penthesilea both became *Neuf Preuses*; Argia, Camille, Cassandra, Clytemenestra, Dido, Hecuba, Helen, Hipsipyle, Jocasta, Lavine, Medea, Penelope, Penthesilea and Polyxena were part of Giovanni Boccaccio's *De Mulieribus Claris* (*c.* 1374); Argia, Camille, Cassandra, Dido, Lavine, Medea, Penelope and Penthesilea appeared in Christine's *Cité des dames*; Andromache, Cassandra, Helen, Medea, Penthesilea and Polyxena featured in Christine's *Epistre Othea*; Camille and Penthesilea were championed in Martin le Franc's *Champion des Dames* (*c.* 1461). In fact, from Christine up to the early sixteenth century these texts (and these women) were an important part of the popular 'imaginative literature written in defence of women that is now ranged under the umbrella term "la querelle des femmes"'.[2] Similarly, historical figures of women with warring connections also continue to appear well after the *romans* first appeared: we could look at Blanche of Castile, Eleanor of Castile, Eleanor of Provence, Isabella of Aragon, Isabella of Castile,

Isabella of France, Isabelle MacDuff, Black Agnes, Joan of Arc, Joan of Navarre, Joanna of Flanders, Richarde de Saluces, Margaret of Anjou or Margaret Beaufort to name but a few. These texts continued to be relevant because the struggle for women to find and exert their role in warfare was also ongoing and the *romans*' exemplars provided some enduring models.

This study is certainly not intended to be the final word on this topic, for the *romans* were surely not alone in their exploration of the many and varied roles and connections that women had in relation to warfare. However, this investigation has yielded particularly fruitful results that give us a new understanding of these particular texts and their diverse material, historical and literary contexts. Incorporating the manuscript context of the texts was especially important in two ways: firstly, it highlighted the importance of looking at the texts not just at the time of their composition (within a twelfth-century Anglo-Norman milieu) but also at the later times of their copying (within a wider thirteenth- and fourteenth-century Franco-Italian context). This helped to uncover the changing ways that the texts were valued and received across different groups and periods and showed that many of the manuscripts had particular connections to women. Secondly, this widened the focus of the research from looking not at the written texts only, but considering the illustrative traditions that often accompanied them, too. Evidence from these illustrations showed that the illustrators (in certain cases working under the influence of a particular patron) were similarly interested in images of women and scenes of warfare in which women appear, demonstrating that there was an artistic appreciation of women's role in warfare, too. The specific physical attention paid to illustrations of women (often resulting in damage to the image) in certain manuscripts further highlights that later readers were similarly engaged with the subjects of these illustrations. Using the historical context of the *romans*' composition also allowed for discussion of possible new sources for the *romans*, specifically by looking at the powerful historical women who were doubtless known to the poets. It is this aspect that allows us to position the findings of this study not just in the space of literary studies, but within the wider field of social history. A large question now remains as to what extent similar debates and discussions might be found in other sources (both literary and historical) if we were to approach them in a similar way. Any claims that there is a dearth of information on medieval women and warfare is not due to a gap in the primary sources, but rather due to a gap in current scholarship. This is an opportunity for further research. Where else could we look and what else could we find? Benoît's epilogue to *Troie* suggests that having reached the end of a long work it is sensible to leave it behind and move on:

> Ci ferons fin, bien est mesure: *Here we shall end our book, which is*
> Auques tient nostre livre e dure.   *right, for it covers much and at great*
> (*Troie*, ll. 30301–02)   *length.*

But while this particular study has come to an end, the work on medieval women and warfare must continue.

Appendix 1: Catalogue of manuscripts

Unless otherwise indicated, information for *Troie* manuscripts is drawn from Marc-René Jung, Elizabeth Morrison, Léopold Constans and the relevant library catalogues;[1] information for the *Enéas* manuscripts has been taken from Raymond J. Cormier and the relevant library catalogues;[2] information for the *Thèbes* manuscripts has come from Aimé Petit and the relevant library catalogues.[3] There are ten fragments of *Troie* (and no fragments of *Enéas* or *Thèbes*) but these are not included.[4] The manuscripts are ordered first by location (alphabetically) and then chronologically with the sigils of my own designation given in parentheses.

Florence, Biblioteca Medicea Laurenziana, MS Plutei XLI.44 (MS F1)

Date: *c.* 1190–1225
Place: Italy
Contents: *Enéas*
Ownership: Unknown
Illustrations: None

Florence, Biblioteca Riccardiana, MS 2433 (MS F2)

Date: *c.* 1344
Place: Florence
Contents: *Hector et Hecule*; *Troie*
Ownership: Lucas Boni of Florence (possibly both scribe and owner)
Illustrations: No formal scheme, but numerous sketches and doodles
Comments: There are several spare folios at the end of *Troie* onto which various hands have written in extracts from a variety of other texts including Latin verses of the *Ave Maria*, a calendar of religious festivals, a hymn by Thomas Aquinas, two Franco-Italian lyrics and a few verses on Alexander the Great.

Geneva, Bibliotheca Bodmeriana, MS Bodmer 18 (MS G)

Date: *c.* 1275–1300
Place: Unknown
Contents: *Troie*; *Thèbes*
Ownership: Sir Thomas Phillipps (1792–1872)
Illustrations: One historiated initial (for *Troie*)
Comments: This is the only copy in which *Thèbes* follows (rather than precedes) *Troie*.

London, BL, MS Additional 30863 (MS L1)

Date: *c.* 1200–20
Place: Champagne
Contents: *Troie*
Ownership: Possibly shared between two fourteenth-century women (or a gift from one to another) as there is a note that reads 'A madame de Martignie madame Maulevrier saluz et bonne amor' (fol. 14^v)
Illustrations: None

London, BL, MS Harley 4482 (MS L2)

Date: *c.* 1250–1300
Place: Amiens or Arras
Contents: *Troie*
Ownership: Edward Harley, Earl of Oxford and Mortimer (1689–1741)
Illustrations: Fifteen historiated initials (connected to the illustrative cycle in MSS P14 and Mn)
Comments: Nine of the manuscript's historiated initials are found in the same place as the historiated initials of MSS P14 and Mn, suggesting a connection between the three.[5] However, Morrison adds that the subjects of the initials do not parallel the visual narratives of those manuscripts.[6]

London, BL, MS Additional 14100 (MS L3)

Date: *c.* 1340–60
Place: Italy
Contents: *Enéas*
Ownership: Arms of the Moro family appear on the flyleaf. Possibly put there by Cristoforo Moro (1390–1471), Doge of Venice
Illustrations: None

London, BL, MS Additional 34114 (MS L4)

Date: *c.* 1375–1400
Place: England
Contents: A *chanson de geste* on the First Crusade; *Enéas*; *Thèbes*; *Le Songe Vert*; *L'Ordène de Chevalerie*
Ownership: Henry Despenser, the 'Fighting Bishop' of Norwich (1341–1406); Maurice Johnson (1815–61)
Illustrations: None
Comments: Despite being the most recent copy of *Thèbes*, the text conserved in this manuscript is believed to be the closest to the twelfth-century original.[7]

Milan, Biblioteca Ambrosiana, MS D55 sup. (MS M)

Date: *c*. 1190–1206
Place: Venice
Contents: *Troie*
Ownership: Geoffrey of Villehardouin (1160–1212) and Milon of Brabant (d. 1224); another thirteenth-century hand has inscribed it with the phrase '[i]ste liber est mei plonbeoli de plombeolis' (*this book is mine, Plonbeoli of Plombeolis*); Gian Vincenzo Pinelli (1535–1601); Cardinal Federico Borromeo (1564–1631)
Illustrations: Seventeen historiated initials
Comments: There is a note at the end of the manuscript (fol. 198^v), dated between 1205 and 1206, explaining that it is to be shared between Geoffrey of Villehardouin and Milon of Brabant (two knights of the Fourth Crusade), which is witnessed by Marino Zeno (the *podestà* of Constantinople).[8]

Montpellier, Bibliothèque interuniversitaire, Section médecine, MS H.251 (MS Mn)

Date: *c*. 1300
Place: Paris or Picardy
Contents: *Thèbes* (probably, but no longer extant);[9] *Troie*; *Enéas*; Wace's *Brut*
Ownership: Cardinal Agostino Trivulzio (1485–1548)
Illustrations: Two miniatures (one for *Enéas* and one for the *Brut*) and twenty-three historiated initials (all for *Troie*, connected to the illustrative cycle of MSS P14 and L2)[10]

Naples, Biblioteca Nazionale Vittorio Emanuele III, MS XIII.C.38 (MS N)

Date: *c*. 1200–50
Place: Unknown
Contents: *Troie*
Ownership: Cardinal Agostino Trivulzio (1485–1548)
Illustrations: None

Nottingham, University Library, MS Mi.LM.6 (MS Nt)

Date: *c*. 1286
Place: Flanders or North-West France
Contents: *Troie*; Gautier d'Arras's *Ille et Galeron*; Heldris of Cornwall's *Roman de Silence*; Alexander of Paris's *Roman d'Alexandre* (fragment); *La Chanson d'Aspremont*; Raoul de Houdenc's *Vengeance Raguidel*; selected *fabliaux* of Gautier le Leu; Marie de France's *Esope* (fragment)
Ownership: Béatrice de Gavre (d. 1315); Anne de Laval (1385–1466); John Talbot, Earl of Shrewsbury (1384–1453); John Bertram of Thorp Kilton (d. 1471)
Illustrations: Eighty-three historiated initials (thirty-three for *Troie*)

Comments: The manuscript was commissioned in Flanders for Béatrice de Gavre, the Countess of Falkemberg, on the occasion of her marriage in 1286 to Guy IX de Laval, a Breton nobleman.[11] It fell into the hands of the English in 1428 during the campaigns of the Hundred Years War when the Laval castle was surrendered to John Talbot, Earl of Shrewsbury.[12] It was rediscovered in 1911 in a box marked 'Old Papers – no value'.[13]

Paris, Bibliothèque de l'Arsenal, MS 3342 (MS P1)

Date: *c.* 1200–25
Place: Unknown
Contents: *Troie*
Ownership: Unknown
Illustrations: 4

Paris, BnF, MS fr. 794 (MS P2)

Date: *c.* 1225–50
Place: Provins (Champagne)
Contents: Chrétien's *Erec et Enide*, *Le Chevalier de la Charrette*, *Cligès* and *Yvain, ou Le Chevalier au Lion*; *Athis et Prophilias*; *Troie*; Wace's *Brut*; Calendre's *Empereurs de Rome*; Chrétien's *Conte du Graal*; *Première Continuation*; *Deuxième Continuation*
Ownership: Unknown
Illustrations: One historiated initial (for *Lancelot, ou Le Chevalier de la Charette*), which is a portrait of Marie de Champagne
Comments: This parchment manuscript is sometimes referred to as the 'Guiot manuscript' because of its scribe, whose signature is found on fol. 105^v.[14]

Paris, Bibliothèque de l'Arsenal, MS 3340 (MS P3)

Date: *c.* 1237
Place: Unknown
Contents: *Troie*
Ownership: Unknown
Illustrations: None

Paris, BnF, MS fr. 2181 (MS P4)

Date: *c.* 1200–1300
Place: Unknown
Contents: *Troie*
Ownership: Unknown
Illustrations: None

148   Appendix 1: Catalogue of Manuscripts

Paris, BnF, MS fr. 1450 (MS P5)

Date: *c*. 1235–65
Place: North France
Contents: *Troie*; *Enéas*; Wace's *Brut* (Part I); Chrétien's *Erec et Enide* and *Le Conte du Graal*; *Première Continuation*; Chrétien's *Cligès*, *Yvain ou le Chevalier au Lion* and *Lancelot ou le Chevalier de la Charrette*; Wace's *Brut* (Part II); Herbert's *Dolopathos*
Ownership: Bertrand Goyon Matignon (there were four Bertrand Goyon Matignons in the thirteenth and fourteenth centuries but it is not clear which one of these Bertrands owned the manuscript)
Illustrations: One historiated initial (for *Enéas*)

MS P6: Paris, BnF, MS fr. 1610

Date: 1264
Place: Paris or Burgundy
Contents: *Troie*
Ownership: Unknown
Illustrations: Thirty-eight miniatures (of which eight are full-page illustrations)[15]
Comments: This manuscript is the oldest to have a full set of miniatures rather than just historiated initials.

Paris, BnF, MS fr. 1553 (MS P7)

Date: *c*. 1285
Place: Picardy
Contents: *Troie*; *De Engerran, Vesque de Cambrai ki fu*; Rutebeuf's *Une Complainte des Jacobins et des Cordeliers*; Gossuin de Metz's *L'Image du Monde en Romans*; Gui de Cambrai's *L'Ystoire de Yozaphas*; extract from the *Chronique dite de Baudouin d'Avesnes*; *Saint Brandainne le Moine*; *Li Ensaignemens des Sains lius d'Outre Mer*; *De Marie et de Marthe*; *Les Enfances Nostre Dame et de Jhesu*; *Des Soinges et des Experimens des Soinges*; *De Adam et Eve Femme*; *De Sainte Anne qui eut III Barons*; Gerbert de Monteuil's *Roman de Gerart de Nevers et de la Violette*; *Romans de Witasse le Moine*; *Le Roman des Sept Sages de Rome*; Alexandre du Pont's *Roman de Mahomet*; *La Vengeance Nostre Seigneur*; *La Vie de Saint Alesin*; *De Sainte Agnes*; *L'Ordène de Chevalerie*; *Le Chevalier au Barisel*; *La Vie de Saint Jehan Paulus*; *De l'Unicorne et du Serpent*; Guillaume le Clerc's *Roman de Fergus*; *Le Lai de l'Espine*; *Courtois d'Arras*; *Auberee*; *Le Epystles des Femes*; Enguerran le Clerc d'Oisi's *Dou Maunier de Aleus*; *Le Prestre Comporté*; *L'Evangile aux Femmes*; *Dou Dieu d'Amours*; Rutebeuf's *Ave Marie*; *Les Quinze Joies Nostre Dame*[16]
Ownership: Cardinal Mazarin (1602–61)
Illustrations: Three miniatures, nineteen historiated initials, eleven diagrams (only one miniature is related to *Troie*)
Comments: This is the earliest example of a manuscript that contains French prose alongside French verse.[17] As with MS P8, it was also owned by Cardinal Mazarin.

Paris, BnF, MS fr. 375 (MS P8)

Date: *c.* 1288
Place: Paris
Contents: *Thèbes*; *Troie*; *Athis et Prophilias*; Jean Bodel's *Les Congés*; Lambert le Tort and Alexandre de Bernay's *Roman d'Alexandre*; Pierre de Saint-Cloud's *Mort d'Alexandre*; Gui de Cambrai's *Vengeance d'Alexandre*; a genealogy of the counts of Boulogne; Wace's *Rou*; *Le Roman de Guillaume d'Angleterre* (possibly by Chrétien de Troyes, although this is debated); *Floire et Blanchefleur*; *Blancandin*; Chrétien's *Cligès* and *Erec et Enide*; *De la Vielle Truande*; Gautier d'Arras's *Ille et Galeron*; Gautier de Coincy's *De Theophilus*; *Amadas et Ydoine*; *De le Castelaine de Vergi*; *Épître Farcie de la Saint-Étienne*; *Loenges Nostre Dame*; *Miracles Nostre Dame*[18]
Ownership: Cardinal Mazarin (1602–61); Jean-Baptiste La Curne de Sainte-Palaye (1697–1781)
Illustrations: None

Paris, BnF, MS fr. 903 (MS P9)

Date: *c.* 1275–1300
Place: Lorraine
Contents: *Troie*; Jehan Malkaraume's *Bible*
Ownership: Philibert de la Mare (1615–87)
Illustrations: None
Comments: This is the only surviving copy of Malkaraume's *Bible*. *Troie* has been inserted into the *Bible* to create an unbroken narrative.[19] At no point does Malkaraume refer to the fact that he is using Benoît's *Troie*. In fact, on the four occasions that Benoît names himself in *Troie*, Malkaraume replaces the name 'Benoît' with his own name, 'Jehans'.[20]

Paris, BnF, MS fr. 1416 (MS P10)

Date: *c.* 1292
Place: Picardy
Contents: *Enéas*; Wace's *Brut*; Nun of Barking's *Vie d'Edouard le Confesseur*
Ownership: Unknown
Illustrations: One historiated initial (for *Enéas*)
Comments: The BnF's online catalogue lists the contents of this manuscript only as *Enéas* and Wace's *Brut*, but it contains an additional third item: the Nun of Barking's *Vie d'Edouard le Confesseur* (*c.* 1163–70).[21] Cataloguers may have previously missed the *Vie* because it has been 'inserted seamlessly' into Wace's text.[22]

Paris, BnF, MS fr. 12600 (MS P11)

Date: *c.* 1285–1300
Place: Northern France
Contents: *Troie*

Ownership: Possibly John II of France (an annotation on fol. 12^r reads 'Johannes dei gracia francorum rex') and possibly either Charles V, Charles VI or Charles VII of France (an annotation on fol. 177^r reads 'Karollus dey gracia')
Illustrations: One miniature and one historiated initial

Paris, BnF, MS fr. 12603 (MS P12)

Date: *c.* 1300
Place: Arras (Picardy)
Contents: *Le Chevalier aux Deux Épées*; Chrétien's *Yvain ou le Chevalier au Lion*; *Enéas*; Wace's *Brut* (fragment); *Enfances Oger le Danois*; *Roman de Fierabras*; selected *fabliaux*; Marie de France's *Fables*
Ownership: Charles de Croÿ, Count of Chimay (1455–1527)
Illustrations: One historiated initial (for *Le Chevalier aux Deux Épées*)
Comments: The final folio has an inscription that describes the contents of the manuscript as 'quatre livres en rime Cest assavoir Du roy Artus Des XII peres de France Du chevalier a deux espeez Et des Fables de ysopet' (*four books in verse relating to King Arthur, the Twelve Fathers of France, the Knight of the Two Swords and Aesop's Fables*) and is signed (in the same hand) by Charles de Croÿ, who was the count (and later prince) of Chimay.[23]

Paris, BnF, MS fr. 784 (MS P13)

Date: *c.* 1300[24]
Place: Paris
Contents: *Thèbes*; *Enéas*
Ownership: Jacques II de Bourbon, Count of La Marche (1370–1438); Jacques d'Armagnac, Duke of Nemours (1433–77)
Illustrations: Two miniatures and two historiated initials (one miniature and one historiated initial each for *Thèbes* and *Enéas*)
Comments: Morrison's work on this manuscript's illustrations and codicology has shown that it can be linked to MS P14; the two codices were either originally one manuscript and later rebound into separate manuscripts or for some reason were originally bound into two volumes.[25]

Paris, BnF, MS fr. 783 (MS P14)

Date: *c.* 1300
Place: Paris
Contents: *Troie*
Ownership: Jacques II de Bourbon, Count of La Marche (1370–1438); Jacques d'Armagnac, Duke of Nemours (1433–77)
Illustrations: One miniature and twenty-six historiated initials (connected to the illustrative cycle in MSS L2 and Mn)[26]
Comments: As mentioned above this manuscript was originally intended to form a complete set with the other two *romans* found in MS P13.

Paris, BnF, MS fr. 821 (MS P15)

Date: *c.* 1300–25
Place: North Italy
Contents: *Hector et Hercule*; Section IV (Greeks and Amazons) from *L'Histoire Ancienne jusqu'à César*; Macé de Troyes's *Distiques de Caton*; *Épître de Saint Bernard*; Bonaventure de Demena's *Consolatio Philosphiae*; *Passion*; *Secret des secrets* (fragment); *Dits des Sages*; *Troie*; Sections V–VI (Troy, Aeneas and Rome) from *L'Histoire Ancienne*; *Landomata*; Section IX (Alexander) from *L'Histoire Ancienne*
Ownership: Library of the dukes of Milan (1426–89)
Illustrations: Numerous medallion portraits (apparently with no specific connection to the texts)

Paris, BnF, MS fr. 19159 (MS P16)

Date: *c.* 1300–50
Place: North France
Contents: *Troie*
Ownership: Unknown
Illustrations: Space left for thirty-nine miniatures but never completed

Paris, BnF, MS fr. 60 (MS P17)

Date: *c.* 1330–40[27]
Place: Paris
Contents: *Thèbes*; *Troie*; *Enéas*
Ownership: Étienne Tabourot, Lord of the Accords (1549–90); Louis XIV of France (1640–1715)
Illustrations: Fifty-three miniatures (fourteen for *Thèbes*, thirty-two for *Troie*, seven for *Enéas*)
Comments: This manuscript was copied in Paris by numerous scribes and its miniatures were added by two prominent Parisian illuminators: the Fauvel Master and Richard de Montbaston. It includes a form of 'introduction' at the start of the collection:

Ci commence li roumans de Tiebes, qui fu racine de Troie la grant, ou il y a moult de merveilles diverses. Item toute l'estoire de Troie la grant, comment elle fu. ij. fois destruite par les Grijois et la cause pour quoi ce fu et les mortalitez qui y furent. Item toute l'histoire de Eneas et d'Ancises, qui s'enfuirent apres la destruction de Troie, et comment leurs oirs peuplerent les regions de deça mer, et	Here begins the roman de Thèbes, that was the origin of the great Troy, where there are many different wonders. Then all the history of the great Troy and how it was destroyed twice by the Greeks and the reason for that and all who died there. Then all the history of Aeneas and Anchises, who fled after Troy's destruction and how their descendants populated

| les granz merveilles qui d'euz issirent. | the regions of the sea and the great wonders that became them there. |
|---|---|//
(fol. 2ʳ)

Paris, BnF, MS fr. 782 (MS P18)

Date: *c.* 1340–50
Place: Verona, Padua or Venice
Contents: *Troie*
Ownership: Unknown
Illustrations: 202 miniatures (same cycle as MS Vn)
Comments: This manuscript is a copy of MS Vn. The main difference is that its illustrations all have captions and rubrics to identify the names of the characters in each miniature. We also know more about its production thanks to Cipollaro's study.[28] She is unable to identify the patron of this manuscript but is able to argue that while MS Vn may have been produced to be sold speculatively at a book market, MS P18 was more likely commissioned specifically by someone who had a relationship with the owner of MS Vn and wanted their own copy.[29]

Paris, BnF, MS nouv. acq. fr. 6774 (MS P19)

Date: *c.* 1350–1400
Place: Italy
Contents: *Troie*; Sections V–VI (Troy, Aeneas and Rome) from *L'Histoire Ancienne*
Ownership: Unknown
Illustrations: None

St Petersburg, Rossiiskaya Natsional'naya Biblioteka, MS fr. F.v.XIV.3 (MS SP1)

Date: *c.* 1340–60
Place: Bologna
Contents: *Troie*
Ownership: Unknown
Illustrations: 168 miniatures
Comments: This manuscript contains the same text as that of MS Vt and its miniatures may be linked to those in MSS Vn and P18. However, it was unfortunately not possible to consult the manuscript due to strict limits placed on its accessibility and the fact that it has not been digitized.

St Petersburg, Rossiiskaya Natsional'naya Biblioteka, MS fr. F.v.XIV.6 (MS SP2)

Date: *c.* 1380–1400
Place: Unknown
Contents: *Troie*

Ownership: Jean d'Averton, Lord of Couldreau (*c.* 1400–99); Charles V, Holy Roman Emperor (1500–58)
Illustrations: None

Vatican City, Biblioteca apostolica Vaticana, MS Reg. Lat. 1505 (MS Vt)

Date: *c.* 1275–1325
Place: Central Italy
Contents: *Troie*
Ownership: Possibly Robert of Anjou (1277–1343); Pierre Bourdelot (1610–85)
Illustrations: 254 miniatures (of which 2 are full-page) and 3 historiated initials
Comments: Hugo Buchthal finds a similarity between these miniatures and those of other manuscripts commissioned by Robert of Anjou, the King of Naples, suggesting that he may also have commissioned this manuscript.[30]

Venice, Biblioteca Nazionale Marciana, MS fr. 17 (MS V1)

Date: *c.* 1330–40
Place: Naples
Contents: *Troie*
Ownership: Francesco I Gonzaga (1366–1407) (possibly inherited from his grandfather, Guido Gonzaga (1290–1369), who also owned MS V2)
Illustrations: 422 miniatures
Comments: Several different artists of varying quality have produced the miniatures. Many of them are incomplete and are sketched outlines only without any pigmentation. They focus on people and animals but pay very little attention to architecture or landscape. Jung notes that their style is similar to the illustrations in a copy of the *L'Histoire Ancienne* (London, BL, MS Royal 20.D.I), which was also made in Naples at around the same time.[31]

Venice, Biblioteca Nazionale Marciana, MS fr. 18 (MS V2)

Date: *c.* 1360–69
Place: North Italy
Contents: *Troie*; *Hector et Hercule*
Ownership: Guido Gonzaga (1290–1369)
Illustrations: Two historiated initials (one for each text)
Comments: The two texts were not originally copied into the same manuscript but were bound together at a later point.[32]

Vienna, Österreichische Nationalbibliothek, MS Cod. 2471 (MS Vn)

Date: *c.* 1330–40
Place: North Italy, possibly Padua or Bologna
Contents: *Troie*

Ownership: Unknown
Illustrations: 199 miniatures (same cycle as MS P18)
Comments: This manuscript was the exemplar for MS P18 and they were probably produced in the same scriptorium.[33] H. J. Hermann and Dagmar Thoss have described its miniatures in detail.[34]

Appendix 2: Manuscript illustrations of women

MS L2

Fol. 109ʳ   Hecuba, Polyxena, Helen and other women mourn at Hector's tomb on the anniversary of his death.
Fol. 151ʳ   Penthesilea's body is thrown into the River Scamander.

MS M

Fol. 104ᵛ   A crowned woman (possibly Helen).
Fol. 156ᵛ   Penthesilea's body lies in state | Two women mourn.

MS Mn

Fol. 80ʳ   Women mourn at the anniversary of Hector's death.
Fol. 106ᵛ   Penthesilea and the Amazons arrive in Troy (damaged).
Fol. 112ʳ   Helen is brought before Priam by Antenor and Aeneas.

MS Nt

Fol. 12ʳ   Woman dressed in white robes holding a bird.
Fol. 92ʳ   Winged mermaid.
Fol. 121ᵛ   Penthesilea kneels before Priam and mourns the news of Hector's death (damaged).

MS P6

Fol. 18ʳ   Hercules and Laomedon in battle | Women and children are killed during the first sack of Troy (full page).
Removed[1] Council of Priam | Paris and the Trojans sail for Greece | Abduction of Helen (full page).
Fol. 90ʳ   Andromache, Priam and Hecuba plead with Hector.
Removed[2] Achilles kills Hector | Women and mourners around the body of Hector (full page).
Fol. 102ʳ   Women and mourners at the tomb of Hector on the anniversary of his death.
Fol. 129ʳ   Achilles and his messenger (to and from Hecuba) | Hecuba instructs Paris to kill Achilles.
Fol. 138ʳ   Penthesilea and the Amazons in battle.

156   Appendix 2: Manuscript Illustrations of Women

| Fol. 154ᵛ | Achilles drags the body of Troilus behind his horse | Ajax and Paris kill each other | Pyrrhus kills Penthesilea (full page). |
| Fol. 155ʳ | Sack of Troy and execution of Priam | Women are given away, execution of Polyxena and execution of Hecuba. |

MS P10

| Fol. 1ʳ | Meeting of Dido and Aeneas. |

MS P13

| Fol. 1ʳ | Jocasta and the birth of Oedipus. |
| Fol. 70ʳ | Dido watches Aeneas and the Trojans leave Carthage | Dido commits suicide. |

MS P14

| Fol. 109ʳ | Women mourn at the anniversary of Hector's death. |
| Fol. 141ʳ | Helen is brought before Priam by Antenor, Aeneas, Anchises and Polydamas. |

MS P17

Fol. 1ʳ	Jocasta with the baby Oedipus	Oedipus abandoned in a forest	Oedipus and the Sphinx	Battle (frontispiece).
Fol. 11ᵛ	Hipsipyle with Tydeus before Adrastus.
Fol. 42ᵛ	Jason fights the dragon	Abduction of Helen	Wooden horse is brought into Troy (frontispiece).
Fol. 47ʳ	Jason, Hercules, Medea and Aeëtes.
Fol. 59ʳ	Abduction of Helen (damaged).
Fol. 79ᵛ	Women remove Hector's armour	Women and Priam at the bedside of Hector.
Fol. 91ʳ	Briseide is handed over by the Trojans to the Greeks.
Fol. 94ʳ	Andromache pleads with Hector.
Fol. 97ᵛ	Women and Priam mourn at the tomb of Hector.
Fol. 101ʳ	Women and Priam mourn at the anniversary of Hector's death.
Fol. 126ʳ	Burning of Troy	Penthesilea's body is thrown into the river.
Fol. 148ᵛ	Burning of Troy	Aeneas sails from Troy	Dido welcomes Aeneas	Dido and Aeneas	Aeneas sails from Carthage	Suicide of Dido (frontispiece).
Fol. 162ʳ	Betrothal of Aeneas and Lavine	Amata and messenger.
Fol. 165ʳ	Aeneas and Evander	Venus gives armour to Aeneas's messenger.
Fol. 182ᵛ	Lavine watches as Aeneas and Turnus fight in single combat (damaged).

MS P18

Fol. 7^r	Medea, Jason, Hercules and Aeëtes.
Fol. 9^r	Aeëtes, Medea and Jason.
Fol. 10^r	Engagement of Jason and Medea.
Fol. 11^r	Jason and Medea in bed (damaged).
Fol. 12^r	Medea gives gifts to Jason	Jason and Medea embrace	Jason and Medea in bed.
Fol. 13^r	Medea watches as Jason sets out for the Golden Fleece.
Fol. 20^r	Hesione and other Trojan women are abducted during the sack of Troy.
Fol. 20^v	Priam and Hecuba learn of the death of Laomedon and abduction of Hesione.
Fol. 31^r	Abduction of Helen from the Temple of Venus.
Fol. 32^r	Paris, Helen and other Trojans sail for Troy.
Fol. 33^r	Paris and Helen at Tenedos.
Fol. 34^r	Paris and Helen are greeted by Priam.
Fol. 67^r	Cassandra mourns Cassibelan and makes her prophecies.
Fol. 77^r	Hecuba, Cassandra and Polyxena meet with Troilus and Paris while Hector speaks with Priam.
Fol. 87^r	Troilus and Briseide lament their separation	Troilus and Briseide embrace.
Fol. 88^r	Briseide is handed over by the Trojans to the Greeks.
Fol. 89^r	Briseide and Diomedes ride together into the Greek camp.
Fol. 90^r	Reunion of Calcas and Briseide.
Fol. 96^v	Women and Master Goz gather around Hector's bedside.
Fol. 99^r	Briseide gives her sleeve to Diomedes.
Fol. 101^r	Andromache pleads with Hector.
Fol. 102^r	Priam pleads with Hector.
Fol. 104^r	Trojan women mourn as Margariton's body is brought back into Troy.
Fol. 105^r	Cassandra and Andromache watch a battle from inside Troy.
Fol. 108^r	Andromache, Priam, Paris and other Trojans mourn around Hector's body.
Fol. 110^r	Women at Hector's funeral.
Fol. 116^r	Achilles sees Polyxena at the anniversary of Hector's death.
Fol. 118^r	Hecuba speaks to Achilles's messenger.
Fol. 119^r	Hecuba speaks with Priam.
Fol. 119^v	Hecuba speaks to Achilles's messenger.
Fol. 136^r	Briseide cares for Diomedes at his bedside.
Fol. 148^r	Hecuba and Paris plot Achilles's death.
Fol. 151^r	Polyxena as a statue above Achilles's tomb.
Fol. 156^r	Women at Paris's funeral.
Fol. 158^r	Penthesilea and the Amazons arrive in Troy and are greeted by Priam.
Fol. 159^r	Penthesilea and the Amazons in battle.
Fol. 163^r	Penthesilea and the Amazons in battle.
Fol. 164^r	Pyrrhus kills Penthesilea.

158 Appendix 2: Manuscript Illustrations of Women

Fol. 165ʳ	The Greeks throw Penthesilea's body into the river.
Fol. 173ʳ	Philemenis departs to escort Penthesilea's funeral cortège back to Femenie.
Fol. 179ʳ	Antenor brings Polyxena before Agamemnon and Ulysses.
Fol. 180ʳ	Execution of Polyxena and Hecuba.
Fol. 184ʳ	Cassandra's prophecies to Agamemnon.
Fol. 193ʳ	Orestes kills Clytemenestra and Egistus.
Fol. 196ʳ	Ulysses meets Circe and Calypso.
Fol. 197ʳ	Ulysses and the sirens (as mermaids).
Fol. 201ʳ	Pyrrhus and Thetis.
Fol. 202ʳ	Andromache flees from Hermione and Menelaus.
Fol. 206ʳ	Penelope by Ulysses's deathbed.

MS Vt

Fol. 11ʳ	Medea outside Jason's bedchamber.
Fol. 12ʳ	Medea and Jason at the Temple of Jupiter | Medea and Jason in bed.
Fol. 12ᵛ	Medea gives gifts to Jason.
Fol. 13ᵛ	Medea watches Jason sail away on his quest for the Golden Fleece.
Fol. 15ʳ	Medea watches Jason return with the Golden Fleece.
Fol. 21ᵛ	Hesione is abducted during the first sack of Troy.
Fol. 33ʳ	Helen and Paris's first meeting in the Temple of Venus (damaged).
Fol. 34ʳ	Abduction of Helen and other Greek women.
Fol. 35ʳ	Helen and the Trojans sail for Troy.
Fol. 36ʳ	Helen and Paris at Tenedon.
Fol. 36ᵛ	Helen and Paris ride to Troy (damaged).
Fol. 37ʳ	Helen and Paris ride into Troy.
Fol. 42³	Cassandra, Hecuba, Andromache and Polyxena. Cassandra holds a scroll of her prophecies.
Fol. 77ʳ	Hector is cared for by Cassandra, Hecuba, Helen, Andromache and Polyxena.
Fol. 78ᵛ	Cassandra watches as the body of Cassibelan is brought into the city.
Fol. 90ᵛ	Polidamas, Troilus, Antenor and Aeneas visit Hecuba, Helen, Andromache and Polyxena.
Fol. 91ᵛ	Antenor, Aeneas, Polidamas and Troilus visit Hecuba, Helen, Andromache and Polyxena. Helen gives a gift to Polidamas and Polyxena embraces Troilus.
Fol. 104ʳ	Briseide is handed over by the Trojans to the Greeks.
Fol. 106ʳ	Briseide inside the Greek camp.
Fol. 108ʳ	Women watch a battle from the towers of Troy.
Fol. 110ʳ	Diomedes's squire gives Troilus's horse to Briseide.
Fol. 112ᵛ	Women at Hector's bedside in the Chamber of Beauties (full page).
Fol. 115ᵛ	Briseide and Diomedes.
Fol. 118ᵛ	Andromache pleads with Hector (damaged).

Appendix 2: Manuscript Illustrations of Women

Fol. 126ʳ	Hecuba, Andromache, Helen, Cassandra, Polyxena, other women and Trojan men mourn over Hector's dead body.
Fol. 128ᵛ	Women and men mourn at Hector's tomb.
Fol. 133ᵛ	Hecuba, Andromache, Helen, Polyxena and Greek men. Probably the anniversary of Hector's death.
Fol. 135ᵛ	Achilles's messenger speaks with Hecuba.
Fol. 136ᵛ	Hecuba speaks with Priam about Achilles's proposal.
Fol. 137⁵	Hecuba speaks with Achilles's messenger, with Polyxena next to the messenger.
Fol. 157ᵛ	Polyxena, Helen, Hecuba and other women care for and remove Troilus's armour and weapons.
Fol. 165ᵛ	Helen, Hecuba, Polyxena, Cassandra, other women and Trojan men mourn over Troilus's dead body.
Fol. 166ᵛ	Hecuba plots the death of Achilles with Paris.
Fol. 168ᵛ	Hecuba plots the death of Achilles with Paris.
Fol. 170ᵛ	Polyxena depicted in effigy over the tomb of Achilles.
Fol. 174ᵛ	Hecuba, Cassandra, Polyxena, Andromache, Helen, other women and Trojan men mourn over Paris's dead body.
Fol. 175ᵛ	Polyxena, Helen, Hecuba, Cassandra, other women and Trojan men mourn at Paris's funeral.
Fol. 178ᵛ	Arrival of Penthesilea and the Amazons, who are met by Paris.
Fol. 179ᵛ	Penthesilea in battle.
Fol. 182ʳ	Penthesilea in battle.
Fol. 183ᵛ	Penthesilea in battle.
Fol. 184ʳ	Penthesilea in battle.
Fol. 185ʳ	Pyrrhus kills Penthesilea.
Fol. 192ᵛ	Helen pleads with Antenor during the sack of Troy.
Fol. 199ʳ	Cassandra and other Trojan women are taken prisoner or killed during the sack of Troy.
Fol. 199ᵛ	Pyrrhus kills Priam	Aeneas finds Polyxena and Hecuba during the sack of the city	Helen is seized by a Greek soldier.
Fol. 200ʳ	Andromache is taken prisoner during the sack of the city	Burning of Troy.
Fol. 200ᵛ	Trojan women wait with the other treasures of Troy for distribution as prizes to the Greeks.
Fol. 201ʳ	Cassandra, Andromache and her children are given away to the Greek nobles.
Fol. 202ᵛ	Polyxena is held prisoner during the Greek deliberations.
Fol. 203ʳ	Execution of Hecuba and Polyxena.
Fol. 203ᵛ	Hecuba's tomb.
Fol. 213ᵛ	Egial speaks with Orestes	Clytemenestra speaks with Orestes.
Fol. 215ʳ	Clytemenestra and Egistus kill Agamemnon.
Fol. 216ʳ	Diomedes arrives home to be reunited with Egial.
Fol. 217ᵛ	Orestes kills Clytemenestra and Egistus.

160   Appendix 2: Manuscript Illustrations of Women

Fol. 218ᵛ	Hermione and Menelaus.
Fol. 224ᵛ	Pyrrhus and Thetis.
Fol. 225ᵛ	Pyrrhus and Thetis.
Fol. 226ᵛ	Pyrrhus and Hermione.
Fol. 227ᵛ	Orestes kills Pyrrhus | Hermione and Orestes | Peleus and Thetis mourn over Pyrrhus's tomb.
Fol. 229ᵛ	Circe and Telegonus.
Fol. 231ʳ	Penelope at Ulysses's bedside.
Fol. 232ᵛ	Circe and Telegonus.

MS V1

Fol. 8ᵛ	Medea at a banquet with Jason and other men.
Fol. 9ʳ	Medea and Jason in conversation.
Fol. 9ᵛ	Medea stands next to her bed.
Fol. 10ʳ	Medea speaks with her maid | Medea in bed while Jason stands next to her.
Fol. 10ᵛ	Medea gives gifts to Jason | Medea and Jason in bed (damaged).
Fol. 11ʳ	Medea gives a parchment to Jason | Jason and Medea kiss.
Fol. 11ᵛ	Jason speaks with Aeëtes | Medea watches Jason sail away.
Fol. 12ᵛ	Medea watches Jason return.
Fol. 18ᵛ	Priam, Hecuba, Cassandra, Polyxena and other Trojans on horses.
Fol. 28ʳ	Helen and her ladies arrive at the Temple of Venus.
Fol. 28ᵛ	Helen and Paris meet for the first time.
Fol. 29ᵛ	Helen and the other ladies are abducted.
Fol. 30ʳ	Helen is led up the gangplank onto the Trojan ships | Helen and the Trojans sail from Greece.
Fol. 31ʳ	Helen asks Paris to release her ladies' husbands.
Fol. 31ᵛ	Helen and Paris speak at Tenedos.
Fol. 32ʳ	Paris and Helen ride towards Troy and are met by Priam.
Fol. 32ᵛ	Helen and the other Trojans ride into Troy.
Fol. 33ʳ	Marriage of Helen and Paris.
Fol. 35ᵛ	Portrait of Helen and other Greek nobles.
Fol. 37ʳ	Portrait of Hecuba, Cassandra, Polyxena, Andromache and Trojan nobles.
Fol. 58ʳ	Women watch a battle from Troy's walls.
Fol. 75ᵛ	Hector has his armour removed by Trojan women.
Fol. 76ʳ	Doctor and women at Hector's bedside.
Fol. 77ᵛ	Cassandra and other women mourn Cassibelan's death.
Fol. 79ʳ	Women watch a battle from Troy's walls.
Fol. 90ᵛ	Hector has his armour removed by Trojan women.
Fol. 91ᵛ	Visit of the Trojan men to the Trojan women.
Fol. 104ʳ	Briseide laments the decision to send her to the Greek camp.
Fol. 104ᵛ	Troilus and Briseide in bed.
Fol. 105ʳ	Briseide packs to go to the Greek camp.

Appendix 2: Manuscript Illustrations of Women 161

Fol. 106^r	Briseide is handed over from the Trojans to the Greeks.
Fol. 107^r	Briseide and Diomedes ride towards Calcas's tent.
Fol. 108^r	Reunion of Briseide and Calcas.
Fol. 108^v	Briseide in the Greek tents.
Fol. 109^r	Women watch a battle from Troy's walls.
Fol. 110^v	Women watch a battle from Troy's walls.
Fol. 111^r	Women watch a battle from Troy's walls.
Fol. 112^r	Diomedes unhorses Troilus	Diomedes's squire gives Troilus's horse to Briseide.
Fol. 112^v	Women watch a battle from Troy's walls.
Fol. 114^r	Women and other Trojans gather around Hector's bedside.
Fol. 115^v	Briseide and Diomedes.
Fol. 116^r	Briseide and Diomedes.
Fol. 116^v	Briseide and Diomedes.
Fol. 118^v	Andromache tells Hector her vision.
Fol. 119^r	Priam pleads with Hector while the Trojan forces ride out of the city.
Fol. 119^v	Andromache speaks to Priam and Hecuba	Andromache and the other Trojan ladies plead with Hector.
Fol. 120^r	Andromache pleads with Hector.
Fol. 120^v	Hector and his squire	Andromache speaks with Priam.
Fol. 125^v	Hector rejoins the fighting as Andromache faints.
Fol. 127^v	Women and other Trojans mourn around Hector's bed.
Fol. 128^r	Women and other Trojans mourn around Hector's bed.
Fol. 129^r	Women and other Trojans mourn around Hector's bed.
Fol. 129^v	Women in attendance at Hector's funeral.
Fol. 137^v	Women in attendance at the anniversary of Hector's death.
Fol. 138^r	Women in attendance at the anniversary of Hector's death. Achilles sees Polyxena.
Fol. 139^v	Hecuba speaks with Achilles's messenger.
Fol. 140^r	Hecuba speaks with Achilles's messenger.
Fol. 140^v	Hecuba speaks with Priam.
Fol. 141^r	Hecuba (and Polyxena) speaks to Achilles's messenger.
Fol. 148^v	Women watching a battle from Troy's walls.
Fol. 158^v	Women at the bedside of Agamemnon and Diomedes.
Fol. 161^v	Troilus has his armour removed by Trojan women.
Fol. 169^v	Women mourn around Troilus's body.
Fol. 170^r	Women mourn around Troilus's body.
Fol. 171^v	Hecuba and Paris plot to kill Achilles.
Fol. 172^r	Hecuba and Paris plot to kill Achilles.
Fol. 175^v	Statue of Polyxena on the tomb of Achilles.
Fol. 179^r	Women mourn around Paris's body.
Fol. 180^v	Penthesilea and the Amazons arrive in Troy and are met by Priam.
Fol. 182^r	Penthesilea and the Amazons in battle.
Fol. 182^v	Penthesilea and the Amazons in battle.
Fol. 185^v	Penthesilea and the Amazons in battle.

Fol. 186ʳ	Penthesilea and the Amazons in battle.
Fol. 187ᵛ	Pyrrhus kills Penthesilea.
Fol. 196ʳ	Penthesilea is recovered from the river	Helen is brought before Priam by Aeneas and Antenor.
Fol. 200ᵛ	Penthesilea's funeral cortège leaves the city.
Fol. 202ᵛ	Women and children are killed during the sack of Troy.
Fol. 203ʳ	Women and children are killed during the sack of Troy.
Fol. 203ᵛ	Pyrrhus kills Priam	Andromache and Cassandra are taken prisoner.
Fol. 204ʳ	Andromache and Cassandra are taken prisoner	Destruction of the city.
Fol. 204ᵛ	Cassandra is given to Agamemnon.
Fol. 205ʳ	Helenus, Andromache and her sons are given to Pyrrhus.
Fol. 206ᵛ	Execution of Polyxena and laments of Hecuba.
Fol. 207ʳ	Protests of Hecuba and her execution.
Fol. 209ᵛ	Final prophecies of Cassandra.
Fol. 217ᵛ	Orestes kills Clytemenestra and Egistus.
Fol. 219ᵛ	Hermione and Menelaus.
Fol. 227ʳ	Escape of Andromache.

MS Vn

Fol. 8ʳ	Medea, Jason, Hercules and Aeëtes.
Fol. 8ᵛ	Aeëtes, Medea and Jason.
Fol. 9ʳ	Engagement of Jason and Medea.
Fol. 10ʳ	Medea in bed while Jason stands next to her.
Fol. 11ʳ	Medea gives gifts to Jason	Jason and Medea embrace	Jason and Medea in bed (damaged).
Fol. 12ʳ	Medea watches Jason set out on his quest for the Golden Fleece.
Fol. 18ʳ	Hesione and other Trojan women are abducted during the sack of Troy.
Fol. 18ᵛ	Priam and Hecuba learn of the death of Laomedon and abduction of Hesione.
Fol. 27ʳ	Abduction of Helen from the Temple of Venus.
Fol. 29ʳ	Paris, Helen and other Trojans sail for Troy.
Fol. 29ᵛ	Paris and Helen at Tenedos.
Fol. 30ʳ	Paris and Helen are greeted by Priam as they ride into Troy.
Fol. 59ʳ	Cassandra mourns Cassibelan and makes her prophecies.
Fol. 68ʳ	Hecuba, Cassandra and Polyxena meet with Troilus and Paris while Hector speaks with Priam.
Fol. 77ʳ	Troilus and Briseide lament their separation	Troilus and Briseide embrace.
Fol. 79ʳ	Briseide is handed over by the Trojans to the Greeks.
Fol. 80ʳ	Briseide and Diomedes ride together into the Greek camp.
Fol. 81ʳ	Reunion of Calcas and Briseide.
Fol. 86ʳ	Women and Master Goz gather around Hector's bedside.
Fol. 87ʳ	Briseide speaks with Diomedes.
Fol. 90ʳ	Andromache pleads with Hector.

Appendix 2: Manuscript Illustrations of Women 163

Fol. 91^r	Priam pleads with Hector.
Fol. 93^r	Trojan women mourn as Margariton's body is brought back into Troy.
Fol. 94^r	Cassandra and Andromache watch a battle from inside Troy.
Fol. 96^r	Andromache, Priam, Paris and other Trojans mourn around Hector's body.
Fol. 99^r	Women in attendance at Hector's funeral.
Fol. 103^r	Achilles sees Polyxena for the first time at the anniversary of Hector's death.
Fol. 107^r	Hecuba speaks to Achilles's messenger.
Fol. 107^v	Hecuba speaks with Priam.
Fol. 108^r	Hecuba speaks to Achilles's messenger.
Fol. 122^r	Briseide cares for Diomedes at his bedside.
Fol. 132^r	Hecuba and Paris plot Achilles's death.
Fol. 136^r	Polyxena as a statue above Achilles's tomb.
Fol. 140^r	Women in attendance at Paris's funeral.
Fol. 141^r	Penthesilea and the Amazons arrive in Troy and are greeted by Priam.
Fol. 143^r	Penthesilea and the Amazons in battle.
Fol. 146^r	Penthesilea and the Amazons in battle.
Fol. 148^r	Pyrrhus kills Penthesilea.
Fol. 149^r	Greeks throw Penthesilea's body into the river.
Fol. 160^r	Execution of Polyxena and Hecuba.
Fol. 161^r	Philemenis departs to escort Penthesilea's funeral cortège back to Femenie.
Fol. 166^r	Women and children are killed during the sack of the city.
Fol. 166^v	Women and children are killed during the sack of the city.
Fol. 167^r	Antenor brings Polyxena before Agamemnon and Ulysses.
Fol. 169^r	Cassandra's prophecies to Agamemnon.
Fol. 177^r	Ulysses meets Circe and Calypso.
Fol. 178^r	Ulysses and the sirens (as mermaids).
Fol. 182^r	Pyrrhus and Thetis.
Fol. 183^r	Andromache flees from Hermione and Menelaus.
Fol. 187^r	Penelope at Ulysses's deathbed.

Notes

Introduction

1. Heather J. Tanner, Laura L. Gathagan and Lois L. Huneycutt, 'Introduction', in Heather J. Tanner (ed), *Medieval Elite Women and the Exercise of Power, 1100–1400: Moving beyond the Exceptionalist Debate* (Cham: Palgrave Macmillan, 2019), pp. 1–18 (p. 15).
2. Benoît de Sainte-Maure, *The Roman de Troie*, trans. by Glyn S. Burgess and Douglas Kelly (Cambridge: D. S. Brewer, 2017), p. iv.
3. Georges Duby, *Les Trois Ordres ou l'Imaginaire du Féodalisme* (Paris: Gallimard, 1978).
4. Theodore Evergates, 'The feudal imaginary of Georges Duby', *Journal of Medieval and Early Modern Studies* 27 (1997), pp. 641–60 (p. 651).
5. Georges Duby, *Love and Marriage in the Middle Ages*, trans. by Jane Dunnett (Chicago: University of Chicago Press, 1996), p. vii. This book had originally been published under the title *Mâle Moyen Âge* in 1988.
6. Evergates, 'The feudal imaginary of Georges Duby', p. 646. See also, Amy Livingstone, 'Pour une revision du "mâle" Moyen Âge de Georges Duby (États-Unis)', *Clio: Histoire, femmes et sociétés* 8 (1998), 1–12.
7. Jean Bodel, *La Chanson des Saisnes*, ed. by Annette Brasseur (Geneva: Droz, 1989), l. 6.
8. The many ways in which the *romans* reflect a medieval rather than a classical world are detailed and analysed in Aimé Petit, *L'Anachronisme dans les Romans Antiques du XIIe siècle: le Roman de Thèbes, le Roman d'Enéas, le Roman de Troie, le Roman d'Alexandre* (Paris: Champion, 2002).
9. The final chapter of Catherine Hanley's study of war and combat in Old French literature includes *Enéas* as part of its corpus, but not *Troie* or *Thèbes*: Catherine Hanley, *War and Combat, 1150–1270: The Evidence from Old French Literature* (Cambridge: Brewer, 2003), pp. 163–225.
10. For a complete survey of the current state of scholarship on the *romans*, see Sophie Harwood, 'Women and war in the Old French Troy tradition: literary and artistic representations of female agency in the *Romans d'Antiquité*' (unpublished PhD thesis, University of Leeds, 2017), pp. 5–9.
11. Sarah Kay, *The Chansons de Geste in the Age of Romance* (Oxford: Clarendon Press, 1995), pp. 25–48. For a later examination of women's role in Old French *chansons de geste*, see Hanley, *War and Combat*, pp. 137–45.
12. Anne D. Hedeman, *The Royal Image: Illustrations of the 'Grandes Chroniques de France', 1272–1422* (Berkeley: University of California Press, 1991); Elizabeth Morrison, 'Illuminations of the *Roman de Troie* and French royal dynastic ambition (1260–1340)' (unpublished PhD thesis, Cornell University, 2002), pp. 82–106; Elizabeth Morrison, 'Linking ancient Troy and medieval France: illuminations of an early copy of the *Roman de Troie*', in *Medieval Manuscripts, Their Makers and Users. A Special Issue of Viator in Honor of Richard and Mary Rouse* (Turnhout: Brepols, 2011), pp. 72–102.
13. For example, in their introduction to their translation of *Troie*, Burgess and Kelly include three pages dedicated to 'women in war'. However, their assessment is that

women's primary representation in the text is as 'exchangeable objects and booty' and that Penthesilea is only able to access the role of warrior and undertake chivalric exploits because she is 'manly' (Benoît, *The Roman de Troie*, trans. by Burgess and Kelly, pp. 26–28). Such a generalization is one that this book seeks to challenge.

14 The only illustrated manuscript I was unable to consult was MS SP1, although my thanks go to Dr Marina Tramet for her support in my quest to reach the Rossiiskaya Natsional'naya Biblioteka, even if it eventually proved unsuccessful. Selected images from MS SP1 are available as reproductions in the work of a few scholars: Jung includes black-and-white copies of eight of its miniatures and he provides a bibliography for four other scholars who have reproduced selected miniatures: Marc-René Jung, *La Légende de Troie en France au Moyen Âge: Analyse des Versions Françaises et Bibliographie Raisonnée des Manuscrits* (Basel: Francke, 1996), pp. 255, 276–90 (plates 21–28). However, due to the poor quality of most of these reproductions, the fact that they represent only a tenth of the manuscript's total illustrations and given that no original research could be carried out, my work does not include this manuscript in its analysis or discussion.

15 Simon Gaunt and Sarah Kay, 'Introduction', in Simon Gaunt and Sarah Kay (eds), *The Cambridge Companion to Medieval French Literature* (Cambridge: Cambridge University Press, 2008), pp. 1–18 (p. 13).

16 Silvère Menegaldo, 'De la traduction à l'invention. La naissance du genre romanesque au XIIe siècle', in Claudio Galderisi (ed), *Translations Médiévales: Cinq siècles de traductions en français au Moyen Âge (XIe–XVe siècles)* (Turnhout: Brepols, 2011), pp. 295–323 (p. 311).

17 Although there was not a complete version there was a short translation (just over a thousand lines and ending after the death of Hector) in the first century, known as the *Ilias Latina*, which was relatively well known during the Middle Ages. It was read in schools during the Carolingian period and continued to be a part of the curriculum in the following centuries: E. R. Curtius, *European Literature and the Latin Middle Ages*, trans. by W. R. Trask (Princeton: Princeton University Press, 1952), pp. 49, 56, 260 and 464; Marco Scaffai, *Baebii Italici Ilias Latina: Introduzione, Edizione Critica, Traduzione Italiana e Commento* (Bologna: Pàtron Editore, 1982), pp. 33–35. It is often found bound in manuscripts with Dares's and Dictys's works: George A. Kennedy, *The Latin Iliad: Introduction, Text, Translation and Notes* (Fort Collins: Privately published, 1998), p. 12. It is possible that Benoît therefore had access to an abridged version of Homer's Trojan story, too.

18 See Edmond Faral, *Recherches sur les Sources Latines des Contes et Romans Courtois du Moyen Âge* (Paris: Champion, 1913), p. 416; Douglas Kelly, 'The invention of Briseide's story in Benoît de Sainte-Maure's *Troie*', *Romance Philology* 48 (1995), pp. 221–41; Tamara F. O'Callaghan, 'Tempering scandal: Eleanor of Aquitaine and Benoît de Sainte-Maure's *Roman de Troie*', in Bonnie Wheeler and John Carmi Parsons (eds), *Eleanor of Aquitaine: Lord and Lady* (New York: Palgrave Macmillan, 2003), pp. 301–17; Aimé Petit, 'Aspects de l'influence d'Ovide sur les romans antiques du XIIe siècle', in Raymond Chevallier (ed), *Présence d'Ovide. Actes du Colloque d'Azay-le-Ferron (26-28 Septembre 1980)* (Paris: Les Belles Lettres, 1982), pp. 219–40 (pp. 220–32).

19 Quotations from and translations of *Daretis Phrygii de excidio Trojae historia* are taken from *The Other Trojan War: Dictys and Dares Parallel Texts*, ed. and trans. by Giles Laurén (Berlin: Sophron, 2012) and are referenced by book and chapter number.

20 Quotations from and translations of *Dictys Cretensis Ephemeridos belli Trojani* are also taken from Laurén's *The Other Trojan War* and are referenced by book and chapter number.
21 Petit, *L'Anachronisme dans les Romans Antiques du XIIe siècle: le Roman de Thèbes, le Roman d'Enéas, le Roman de Troie, le Roman d'Alexandre*.
22 Helen Nicholson, *Medieval Warfare: Theory and Practice of War in Europe, 300–1500* (Basingstoke: Palgrave Macmillan, 2003), p. 102.
23 Roger Dragonetti, *Le Mirage des Sources: L'Art du Faux dans le Roman Medieval* (Paris: Editions du Seuil, 1987), pp. 47–48; Menegaldo, 'De la traduction à l'invention', pp. 295–323.
24 F. M. Warren, 'On the Latin sources of *Thèbes* and *Enéas*', *Publications of the Modern Language Association of America* 16 (1901), pp. 375–87 (pp. 375–79).
25 Dominique Battles, *The Medieval Tradition of Thèbes: History and Narrative in the Old French Roman de Thèbes, Boccaccio, Chaucer and Lydgate* (New York: Routledge, 2004), pp. 19–25.
26 Joan M. Ferrante and Robert W. Hanning, 'Introduction', in Joan M. Ferrante and Robert W. Hanning (trans), *The Romance of Thebes* (Tempe: ACMRS, 2018), pp. 1–50 (p. 9).
27 This fact has also been noted by Ferrante and Hanning, who include their own comparison of the women from *Thèbes* and the women from the *Thebaid* in their introduction to their new translation of the text. See Ferrante and Hanning, 'Introduction', pp. 16–20.
28 References to the *Thebaid* use J. H. Mozley's edition and are referred to by book and line number.
29 See Battles, *The Medieval Tradition of Thèbes*, pp. 19–60; Faral, *Recherches*, p. 63; Petit, 'Aspects de l'influence d'Ovid', pp. 220–32.
30 See, for example, Raymond J. Cormier, *One Heart, One Mind: The Rebirth of Virgil's Hero in Medieval French Romance* (Oxford, MI: University of Mississippi Press, 1973); Raymond J. Cormier, 'An example of twelfth-century *adaptatio*: the *Roman d'Enéas*-author's ese of glossed *Aeneid* manuscripts', *Revue d'Histoire des Textes* 19 (1989), pp. 277–89; Raymond J. Cormier, 'Classical continuity and transposition in two twelfth-century adaptations of the *Aeneid*', *Symposium: A Quarterly Journal in Modern Literatures* 47 (1994), pp. 261–74; Jessie Crosland, '*Enéas* and the *Aeneid*', *The Modern Language Review* 29 (1934), pp. 282–90; Edmond Faral, 'Ovide et quelques autres sources du *Roman d'Enéas*', *Romania* 40 (1911), pp. 161–234; Francine Mora-Lebrun, 'Sources de l'*Enéas*: La tradition exégétique et le modèle épique latin', in Jean Dufournet (ed), *Relire le Roman d'Enéas* (Paris: Champion, 1985), pp. 83–104; Barbara Nolan, 'The judgement of Paris in the *Roman d'Énéas*: a new look at sources and significance', *Classical Bulletin* 56 (1980), pp. 52–56; Barbara Nolan, 'Ovid's *Heroides* contextualized: foolish love and legitimate marriage in the *Roman d'Enéas*', *Mediaevalia* 13 (1989), pp. 157–87; Nancy P. Pope, 'The *Aeneid* and the *Roman d'Enéas*: a medieval translator at work', *Papers on Language and Literature* 16 (1980), pp. 243–49; Jerome Singerman, *Under Clouds of Poesy: Poetry and Truth in French and English Reworkings of the Aeneid, 1160–1513* (New York: Garland, 1986).
31 For Dido, see Marilynn Desmond, *Reading Dido: Gender, Textuality and the Medieval Aeneid* (Minneapolis: University of Minnesota Press, 1994), pp. 114–15; Singerman, *Under Clouds of Poesy*, pp. 49–52 and p. 114. For Lavine, see Faral, 'Ovide et quelques autres sources', *passim*; Nolan, 'Ovid's *Heroides*', pp. 157–87; Petit, 'Aspects de l'influence d'Ovide', pp. 219–40.
32 There is a lot of recent scholarship on the topic of women and power in the twelfth century. For example, see Judith A. Green, 'Aristocratic women in early twelfth-century England', in C. Warren Hollister (ed), *Anglo-Norman Political Culture and*

the *Twelfth-Century Renaissance: Proceedings of the Borchard Conerence on Anglo-Norman History, 1995* (Woodbridge: Boydell Press, 1997), pp. 59–82 and 'Duchesses of Normandy in the eleventh and twelfth centuries', in David Crouch and Kathleen Thompson (eds), *Normandy and Its Neighbours, 900–1250: Essays for David Bates* (Turnhout: Brepols, 2011), pp. 43–59; Lois L. Huneycutt, 'Female succession and the language of power in the writings of twelfth-century churchmen', in John Carmi Parsons (ed), *Medieval Queenship* (Stroud: Alan Sutton, 1994), pp. 189–201; Susan M. Johns (ed), *Noblewomen, Aristocracy and Power in the Twelfth-Century Anglo-Norman Realm* (Manchester: Manchester University Press, 2003); Pauline Stafford, 'The portrayal of royal women in England, mid-tenth to mid-twelfth centuries', in John Carmi Parsons (ed), *Medieval Queenship* (Stroud: Alan Sutton, 1994), pp. 143–67; R. N. Swanson, *The Twelfth-Century Renaissance* (Manchester: Manchester University Press, 1999), pp. 188–206; Heather J. Tanner (ed), *Medieval Elite Women and the Exercise of Power, 1100–1400: Moving beyond the Exceptionalist Debate* (Cham: Palgrave Macmillan, 2019).

Chapter 1

1   A complete manuscript catalogue with details of all the manuscripts discussed in this chapter is available as Appendix 1. This only takes into consideration complete copies of the texts and does not include manuscript fragments.
2   This is the view in Emmanuèle Baumgartner and Françoise Veillard, see Benoît de Sainte-Maure, 'Introduction', Emmanuele Baumgartner and Françoise Veillard (eds), *Le Roman de Troie* (Paris: Librairie Générale Française, 1998), pp. 5–29 (p. 6); Catherine Desprès Caubrière, 'L'enjeu triangulaire de la trame romanesque du *Roman d'Énéas*', *Çédille* 9 (2013), pp. 129–44 (p. 136); F. A. G. Cowper, 'Date and dedication of the *Roman de Troie*', *Modern Philology* 27 (1930), pp. 379–82; Raymond J. Cormier, 'Pagan versus Christian values in the *Roman d'Enéas*', *Medievalia et Humanistica* 33 (2007), pp. 63–86 (p. 64); Marilynn Desmond, 'History and fiction: the narrativity and historiography of the Matter of Troy', in William Burgwinkle, Nicholas Hammond and Emma Wilson (eds), *The Cambridge History of French Literature* (Cambridge: Cambridge University Press, 2011), pp. 139–44 (p. 141); Peter Dronke, 'Peter of Blois and poetry at the court of Henry II', *Mediaeval Studies* 38 (1976), pp. 185–235 (p. 186); Joan M. Ferrante and Robert W. Hanning, 'Introduction', in Joan M. Ferrante and Robert W. Hanning (trans), *The Romance of Thebes* (Tempe: ACMRS, 2018), pp. 1–50 (p. 4); Judith Haas, 'Trojan sodomy and the politics of marriage in the *Roman d'Enéas*', *Exemplaria* 20 (2008), pp. 48–71 (p. 59); Rita Lejeune, 'Rôle littéraire d'Aliénor d'Aquitaine et de sa famille', *Cultura Neolatina* 14 (1954), pp. 5–57 (p. 22); Francine Mora-Lebrun, 'Introduction', in Francine Mora Lebrun (ed), *Le Roman de Thebes* (Paris: Livre de Poche, 1995), pp. 5–32 (p. 7); Aimé Petit, 'Introduction', in *Le Roman d'Enéas*, ed. by Aimé Petit (Paris: Livre de Poche, 1997), pp. 7–21 (p. 9); Zrinka Stahuljak, *Bloodless Genealogies of the French Middle Ages: Translation, Kinship and Metaphor* (Gainesville: University Press of Florida, 2005), pp. 36–78.
3   See Benoît de Saint-Maure, *Roman de Troie*, ed. by Léopold Constans, 6 vols (Paris: Société des Anciens Textes Français, 1904–12), Vol. 6, p. 189 and Cowper, 'Date and dedication', p. 380.
4   Tamara F. O'Callaghan, 'Tempering scandal: Eleanor of Aquitaine and Benoît de Sainte-Maure's *Roman de Troie*', in Bonnie Wheeler and John Carmi Parsons (eds), *Eleanor of Aquitaine: Lord and Lady* (New York: Palgrave Macmillan, 2003), pp. 301–17 (p. 303).

5   Elizabeth. E. R. Brown, 'Eleanor of Aquitaine: parent, queen, and duchess', in William W. Kibler (ed), *Eleanor of Aquitaine: Patron and Politician* (Austin: University of Texas Press, 1976), pp. 9–34 (p. 10).
6   Karen M. Broadhurst, 'Henry II of England and Eleanor of Aquitaine: patrons of literature in French?', *Viator* 27 (1996), pp. 53–84 (p. 73).
7   It is omitted from MSS L1, P1, N, P2, P5, P9, L2, P11, P14, Mn and P15. Benoît, *Troie*, VI, pp. 25 and 189.
8   Transcribed by Constans in Benoît, Troie, VI, p. 25.
9   Cowper, 'Date and dedication', p. 382.
10 For more on the decline of Eleanor's reputation in the thirteenth and fourteenth centuries, see Michael R. Evans, *Inventing Eleanor: The Medieval and Post-Medieval Image of Eleanor of Aquitaine* (London: Bloomsbury, 2014), Chapters 1–2; Peggy McCracken, 'Scandalising desire: Eleanor of Aquitaine and the chroniclers', in Wheeler and Parsons (eds), *Eleanor of Aquitaine*, pp. 247–63; Fiona Tolhurst, 'What ever happened to Eleanor? Reflections of Eleanor of Aquitaine in Wace's *Roman de Brut* and Lawman's *Brut*', in Wheeler and Parsons (eds), *Eleanor of Aquitaine*, pp. 319–36.
11 The identity of the patron in the Fécamp Psalter's portrait has not been definitively confirmed but the argument for Eleanor is highly persuasive with compelling evidence and I see no reason not to accept it. See Jesús Rodríguez Viejo, 'Royal manuscript patronage in late Ducal Normandy: a context for the female patron portrait of the Fécamp Psalter (*c.* 1180)', *Cerae* 3 (2016), pp. 1–35.
12 There is a note at the end of the manuscript (on fol. 198^v), dated between 1205 and 1206, explaining that the copy is to be shared between Geoffrey of Villehardouin and Milon of Brabant (another knight of the Fourth Crusade), which is witnessed by Marino Zeno (the *podestà* of Constantinople).
13 For more on the relationship between Eleanor and Marie de Champagne, see John F. Benton, 'The court of Champagne as literary centre', *Speculum* 36 (1961), pp. 551–91 (pp. 580–89). Lejeune, 'Rôle littéraire', pp. 324–28; June Hall Martin McCash, 'Marie de Champagne and Eleanor of Aquitaine: a relationship reexamined', *Speculum* 54 (1979), pp. 698–711; Ralph V. Turner, 'Eleanor of Aquitaine and her children: an inquiry into medieval family attachment', *Journal of Medieval History* 14 (1988), pp. 321–35.
14 See Baumgartner and Veillard, 'Introduction', p. 5; Broadhurst, 'Henry II of England', p. 67; Charles H. Haskins, 'Henry II as a patron of literature', in A. G. Little and F. M. Powicke (eds), *Essays in Medieval History Presented to Thomas Frederick Tout* (Manchester: Clark Edinburgh, 1925), pp. 71–77; Lejeune, 'Rôle littéraire', pp. 5–57; Bénédicte Milland-Bove, 'Aliénor d'Aquitaine: femme de lettres ou homme d'État?', *Arts, Recherches et Créations* 303 (2004), pp. 157–61 (p. 158).
15 Quotations from the *Rou* are taken from Wace, *Le Roman de Rou*, ed. by A. J. Holden, 3 vols (Paris: Picard, 1970–73).
16 Quotations from the *Chronique* come from Benoît de Sainte-Maure, *Chronique des ducs de Normandie par Benoit*, ed. by Carin Fahlin, 4 vols (Uppsala: Almqvist & Wiksell, 1951–79).
17 These manuscripts are MSS P2, P5, P10, P12 and Mn.
18 For more on prospective patronage, see Ian Short, 'Patrons and polyglots: French literature in twelfth-century England', in Marjorie Chibnall (ed), *Anglo-Norman Studies XIV: Proceedings of the Battle Conference 1991* (Woodbridge: Boydell Press, 1992), pp. 229–49 (p. 232).
19 This couplet is not found in MS L4, the base manuscript for Mora-Lebrun's edition, and this quotation is therefore taken from Constans's edition: *Thèbes: Le roman de Thèbes*, ed. by Léopold Constans, 2 vols (Paris: Librairie de Firmin Didot, 1890).

20 Reto Roberto Bezzola, *Les Origines et la Formation de la Littérature Courtoise en Occident* (Paris: H. Champion, 1963), p. 271.
21 Highlighted in Aimé Petit, *Naissances du Roman: Les Techniques Littéraires dans les Romans Antiques du XIIe siècle* (Paris: Champion-Slatkine, 1985), pp. 1085–87.
22 Benoît, *Troie*, VI, p. 33.
23 For more on the additions and omissions to this manuscript, see Marc-René Jung, *La Légende de Troie en France au Moyen Âge: Analyse des Versions Françaises et Bibliographie Raisonnée des Manuscrits* (Basel: Francke, 1996), pp. 82–84.
24 Desmond, 'History and fiction', p. 142; Richard Waswo, 'Our ancestors, the Trojans: inventing cultural identity in the Middle Ages', *Exemplaria: A Journal of Theory in Medieval and Renaissance Studies* 7 (1995), pp. 269–90.
25 Several fragments of *Troie* are written in an Anglo-Norman hand, another fragment of *Troie* was copied by a Walloon scribe and an additional *Troie* fragment was written by a Catalan scribe. Since there are no complete manuscripts written by Anglo-Norman, Walloon or Catalan scribes, this suggests that the extant complete manuscripts are not necessarily representative of the spread of these texts throughout Europe during the Middle Ages. For more on the fragments, see Jung, *La Légende*, pp. 306–30.
26 The Anjou manuscript of the *Chronique* is Tours, Bibliothèque municipale, MS 903 (c. 1180–1200) and the other manuscript is London, BL, Harley MS 1717 (c. 1200–1250).
27 Elizabeth Morrison, 'Illuminations of the *Roman de Troie* and French royal dynastic ambition (1260–1340)' (unpublished PhD thesis, Cornell University, 2002), pp. 82–106 and 'Linking ancient Troy and medieval France: illuminations of an early copy of the *Roman de Troie*', in *Medieval Manuscripts, Their Makers and Users. A Special Issue of Viator in Honor of Richard and Mary Rouse* (Turnhout: Brepols, 2011), pp. 72–102. For more on the Capetians and their Trojan ancestry, see Colette Beaune, *The Birth of an Ideology: Myths and Symbols of Nation in Late-Medieval France* (Berkeley: University of California Press, 1991), pp. 226–44; Bernard Guenée, 'Les généalogies entre l'histoire et la politique: la fierté d'être Capétien, en France, au Moyen Âge', *Annales: Economies, Sociétés, Civilisations* 33 (1978), pp. 450–77 (p. 452).
28 Anne D. Hedeman, *The Royal Image: Illustrations of the 'Grandes Chroniques de France', 1272–1422* (Berkeley: University of California Press, 1991), pp. 12–15.
29 This table can be cross-referenced with Appendices 1 and 2 for more detailed information.
30 These illustrations are a series of unidentified medallion-style portraits that are unrelated to the manuscript's texts.
31 Spaces for miniatures were left but the illustrations were never completed. Morrison has noted all the spaces where miniatures were planned in MS P16 and has transcribed the rubrics that accompany these spaces (and would have accompanied the miniatures). Morrison, 'Illuminations of the *Roman de Troie*', pp. 268–72.
32 Fredegar, *Fredegarii et Aliorum Chronica*, ed. by Bruno Krusch (Hannover: Bibliopolii Hahniani, 1888), pp. 45–47.
33 Nennius, *Nennius et l'Historia Brittonum*, ed. by Ferdinand Lot (Paris: BEHE, 1934), pp. 154–55.
34 Geoffrey of Monmouth, *The History of the Kings of Britain*, trans. by Lewis Thorpe (London: Penguin, 1966), p. 53.
35 Beaune, *The Birth of an Ideology*, p. 226.
36 For more on MS P18's dialect, see Constanza Cipollaro, 'Turone di Maxio, miniature del *Roman de Troie* di Parigi (BnF, MS fr. 782), *Codices Manuscripti* 33 (2012), pp. 16–22 (p. 16).
37 See Appendix 2 for details on the women who appear in the manuscript illustrations.

38 For more on the *Preuses* topos, Sophie Cassagnes-Brouquet, *Chevaleresses: Une Chevalerie au Féminin* (Paris: Perrin, 2013), pp. 154–67 and Horst Schroeder, *Der Topos der Nine Worthies in Literatur und Bildender Kunst* (Göttingen: Vandenhoeck & Ruprecht, 1971), pp. 168–203.
39 The catalogue of manuscript in Appendix 1 gives complete details on the contents of each manuscript.
40 See Appendix 1 for a transcription of this 'introduction'.
41 However, the addition of *Dolopathos* at the end does break this chronological narrative somewhat, the *Brut* finishing with the story of the seventh-century Cadwaladr, whereas the Seven Wise Masters of the *Dolopathos* were supposed to have lived around 100 BCE.
42 Petit, *L'Anachronisme dans les Romans Antiques, passim* and 'La chevalerie au prisme de l'Antiquité', *Revue des Langues Romanes* 110 (2006), pp. 17–34.
43 Jung, *La Légende*, p. 196.
44 For more information on the way that such classical texts were reinterpreted, see Renate Blumenfeld-Kosinski, *Reading Myth: Classical Mythology and Its Interpretations in Medieval French Literature* (Cambridge: Cambridge University Press, 1998), Chapter 1.
45 Jean Ogée, *Dictionnaire Historique et Géographique de la Province de Bretagne*, 2 vols (Rennes: Molliex, 1843–53), Vol. 2, p. 15.
46 A. D. Carr, 'Wales', in Michael Jones (ed), *The New Cambridge Medieval History VI c. 1300–1415* (Cambridge: Cambridge University Press, 2000), pp. 334–44 (pp. 341–42).
47 F. A. G. Cowper, 'Origins and peregrinations of the Laval-Middleton manuscript', *Nottingham Mediaeval Studies* 3 (1959), pp. 3–18 (pp. 12–13).
48 See Appendix 1 for more information.
49 Jung, *La Légende*, pp. 122–23.
50 Ibid., p. 123.
51 Ibid., p. 122.
52 Kathryn M. Rudy, 'Kissing images, unfurling rolls, measuring wounds, sewing badges and carrying talismans: considering some Harley manuscripts through the physical rituals they reveal', *Electronic British Library Journal* (2011), 1–56 (p. 30), http://www.bl.uk/eblj/2011articles/articles.html [accessed 1 June 2017].
53 British Library description, http://www.bl.uk/catalogues/illuminatedmanuscripts/ILLUMIN.ASP?Size=mid&IllID=30781 [accessed 5 July 2017]. The description was subsequently updated at some point between July 2017 and October 2019 and now reads 'knights beside a dead body perhaps Penthesilea'. It is interesting that despite the update they have kept a cautionary 'perhaps' in their description.
54 For more on the iconology of hair, including the ways in which virgin women were depicted, see Roberta Milliken, *Ambiguous Locks: An Iconology of Hair in Medieval Art and Literature* (London: McFarland & Company, 2012), p. 226.
55 Jung, *La Légende*, p. 112.
56 Ibid., p. 113.
57 Ibid.
58 Anne Derbes and Mark Sandona, 'Amazons and crusaders: the *Histoire Universelle* in Flanders and the Holy Land', in Daniel H. Weiss and Lisa Mahoney (eds), *France and the Holy Land: Frankish Culture and the End of the Crusades* (Baltimore: Hopkins University Press, 2004), pp. 187–229 (pp. 216–17, n. 3). For more on Penthesilea's white caparison as an identifier see Sophie Harwood, 'Swans and Amazons: Penthesilea and the case for women's heraldry in medieval culture', *The Mediaeval Journal* 7 (2017), pp. 61–87 (pp. 64–68).

59　Jung misidentifies both the top and bottom registers of this illustration: he describes the top register as Paris removing the body of Deiphobus from the battlefield (when it is actually Achilles dragging the body of Troilus) and the bottom register as the death of Troilus: Jung, *La Légende*, p. 222. Elizabeth Morrison clarifies this error in Morrison, 'Illuminations of the *Roman de Troie*', pp. 133-34.
60　Jung, *La Légende*, p. 225.
61　These nine are detailed in Appendix 2.
62　Highlighted by Jung, *La Légende*, p. 184.
63　The link between these three manuscripts' illustrative schemes is made by Morrison in 'Illuminations of the *Roman de Troie*', pp. 160-80.
64　Jung reproduces these lines in *La Légende*, pp. 82-84.

Chapter 2

1　Christine de Pizan, *Le Livre des Trois Vertus*, ed. by Charity Cannon Willard and Eric Hicks (Paris: Champion, 1989), Part I, Chapter 9.
2　For more on this story, see F. Donald Logan, *Runaway Religious in Medieval England, 1240-1540* (Cambridge: Cambridge University Press, 1996), pp. 85-86.
3　For the varying implications and meaning of abduction, see Christopher Cannon, '*Raptus* in the Chaumpaigne Release and a newly discovered document concerning the life of Geoffrey Chaucer', *Speculum* 68 (1993), pp. 74-94 and J. B. Post, 'Ravishment of women and the statutes of Westminster', in J. H. Baker (eds), *Legal Records and the Historian* (London: Royal Historical Society, 1978), pp. 150-64.
4　Philippe Logié, 'L'oubli d'Hésione ou le fatal aveuglement: le jeu du *tort* et du *droit* dans le *Roman de Troie* de Benoît de Sainte Maure', *Le Moyen Âge* 108 (2002), pp. 235-52.
5　Ibid., p. 240.
6　For more on the exchange of women as prizes, see Roberta L. Krueger, *Women Readers and the Ideology of Gender in Old French Verse Romance* (Cambridge: Cambridge University Press, 1993), pp. 128-55; Peggy McCracken, *The Romance of Adultery: Queenship and Sexual Transgression in Old French Literature* (Philadelphia: University of Pennsylvania Press, 1998), pp. 84-118. For an overview of this topic in Middle English Romance see Corinne Saunders, 'A matter of consent: middle English Romance and the law of *raptus*', in Noël James Menuge (ed), *Medieval Women and the Law* (Woodbridge: Boydell Press, 2000), pp. 105-124.
7　For more on *Enéas* and the courtly love tradition, see Helen C. R. Laurie, '*Enéas* and the doctrine of courtly love', *The Modern Language Review* 64 (1969), pp. 283-94. For more on the development of the *fin amors* concept in general, see Roger Boase, *The Origin and Meaning of Courtly Love: A Critical Study* (Manchester: Manchester University Press, 1977). For a more recent feminist revision of the courtly love in the Old French tradition, see E. Jane Burns, 'Courtly love: who needs it? Recent feminist work in the medieval French tradition', *Signs* 27 (2001), pp. 23-57.
8　*History of William Marshal*, ed. by A. J. Holden and D. Crouch, trans. by S. Gregory (3 vols) (London: Anglo-Norman Text Society, 2002-06), Vol. I, ll. 3466-67. Quoted in David Crouch, *Tournament* (London: Hambledone Continuum, 2006), p. 56.
9　This is part of what Nicholson characterizes as 'individual reasons for waging war', which also includes the desire of individuals to win prestige, wealth, admiration, or notoriety in art and literature. See Helen Nicholson, *Medieval Warfare: Theory and Practice of War in Europe, 300-1500* (Basingstoke: Palgrave Macmillan, 2003), p. 2.

10 Crouch, *Tournament*, p. 157.
11 Ibid., p. 157.
12 E. Jane Burns, *Courtly Love Undressed: Reading through Clothes in Medieval French Culture* (Philadelphia: University of Pennsylvania Press, 2002), p. 4.
13 In MS L4, there is an added detail that the women scratch at the walls specifically using their fingernails (see Mora-Lebrun's edition, l. 11908).
14 Both these episodes are highlighted in Catherine Hanley, *War and Combat, 1150-1270: The Evidence from Old French Literature* (Cambridge: Brewer, 2003), p. 86.
15 Maurice Keen, *Chivalry* (New Haven: Yale University Press, 1984), pp. 1-4.
16 Richard W. Kaeuper, *Medieval Chivalry* (Cambridge: Cambridge University Press, 2016), p. 63.
17 Ibid., pp. 155-207.
18 Craig Taylor, *Chivalry and the Ideals of Knighthood in France during the Hundred Years War* (Cambridge: Cambridge University Press, 2013), p. 121.
19 See, for example, Leo Braudy, *From Chivalry to Terrorism: War and the Changing Nature of Masculinity* (New York: Vintage Books, 2003); Stefan Dudink and Josh Tosh (eds), *Masculinities in Politics and War: Gendering Modern History* (Manchester: Manchester University Press, 2004); Robert A. Nye, 'Western masculinities in war and peace', *The American Historical Review* 112 (2007), pp. 417-38.
20 Nancy C. M. Hartsock, 'Masculinity, heroism and the making of war', in A. Harris and Y. King (eds), *Rocking the Ship of State: Towards a Feminist Peace Politics* (Boulder: Westview Press, 1989), pp. 133-52; Joshua S. Goldstein, *War and Gender* (Cambridge: Cambridge University Press, 2001).
21 Ruth Mazo Karras, *From Boys to Men: Formations of Masculinity in Late Medieval Europe* (Philadelphia: University of Pennsylvania Press, 2003), p. 3 and 21.
22 Ibid., p. 62.
23 Kimberly Hutchings, 'Making sense of masculinity and war', *Men and Masculinities* 10 (2008), pp. 389-404 (p. 389).
24 Ibid., p. 389.
25 Christine, *Livre des Trois Vertus*, Part I, Chapter 9.
26 Andromache's scene appears in MSS P6, P17, Vt, P18 and Vn while Priam's scene appears in MSS P6, Vt, P18 and Vn. These will be discussed further in chapter six.
27 This anniversary service appears in seven manuscripts: MSS P6, P8, P18, Vt, Mn, L2 and Vn.

Chapter 3

1 Rory Cox, 'Asymmetric warfare and military conduct in the Middle Ages', *Journal of Medieval History* 38 (2012), pp. 100-25 (p. 104).
2 H. E. J. Cowdrey, 'The Peace and Truce of God in the eleventh century', *Past and Present* 46 (1970), pp. 42-67 and T. Head and R. Landes (eds), *The Peace of God: Social Violence and Religious Response in France around the Year 1000* (Ithaca: Cornell University Press, 1992).
3 For more on the problem of noncombatants in the Middle Ages, see Christopher Allmand, 'War and the non-combatant in the Middle Ages', in Maurice Keen (ed), *Medieval Warfare: A History* (Oxford: Oxford University Press, 1999), pp. 253-72; David J. Hay, '"Collateral damage?" Civilian casualties in the early ideologies of chivalry and crusade', in Niall Christie and Maya Yazigi (eds), *Noble Ideals and Bloody Realities: Warfare in the Middle Ages* (Leiden: Brill, 2006), pp. 3-25; James Johnson,

'The meaning of non-combatant immunity in the Just War/Limited War tradition', *Journal of the American Academy of Religion* 39 (1971), pp. 151-70.
4   Hay, 'Collateral Damage?', p. 11. There is a caveat to this, which is that this definition only holds if the individual is not subsequently presented in a fashion fitting for a knight or soldier: for example, *Thèbes* has an example of a warrior-bishop, while *Enéas* and *Troie* both have female warriors. These individuals would then lose their right to 'immunity' and are considered as combatants.
5   See Catherine Hanley, 'The portrayal of warfare in Old French literature c. 1150 – c. 1270' (unpublished PhD thesis, University of Sheffield, 2001) p. 183.
6   Quotations from Raymond are taken from *Recueil des historiens des croisades. I: Historiens occidentaux*, III (Paris: Impr. Royale, 1866) and are referenced by chapter and paragraph. Translations are from Raymond d'Aguilers, *Historia Francorum qui ceperunt Iherusalem*, trans. by John Hugh Hill and Laurita L. Hill (Philadelphia: American Philosophical Society, 1968).
7   Quotations from Fulcher of Chartres's *Historia Hierosolymitana* are taken from *Recueil des historiens des croisades. I: Historiens occidentaux*, III and are referenced by chapter and paragraph. Translations are from Fulcher of Chartres, A *History of the Expedition to Jerusalem, 1095-1127*, trans. by Frances Rita Ryan (Knoxville: University of Tennessee Press, 1969).
8   Quotations from and translations of the *Gesta* are taken from *Gesta Francorum et aliorum Hierosolimitanorum: The Deeds of the Franks and the Other Pilgrims to Jerusalem*, ed. and trans. by Rosalind Hill (Oxford: Clarendon Press, 1967).
9   Dominique Battles, *The Medieval Tradition of Thèbes: History and Narrative in the Old French Roman de Thèbes, Boccaccio, Chaucer and Lydgate* (New York: Routledge, 2004), pp. 19-25.
10 Revelation 14:20. This connection was highlighted by Hill and Hill in their edition of Raymond, *Historia Francorum qui ceperunt Iherusalem*, p. 128, n. 22. For more on the ways in which the Jerusalem massacre has been described and interpreted over the centuries and the ways in which these chronicle accounts were influenced by biblical topoi, see Benjamin Z. Kedar, 'The Jerusalem massacre of July 1099 in the western historiography of the crusades', *Crusades* 3 (2004), pp. 15-75.
11 Quotations from the *Cantilène* are taken from L. C. Porter, 'The "Cantilène de Sainte Eulalie": phonology and graphemics', *Studies in Philology* 57 (1960), pp. 587-96 (pp. 589-90).
12 Martha Easton, 'Pain, torture and death in the Huntingdon Library *Legenda aurea*', in Samantha J. E. Riches and Sarah Salih (eds), *Gender and Holiness: Men, Women and Saints in Late Medieval Europe* (London: Routledge, 2002), pp. 49-64 (p. 61). See also, Florike Egmond, 'Execution, dissection, pain and infamy: a morphological investigation', in Florike Egmond and Robert Zwijnenberg (eds), *Bodily Extremities: Preoccupations with the Human Body in Early Modern European Culture* (Aldershot: Ashgate, 2003), pp. 92-127; Klaus P. Jankofsy, 'Public executions in England in the late Middle Ages: the indignity and dignity of death', *Omega: Journal of Death and Dying* 10 (1980), pp. 43-57; Katherine Royer, 'The body in parts: reading the execution ritual in late medieval England', *Historical Reflections* 29 (2003), pp. 319-39.
13 For more on public executions and the relationship to punishment and dishonour, see Egmond, 'Execution, dissection, pain and infamy', pp. 92-127.
14 The corresponding illustration in MS Vn is on fol. 160^r.
15 Quotations from the *Aeneid* are from Virgil, *The Aeneid*, ed. by J. W. Mackail (Oxford: Clarendon Press, 1930) and translations are from Virgil, *The Aeneid of Virgil*, trans. by Allen Mandelbaum (Berkeley: University of California Press, 1981).

16 Juanita Feros Ruys, '"He who kills himself liberates a wretch": Abelard on Suicide', in Babette S. Hellemans (ed), *Rethinking Abelard: A Collection of Critical Essays* (Leiden: Brill, 2014), pp. 230–50.
17 The first recorded burning, for the crime of heresy, was recorded in 1022 in Orléans (see Michael D. Barbezat, 'The fires of hell and the burning of heretics in the accounts of the executions at Orleans in 1022', *Journal of Medieval History* 40 (2014), pp. 399–420). Burning was used relatively infrequently in the twelfth century, but from the thirteenth century it became 'standard' punishment for those accused of witchcraft or heresy (see Anita Obermeier, 'Witches and the myth of the medieval *Burning Times*', in Stephen Harris and Bryon L. Grigsby (eds), *Misconceptions about the Middle Ages* (New York: Routledge, 2008), pp. 218–29). Of course, most famously and perhaps most pertinently given the subject of this book, Joan of Arc was executed by the English by being burned at the stake in May 1431.
18 See, for example, Matthew Bennett and Katherine Weikert (eds), *Medieval Hostageship c. 700–1500* (New York: Routledge, 2016); Yvonne Friedman, *Encounter between Enemies: Captivity and Ransom in the Latin Kingdom of Jerusalem* (Leiden: Brill, 2002); Adam J. Kosto, *Hostages in the Middle Ages* (Oxford: Oxford University Press, 2012).
19 Kosto, *Hostages*, p. 2.
20 Yvonne Friedman, 'Captivity and ransom: the experience of women', in Susan B. Edgington and Sarah Lambert (eds), *Gendering the Crusades* (Cardiff: University of Wales Press, 2001), pp. 121–39 (p. 121).
21 John Gillingham, 'Women, children and the profits of war', in Janet L. Nelson and others (eds), *Gender and Historiography: Studies in the Earlier Middle Ages in Honour of Pauline Stafford* (London: Institute of Historical Research, 2012), pp. 61–74 (p. 61).
22 Ibid., p. 61.
23 Robert Bartlett, *The Making of Europe: Conquest, Colonization and Cultural Change 950–1350* (London: Penguin, 1994), p. 303 (cited in Gillingham, 'Women, children and the profits of war', p. 73).
24 This is the first usage recorded by the Anglo-Norman On-Line Hub, https://anglo-norman.net.
25 Although we can assume that Helenus is not a child (he is older than Troilus) and therefore would be eligible to be a knight like his brothers, he does not take up arms at any point. Illustrations of Helenus tend to depict him dressed in the habit of a monk or with the tonsure of a monk (MS Vt fol. 201^r and MS V1 fol. 205^r). There is no textual suggestion that he is a religious figure (and certainly in the classical sources he could not have been a monk) and so the illustrators seem to have fixed on this way of representing him as a way to explain why a nobleman of fighting age was not a knight.
26 For example, in the early thirteenth century, Margaret and Isabella of Scotland were part of a peace agreement and had been deliberately held by the king for the purpose of such strategic marriages. See Katherine Weikert, 'The princesses who might have been hostages: the custody and marriages of Margaret and Isabella of Scotland, 1209–1220s', in Bennett and Weikert (eds), *Medieval Hostageship*, pp. 237–71 (p. 239).
27 See Anne-Marie Eddé, *Saladin* (Cambridge: Harvard University Press, 2011), p. 299; Friedman, *Encounter between Enemies*, p. 162; Natasha R. Hodgson, *Women, Crusading and the Holy Land in Historical Narrative* (Woodbridge: Boydell Press, 2007), p. 43.
28 Translation from Francesco Gabrielli, *Arab Historians of the Crusades* (Berkeley: University of California Press, 1969), pp. 162–63.

29 For more on the question of enslavement in medieval Christian and Muslim communities, see Olivia R. Constable, 'Muslim Spain and Mediterranean slavery: the medieval slave trade as an aspect of Muslim-Christian relations', in Scott Waugh (ed), *Christendom and Its Discontents* (Berkeley: University of California Press, 1998), pp. 264–84; John Gillingham, 'Christian warriors and the enslavement of fellow Christians', in Martin Aurell and Catalina Girbea (eds), *Chevalerie et Christianisme aux XIIe et XIIIe siècles* (Rennes: Presses Universitaires de Rennes, 2011), pp. 237–56; Jacques Heers, *Esclaves et Domestiques au Moyen Âge dans le Monde Méditerranéen* (Paris: Fayard, 1981); Sally McKee, 'Inherited status and slavery in late medieval Italy and Venetian Crete', *Past and Present* 182 (2004), pp. 31–53 and 'Slavery', in Judith M. Bennett and Ruth Mazo Karras (eds), *The Oxford Handbook of Women and Gender in Medieval Europe* (Oxford: Oxford University Press, 2013), pp. 281–94; William D. Phillips, *Slavery in Medieval and Early Modern Iberia* (Philadelphia: University of Pennsylvania Press, 2014); Susan Mosher Stuard, 'Ancillary evidence for the decline of medieval slavery', *Past and Present* 149 (1995), pp. 3–28; David Wyatt, *Slaves and Warriors in Medieval Britain and Ireland, 800–1200* (Leiden: Brill, 2009).

30 For an English translation of Aucassin et Nicolette (with the original Old French in facing page), see Sturges's edition listed in the bibliography.

31 For example, see Corinne J. Saunders, *Rape and Ravishment in the Literature of Medieval England* (Cambridge: Cambridge University Press, 2001); James A. Brundage, *Sex, Law and Marriage in the Middle Ages* (Aldershot: Variorum, 1993); Kathryn Gravdal, *Ravishing Maidens: Writing Rape in Medieval French Literature and Law* (Philadelphia: University of Pennsylvania Press, 1991); Kim M. Phillips, 'Written on the body: reading rape from the twelfth to fifteenth centuries', in Noël James Menuge (ed), *Medieval Women and Law* (Woodbridge: Boydell Press, 2000), pp. 125–44; Elizabeth Robertson and Christine M. Rose (eds), *Representing Rape in Medieval and Early Modern Literature* (New York: Palgrave Macmillan, 2001); Diane Wolfthal, *Images of Rape: The 'Heroic' Tradition and Its Alternatives* (Cambridge: Cambridge University Press, 1999).

32 James A. Brundage, *Law, Sex and Christian Society in Medieval Europe* (Chicago: University of Chicago Press, 2009), p. 48.

33 Ibid., p. 148.

34 J. B. Post, 'Ravishment of women and the statutes of Westminster', in J. H. Baker (eds), *Legal Records and the Historian* (London: Royal Historical Society, 1978), pp. 150–64; Sue Sheridan Walker, 'Punishing convicted ravishers: statutory strictures and actual practice in thirteenth- and fourteenth-century England', *Journal of Medieval History* 13 (1987), pp. 237–50.

35 For the varying implications and meaning of abduction, see the first section of the previous chapter. See also, Christopher Cannon, '*Raptus* in the Chaumpaigne Release and a newly discovered document concerning the life of Geoffrey Chaucer', *Speculum* 68 (1993), pp. 74–94 and Post, 'Ravishment of women and the statutes of Westminster'.

36 Friedman, *Encounters between Enemies*, p. 169.

37 See, for example, Anne Curry, 'The theory and practice of female immunity in the medieval West', in Elizabeth D. Heineman (ed), *Sexual Violence in Conflict Zones: from the Ancient World to the Era of Human Rights* (Philadelphia: University of Pennsylvania Press, 2011), pp. 173–88; Richard W. Kaeuper, *Chivalry and Violence in Medieval Europe* (Oxford: Oxford University Press, 1999), pp. 225–30; Corinne Saunders, 'Sexual violence in wars: the Middle Ages', in Hans-Henning Kortüm (ed), *Transcultural Wars from the Middle Ages to the Twenty-First Century* (Berlin: Akademie Verlag, 2006), pp. 151–64.

38 Wolfthal, *Images of Rape*, p. 101.
39 Kenneth Varty, 'The giving and withholding of consent in late twelfth-century French literature', *Reading Medieval Studies* 12 (1986), pp. 27–49 (pp. 36–37). For more on rape in medieval canon law, see Brundage, 'Rape and marriage', pp. 62–75; Wolfthal, *Images of Rape*, pp. 99–126.
40 Varty, 'The giving and withholding of consent', p. 37.
41 Gravdal, *Ravishing Maidens*, p. 42.
42 Ibid., p. 44.
43 *La Fille du Comte de Ponthieu*, trans. by Danielle Quéruel, in Danielle Régnier-Bohler (ed), *Splendeurs de la Cour de Bourgogne: Récits et Chroniques* (Paris: Laffont, 1995), pp. 415–65, sections 16–17.
44 Ralph V. Turner, *Eleanor of Aquitaine: Queen of France, Queen of England* (London: Yale University Press, 2011), p. 107.
45 Bruce L. Venarde, *Women's Monasticism and Medieval Society: Nunneries in France and England, 890–1215* (Ithaca: Cornell University Press, 1997), p. 96.
46 Orderic Vitalis, *The Ecclesiastical History of England and Normandy*, trans. by Thomas Forester (London: H. G. Bohn, 1856), Vol. 6, p. 59, n. 3.
47 For more on Eleanor's semi-retirement to Fontevraud, see Jean-Marc Bienvenu, 'Aliénor d'Aquitaine et Fontevraud', *Cahiers de Civilisation Médiévale* 113 (1984), pp. 15–27 (p. 23); Edmond-René Labande, 'Pour une image véridique d'Aliénor d'Aquitaine', *Bulletin de la Société des Antiquaires de l'Ouest* 4 (1952), pp. 175–234 (p. 224); Turner, *Eleanor of Aquitaine*, pp. 275–77.
48 Venarde, *Women's Monasticism*, p. 75.
49 Yves Gravelle, 'Le problème des prisonniers pendant les croisades orientales, 1095–1192' (unpublished master's thesis, University of Sherbrooke, 1999), p. 104.
50 Matthew Strickland, *War and Chivalry: The Conduct and Perception of War in England and Normandy, 1066–1217* (Cambridge: Cambridge University Press, 1996), pp. 274 and 283.

Chapter 4

1 See Christoph T. Maier, 'The roles of women in the crusade movement: a survey', *Journal of Medieval History* 30 (2004), pp. 61–82; Helen Nicholson, 'Women on the Third Crusade', *Journal of Medieval History* 23 (1997), pp. 335–49; Jean A. Truax, 'Anglo-Norman women at war: valiant soldiers, prudent strategists or charismatic leaders?', in Donald J. Kagay and L. J. Andrew Villalon (eds), *The Circle of War in the Middle Ages* (Woodbridge: Boydell Press, 1999), pp. 111–25 (p. 114).
2 For women's role in sieges, see Catherine Hanley, *War and Combat, 1150–1270: The Evidence from Old French Literature* (Cambridge: Brewer, 2003), p. 45.
3 These episodes are described in detail in Sophie Harwood, '"I will lead you to the river": women, water and warfare in the *Roman de Thèbes* and early chronicles of the First Crusade', *Open Library of Humanities* 4(2):15 (2018), pp. 1–22.
4 Guibert of Nogent, *The Deeds of God through the Franks*, trans. by Robert Levine (Woodbridge: Boydell Press, 1997), p. 66.
5 Susan B. Edgington and Carol Sweetenham, *The Chanson d'Antioche: An Old French Account of the First Crusade* (Farnham: Ashgate, 2011), p. 74.
6 William of Tyre, *A History of Deeds Done beyond the Sea*, trans. by Emily A. Babcock and A. C. Krey (New York: Columbia University Press, 1943).

7   Oliver of Paderborn, *The Capture of Damietta*, trans. by John J. Gavigan (Philadelphia: University of Pennsylvania Press, 1948), p. 38.
8   Sarah Lambert, 'Crusading or Spinning', in Susan B. Edgington and Sarah Lambert (eds), *Gendering the Crusades* (Cardiff: University of Wales Press, 2001), pp. 1–15 (p. 8).
9   Charles R. Glasheen, 'Provisioning Peter the Hermit: from Cologne to Constantinople, 1096', in John H. Pryor (ed), *Logistics of Warfare in the Age of the Crusades: Proceedings of a Workshop Held at the Centre for Medieval Studies, University of Sydney, 30 September to 4 October 2002* (Aldershot: Ashgate, 2006), pp. 119–30 (p. 121).
10 This episode is described in more detail in Harwood, 'I will lead you', pp. 10–11.
11 See Joshua Prawer, *A History of the Latin Kingdom of Jerusalem* (London: Weidenfeld and Nicolson, 1972), pp. 2 and 18 and Elizabeth Siberry, *Criticism of Crusading 1095–1274* (Oxford: Clarendon, 1985), p. 45.
12 Keren Caspi-Reisfeld, 'Women warriors during the crusades, 1095–1254', in Susan B. Edgington and Sarah Lambert (eds), *Gendering the Crusades* (Cardiff: University of Wales Press, 2001), pp. 94–107 (p. 97).
13 Helen Nicholson, *Medieval Warfare: Theory and Practice of War in Europe, 300–1500* (Basingstoke: Palgrave Macmillan, 2003), p. 63.
14 Constans's edition of *Troie*, using MS V2 as his base manuscript, gives the name of the doctor at this point as 'Broz', while Baumgartner and Vielliard's edition, using MS M as their base, gives it as 'Brot'. However, Constans notes that MSS P5 and P9 both give alternatives of 'Goz' at this point. Given that there is no ambiguity in the name the first time the doctor appears (all the manuscripts agree on 'Goz') and there would not appear to be any particular purpose in replacing one doctor with another, I have chosen to retain the name 'Goz' throughout, following MSS P5 and P9.
15 Monica H. Green, 'Women's medical practice and health care in medieval Europe', in Judith M. Bennett and others (eds), *Sisters and Workers in the Middle Ages* (Chicago: University of Chicago Press, 1989), pp. 39–78 (p. 44).
16 Joanna Phillips discusses the possibility of women as medical practitioners in her study of sickness and health during crusader campaigns and concludes that while it is possible to infer their contribution to medical care, it is not currently possible to confirm it: Joanna Phillips, 'The experience of sickness and health during crusader campaigns to the eastern Mediterranean, 1095–1274'. (unpublished PhD thesis, University of Leeds, 2017), pp. 75–77.
17 Jean de Joinville, *Histoire de Saint Louis*, ed. by Natalis de Wailly, 12th edition (Paris: F. Didot, 1874), Book 62, paragraph 310. This event is discussed by Phillips, and the identity of the woman may have been Hersende, the female physician who is known to have attended Louis on his crusade (Phillips, 'The experience of sickness', p. 242). For more on Hersende, see Piers D. Mitchell, *Medicine in the Crusades: Warfare, Wounds and the Medieval Surgeon* (Cambridge: Cambridge University Press, 2004), p. 19.
18 Monica H. Green, 'Women's medical practice and health care in medieval Europe', *Signs* 14 (1989), pp. 434–73 (p. 450).
19 April Harper, 'The image of the female healer in western vernacular literature of the Middle Ages', *Social History of Medicine* 24 (2011), pp. 108–24 (p. 110).
20 The subject of women's medical practice in general (outside the specific confines of warfare) has received a considerable amount of attention. For a thorough survey of scholarship, see Monica H. Green, 'Bibliography on medieval women, gender and medicine (1985–2009)', *Digital Library of Sciència.cat*, Universitat de Barcelona, http://wwww.sciencia.cat/biblioteca/documents/Green_CumulativeBib_Feb2010.pdf [accessed 24 November 2018].

21 For analysis of the tombs in *Enéas* and *Troie*, see Emmanuèle Baumgartner, 'Tombeaux pour guerriers et Amazones. Sur un motif descriptif de l'*Enéas* et du *Roman de Troie*', in Guy Mermier (ed), *Contemporary Readings of Medieval Literature* (Ann Arbor: University of Michigan Press, 1989), pp. 37–50; Daniel Poirion, 'De l'*Enéide* à l'*Enéas*', *Cahiers de Civilisation Médiévale* 19 (1976), pp. 213–29 (pp. 221–24); Charles Ridoux, 'Trois exemples d'une approche symbolique: le tombeau de Camille, le nain Frocin, le lion', in *Et c'est la Fin pour quoy sommes Ensemble: Hommage à Jean Dufournet* (Paris: Champion, 1993), pp. 1217–21.

22 In Sandy Bardsley's somewhat infamous response to John Hatcher during an exchange over her research on gender and wage differentiation in late medieval England, she relates her experiences as a gravedigger during which she learnt that 'stamina was at least as important for the job as brute strength' and that the male gravediggers on her team 'were only slightly faster over the course of a day': Sandy Bardsley, 'Women's work reconsidered: gender and wage differentiation in late medieval England: a reply', *Past and Present* 173 (2001), pp. 199–202 (p. 201).

23 These differences are outlined in more detail in Joan M. Ferrante and Robert W. Hanning, 'Introduction', in *The Romance of Thebes*, trans. by Joan M. Ferrante and Robert W. Hanning (Tempe: ACMRS, 2018), pp. 1–50 (p. 31).

24 See Jennie Hooper, 'The "Rows of Battle-Swan": the aftermath of battle in Anglo-Saxon art' in Matthew Strickland (ed), *Armies, Chivalry and Warfare in Medieval Britain and France* (Stamford: Paul Watkins, 1998), pp. 82–99.

25 Jean Froissart, *Chroniques, Livres I et II*, ed. by Peter F. Ainsworth and George T. Diller (Paris: Livre de Poche, 2001), pp. 589–90; Monstrelet, *Chronique d'Enguerran de Monstrelet*, ed. by Louis Douët-d'Arcq, Vol. 3, p. 121; both cited in Anne Curry and Glenn Foard, 'Where are the dead of medieval battles? A preliminary survey', *Journal of Conflict Archaeology* 11 (2016), pp. 61–77 (pp. 64–65).

26 Curry and Foard provide more details on these methods and those who are known to have been treated in this way: Curry and Foard, 'Where are the dead', p. 65.

27 Tim Sutherland and Simon Richardson, 'Arrows point to mass graves: finding the dead from the Battle of Towton', in Douglas D. Scott, Lawrence Edward Babits and Charles M. Haeker (eds), *Fields of Conflict: Battlefield Archaeology from the Roman Empire to the Korean War* (Westport: Praeger Security International, 2007), pp. 160–73.

28 Curry and Foard, 'Where are the dead', p. 68.

29 Ibid., p. 66.

30 Ibid., p. 70.

31 Burgess and Kelly translate 'gent' as 'men' here, but I have chosen to translate it as 'people' and I cannot find any indication to suggest that women from Troy did not also assist in this task: Benoît de Sainte-Maure, *The Roman de Troie*, trans. by Glyn S. Burgess and Douglas Kelly (Cambridge: D. S. Brewer, 2017), p. 169.

32 Michael R. Evans, '"Unfit to bear arms": the gendering of arms and armour in accounts of women on crusade', in Susan B. Edgington and Sarah Lambert (eds), *Gendering the Crusades* (Cardiff: University of Wales Press, 2001), pp. 45–58 (p. 45).

33 Natasha R. Hodgson, *Women, Crusading and the Holy Land in Historical Narrative* (Woodbridge: Boydell Press, 2007), p. 106.

34 Alan V. Murray, 'Sex, death and the problem of single women in the armies of the First Crusade', in Ruthy Gertwagen and Elizabeth Jeffreys (eds), *Shipping, Trade and Crusade in the Medieval Mediterranean: Studies in Honour of John Pryor* (Farnham: Ashgate, 2012), pp. 255–70 (pp. 266–68).

35 The illustration also includes Antenor, though the text does not describe him as being present. Aeneas and Antenor are often pictured together, so the illustrator could have assumed he was also present without any textual specificity on this. The lady on the far right is not given a name and is probably intended to represent the other nameless noblewomen who are described as being present in the room, too.
36 The corresponding image from MS Vn is almost identical and therefore only one is reproduced.
37 Robert the Monk, *History of the First Crusade: Historia Iherosolimitana*, trans. by Carol Sweetenham (Aldershot: Ashgate, 2006), Book V, Chapters 6-7.
38 Albert of Aachen, *Historia Ierosolimitana: History of the Journey to Jerusalem*, ed. and trans. by Susan B. Edgington (Oxford: Oxford University Press, 2007), pp. 208-10.
39 Constance Brittain Bouchard, 'Eleanor's divorce from Louis VII: the uses of consanguinity', in Bonnie Wheeler and John C. Parsons (eds), *Eleanor of Aquitaine: Lord and Lady* (New York: Palgrave Macmillan, 2003), pp. 223-35 (p. 225).
40 David S. Bachrach, 'The royal crossbow makers of England, 1204-72', *Nottingham Medieval Studies* 47 (2003), pp. 168-97; Malcolm Mercer, 'King's armourers and the growth of the armourer's craft in early fourteenth-century London', in J. S. Hamilton (ed), *Fourteenth Century England, VIII* (Woodbridge: Boydell Press, 2014), pp. 1-20; Mario Scalini, 'Armi e armature', in Enrico Castelnuovo and Giuseppe Sergi (ed), *Arti e Storia nel Medioevo, 2: Del costruire. Tecniche, artisti, artigiani, committenti* (Turin: Einaudi, 2003), pp. 441-53. These studies describe crafts and industries for the manufacture of arms and armaments that appear to be exclusively occupied by men.
41 Shulamith Shahar, *The Fourth Estate: A History of Women in the Middle Ages* (London: Methuen, 1983), pp. 191-92; P. J. P. Goldberg, *Women, Work and Life Cycle in a Medieval Economy: Women in York and Yorkshire c. 1300-1520* (Oxford: Clarendon Press, 1992), pp. 91-96 and 128. Goldberg's findings come from Yorkshire specifically, but there is nothing to suggest that similar findings would not be possible if similar research techniques and methodologies were to be applied in other geographic regions.
42 Oliver, *The Capture of Damietta*, p. 38; *La Chanson d'Antioche*, ed. by Suzanne Duparc-Quioc, 2 vols (Paris: Librairie Orientaliste Paul Geuthner, 1977), Vol. 1, l. 8936.
43 Fulcher of Chartres, *Historia Hierosolymitana*, Book 3, Chapter 17, Paragraph 3. References to Fulcher's *Historia* are taken from *Recueil des historiens des croisades. I: Historiens occidentaux* (Paris: Impr. Royale, 1866), Vol. 3 and are referenced by chapter and paragraph.
44 This episode is highlighted in Hanley, *War and Combat*, p. 86.
45 Ibid.
46 Albert of Aachen, *Historia Ierosolimitana*, Book 6, Paragraph 3.
47 Ambroise, *L'Estoire de la Guerre Sainte*, ed. by Catherine Croizy-Naquet (Paris: Honoré Champion, 2014), ll. 3620-60.
48 Ibid., ll. 3635-60.
49 Bernard S. Bachrach and David S. Bachrach, *Warfare in Medieval Europe c. 400-c. 1453* (London: Routledge, 2017), p. 346.
50 Anne Curry, 'Soldiers' wives in the Hundred Years War', in Peter R. Coss and Christopher Tyerman (eds), *Soldiers, Nobles and Gentlemen: Essays in Honour of Maurice Keen* (Woodbridge: Boydell Press, 2009), pp. 198-214 (p. 205).
51 The first story comes from Paris, BnF, MS fr. 26060/2710 (entry for December 1435-January 1436) and the second comes from Archives Communales de Mantes CC 22 (1422-23), fol. 38. Both cited in Curry, 'Soldiers' wives', p. 205, nn. 33-34.

52 In return Venus agrees to go to bed with Vulcan, something that she has not done for seven years (*Enéas*, ll. 4426–39).
53 For a thorough survey of such gift exchanges, see Monica L. Wright, *Weaving Narrative: Clothing in Twelfth-Century French Romance* (Philadelphia: Pennsylvania State University Press, 2009), pp. 79–122.
54 Ibid., p. 83.
55 Renate Blumenfeld-Kosinski, 'The gods as metaphor in the *Roman de Thèbes*', *Modern Philology* 83 (1985), pp. 1–11.
56 E. Jane Burns, 'Magical politics from Poitou to Armenia: Mélusine, Jean de Berry and the Eastern Mediterranean', *Journal of Medieval and Early Modern Studies* 43 (2013), pp. 275–301.

Chapter 5

1 For more on this work and the historical women that are connected to it, see Holger Petersen Dyggve, 'Personnages historiques figurant dans la poésie lyrique française des XIIe et XIIIe siècles: deux dames du *Tournoiement* de Huon d'Oisi', *Neuphilologische Mitteilungen* 41 (1940), pp. 157–180.
2 For a general overview of the 'Tournament of Ladies' topos, see Sophie Cassagnes-Brouquet, *Chevaleresses: Une Chevalerie au Féminin* (Paris: Perrin, 2013), pp. 79–110. For a specific discussion of four thirteenth-century narratives, see Helen Solterer, 'Figures of female militancy in medieval France', *Signs* 16 (1991), pp. 522–49.
3 For more on gender and *Silence* see, Robert L. A. Clark, 'Queering gender and naturalizing class in the *Roman de Silence*, *Arthuriana* 12 (2002), pp. 50–63; Simon Gaunt, 'The significance of Silence', *Paragraph* 13 (1990), pp. 202–16; Roberta L. Krueger, *Women Readers and Ideology of Gender in Old French Verse Romance* (Cambridge: Cambridge University Press, 1993), pp. 101–27; Peggy McCracken, '"The boy who was a girl": reading gender in the *Roman de Silence*', *Romanic Review* 85 (1994), pp. 517–46; Lorraine Kochanske Stock, '"Arms and the (wo)man" in medieval romance: the gendered arming of female warriors in the *Roman d'Enéas* and Heldris's *Roman de Silence*', *Arthuriana* 5 (1995), pp. 56–83; Lorraine Kochanske Stock, 'The importance of being gender "stable": masculinity and feminine empowerment in *Le Roman de Silence*', *Arthuriana* 7 (1997), pp. 7–34; Elizabeth A. Waters, 'The third path: alternative sex, alternative gender in *Le Roman de Silence*', *Arthuriana* 7 (1997), pp. 35–46.
4 For more on the *Preuses* topos, see Cassagnes-Brouquet, *Chevaleresses*, pp. 154–67; Horst Schroeder, *Der Topos der Nine Worthies in Literatur und bildender Kunst* (Göttingen: Vandenhoeck & Ruprecht, 1971), pp. 168–203.
5 Plato, *The Republic*, trans. by Benjamin Jowett, http://classics.mit.edu/Plato/republic.6.v.html [accessed 1 July 2018], Book 5.
6 James M. Blythe, 'Women in the military: scholastic arguments and medieval images of female warriors', *History of Political Thought* 22 (2001), pp. 242–69 (p. 243).
7 Aristotle, *Politics*, trans. by H. Rackham, 23 vols (Cambridge, MA: Harvard University Press, 1944), Vol. 21, Book 1, Section 1254b.
8 Blythe, 'Women in the military', p. 242.
9 For examples, see Megan McLaughlin, 'The woman warrior: gender, warfare and society in medieval Europe', *Women's Studies: An Interdisciplinary Journal* 17 (1990), pp. 193–209 (p. 194).

10 Peter the Venerable, 'Letter 115', in *The Letters of Abelard and Heloise*, ed. and trans. by Betty Radice, rev. edition (New York: Prentice Hall, 2003), pp. 279–80.
11 Marbod of Rennes, *The Book with Ten Chapters*, Chapter 4. Cited by Alcuin Blamires (ed), *Women Defamed and Women Defended: An Anthology of Medieval Texts* (Oxford: Clarendon Press, 1992), p. 231.
12 McLaughlin, 'The woman warrior', p. 194.
13 Albertus Magnus, *Commentarium in Octo Libris Politicorum Aristotelis*, in *Opera Omnia* (London: Publisher unknown, 1651), Vol. 4, Book 2, Ch. 3, p. 79.
14 For a summary of Ptolemy of Lucca's and Giles of Rome's views on women warriors see Blythe, 'Women in the military', pp. 253–56.
15 Ptolemy of Lucca, *On the Government of Rules (De Regimine Principum)*, with Portions Attributed to Thomas Aquinas, trans. by James M. Blythe (Philadelphia: University of Pennsylvania Press, 1997), Book 4, Section 5, Paragraph 8.
16 Blythe, 'Women in the military', pp. 265–66.
17 Natasha R. Hodgson, *Women, Crusading and the Holy Land in Historical Narrative* (Woodbridge: Boydell Press, 2007), pp. 109–110.
18 Maureen Purcell, 'Women crusaders: a temporary canonical aberration', in L. O. Frappell (ed), *Principalities, Powers and Estates* (Adelaide: Adelaide University Union Press, 1979), pp. 57–67 (pp. 59–61).
19 For more on these accounts, see Matthew Bennett, 'Virile Latins, effeminate Greeks and strong women: gender definitions on crusade?', in Susan B. Edgington and Sarah Lambert (eds), *Gendering the Crusades* (Cardiff: University of Wales Press, 2001), pp. 16–30; Keren Caspi-Reisfeld, 'Women warriors during the crusades, 1095–1254', in Edgington and Lambert(ed), *Gendering the Crusades*, pp. 94–107 (p. 98); Cassagnes-Brouquet, *Chevaleresses*, pp. 45–48; Michael R. Evans, '"Unfit to bear arms": the gendering of arms and armour in accounts of women on crusade', in Edgington and Lambert (ed), *Gendering the Crusades*, pp. 45–58 (p. 46); Christoph T. Maier, 'The roles of women in the crusade movement: a survey', *Journal of Medieval History* 30 (2004), pp. 61–82 (p. 68).
20 See Leigh Ann Craig, '"Stronger than men and braver than knights": women and the pilgrimages to Jerusalem and Rome in the later Middle Ages', *Journal of Medieval History* 29 (2003), pp. 153–75 and Helen J. Nicholson, 'Women's involvement in the crusades', in Adrian J. Boas (ed), *The Crusader World* (Abingdon: Routledge, 2016), pp. 54–67.
21 For more on women and the military orders, see Cassagnes-Brouquet, *Chevaleresses*, pp. 52–78; Anthony Luttrell and Helen Nicholson, *Hospitaller Women in the Middle Ages* (Aldershot: Ashgate, 2006); Helen Nicholson, 'Templar attitudes towards women', *Medieval History*, 1 (1991), pp. 74–80; Helen Nicholson, 'Women in Templar and Hospitaller commanderies', in Anthony Luttrell and Léon Pressouyre (eds), *La Commanderie, Institution des Ordres Militaires dans l'Occident Medieval* (Paris: Comité des Travaux Historiques et Scientifiques, 2002), pp. 125–34. For more on women and the chivalric orders, see Peter J. Begent, 'Ladies of the Garter', *The Coat of Arms* 8 (1989), pp. 16–22 and Cassagnes-Brouquet, *Chevaleresses*, pp. 111–35.
22 Cassagnes-Brouquet, *Chevaleresses*, pp. 24–27 (p. 25).
23 David J. Hay, *The Military Leadership of Matilda of Canossa, 1046–1115* (Manchester: Manchester University Press, 2010), p. 241.
24 Ibid., p. 253.
25 Much has been written about Matilda's role in the Anarchy, although it is sometimes hidden in chapters and books purporting to be about Stephen. See, for example, Jim Bradbury, *Stephen and Matilda: The Civil War of 1139–53* (Stroud: The History Press,

2005); Marjorie Chibnall, *The Empress Matilda: Queen Consort, Queen Mother and Lady of the English* (Oxford: Blackwell, 1993); Edmund King, *The Anarchy of King Stephen's Reign* (Oxford: Clarendon Press, 1994); Edmund King, *King Stephen* (New Haven: Yale University Press, 2010); Keith J. Stringer, *The Reign of Stephen: Kingship, Warfare and Government in Twelfth-Century England* (London: Routledge, 1993); Graeme J. White, *King Stephen's Reign (1135-54)* (Woodbridge: Boydell Press, 2008). Catherine Hanley's recently published biography of Matilda makes a welcome and much-needed focused contribution to the scholarship on Matilda: Catherine Hanley, *Matilda: Empress, Queen, Warrior* (New Haven: Yale University Press, 2019).

26   Chibnall, *The Empress Matilda*, pp. 158-65.
27   Judith A. Green, 'Duchesses of Normandy in the eleventh and twelfth centuries', in David Crouch and Kathleen Thompson (eds), *Normandy and Its Neighbours, 900-1250: Essays for David Bates* (Turnhout: Brepols, 2011), pp. 43-59 (p. 53).
28   Green, 'Duchesses of Normandy', p. 52.
29   Patricia Dark, '"A woman of subtlety and a man's resolution": Matilda of Boulogne in the power struggles of the Anarchy', in Brenda Bolton and Christine Meek (eds), *Aspects of Power and Authority in the Middle Ages* (Turnhout: Brepols, 2007), pp. 147-64.
30   For more on political expectations of women see Amalie Fößel, 'The political traditions of female rulership in medieval Europe', in Judith M. Bennett and Ruth Mazo Karras (eds), *The Oxford Handbook of Women and Gender in Medieval Europe* (Oxford: Oxford University Press, 2013), pp. 68-83.
31   For more on Sibylla and full references to the primary sources, see Cassagne-Brouquet, *Chevaleresses*, pp. 30-31 and p. 209, nn. 37-38.
32   Conor Kostick highlights the problems with primary sources for Eleanor's role on the Second Crusade in his chapter 'Eleanor of Aquitaine and the women of the Second Crusade', in Conor Kostick (ed), *Medieval Italy, Medieval and Early Modern Women: Essays in Honour of Christine Meek* (Dublin: Four Courts Press, 2010), pp. 195-205.
33   Niketas Choniates, *'O City of Byzantium:' Annals of Niketas Choniates*, ed. and trans. Harry J. Magoulias (Detroit: Wayne State University Press, 1984), p. 35.
34   Michael R. Evans, 'Penthesilea on the Second Crusade: is Eleanor of Aquitaine the Amazon queen of Niketas Choniates?', *Crusades* 8 (2009), pp. 23-30.
35   Peggy McCracken, 'Scandalising desire: Eleanor of Aquitaine and the chroniclers', in Bonnie Wheeler and John Carmi Parsons (eds), *Eleanor of Aquitaine: Lord and Lady* (New York: Palgrave Macmillan, 2003), pp. 247-63.
36   Ibid., pp. 248-55.
37   See Kostick, 'Eleanor of Aquitaine', pp. 203-05.
38   Quotation from Ovid, *Metamophoses*, Book 2, ll. 411-12. Highlighted in Alison Sharrock, 'Warrior women in Roman epic', in Jacqueline Fabre-Serris and Alison Keith (eds), *Women and War in Antiquity* (Baltimore: Johns Hopkins University Press, 2015), pp. 157-78 (p. 168).
39   For more on Judith in these sources, see Peggy L. Curry, 'Representing the biblical Judith in literature and art: an intertextual cultural critique' (unpublished PhD thesis, University of Massachusetts Amherst, 1994); Cassagnes-Brouquet, *Chevaleresses*, pp. 136-39; Peter J. Lucas, '*Judith* and the woman hero', *The Yearbook of English Studies* 22 (1992), pp. 17-27 (p. 17).
40   There is a substantial amount of scholarly work on medieval ethical and moral attitudes to military conduct and martial behaviour. See, for example, Maria Grazia Cammarota, 'War and the "agony of conscience" in Ælfric's writings', *Mediaevistik* 26 (2014), pp. 87-110; H. E. John Cowdrey, 'Christianity and the morality of warfare during the first century of crusading', in Marcus Bull and Norman Housley (eds), *The*

Experience of Crusading, 1: Western Approaches (Cambridge: Cambridge University Press, 2003), pp. 175–92; Rory Cox, 'Asymmetric warfare and military conduct in the Middle Ages', *Journal of Medieval History* 38 (2012), pp. 100–25; Thomas K. Heebøll-Holm, 'Apocalypse then? The First Crusade, traumas of war and Thomas de Marle', in Kerstin Hundahl, Lars Kjær and Niels Lund (eds), *Denmark and Europe in the Middle Ages, c. 1000–1525: Essays in Honour of Professor Michael H. Gelting* (Farnham: Ashgate, 2014), pp. 237–54; James Johnson, 'Thinking morally about war in the Middle Ages and today', in Henrik Syse and Gregory M. Reichberg (eds), *Ethics, Nationalism and Just War: Medieval and Contemporary Perspectives* (Washington, DC: Catholic University of America Press, 2007), pp. 3–10; Richard W. Kaeuper, *Medieval Chivalry* (Cambridge: Cambridge University Press, 2016), pp. 155–207; Maurice Keen, *Chivalry* (New Haven: Yale University Press, 1984), pp. 219–37.

41 Keen, *Chivalry*, p. 2.
42 In MS L4, this line is rendered as 'Et demenoit moult grant barnage' (l. 4053 in Aimé Petit's edition). Petit translates this line as '*she had very noble manners*', but 'barnage' could also mean an assembly of barons or a military unit, meaning that this line could also be translated as '*she had many barons in her retinue*'.
43 The translation of 'chevalerie' presents a particular challenge to translators into English, which is why it has been left as *chevalerie* here. It could be translated as the concept of 'chivalry', or as 'knighthood' or 'knightliness', or simply as 'horsemanship;' the *Dictionnaire Étymologique de l'Ancien Français* gives all these possible translations for a mid-twelfth-century context. However, as chivalry became increasingly discussed and conceptualized during the Middle Ages and after the circulation of texts such as the *Ordène*, Ramon's *Libre* and Geoffrey's *Livre*, it is probable that later readers and audiences of *Enéas*, when they heard or saw the word *chevalerie*, would have been thinking of the virtues and qualities that were associated with this as a way of life, rather than purely associating it with horsemanship or being a mounted warrior. Petit's modern French translation of *Enéas* is able to retain the word *chevalerie* as the modern French 'chevalerie' also retains the double meaning of both 'chivalry' and 'knighthood', thereby avoiding the need to choose between the two, although this does exclude the possibility of the less value-loaded term of simple 'horsemanship'.
44 Cassagne-Brouquet, *Chevaleresses*, p. 9.
45 See their respective entries in the *Dictionnaire Étymologique de l'Ancien Français*.
46 Female knights are relatively fortunate the feminine equivalent of *chevalier* appeared in the Middle Ages. The feminine forms of many other vocations, such as author, doctor, mayor, firefighter, engineer or police officer, were only officially recognized by the Academie Française in February 2019!
47 For more on the semantic range of *chevalier*, see Glyn S. Burgess, 'The term "chevalerie" in twelfth-century French', in Peter Rolfe Monks and D. D. R. Owen (eds), *Medieval Codicology, Iconography, Literature and Translation: Studies for Keith Val Sinclair* (Leiden: Brill, 1994), pp. 343–58; Jean Flori, 'La notion de chevalerie dans les *chansons de geste* du 12e siècle, *Le Moyen Âge* 81 (1975), pp. 211–44 (pp. 219–44); Gillian Gaughan, 'Rank and social status in non-Arthurian Romance of the late twelfth and early thirteenth centuries' (unpublished PhD thesis, University of Liverpool, 1987), p. 203.
48 Erich Auerbach, *Literary Language and Its Public in Late Latin Antiquity and the Middle Ages* (New York: Pantheon Books, 1965), pp. 190–91.
49 Jessie Crosland, '*Enéas* and the *Aeneid*', *The Modern Language Review* 29 (1934), pp. 282–90 (p. 289).

50 These manuscripts are MSS M, P6, L2, Nt, Mn, Vt, P17, V1, Vn and P18 and all the illustrations are described in Appendix 2. It is almost certain that MS SP1 also contains illustrations of Penthesilea given that it contains over three hundred illustrations and has been connected to MS Vt (which itself contains six illustrations of Penthesilea). However, as mentioned in the introduction, I am excluding it from my discussion due to its inaccessibility.
51 For more on Penthesilea's heraldic identifiers, see Sophie Harwood, 'Swans and Amazons: the case of Penthesilea and women's heraldry in medieval culture', *The Mediaeval Journal* 7 (2017), pp. 61–87.
52 The perfidy of the Greeks is demonstrated through the dastardliness of their actions in battle, such as attacking from behind or unceremoniously dragging the body of a noble behind a horse: Elizabeth Morrison, 'Illuminations of the *Roman de Troie* and French royal dynastic ambition (1260–1340)' (unpublished PhD thesis, Cornell University, 2002), p. 117.
53 The link between these three manuscripts' illustrative schemes is made by Morrison in 'Illuminations of the *Roman de Troie*', pp. 160–80.
54 Miri Rubin, *Mother of God: A History of the Virgin Mary* (New Haven: Yale University Press, 2009), pp. 22–31.
55 G. Laris Auguste Grisay and M. Dubois-Stasse (eds), *Les Dénominations de la Femme dans les Anciens Textes Littéraires Français* (Gembloux: J. Ducolot, 1969), pp. 156–66.
56 Ibid., p. 187.
57 Carolyne Larrington, *Women and Writing in Medieval Europe: A Sourcebook* (London: Routledge, 1995), p. 50.
58 Isidore of Seville, *Etymologies*, 11.2.23, in Blamires, *Woman Defamed and Woman Defended*, p. 43.
59 Kelly DeVries, 'A woman as leader of men: Joan of Arc's military career', in Bonnie Wheeler and Charles T. Wood (eds), *Fresh Verdicts on Joan of Arc* (New York: Garland, 1996), pp. 3–18 (p. 12).
60 For more on reformed virginity, see Christine Reno, 'Virginity as an ideal in Christine de Pizan's *Cité des dames*', in Diane Bornstein (ed), *Ideals for Women in the Works of Christine de Pizan* (Detroit: Michigan Consortium for Medieval and Early Modern Studies, 1981), pp. 69–90 (p. 76). For more on honorary virginity, see Jocelyn Wogan-Browne, *Saints' Lives and Women's Literary Culture, 1150–1300: Virginity and Its Authorizations* (Oxford: Oxford University Press, 2001), pp. 123–50.
61 Anke Bernau, Ruth Evans and Sarah Salih (eds), 'Introduction: Virginities and virginity studies', in Anke Bernau, Ruth Evans and Sarah Salih (eds), *Medieval Virginities* (Cardiff: University of Wales Press, 2003), pp. 1–13 (p. 2).
62 Despite Semiramis's position as a *Preuse*, she is frequently depicted in both classical and medieval sources as a lustful woman with questionable morals due to this lasciviousness. Her active sexuality does not therefore go unnoticed or unjudged; clearly it is seen as inappropriate: Deborah Levine Gera, *Warrior Women: The Anonymous Tractatus De Mulieribus* (Leiden: Brill, 1997), p. 65.
63 Jocelyn Wogan-Browne, 'Chaste bodies: frames and experiences', in Sarah Kay and Miri Rubin (eds), *Framing Medieval Bodies* (Manchester: Manchester University Press, 1994), pp. 24–42 (p. 24).
64 Ibid., p. 24.
65 See Kathleen Coyne Kelly, *Performing Virginity and Testing Chastity in the Middle Ages* (London: Routledge, 2000), p. 5.

66 See, for example, Simon Gaunt, *Gender and Genre in Medieval French Literature* (Cambridge: Cambridge University Press, 1995), pp. 180–233; Kathryn Gravdal, *Ravishing Maidens: Writing Rape in Medieval French Literature and Law* (Philadelphia: University of Pennsylvania Press, 1991), pp. 21–41.
67 Sarah Salih, *Versions of Virginity in Late Medieval England* (Cambridge: D. S. Brewer, 2001), pp. 46–50.
68 Karen Cherewatuk, 'Born-again virgins and holy bastards: Bors and Elyne and Lancelot and Galahad', *Arthuriana* 11 (2001), pp. 52–64 (p. 53).
69 See John H. Arnold, 'The labour of continence: masculinity and clerical virginity', in Bernau, Evans and Salih (eds), *Medieval Virginities*, (Cardiff, 2003), pp. 102–18; Kelly, *Performing Virginity*, pp. 91–118.
70 See Kelly, *Performing Virginity*, p. 5.
71 This was highlighted in Cherewatuk, 'Born-Again virgins', pp. 55–56.
72 Jessica Grady, 'Power, courtly love and a lack of heirs: Guinevere and medieval queens' (unpublished master's thesis, Marshall University, 2009).
73 See John Carmi Parsons, 'Damned if she didn't and damned when she did: bodies, babies and bastards in the lives of two queens of France', in Bonnie Wheeler and John Carmi Parsons (eds), *Eleanor of Aquitaine: Lord and Lady* (New York: Palgrave Macmillan, 2003), pp. 265–99.
74 David M. Halperin, *One Hundred Years of Homosexuality: And Other Essays on Greek Love* (New York: Routledge, 1990), p. 76.
75 See Gaunt, *Gender and Genre*, pp. 22–70.
76 Robert Mills, 'Can the virgin martyr speak?', in Bernau, Evans and Salih (eds), *Medieval Virginities*, (Cardiff, 2003), pp. 187–213 (p. 188).
77 See Morrison, 'Illuminations of the *Roman de Troie*', pp. 215–17.
78 See Craig Taylor, 'The Salic Law, French queenship, and the defense of women in the late Middle Ages', *French Historical Studies* 29 (2006), pp. 543–64.
79 Taylor, 'The Salic Law', pp. 549 and 554.
80 For example, Isabella of France claimed that her son, Edward III of England, had the strongest right to claim the French throne as she was the direct descendent of Philip IV of France, which was disputed partly on the grounds of Salic Law and ultimately became one of the key reasons for the outbreak of the Hundred Years War (1337–1453). Or Isabeau of Bavaria, wife of Charles VI of France, whose prominence in government from 1402 to 1420 was unparalleled, and whose grandson, Henry VI of England, became the (disputed) king of France from 1422 to 1453 thanks to a treaty signed by Isabeau and Charles VI in 1420 and a claim through his mother (Isabeau's daughter) – again a direct snub to Salic Law.
81 Taylor, 'The Salic Law', p. 559.
82 Cassagnes-Brouqet, *Chevaleresses*, p. 153.
83 It is illustrated in thirty-five miniatures across eight manuscripts: once in MS P6, once in MS P8, once in MS Mn, twice in MS L2, seven times in MS Vt, eleven times in MS V1, six times in MS Vn and six times in MS P17.
84 The corresponding illustration in MS P18 is found on fol. 173^r and is almost identical to that of MS Vn.
85 Dagmar Thoss, *Benoît de Sainte-Maure: Roman de Troie (Österreichische Nationalbibliothek, Wien, Codex 2571)* (Munich: Lengenfelder, 1989), p. 34. Thoss reorders the folio numbers of the manuscript to reflect its original codicological structure whereas I have followed the folio numbers given by the ÖN in their online catalogue. I have therefore given a folio reference of 161^r for Figure 29 whereas Thoss identifies this illustration on fol. 166^r.

86 For Ulrich's exploits as Venus, see Ulrich von Liechtenstein, *The Service of Ladies*, trans. by J. W. Thomas (Woodbridge: Boydell, 2004), pp. 473–80; for the knights of the Round Table dressed as Amazons, see Ad Putter, 'Transvestite knights in medieval life and history', in Jeffrey Jerome Cohen and Bonnie Wheeler (eds), *Becoming Male in the Middle Ages* (New York: Garland Publishing, 1997), pp. 279–302 (p. 283).

Chapter 6

1 For their role as regents and consorts, see Amalie Fößel, 'The political tradition of female rulership', in Judith M. Bennett and Ruth Mazo Karras (eds), *The Oxford Handbook of Women and Gender in Medieval Europe* (Oxford: Oxford University Press, 2013), pp. 68–83 (pp. 77–80). For their role at council meetings see Lois L. Huneycutt, 'Female succession and the language of power in the writings of twelfth-century churchmen', in John Carmi Parsons (ed), *Medieval Queenship* (New York: St. Martin's Press, 1998), pp. 189–201 (pp. 189–90).
2 For more on this rebellion and Matilda's role, see William M. Aird, *Robert 'Curthose,' Duke of Normandy (c. 1050–1134)* (Woodbridge: Boydell Press, 2008), pp. 84–91.
3 Green, 'Duchesses of Normandy', p. 48.
4 Ibid.
5 Ibid., p. 49, n. 35.
6 Kimberly A. LoPrete, *Adela of Blois: Countess and Lord (c. 1067–1137)* (Dublin: Four Courts Press, 2007), Chapter 4.
7 Ibid., Chapter 6.
8 Lois L. Huneycutt, *Matilda of Scotland: A Study in Medieval Queenship* (Woodbridge: Boydell Press, 2003), p. 73.
9 Ibid., p. 74.
10 Ibid., pp. 75–78.
11 Alan V. Murray, 'Women in the royal succession of the Latin Kingdom of Jerusalem (1099–1291)', in *Mächtige Frauen? Königinnen und Fürstinnen im Europäischen Mittelalter (11.–14. Jahrhundert)* (Ostfildern: J. Thorbecke, 2015), pp. 131–62 (p. 133).
12 Ibid., p. 144.
13 William of Tyre, *Chronicon*, Book 16, Chapter 3 (cited and translated in Murray, 'Women in the royal succession', p. 142).
14 Murray, 'Women in the royal succession', p. 144, n. 42.
15 William of Tyre, *Chronicon*, Book XIII, Chapter 27; Book XIV, Chapter 4; Book XIV, Chapter 20. Cited and translated in Thomas Asbridge, 'Alice of Antioch: a case study of female power in the twelfth century', in Peter Edbury and Jonathan Phillips (eds), *The Experience of Crusading: Defining the Crusader Kingdom* (Cambridge: Cambridge University Press, 2003), pp. 29–47 (p. 29).
16 Asbridge, 'Alice of Antioch', pp. 42–44.
17 Sally Burch North, 'The role of advice in Marie de France's *Eliduc*', in Sally Burch North (ed), *Studies in Medieval French Language and Literature Presented to Brian Woledge* (Geneva: Droz, 1988), pp. 111–34 (pp. 113–14).
18 François-Louis Ganshof, *Qu'est-ce que la Féodalité?*, 4th edition (Brussels: Presses Universitaires de Bruxelles, 1968), p. 87; Dominique Boutet, 'Carrefours idéologiques de la royauté arthurienne', *Cahiers de Civilisation Médiévale* 27 (1985), pp. 3–17.

19   For full details and analysis of the individual scenes within these texts, see Catherine Hanley, *War and Combat, 1150-1270: The Evidence from Old French Literature* (Cambridge: Brewer, 2003), pp. 139-44.
20   Karen Pratt, 'The image of the queen in Old French literature', in Anne Duggan (ed), *Queens and Queenship in Medieval Europe* (Woodbridge: Boydell Press, 2002), pp. 235-62 (pp. 248-49).
21   This is the case in the versions of Hyginus, Aeschylus and Euripides.
22   The corresponding illustration found in MS Vn on fol. 59^r is almost identical and so only one is described here and reproduced.
23   See, for example, Colum Hourihane (ed), *Looking Beyond: Visions, Dreams and Insights in Medieval Art and History* (Princeton: Princeton University Press, 2010); Jesse Keskiaho, *Dreams and Visions in the Early Middle Ages: The Reception and Use of Patristic Ideas, 400-900* (Cambridge: Cambridge University Press, 2015).
24   These sixteen are: Jason setting sail on his quest for the golden fleece (fol. 49^v), the first sack of Troy and the death of Laomedon (fol. 51^r), the reconstruction of Troy (fol. 54^r), Priam's council and decision for Paris to go to Greece (fol. 57^v), a sea battle (fol. 68^r), Priam and his knights riding out from Troy (fol. 72^r), two battles (fols. 73^v and 77^r), Hector injured in bed (fol. 79^r), two battles (fols. 81^r and 84^r), Andromache trying to stop Hector going to battle (fol. 94^r), two battles (fols. 107^r and 113^r), Penthesilea's body being thrown into the river (fol. 126^r), Pyrrhus killing Priam (fol. 131^v).
25   The quality of this image is quite poor and therefore has not been chosen for reproduction here. However, all images from MS Vt can be viewed free of charge via a digitized copy of the manuscript on the BAV's website.
26   The corresponding identical image in MS Vn is found on fol. 90^r.
27   For a survey of medieval artistic representations of the Virgin Mary (and in particular the image of Mary as mother), see Timothy Verdon, *Mary in Western Art* (Washington, DC: Pope John Paul II Cultural Center, 2006), pp. 124-43.
28   For more on the iconology of hair, including the ways in which virgin women were depicted, see Roberta Milliken, *Ambiguous Locks: An Iconology of Hair in Medieval Art and Literature* (London: McFarland & Company, 2012), p. 226.
29   Quotations from the *Epistre* are taken from Christine de Pizan, *Epistre Othea*, ed. by Gabriella Parussa (Geneva: Droz, 1999) and are referenced by text and line number.
30   Jim Bradbury, *The Medieval Siege* (Woodbridge: Boydell Press, 1992), p. 316. Bradbury gives examples of the perils suffered by negotiators (such as death or imprisonment) from the Merovingian age up to Henry V of England's reign. For more on the role of envoys and negotiators in general, see J. E. M. Benham, *Peacemaking in the Middle Ages: Principles and Practice* (Manchester: Manchester University Press, 2011), pp. 115-42.
31   See, for example, Kimberley A. LoPrete, 'Adela of Blois: familial alliances and female lordship', in Theodore Evergates (ed), *Aristocratic Women in Medieval France* (Philadelphia: University of Pennsylvania Press, 1999), pp. 7-43; John Gillingham, 'Love, marriage and politics in the twelfth century', *Forum for Modern Language Studies* 25 (1989), pp. 292-303; John Carmi Parsons, 'Mothers, daughters, marriage, power: some Plantagenet evidence, 1150-1500', in John Carmi Parsons (ed), *Medieval Queenship* (New York: St. Martin's Press, 1998), pp. 63-78.
32   Mozley's translation of the *Thebaid* translates 'geminae [...] tigres' (*Thebaid*, VII, l. 564) as 'two tigers', but the grammatically feminine form of the Latin (as opposed to what would be the masculine form of *gemini tigris*) indicates that they should correctly be identified as twin tigresses.

33 As mentioned in Chapter 1, MS P8 is one of the manuscripts that contains numerous other narrative texts alongside *Thèbes*, while MS G is the manuscript that has had its 'quality and accuracy' called into question by at least one editor. See Chapter 1 and Appendix 1 for more details.
34 This quotation (and line reference) is taken from Francine Mora-Lebrun's edition of *Thèbes*.
35 For a detailed discussion of its etymology and development in the Middle Ages, see William Sayers, 'The Wyvern', *Neuphilologische Mitteilungen* 109 (2008), pp. 457–65. Sayers explains that the word *guivre* appears in twelfth-century texts such as the *Chanson de Roland*, Guillaume de Berneville's *Vie de Saint Gilles*, the *Roman de Claris et Laris* and *Thèbes* to represent some kind of aggressive and exotic beast, before tracing its development in later centuries to become a two-legged winged serpentine-dragon known as a *wyvern* in English heraldry.
36 Aimé Petit, *Naissances du Roman: Les Techniques Littéraires dans les Romans Antiques du XIIe siècle* (Paris: Champion-Slatkine, 1985), pp. 1085–87.
37 See Daniel Power, 'The stripping of a queen: Eleanor of Aquitaine in the thirteenth-century Norman tradition', in Marcus Bull and Catherine Léglu (eds), *The World of Eleanor of Aquitaine: Literature and Society in South France between the Eleventh and Thirteenth Centuries* (Woodbridge: Boydell Press, 2005), pp. 115–36 (pp. 126–33). I am grateful to one of the anonymous early reviewers of this book for suggesting this connection.
38 Robert Scheller, 'The *Lit de Justice* or how to sit on a bed of estate', in *Annus Quadriga Mundi: Opstellen over misseleeuwse kunst opgedragen aan prof. de. Anna C. Esmeijer* (Utrecht: De Walburg Pers, 1989), pp. 193–202. Similarly, Anne D. Hedeman's study of the earliest manuscript of Pierre Salmon's *Réponses à Charles Vi et Lamentation au roi sur son état* (Paris, BnF, MS fr. 23279) reveals Charles VI of France frequently depicted as lying or sitting on his bed while in conversation with Salmon: Anne D. Hedeman, 'Pierre Salmon's advice for a king', *Gesta* 32 (1993), pp. 113–23.
39 Isabel Alfonso Antón, 'The language and practice of negotiation in medieval conflict resolution', in Belle S. Tuten and Tracey L. Billado (eds), *Feud, Violence and Practice: Essays in Medieval Studies in Honour of Stephen D. White* (Farnham: Ashgate, 2010), pp. 158–74; Benham, *Peacemaking in the Middle Ages*; John Gillingham, 'The meetings of the kings of France and England, 1066–1204', in David Crouch and Kathleen Thompson (eds), *Normandy and Its Neighbours, 900–1250* (Turnhout: Brepols, 2011), pp. 17–42; Christopher J. Holdsworth, 'Peacemaking in the twelfth century', in Christopher Harper-Bill (ed), *Anglo-Norman Studies XIX: Proceedings of the Battle Conference, 1996* (Woodbridge: Boydell Press, 1997), pp. 1–18; Christopher J. Holdsworth, 'War and peace in the twelfth century: the reign of Stephen reconsidered', in Brian Patrick McGuire (ed), *War and Peace in the Middle Ages* (Copenhagen: C. A. Reitzels Forlag, 1987) pp. 67–93; Maurice Keen, 'War, peace and chivalry', in McGuire (ed), *War and Peace*, pp. 94–117; Esther Pascua, 'Peace among equals: war and treaties in twelfth-century Europe', in Philip de Souza and John France (eds), *War and Peace in Ancient and Medieval History* (Cambridge: Cambridge University Press, 2008), pp. 193–210.
40 Holdsworth, 'Peacemaking in the twelfth century', pp. 1–18.
41 Extract taken from Christine de Pizan, *Le Livre des Trois Vertus*, ed. by Charity Cannon Willard and Eric Hicks (Paris: Champion, 1989).

42 A full analysis of these scenes is given in Hanley, *War and Combat*, pp. 140–43.
43 Kimberly A. LoPrete, 'Adela of Blois: familial alliances and female lordship', in Evergates (ed), *Aristocratic Women*, pp. 7–43 (p. 23).
44 Laurence W. Marvin, *The Occitan War: A Military and Political History of the Albigensian Crusade, 1209–18* (Cambridge: Cambridge University Press, 2008), pp. 69–93.
45 *La Chanson de la Croisade Albigeoise*, ed. by Henri Gougaud (Paris: Librairie Générale Française, 1989), p. 38. Cited in Sophie Cassagnes-Brouquet, *Chevaleresses: Une Chevalerie au Féminin* (Paris: Perrin, 2013), pp. 49–51 and p. 212, n. 49.
46 See Hanley, *War and Combat*, p. 88.

Conclusion

1 For more on women's monasticism in the High Middle Ages, see Cordula van Wyhe (ed), *Female Monasticism in Early Modern Europe: An Interdisciplinary View* (Aldershot: Ashgate, 2008) and Bruce L. Venarde, *Women's Monasticism and Medieval Society: Nunneries in France and England, 890–1215* (Ithaca: Cornell University Press, 1997).
2 Helen J. Swift, *Gender, Writing and Performance: Men Defending Women in Late Medieval France (1440–1538)* (Oxford: Clarendon Press, 2008), p. 2.

Appendix 1

1 Marc-René Jung, *La Légende de Troie en France au Moyen Âge: Analyse des Versions Françaises et Bibliographie Raisonnée des Manuscrits* (Basel: Francke, 1996); Elizabeth Morrison, 'Illuminations of the *Roman de Troie* and French royal dynastic ambition (1260–1340)' (unpublished PhD thesis, Cornell University, 2002); Benoît de Saintemaure, *Le Roman de Troie*, ed. by Léopold Constans, 6 vols (Paris: Société des Anciens Textes Français, 1904–12).
2 Raymond J. Cormier, 'Gleanings on the manuscript tradition of the *Roman d'Enéas*', *Manuscripta* 18 (1974), pp. 42–47.
3 Aimé Petit, 'La réception de la *Thébaïde* à travers la tradition manuscrite du *Roman de Thèbes*', in Dominique Boutet and others (eds), *'Plaist vos Oïr Bone Cançon Vallant?' Mélanges de Langue et de Littérature Médiévales offerts à François Suard* (Lille: Université Charles-de-Gaulle Lille 3, 1999), pp. 703–12.
4 Information on the fragments can be found in Jung, *La Légende*, pp. 306–30.
5 Jung, *La Légende*, p. 112.
6 Morrison, 'Illuminations of the *Roman de Troie*', p. 177.
7 Petit, 'Introduction' to *Enéas*, p. 34.
8 For more on the connections between these three men, see Jean Longnon, *Les Compagnons de Villehardouin* (Geneva: Librairie Droz, 1978), pp. 48–49.
9 The manuscript is incomplete at the beginning and Jung suggests that *Thèbes* would probably have originally occupied this space: Jung, *La Légende*, p. 117.
10 See the comments for the catalogue entry of MS L2.
11 F. A. G. Cowper, 'Origins and peregrinations of the Laval-Middleton manuscript', *Nottingham Mediaeval Studies* 3 (1959), pp. 3–18 (pp. 7–8).
12 Ibid., pp. 12–13.

13 Ibid., p. 17.
14 For more on this manuscript and its scribe, see Mario Roques, 'Le manuscrit fr. 794 de la Bibliothèque nationale et le scribe Guyot', *Romania* 73 (1952), pp. 177–99.
15 Four of the full-page miniatures were cut out of the manuscript in 1850 to be sold to a private collector. The missing four are reproduced in black and white in Hugo Buchthal, *Historia Troiana: Studies in the History of Mediaeval Secular Illustration* (London: Warburg Institute, 1971), plates 4–5.
16 Despite the rather eclectic grouping of texts, Morrison confirms that nonetheless they were 'a planned grouping, for most of the texts begin on the same folio on which the last one ended' and that the same illustrator has been used throughout: Morrison, 'Illuminations of the *Roman de Troie*', p. 156, n. 46.
17 For a detailed description of this manuscript, see Yvan G. Lepage, 'Un recueil français de la fin du XIIIe siècle (Paris, BnF, fr. 1553)', *Scriptorium* 29 (1975), pp. 23–46.
18 Several scholars have conducted studies on the manuscript's contents. See Isabelle Delage-Béland, 'Une conquête problématique: Le statut ambigu de la fiction dans le manuscrit Paris, BNF, fr. 375, un recueil de *romans*', in Olivier Collet, Francis Gingras and Richard Trachsler (eds), *Lire en context: Enquête sur les manuscrits de fabliaux* (Montreal: Les Presses de l'Université de Montréal, 2012), pp. 95–113; Aimé Petit, 'A commentary on some singular aspects of Manuscript A (BnF 375) of the *Roman de Thèbes*', *Le Moyen Âge* 119 (2013), pp. 597–620; Mary Rouse and Richard Rouse, 'The crusade as context: the manuscripts of *Athis et Prophilias*', in Keith Busby and Christopher Kleinhenz (eds), *Courtly Arts and the Art of Courtliness: Selected Papers from the Eleventh Triennial Congress of the International Courtly Literature Society, University of Wisconsin-Madison, 29 July–4 August 2004* (Cambridge: D. S. Brewer, 2006), pp. 49–103.
19 The *Bible* occupies fols. 1–54 and 182–203; *Troie* occupies fols. 54–181: Jung, *La Légende*, pp. 199–200.
20 Jehan Malkaraume, *La Bible de Jehan Malkaraume (Ms. Paris, Bibl. Nat. fr. 903) (XIIIe/XIVe siècle)*, ed. by Jean Robert Smeets, 2 vols (Amsterdam: Van Gorcum, 1978), Vol. 1, p. 10.
21 The presence of this text within this manuscript was highlighted to me by Delbert W. Russell in 'The cultural context of the French prose *Remaniement* of the *Life of Edward the Confessor by a Nun of Barking Abbey*', in Jocelyn Wogan-Browne (ed), *Language and Culture in Medieval Britain: The French of England c. 1100–c. 1500* (York: Boydell and Brewer, 2009), pp. 290–302 (p. 290).
22 Russell, 'The cultural context', p. 290.
23 For a survey of other manuscripts and books owned by Charles de Croÿ, see Hanno Wijsman, *Luxury Bound: Illustrated Manuscript Production and Noble and Princely Book Ownership in the Burgundian Netherlands (1400–1550)* (Turnhout: Brepols, 2010), pp. 324–27.
24 There are questions over the dating of this manuscript, but *c*. 1300 seems the most likely based on the various arguments. See Petit, 'La réception de la *Thebaïde*', pp. 711–12.
25 Morrison, 'Illuminations of the *Roman de Troie*', p. 160.
26 For more on the illustrative connection between MSS P14, L2 and Mn, see the comments in Appendix 1 for the entry of MS L2.
27 Petit edited this manuscript for his edition of *Enéas* and believed that it was copied at the end of the fourteenth century: Petit, 'Introduction' to *Enéas*, p. 23. However, Jung's identification of the Fauvel Master meant that a more likely dating is between 1315 and 1340, which is when the Fauvel Master was active: Jung, *La Légende*,

pp. 147–49. Morrison's study explains that Richard de Montbaston was also involved in its illustrations and that the only time both he and the Fauvel Master could have worked together was between 1330 and 1340: Morrison, 'Illuminations of the *Roman de Troie*', pp. 207–11. Given Morrison's detailed analysis of this manuscript's illustrations I am inclined to follow her dating.
28 Cipollaro, 'Turone di Maxio', pp. 16–22.
29 Ibid., p. 17.
30 Buchthal, *Historia Troiana*, p. 14.
31 Jung, *La Légende*, p. 290.
32 Ibid., p. 292.
33 Buchthal, *Historia Troiana*, p. 14. Refer to the catalogue entry for MS P18 for further details and references.
34 H. J. Hermann, *Die Italienischen Handschriften des Dugento und Trecento* (Leipzig: Hiersemann, 1928), Vol. 2, pp. 136–52 and Dagmar Thoss, *Benoît de Sainte-Maure: Roman de Troie (Österreichische Nationalbibliothek, Wien, Codex 2571)* (Munich: Lengenfelder, 1989).

Appendix 2

1 The folio containing this miniature was removed from the manuscript in 1850 and is held in the private collection of J. H. van Heek at Huis Bergh Castle in 's-Heerenberg.
2 See note above.

Bibliography

Manuscripts

Florence, Biblioteca Riccardiana, 2433 (MS F2).
Florence, Biblioteca Medicea Laurenziana, Plut. XLI, cod. 44 (MS F1).
Geneva, Bibliotheca Bodmeriana, Bodmer 18 (MS G).
London, British Library, Additional 14100 (MS L3).
London, British Library, Additional 30863 (MS L1).
London, British Library, Additional 34114 (MS L4).
London, British Library, Harley 4482 (MS L2).
Milan, Biblioteca Ambrosiana, D55 sup. (MS M).
Montpellier, Bibliothèque Interuniversitaire, Section Médecine, H. 251 (MS Mn).
Naples, Biblioteca Nazionale Vittorio Emanuele III, XIII cod. 38 (MS N).
Nottingham, University Library, Mi. LM. 6 (MS Nt).
Paris, Bibliothèque de l'Arsenal, 3340 (MS P3).
Paris, Bibliothèque de l'Arsenal, 3342 (MS P1).
Paris, Bibliothèque nationale de France, fr. 60 (MS P17).
Paris, Bibliothèque nationale de France, fr. 375 (MS P8).
Paris, Bibliothèque nationale de France, fr. 782 (MS P18).
Paris, Bibliothèque nationale de France, fr. 783 (MS P14).
Paris, Bibliothèque nationale de France, fr. 784 (MS P13).
Paris, Bibliothèque nationale de France, fr. 794 (MS P2).
Paris, Bibliothèque nationale de France, fr. 821 (MS P15).
Paris, Bibliothèque nationale de France, fr. 903 (MS P9).
Paris, Bibliothèque nationale de France, fr. 1416 (MS P10).
Paris, Bibliothèque nationale de France, fr. 1450 (MS P5).
Paris, Bibliothèque nationale de France, fr. 1553 (MS P7).
Paris, Bibliothèque nationale de France, fr. 1610 (MS P6).
Paris, Bibliothèque nationale de France, fr. 2181 (MS P4).
Paris, Bibliothèque nationale de France, fr. 12600 (MS P11).
Paris, Bibliothèque nationale de France, fr. 12603 (MS P12).
Paris, Bibliothèque nationale de France, fr. 19159 (MS P16).
Paris, Bibliothèque nationale de France, nouv. acq. fr. 6774 (MS P19).
Saint Petersburg, Rossijskaja Nacional'naja Biblioteka, fr. F. v. XIV. 3 (MS SP1).
Saint Petersburg, Rossijskaja Nacional'naja Biblioteka, fr. F. v. XIV. 6 (MS SP2).
Vatican City, Biblioteca apostolica Vaticana, Reg. Lat. 1505 (MS Vt).
Venice, Biblioteca Nazionale Marciana, fr. 17 (MS V1).
Venice, Biblioteca Nazionale Marciana, fr. 18 (MS V2).
Vienna, Österreichische Nationalbibliothek, Cod. 2471 (MS Vn).

Primary texts and translations

Abelard and Heloise, *The Letters of Abelard and Heloise*, ed. and trans. by Betty Radice (New York: Prentice Hall, 2003).
Albert of Aachen, *Historia Ierosolimitana: History of the Journey to Jerusalem*, ed. and trans. by Susan B. Edgington (Oxford: Oxford University Press, 2007).
Ambroise, *L'estoire de la Guerre Sainte*, ed. by Catherine Croizy-Naquet (Paris: Honoré Champion, 2014).
Aristotle, *Politics*, trans. by H. Rackham, 23 vols (Cambridge, MA: Harvard University Press, 1944).
Aucassin and Nicolette, ed. and trans. by Robert S. Sturges (East Lansing: Michigan State University Press, 2015).
Benoît de Sainte-Maure, *Le Roman de Troie*, ed. by Léopold Constans, 6 vols (Paris: Société des Anciens Textes Français, 1904–12).
Benoît de Sainte-Maure, *Chronique des ducs de Normandie par Benoît*, ed. by Carin Fahlin, 4 vols (Uppsala: Almqvist & Wiksell, 1951–79).
Benoît de Sainte-Maure, *Le Roman de Troie*, selections, ed. and trans. by Emmanuèle Baumgartner and Françoise Vielliard (Paris: Librairie Générale Française, 1998).
Benoît de Sainte-Maure, *The Roman de Troie*, trans. by Glyn S. Burgess and Douglas Kelly (Cambridge: D. S. Brewer, 2017).
La Chanson d'Antioche, ed. by Suzanne Duparc-Quioc, 2 vols (Paris: Librairie Orientaliste Paul Geuthner, 1977).
La Chanson d'Antioche: An Old French Account of the First Crusade, ed. and trans. by Susan B. Edgington and Carol Sweetenham (Farnham: Ashgate, 2011).
La Chanson de la Croisade Albigeoise, ed. by Henri Gougaud (Paris: Librairie Générale Française, 1989).
Chrétien de Troyes, *Œvres complètes*, ed. and trans. by Anne Berthelot and others (Paris: Gallimard, 1994).
Christine de Pizan, *La Città delle Dame*, ed. by Earl Jeffrey Richards and trans. by Patrizia Caraffi (Milan: Luni, 1997).
Christine de Pizan, *Le Livre des Trois Vertus*, ed. by Charity Cannon Willard and Eric Hicks (Paris: Champion, 1989).
Christine de Pizan, *The Book of the City of Ladies*, trans. by Rosalind Brown-Grant (London: Penguin Books, 1999).
Christine de Pizan, *Epistre Othea*, ed. by Gabriella Parussa (Geneva: Droz, 1999).
Dares and Dictys, *The Other Trojan War: Dictys and Dares Parallel Texts*, ed. and trans. by Giles Laurén (Berlin: Sophron, 2012).
Eneas: A Twelfth-Century French Romance, trans. by John A. Yunck (New York: Columbia University Press, 1974).
La Fille du Comte de Ponthieu, trans. by Danielle Quéruel, in Danielle Régnier-Bohler (ed), *Splendeurs de la Cour de Bourgogne: Récits et Chroniques* (Paris: Laffont, 1995).
Fredegar, *Fredegarii et Aliorum Chronica*, ed. by Bruno Krusch (Hannover: Bibliopolii Hahniani, 1888).
Fulcher of Chartres, *Historia Hierosolymitana*, from *Recueil des historiens des croisades* (Paris: Impr. Royale, 1866), Vol. 3.
Fulcher of Chartres, *A History of the Expedition to Jerusalem, 1095–1127*, trans. by Frances Rita Ryan (Knoxville: University of Tennessee Press, 1969).

Geoffrey of Monmouth, *The History of the Kings of Britain*, trans. by Lewis Thorpe (London: Penguin, 1966).
Gesta Francorum et aliorum Hierosolimitanorum: The Deeds of the Franks and the Other Pilgrims to Jerusalem, ed. and trans. by Rosalind Hill (Oxford: Clarendon Press, 1967).
Guibert of Nogent, *The Deeds of God through the Franks*, trans. by Robert Levine (Woodbridge: Boydell Press, 1997).
Heldris of Cornwall, *Le Roman de Silence*, ed. by Lewis Thorpe (Cambridge: Heffer, 1972).
Heldris of Cornwall, *Le Roman de Silence*, ed. and trans. by Sarah Roche-Mahdi (East Lansing: Michigan State University Press, 1992).
History of William Marshal, ed. by A. J. Holden and D. Crouch, trans. by S. Gregory (3 vols) (London: Anglo-Norman Text Society, 2002–06).
Jean Bodel, *La Chanson des Saisnes*, ed. by Annette Brasseur (Geneva: Droz, 1989).
Jean de Joinville, *Histoire de Saint Louis*, ed. by Natalis de Wailly, edition (Paris: F. Didot, 1874).
Jehan Le Fèvre, *The Book of Gladness / Le Livre de Leesce*, ed. and trans. by Linda Burke (Jefferson: McFarland & Company, 2013).
Jehan Malkaraume, *La Bible de Jehan Malkaraume (Ms. Paris, Bibl. Nat. fr. 903) (XIIIe/XIVe siècle)*, ed. by Jean Robert Smeets, 2 vols (Amsterdam: Van Gorcum, 1978).
Nennius, *Nennius et l'Historia Brittonum*, ed. by Ferdinand Lot (Paris: BEHE, 1934).
Niketas Choniates, *'O City of Byzantium:' Annals of Niketas Choniates*, ed. and trans. by Harry J. Magoulias (Detroit: Wayne State University Press, 1984).
Oliver of Paderborn, *The Capture of Damietta*, trans. by John J. Gavigan (Philadelphia: University of Pennsylvania Press, 1948).
Orderic Vitalis, *The Ecclesiastical History of England and Normandy*, trans. by Thomas Forester, 6 vols (London: H. G. Bohn, 1856).
Plato, *The Republic*, trans. by Benjamin Jowett, http://classics.mit.edu/Plato/republic.6.v.html [accessed 1 April 2017].
Raymond d'Aguilers, *Historia Francorum qui ceperunt Iherusalem*, trans. by John Hugh Hill and Laurita L. Hill (Philadelphia: American Philosophical Society, 1968).
Recueil des Historiens des Croisades. I: Historiens Occidentaux, 3 vols (Paris: Impr. Royale, 1866), Vol. 3.
Renaut de Beaujeu, *Le Bel Inconnu*, ed. by Michèle Perret and trans. by Michèle Perret and Isabelle Weill (Paris, 2003).
Robert the Monk, *History of the First Crusade: Historia Iherosolimitana*, trans. by Carol Sweetenham (Aldershot: Ashgate, 2006).
Le Roman d'Enéas, ed. by J. J. Salverda de Grave, 2 vols (Paris: É. Champion, 1925–29).
Le Roman d'Enéas, ed. and trans. by Aimé Petit (Paris: Livre de Poche, 1997).
Le Roman de Thèbes, ed. by Léopold Constans, 2 vols (Paris: Librairie de Firmin Didot, 1890).
Le Roman de Thèbes, ed. and trans. by Francine Mora-Lebrun (Paris: Livre de Poche, 1995).
Le Roman de Thèbes, ed. and trans. by Aimé Petit (Paris: H. Champion, 2008).
Le Roman de Thèbes: Manuscript A (BnF, fr. 375), ed. by Luca di Sabatino (Paris: Classiques Garnier, 2016).
The Romance of Thebes, trans. by Joan M. Ferrante and Robert W. Hanning (Tempe: ACMRS, 2018).
The Story of Thebes, trans. by John Smartt Coley (New York: Garland, 1986).
Statius, *Silvae and Thebaid*, ed. and trans. by J. H. Mozley, 2 vols (Cambridge, MA: Harvard University Press, 1967).
Ulrich von Liechtenstein, *The Service of Ladies*, trans. by J. W. Thomas (Woodbridge: Boydell, 2004).
Virgil, *The Aeneid*, ed. by J. W. Mackail (Oxford: Clarendon Press, 1930).

Virgil, *The Aeneid of Virgil*, trans. by Allen Mandelbaum (Berkeley: University of California Press, 1981).
Wace, *Le Roman de Rou*, ed. by A. J. Holden, 3 vols (Paris: Picard, 1970–73).
Wace, *Le Roman de Brut: A History of the British*, ed. and trans. by Judith Weiss (Exeter: University of Exeter Press, 1999).
Wace, *The Roman de Rou*, ed. and trans. by Glyn S. Burgess and Anthony Holden (St Helier: Société Jersiaise, 2002).
William of Tyre, *A History of Deeds Done beyond the Sea by William, Archbishop of Tyre*, trans. by Emily Atwater Babcock and A. C. Krey (New York: Columbia University Press, 1943).

Secondary sources

Adams, Alison, 'Destiny, love and the cultivation of suspense: the *Roman d'Enéas* and Aimon de Varennes', *Florimont*', *Reading Medieval Studies* 5 (1979), pp. 57–69.
Adler, Alfred, 'Militia and Amor in the *Roman de Troie*', *Romanische Forschungen* 72 (1960), pp. 14–29.
Aird, William M., *Robert 'Curthose,' Duke of Normandy (c. 1050–1134)* (Woodbridge: Boydell Press, 2008).
Allmand, Christopher, 'War and the non-combatant in the Middle Ages', in Maurice Keen (ed), *Medieval Warfare: A History* (Oxford: Oxford University Press, 1999), pp. 253–72.
Antón, Isabel Alfonso, 'The language and practice of negotiation in medieval conflict resolution', in Belle S. Tuten and Tracey L. Billado (eds), *Feud, Violence and Practice: Essays in Medieval Studies in Honour of Stephen D. White* (Farnham: Ashgate, 2010), pp. 158–74.
Arnold, John H., 'The labour of continence: masculinity and clerical virginity', in Anke Bernau, Ruth Evans and Sarah Salih (eds), *Medieval Virginities* (Cardiff: University of Wales Press, 2003), pp. 102–18.
Asbridge, Thomas, 'Alice of Antioch: a case study of female power in the twelfth century', in Peter Edbury and Jonathan Phillips (eds), *The Experience of Crusading: Defining the Crusader Kingdom* (Cambridge: Cambridge University Press, 2003), pp. 29–47.
Auerbach, Erich, *Literary Language and Its Public in Late Latin Antiquity and the Middle Ages* (New York: Pantheon Books, 1965).
Bachrach, Bernard S. and David S. Bachrach, *Warfare in Medieval Europe c. 400–c. 1453* (London: Routledge, 2017).
Bachrach, David S., 'The royal crossbow makers of England, 1204–72', *Nottingham Medieval Studies* 47 (2003), pp. 168–97.
Barbezat, Michael D., 'The fires of hell and the burning of heretics in the accounts of the executions at Orleans in 1022', *Journal of Medieval History* 40 (2014), pp. 399–420.
Bardsley, Sandy, 'Women's work reconsidered: gender and wage differentiation in late medieval England: a reply', *Past and Present* 173 (2001), pp. 199–202.
Bartlett, Robert, *The Making of Europe: Conquest, Colonization and Cultural Change 950–1350* (London: Penguin, 1994).
Baswell, Christopher, 'Men in the *Roman d'Enéas*: the construction of empire', in Clare A. Lees (ed), *Medieval Masculinities: Regarding Men in the Middle Ages* (Minneapolis: University of Minnesota Press, 1994), pp. 149–68.

Battles, Dominique, 'Trojan Elements in the Old French *Roman de Thèbes*', *Neophilologus* 85 (2001), pp. 163–76.
Battles, Dominique, *The Medieval Tradition of Thebes: History and Narrative in the OF Roman de Thèbes, Boccaccio, Chaucer and Lydgate* (New York: Routledge, 2004).
Baumgartner, Emmanuèle, 'Tombeaux pour guerriers et Amazones. Sur un motif descriptif de l'*Enéas* et du *Roman de Troie*', in Guy Mermier (ed), *Contemporary Readings of Medieval Literature* (Ann Arbor: University of Michigan Press, 1989), pp. 37–50.
Baumgartner, Emmanuèle and Laurence Harf-Lancner (eds), *Entre Fiction et Histoire: Troie et Rome au Moyen Âge* (Paris: Presses de la Sorbonne Nouvelle, 1997).
Beaune, Colette, *The Birth of an Ideology: Myths and Symbols of Nation in Late-Medieval France* (Berkeley: University of California Press, 1991).
Benham, J. E. M., 'Anglo-French peace conferences in the twelfth century', in John Gillingham (ed), *Anglo-Norman Studies XXVII: Proceedings of the Battle Conference, 2004* (Woodbridge: Boydell Press, 2005), pp. 52–67.
Benham, J. E. M., *Peacemaking in the Middle Ages: Principles and Practice* (Manchester: Manchester University Press, 2011).
Bennett, Matthew, 'Virile Latins, effeminate Greeks and strong women: gender definitions on crusade?' in Susan B. Edgington and Sarah Lambert (eds), *Gendering the Crusades* (Cardiff: University of Wales Press, 2001), pp. 16–30.
Bennett, Matthew and Katherine Weikert (eds), *Medieval Hostageship c. 700–1500* (New York: Routledge, 2016).
Benton, John F., 'The court of Champagne as literary centre', *Speculum* 36 (1961), pp. 551–91.
Bernau, Anke, Ruth Evans and Sarah Salih (eds), *Medieval Virginities* (Cardiff: University of Wales Press, 2003).
Bezzola, Reto Roberto, *Les Origines et la Formation de la Littérature Courtoise en Occident*. (Paris: H. Champion, 1963).
Bienvenu, Jean-Marc, 'Aliénor d'Aquitaine et Fontevraud', *Cahiers de Civilisation Médiévale* 113 (1984), pp. 15–27.
Blamires, Alcuin (ed), *Woman Defamed and Woman Defended: An Anthology of Medieval Texts* (Oxford: Clarendon Press, 1992).
Blumenfeld-Kosinski, Renate, 'The gods as metaphor in the *Roman de Thèbes*', *Modern Philology* 83 (1985), pp. 1–11.
Blumenfeld-Kosinski, Renate, *Reading Myth: Classical Mythology and Its Interpretations in Medieval French Literature* (Cambridge: Cambridge University Press, 1998).
Blythe, James M., 'Women in the military: scholastic arguments and medieval images of female warriors', *History of Political Thought* 22 (2001), pp. 242–69.
Boase, Roger, *The Origin and Meaning of Courtly Love: A Critical Study* (Manchester: Manchester University Press, 1977).
Bouchard, Constance Brittain, 'Eleanor's divorce from Louis VII: the uses of consanguinity', in Bonnie Wheeler and John C. Parsons (eds), *Eleanor of Aquitaine: Lord and Lady* (New York: Palgrave Macmillan, 2003), pp. 223–35.
Boutet, Dominique, 'Carrefours idéologiques de la royauté arthurienne', *Cahiers de Civilisation Médiévale* 27 (1985), pp. 3–17.
Bradbury, Jim, *The Medieval Siege* (Woodbridge: Boydell Press, 1992).
Bradbury, Jim, *Stephen and Matilda: The Civil War of 1139–53* (Stroud: The History Press, 2005).
Braudy, Leo, *From Chivalry to Terrorism: War and the Changing Nature of Masculinity* (New York: Vintage Books, 2003).

Broadhurst, Karen M., 'Henry II of England and Eleanor of Aquitaine: patrons of literature in French?', *Viator* 27 (1996), pp. 53–84.

Brown, Elizabeth. E. R., 'Eleanor of Aquitaine: parent, queen, and duchess', in William W. Kibler (ed), *Eleanor of Aquitaine: Patron and Politician* (Austin: University of Texas Press, 1976), pp. 9–34.

Brundage, James A., 'Rape and marriage in the medieval canon law', *Revue du Droit Canonique* 28 (1978), pp. 62–75.

Brundage, James A., *Sex, Law and Marriage in the Middle Ages* (Aldershot: Variorum, 1993).

Brundage, James A., *Law, Sex and Christian Society in Medieval Europe* (Chicago: University of Chicago Press, 2009).

Buchthal, Hugo, *Historia Troiana: Studies in the History of Mediaeval Secular Illustration* (London: Warburg Institute, 1971).

Burgess, Glyn S., 'The term "chevalerie" in twelfth-century French', in Peter Rolfe Monks and D. D. R. Owen (eds), *Medieval Codicology, Iconography, Literature and Translation: Studies for Keith Val Sinclair* (Leiden: Brill, 1994), pp. 343–58.

Burns, E. Jane, 'Courtly love: who needs it? Recent feminist work in the medieval French tradition', *Signs* 27 (2001), pp. 23–57.

Burns, E. Jane, *Courtly Love Undressed: Reading through Clothes in Medieval French Literature* (Philadelphia: University of Pennsylvania Press, 2002).

Burns, E. Jane, 'Magical politics from Poitou to Armenia: Mélusine, Jean de Berry and the eastern Mediterranean', *Journal of Medieval and Early Modern Studies* 43 (2013), pp. 275–301.

Cammarota, Maria Grazia, 'War and the "agony of conscience" in Ælfric's writings', *Mediaevistik* 26 (2014), pp. 87–110.

Cannon, Christopher, '*Raptus* in the Chaumpaigne Release and a newly discovered document concerning the life of Geoffrey Chaucer', *Speculum* 68 (1993), pp. 74–94.

Cardini, Franco, 'The warrior and the knight', in Jacques Le Goff (ed), *The Medieval World* (London: Collins & Brown, 1990), pp. 75–111.

Carr, A. D., 'Wales', in Michael Jones (ed), *The New Cambridge Medieval History VI c. 1300–1415* (Cambridge: Cambridge University Press, 2000), pp. 334–44.

Caspi-Reisfeld, Keren, 'Women warriors during the crusades, 1095–1254', in Susan B. Edgington and Sarah Lambert (eds), *Gendering the Crusades* (Cardiff: University of Wales Press, 2001), pp. 94–107.

Cassagnes-Brouquet, Sophie, 'Penthésilée, reine des Amazones et Preuse, une image de la femme guerrière à la fin du Moyen Âge', *Clio: Histoire, femmes et sociétés* 20 (2004), 169–79.

Cassagnes-Brouquet, Sophie, *Chevaleresses: Une chevalerie au féminin* (Paris: Perrin, 2013).

Cherewatuk, Karen, 'Born-again virgins and holy bastards: Bors and Elyne and Lancelot and Galahad', *Arthuriana* 11 (2001), pp. 52–64.

Chibnall, Marjorie, *The Empress Matilda: Queen Consort, Queen Mother and Lady of the English* (Oxford: Blackwell, 1993).

Cipollaro, Costanza, 'Turone di Maxio, miniatore del *Roman de Troie* di Parigi (Bibliothèque nationale de France, ms français 782), *Codices Manuscripti* 33 (2012), pp. 16–22.

Constable, Olivia R., 'Muslim Spain and Mediterranean slavery: the medieval slave trade as an aspect of Muslim-Christian relations', in Scott Waugh (ed), *Christendom and Its Discontents* (Berkeley: University of California Press, 1998), pp. 264–84.

Cormier, Raymond J., *One Heart, One Mind: The Rebirth of Virgil's Hero in Medieval French Romance* (Oxford, MI: University of Mississippi Press, 1973).
Cormier, Raymond J., 'Gleanings on the manuscript tradition of the *Roman d'Enéas*', *Manuscripta* 18 (1974), pp. 42–47.
Cormier, Raymond J., 'An example of twelfth-century *adaptatio*: the *Roman d'Enéas* author's use of glossed *Aeneid* manuscripts', *Revue d'Histoire des Textes* 19 (1989), pp. 277–89.
Cormier, Raymond J., 'Classical continuity and transposition in two twelfth-century adaptations of the *Aeneid*', *Symposium: A Quarterly Journal in Modern Literatures* 47 (1994), pp. 261–74.
Cormier, Raymond J., 'Pagan versus Christian values in the *Roman d'Enéas*', *Medievalia et Humanistica* 33 (2007), pp. 63–86.
Cormier, Raymond J., 'A propos de Lavine amoureuse: le savoir sentimental feminine et cognitive', *Bien Dire et Bien Aprandre* 24 (2007), pp. 57–70.
Cowdrey, H. E. J., 'The Peace and Truce of God in the eleventh century', *Past and Present* 46 (1970), pp. 42–67.
Cowdrey, H. E. J., 'Christianity and the morality of warfare during the first century of crusading', in Marcus Bull and Norman Housley (eds), *The Experience of Crusading, 1: Western Approaches* (Cambridge: Cambridge University Press, 2003), pp. 175–92.
Cowper, Frederick A. G., 'Date and dedication of the *Roman de Troie*', *Modern Philology* 27 (1929–1930), pp. 379–83.
Cowper, Frederick A. G., 'Origins and peregrinations of the Laval-Middleton manuscript', *Nottingham Mediaeval Studies* 3 (1959), pp. 3–18.
Cox, Rory, 'Asymmetric warfare and military conduct in the Middle Ages', *Journal of Medieval History* 38 (2012), pp. 100–25.
Craig, Leigh Ann, '"Stronger than men and braver than knights": women and the pilgrimages to Jerusalem and Rome in the later Middle Ages', *Journal of Medieval History* 29 (2003), pp. 153–75.
Croizy-Naquet, Catherine, 'La forteresse de tentes troyennes dans *Le Roman d'Enéas* (vv. 7281-7352)', *Bien dire et bien aprandre* 9 (1991), pp. 73–89.
Croizy-Naquet, Catherine, 'Les amours d'Achille et de Polyxène dans le *Roman de Troie*', in Rosanna Brusegan and others (eds), *L'Antichità nella Cultura Europea del Medioevo. L'Antiquité dans la Culture Européenne du Moyen Âge* (Greifswald, 1998), pp. 31–42.
Crosland, Jessie, '*Enéas* and the *Aeneid*', *The Modern Language Review* 29 (1934), pp. 282–90.
Crouch, David, *Tournament* (London: Hambledone Continuum, 2006).
Curry, Anne, 'Soldiers' wives in the Hundred Years War', in Peter R. Coss and Christopher Tyerman (eds), *Soldiers, Nobles and Gentlemen: Essays in Honour of Maurice Keen* (Woodbridge: Boydell Press, 2009), pp. 198–214.
Curry, Anne, 'The theory and practice of female immunity in the medieval west', in Elizabeth D. Heineman (ed), *Sexual Violence in Conflict Zones: From the Ancient World to the Era of Human Rights* (Philadelphia: University of Pennsylvania Press, 2011), pp. 173–88.
Curry, Anne and Glenn Foard, 'Where are the dead of medieval battles? A preliminary survey', *Journal of Conflict Archaeology* 11 (2016), pp. 61–77.
Curry, Peggy L., 'Representing the biblical Judith in literature and art: an intertextual cultural critique' (unpublished PhD thesis, University of Massachusetts Amherst, 1994).
Curtius, E. R., *European Literature and the Latin Middle Ages*, trans. by W. R. Trask (Princeton: Princeton University Press, 1952).

Dark, Patricia, '"A woman of subtlety and a man's resolution": Matilda of Boulogne in the power struggles of the Anarchy', in Brenda Bolton and Christine Meek (eds), *Aspects of Power and Authority in the Middle Ages* (Turnhout: Brepols, 2007), pp. 147–64.

Delage-Béland, Isabelle, 'Une conquête problématique: le statut ambigu de la fiction dans le manuscript Paris, BNF, fr. 375, un recueil de *romans*', in Olivier Collet, Francis Gingras and Richard Trachsler (eds), *Lire en Context: Enquête sur les Manuscrits de Fabliaux* (Montreal: Les Presses de l'Université de Montréal, 2012), pp. 95–113.

Derbes, Anne and Mark Sandona, 'Amazons and crusaders: the *Histoire Universelle* in Flanders and the Holy Land', in Daniel H. Weiss and Lisa Mahoney (eds), *France and the Holy Land: Frankish Culture and the End of the Crusades* (Baltimore: Hopkins University Press, 2004), pp. 187–229.

Desmond, Marilynn, *Reading Dido: Gender, Textuality and the Medieval 'Aeneid'* (Minneapolis: University of Minnesota Press, 1994).

Desmond, Marilynn, 'History and fiction: the narrativity and historiography of the matter of Troy', in William Burgwinkle, Nicholas Hammond and Emma Wilson (eds), *The Cambridge History of French Literature* (Cambridge: Cambridge University Press, 2011), pp. 139–44.

Després Caubrière, Catherine, 'L'enjeu triangulaire de la trame romanesque du *Roman d'Enéas*', *Cédille* 9 (2013), 129–44.

DeVries, Kelly, 'A woman as leader of men: Joan of Arc's military career', in Bonnie Wheeler and Charles T. Wood (eds), *Fresh Verdicts on Joan of Arc* (New York: Garland, 1996), pp. 3–18.

Donovan, L. G., *Recherches sur 'Le Roman de Thèbes'* (Paris: Société d'Edition d'Enseignement Supérieur, 1975).

Dragonetti, Roger, *Le Mirage des Sources: L'Art du Faux dans le Roman Médiéval* (Paris: Editions du Seuil, 1987).

Dronke, Peter, 'Peter of Blois and poetry at the court of Henry II', *Mediaeval Studies* 38 (1976), pp. 185–235.

Duby, Georges, *Les Trois Ordres ou l'Imaginaire du Féodalisme* (Paris: Gallimard, 1978).

Duby, Georges, *Love and Marriage in the Middle Ages*, trans. by Jane Dunnett (Chicago: University of Chicago Press, 1996).

Dudink, Stefan and Josh Tosh (eds), *Masculinities in Politics and War: Gendering Modern History* (New York: Vintage Books, 2003).

Dyggve, Holger Petersen, 'Personnages historiques figurant dans la poésie lyrique française des XIIe et XIIIe siècles: deux dames du *Tournoiement* de Huon d'Oisi', *Neuphilologische Mitteilungen* 41 (1940), pp. 157–80.

Easton, Martha, 'Pain, torture and death in the Huntingdon Library *Legenda Aurea*', in Samantha J. E. Riches and Sarah Salih (eds), *Gender and Holiness: Men, Women and Saints in Late Medieval Europe* (London: Routledge, 2002), pp. 49–64.

Eckman, Zoe, 'An oppressive silence: the evolution of the raped woman in medieval France and England', *Historian: Journal of the Undergraduate History Department at New York University* 50 (2009), pp. 68–77.

Eddé, Anne-Marie, *Saladin* (Cambridge: Harvard University Press, 2011).

Edgington, Susan B. and Sarah Lambert (eds), *Gendering the Crusades* (Cardiff: University of Wales Press, 2001).

Egmond, Florike, 'Execution, dissection, pain and infamy: a morphological investigation', in Florike Egmond and Robert Zwijnenberg (eds), *Bodily Extremities: Preoccupations with the Human Body in Early Modern European Culture* (Aldershot: Ashgate, 2003), pp. 92–127.

Evans, Michael R., '"Unfit to bear arms": the gendering of arms and armour in accounts of women on crusade', in Susan B. Edgington and Sarah Lambert (eds), *Gendering the Crusades* (Cardiff: University of Wales Press, 2001), pp. 45–58.
Evans, Michael R., 'Penthesilea on the Second Crusade: is Eleanor of Aquitaine the Amazon queen of Niketas Choniates?', *Crusades* 8 (2009), pp. 23–30.
Evans, Michael R., *Inventing Eleanor: The Medieval and Post-Medieval Image of Eleanor of Aquitaine* (London: Bloomsbury, 2014).
Evergates, Theodore (ed), 'The feudal imaginary of Georges Duby', *Journal of Medieval and Early Modern Studies* 27 (1997), pp. 641–60.
Evergates, Theodore, *Aristocratic Women in Medieval France* (Philadelphia: University of Pennsylvania Press, 1999).
Faral, Edmond, 'Ovide et quelques autres sources du *Roman d'Enéas*', *Romania* 40 (1911), pp. 161–234.
Faral, Edmond, 'Compte rendu: *Le Roman de Troie*, par Constans', *Romania* 42 (1913), pp. 88–106.
Faral, Edmond, *Recherches sur les Sources Latines des Contes et Romans Courtois du Moyen Âge* (Paris: Champion, 1913).
Flori, Jean, 'La notion de chevalerie dans les *chansons de geste* du 12e siècle', *Le Moyen Âge* 81 (1975), pp. 211–44.
Flori, Jean, 'La notion de la chevalerie dans les romans de Chrétien de Troyes', *Romania* 114 (1996), pp. 289–315.
Flori, Jean, *Chevaliers et chevalerie au Moyen Âge* (Paris: Hachette, 1998).
Flori, Jean, 'Knightly society', in David Luscombe and Jonathan Riley-Smith (eds), *The New Cambridge Medieval History IV, c. 1024–c. 1198, Part I* (Cambridge: Cambridge University Press, 2004), pp. 148–84.
Forey, Alan, 'Women and the military orders in the twelfth and thirteenth centuries', in Anthony Luttrell and Helen Nicholson (eds), *Hospitaller Women in the Middle Ages* (Aldershot: Ashgate, 2006), pp. 43–70.
Fößel, Amalie, 'The political traditions of female rulership in medieval Europe', in Judith M. Bennett and Ruth Mazo Karras (eds), *The Oxford Handbook of Women and Gender in Medieval Europe* (Oxford: Oxford University Press, 2013), pp. 68–83.
Franchet d'Esperty, Sylvie, 'La *Thébaïde* de Stace et ses rapports avec le *Roman de Thèbes* (prologue, épilogue et causalité)', *Information Littéraire* 2 (2003), pp. 4–10.
Friedman, Yvonne, 'Women in captivity and their ransom during the crusader period', in Michael Goodich, Sophia Menache and Sylvia Schein (eds), *Cross Cultural Convergences in the Crusader Period: Essays Presented to Aryeh Grabois on His Sixtieth Birthday* (New York: P. Lang, 1995), pp. 75–87.
Friedman, Yvonne, 'Captivity and ransom: the experience of women', in Susan B. Edgington and Sarah Lambert (eds), *Gendering the Crusades* (Cardiff: University of Wales Press, 2001), pp. 121–39.
Friedman, Yvonne, *Encounter between Enemies: Captivity and Ransom in the Latin Kingdom of Jerusalem* (Leiden: Brill, 2002).
Gabrielli, Francesco, *Arab Historians of the Crusades* (Berkeley: University of California Press, 1969).
Ganshof, François-Louis, *Qu'est-ce que la Féodalité?*, 4th edition (Brussels: Presses Universitaires de Bruxelles, 1968).
Gaughan, Gillian, 'Rank and social status in non-Arthurian Romance of the late twelfth and early thirteenth centuries' (unpublished PhD thesis, University of Liverpool, 1987).
Gaunt, Simon, 'The significance of Silence', *Paragraph* 13 (1990), pp. 202–16.

Gaunt, Simon, *Gender and Genre in Medieval French Literature* (Cambridge: Cambridge University Press, 1995).
Gaunt, Simon, *Love and Death in Medieval French and Occitan Courtly Literature: Martyrs to Love* (Oxford: Oxford University Press, 2006).
Gera, Deborah Levine, *Warrior Women: The Anonymous Tractatus De Mulieribus* (Leiden: Brill, 1997).
Gillingham, John, 'Love, marriage and politics in the twelfth century', *Forum for Modern Language Studies* 25 (1989), pp. 292–303.
Gillingham, John, 'Christian warriors and the enslavement of fellow Christians', in Martin Aurell and Catalina Girbea (eds), *Chevalerie et Christianisme aux XIIe et XIIIe siècles* (Rennes: Presses Universitaires de Rennes, 2011), pp. 237–56.
Gillingham, John, 'The meetings of the kings of France and England, 1066–1204', in David Crouch and Kathleen Thompson (eds), *Normandy and Its Neighbours, 900–1250* (Turnhout: Brepols, 2011), pp. 17–42.
Gillingham, John, 'Women, children and the profits of war', in Janet L. Nelson and Susan Reynolds (eds), *Gender and Historiography: Studies in the History of the Earlier Middle Ages in Honour of Pauline Stafford* (London: Institute of Historical Research, 2012), pp. 61–74.
Gillingham, John, 'Crusading warfare, chivalry and the enslavement of women and children', in Gregory Halfond (ed), *The Medieval Way of War: Studies in Medieval Military History in Honour of Bernard S. Bachrach* (Farnham: Ashgate, 2015), pp. 133–52.
Glasheen, Charles R., 'Provisioning Peter the Hermit: from Cologne to Constantinople, 1096', in John H. Pryor (ed), *Logistics of Warfare in the Age of the Crusades: Proceedings of a Workshop Held at the Centre for Medieval Studies, University of Sydney, 30 September to 4 October 2002* (Aldershot: Ashgate, 2006), pp. 119–30.
Goldberg, P. J. P., *Women, Work and Life Cycle in a Medieval Economy: Women in York and Yorkshire c. 1300–1520* (Oxford: Clarendon Press, 1992).
Goldstein, Joshua S., *War and Gender* (Cambridge: Cambridge University Press, 2001).
Gottlieb, Rebecca, 'Why we can't "do without" *Camille*', in Aldo S. Bernardo and Saul Levin (eds), *The Classics in the Middle Ages: Papers of the Twentieth Annual Conference of the Center for Medieval and Early Renaissance Studies* (Binghamton, NY: CMERS, 1990), pp. 153–64.
Gravdal, Kathryn, *Ravishing Maidens: Writing Rape in Medieval French Literature and Law* (Philadelphia: University of Pennsylvania Press, 1991).
Gravelle, Yves, 'Le problème des prisonniers pendant les croisades orientales, 1095–1192' (unpublished master's thesis, University of Sherbrooke, 1999).
Green, Judith A., 'Aristocratic women in early twelfth-century England', in C. Warren Hollister (ed), *Anglo-Norman Political Culture and the Twelfth-Century Renaissance: Proceedings of the Borchard Conference on Anglo-Norman History, 1995* (Woodbridge: Boydell Press, 1997), pp. 59–82.
Green, Judith A., 'Duchesses of Normandy in the eleventh and twelfth centuries', in David Crouch and Kathleen Thompson (eds), *Normandy and Its Neighbours, 900–1250: Essays for David Bates* (Turnhout: Brepols, 2011), pp. 43–59.
Green, Monica H., *Women's Healthcare in the Medieval West* (Aldershot: Ashgate, 2000).
Green, Monica H., 'Women's medical practice and health care in medieval Europe', in Judith M. Bennett and others (eds), *Sisters and Workers in the Middle Ages* (Chicago: University of Chicago Press, 1989), pp. 39–78.
Grisay, Auguste, G. Laris and M. Dubois-Stasse (eds), *Les Dénominations de la Femme dans les Anciens Textes Littéraires Français* (Gembloux: J. Ducolot, 1969).

Guenée, Bernard, 'Les généalogies entre l'histoire et la politique: la fierté d'être Capétian, en France, au Moyen Âge', *Annales: Economies, Sociétés, Civilisations* 33 (1978), pp. 450–77.
Haas, Judith, 'Trojan sodomy and the politics of marriage in the *Roman d'Enéas*', *Exemplaria* 20 (2008), pp. 48–71.
Halperin, David M., *One Hundred Years of Homosexuality: And Other Essays on Greek Love* (New York: Routledge, 1990).
Hanley, Catherine, 'The portrayal of warfare in Old French literature *c.* 1150–*c.* 1270' (unpublished PhD thesis, University of Sheffield, 2001).
Hanley, Catherine, *War and Combat, 1150–1270: The Evidence from Old French Literature* (Cambridge: Brewer, 2003).
Hanley, Catherine, *Matilda: Empress, Queen, Warrior* (New Haven: Yale University Press, 2019).
Hartsock, Nancy C. M., 'Masculinity, heroism and the making of war', in A. Harris and Y. King (eds), *Rocking the Ship of State: Towards a Feminist Peace Politics* (Boulder: Westview Press, 1989), pp. 133–52.
Harwood, Sophie, 'Swans and Amazons: Penthesilea and the case for women's heraldry in medieval culture', *The Mediaeval Journal* 7 (2017), pp. 61–87.
Harwood, Sophie, '"I will lead you to the river": women, water and warfare in the *Roman de Thèbes* and early chronicles of the first crusade', *Open Library of Humanities* 4(2):15 (2018), pp. 1–22.
Haskins, Charles H., 'Henry II as a patron of literature', in A. G. Little and F. M. Powicke (eds), *Essays in Medieval History Presented to Thomas Frederick Tout* (Manchester: Clark Edinburgh, 1925), pp. 71–77.
Hay, David J., 'Gender bias and religious intolerance in accounts of the "massacres" of the First Crusade', in Michael Gervers and James M. Powell (eds), *Tolerance and Intolerance: Social Conflict in the Age of the Crusades* (Syracuse: Syracuse University Press, 2001), pp. 3–10.
Hay, David J., 'Canon laws regarding female military commanders up to the time of Gratian: some texts and their historical contexts', in Mark D. Meyerson and others (eds), *A Great Effusion of Blood?: Interpreting Medieval Violence* (Toronto: University of Toronto Press, 2004), pp. 287–314.
Hay, David J., '"Collateral damage?" Civilian casualties in the early ideologies of chivalry and crusade', in Niall Christie and Maya Yazigi (eds), *Noble Ideals and Bloody Realities: Warfare in the Middle Ages* (Leiden: Brill, 2006), pp. 3–25.
Hay, David J., *The Military Leadership of Matilda of Canossa, 1046–1115* (Manchester: Manchester University Press, 2010).
Hedeman, Anne D., *The Royal Image: Illustrations of the 'Grandes Chroniques de France,' 1272–1422* (Berkeley: University of California Press, 1991).
Hedeman, Anne D., 'Pierre Salmon's advice for a king', *Gesta* 32 (1993), pp. 113–23.
Heebøll-Holm, Thomas K., 'Apocalypse then? The First Crusade, traumas of war and Thomas de Marle', in Kerstin Hundahl, Lars Kjær and Niels Lund (eds), *Denmark and Europe in the Middle Ages, c. 1000–1525: Essays in Honour of Professor Michael H. Gelting* (Farnham: Ashgate, 2014), pp. 237–54.
Heers, Jacques, *Esclaves et Domestiques au Moyen Âge dans le Monde Méditerranéen* (Paris: Fayard, 1981).
Hermann, H. J., *Die Italienischen Handschriften des Dugento und Trecento*, 2 vols (Leipzig: Hiersemann, 1928).
Hodgson, Natasha R., *Women, Crusading and the Holy Land in Historical Narrative* (Woodbridge: Boydell Press, 2007).

Holdsworth, Christopher J., 'Peacemaking in the twelfth century', in Christopher Harper-Bill (ed), *Anglo-Norman Studies XIX: Proceedings of the Battle Conference, 1996* (Woodbridge: Boydell Press, 1997), pp. 1–18.
Hourihane, Colum (ed), *Looking Beyond: Visions, Dreams and Insights in Medieval Art and History* (Princeton: Princeton University Press, 2010).
Huneycutt, Lois L., 'Images of queenship in the High Middle Ages', *The Haskins Society Journal: Studies in Medieval History* 1 (1989), pp. 61–71.
Huneycutt, Lois L., 'Female succession and the language of power in the writings of twelfth-century churchmen', in John Carmi Parsons (ed), *Medieval Queenship* (New York: St. Martin's Press, 1998), pp. 189–201.
Huneycutt, Lois L., *Matilda of Scotland: A Study in Medieval Queenship* (Woodbridge: Boydell Press, 2003).
Hutchings, Kimberley, 'Making sense of masculinity and war', *Men and Masculinities* 10 (2008), pp. 389–404.
Jankofsy, Klaus P., 'Public executions in England in the late Middle Ages: the indignity and dignity of death', *Omega: Journal of Death and Dying* 10 (1980), pp. 43–57.
Johns, Susan M. (ed), *Noblewomen, Aristocracy and Power in the Twelfth-Century Anglo-Norman Realm* (Manchester: Manchester University Press, 2003).
Johnson, James, 'The meaning of non-combatant immunity in the Just War / Limited War tradition', *Journal of the American Academy of Religion* 39 (1971), pp. 151–70.
Johnson, James, 'Thinking morally about war in the Middle Ages and today', in Henrik Syse and Gregory M. Reichberg (eds), *Ethics, Nationalism and Just War: Medieval and Contemporary Perspectives* (Washington, DC: Catholic University of America Press, 2007), pp. 3–10.
Jung, Marc-René, *La Légende de Troie en France au Moyen Âge: Analyse des Versions Françaises et Bibliographie Raisonnée des Manuscrits* (Basel: Francke, 1996).
Kaeuper, Richard W., *Chivalry and Violence in Medieval Europe* (Oxford: Oxford University Press, 1999).
Kaeuper, Richard W., *Medieval Chivalry* (Cambridge: Cambridge University Press, 2016).
Karras, Ruth Mazo, *From Boys to Men: Formations of Masculinity in Late Medieval Europe* (Philadelphia: University of Pennsylvania Press, 2003).
Kay, Sarah, *The Chansons de Geste in the Age of Romance* (Oxford: Clarendon Press, 1995).
Kedar, Benjamin Z., 'The Jerusalem Massacre of July 1099 in the western historiography of the crusades', *Crusades* 3 (2004), pp. 15–75.
Keen, Maurice, *Chivalry* (New Haven: Yale University Press, 1984).
Kelly, Douglas, 'The invention of Briseide's story in Benoît de Sainte-Maure's *Troie*', *Romance Philology* 48 (1995), pp. 221–41.
Kelly, Douglas, 'Perspectives on women in war in twelfth-century Troy', in Myriam Watthée-Delmotte and Paul-Augustin Deproost (eds), *Imaginaires du Mal* (Paris: Les Éditions du Cerf, 2000), pp. 115–31.
Kelly, Kathleen Coyne, *Performing Virginity and Testing Chastity in the Middle Ages* (London: Routledge, 2000).
Kennedy, George A., *The Latin Iliad: Introduction, Text, Translation and Notes* (Fort Collins: Privately published, 1998).
Keskiaho, Jesse, *Dreams and Visions in the Early Middle Ages: The Reception and Use of Patristic Ideas, 400–900* (Cambridge: Cambridge University Press, 2015).
Kibler, William W. (ed), *Eleanor of Aquitaine: Patron and Politician* (Austin: University of Texas Press, 1976).
King, Edmund, *The Anarchy of King Stephen's Reign* (Oxford: Clarendon Press, 1994).

King, Edmund, *King Stephen* (New Haven: Yale University Press, 2010).
Kostick, Conor, 'Eleanor of Aquitaine and the women of the Second Crusade', in Conor Kostick (ed), *Medieval Italy, Medieval and Early Modern Women: Essays in Honour of Christine Meek* (Dublin: Four Courts Press, 2010), pp. 195–205.
Kosto, Adam J., *Hostages in the Middle Ages* (Oxford: Oxford University Press, 2012).
Krueger, Roberta L., *Women Readers and the Ideology of Gender in Old French Verse Romance* (Cambridge: Cambridge University Press, 1993).
Labande, Edmond-René, 'Pour une image véridique d'Aliénor d'Aquitaine', *Bulletin de la Société des Antiquaires de l'Ouest* 4 (1952), pp. 175–234.
Larrington, Carolyne, *Women and Writing in Medieval Europe: A Sourcebook* (London: Routledge, 1995).
Laurie, Helen C. R., '*Enéas* and the doctrine of courtly love', *The Modern Language Review* 64 (1969), pp. 283–94.
Lees, Clare A. (ed), *Medieval Masculinities: Regarding Men in the Middle Ages* (Minneapolis: University of Minnesota Press, 1994).
Lejeune, Rita, 'Rôle littéraire d'Aliénor d'Aquitaine et de sa famille', *Cultura Neolatina* 14 (1954), pp. 5–57.
Lejeune, Rita, 'Rôle littéraire de la famille d'Aliénor d'Aquitaine', *Cahiers de Civilisation Médiévale* 1 (1958), pp. 319–37.
Lepage, Yvan G., 'Un recueil français de la fin du XIIIe siècle (Paris, Bibliothèque Nationale, fr. 1553)', *Scriptorium* 29 (1975), pp. 23–46.
Livingstone, Amy, 'Pour une revision du "mâle" Moyen Âge de Georges Duby (États-Unis)', *Clio: Histoire, femmes et sociétés* 8 (1998), 1–12.
Logan, F. Donald, *Runaway Religious in Medieval England, 1240–1540* (Cambridge: Cambridge University Press, 1996).
Logié, Philippe, *L'Enéas: Une Traduction au Risque de l'Invention* (Paris: Champion, 1999).
Logié, Philippe, 'L'oubli d'Hésione ou le fatal aveuglement: le jeu du tort et du droit dans le *Roman de Troie* de Benoît de Sainte Maure', *Le Moyen Âge* 108 (2002), pp. 235–52.
Longnon, Jean, *Les Compagnons de Villehardouin* (Geneva: Librairie Droz, 1978).
LoPrete, Kimberley A., 'Adela of Blois: familial alliances and female lordship', in Theodore Evergates (ed), *Aristocratic Women in Medieval France* (Philadelphia: University of Pennsylvania Press, 1999), pp. 7–43.
LoPrete, Kimberley A., 'The gender of lordly women: the case of Adela of Blois', in Christine Meek and Catherine Lawless (eds), *Studies on Medieval and Early Modern Women: Pawns or Players* (Dublin: Four Courts Press, 2003), pp. 90–110.
LoPrete, Kimberley A., *Adela of Blois: Countess and Lord (c. 1067–1137)* (Dublin: Four Courts Press, 2007).
Maddicott, J. R., *Simon de Montfort* (Cambridge: Cambridge University Press, 1994).
Maier, Christopher T., 'The roles of women in the crusade movement: a survey', *Journal of Medieval History* 30 (2004), pp. 61–82.
Marchello-Nizia, Christiane, 'De l'*Enéide* à l'*Enéas*: les attributs du fondateur', in *Lectures Médiévales de Virgile. Actes du Colloque Organisé par l'Ecole Française de Rome (Rome, 25–28 octobre 1982)* (Rome: École Française de Rome, 1985), pp. 251–66.
Marvin, Laurence W., *The Occitan War: A Military and Political History of the Albigensian Crusade, 1209–18,* (Cambridge: Cambridge University Press, 2008).
McCash, June Hall Martin, 'Marie de Champagne and Eleanor of Aquitaine: a relationship reexamined', *Speculum* 54 (1979), pp. 698–711.
McCash, June Hall Martin (ed), *The Cultural Patronage of Medieval Women* (Athens, GA: University of Georgia Press, 1996), pp. 1–49.

McCracken, Peggy, '"The boy who was a girl": reading gender in the *Roman de Silence*', *Romanic Review* 85 (1994), pp. 517–46.
McCracken, Peggy, *The Romance of Adultery: Queenship and Sexual Transgression in Old French Literature* (Philadelphia: University of Pennsylvania Press, 1998).
McCracken, Peggy, 'Scandalising desire: Eleanor of Aquitaine and the chroniclers', in Bonnie Wheeler and John Carmi Parsons (eds), *Eleanor of Aquitaine: Lord and Lady* (New York: Palgrave Macmillan, 2003), pp. 247–63.
McGuire, Brian Patrick (ed), *War and Peace in the Middle Ages* (Copenhagen: C. A. Reitzels Forlag, 1987).
McKee, Sally, 'Inherited status and slavery in late medieval Italy and Venetian Crete', *Past and Present* 182 (2004), pp. 31–53.
McKee, Sally, 'Slavery', in Judith M. Bennett and Ruth Mazo Karras (eds), *The Oxford Handbook of Women and Gender in Medieval Europe* (Oxford: Oxford University Press, 2013), pp. 281–94.
McLaughlin, Megan, 'The woman warrior: gender, warfare and society in medieval Europe', *Women's Studies* 17 (1990), pp. 193–209.
Menegaldo, Silvère, 'De la traduction à l'invention: La naissance du genre romanesque au XIIe siècle', in Claudio Galderisi (ed), *Translations Médiévales: Cinq Siècles de Traductions en Français au Moyen Âge (XIe–XVe siècles)* (Turnhout: Brepols, 2011), pp. 295–323.
Mercer, Malcolm, 'King's armourers and the growth of the armourer's craft in early fourteenth-century London', in J. S. Hamilton (ed), *Fourteenth Century England, VIII* (Woodbridge: Boydell Press, 2014), pp. 1–20.
Milliken, Roberta, *Ambiguous Locks: An Iconology of Hair in Medieval Art and Literature* (London: McFarland & Company, 2012).
Mitchell, Piers D., *Medicine in the Crusades: Warfare, Wounds and the Medieval Surgeon* (Cambridge: Cambridge University Press, 2004).
Mora-Lebrun, Francine, 'Sources de l'*Enéas*: La tradition exégétique et le modèle épique latin', in Jean Dufournet (ed), *Relire le 'Roman d'Enéas'* (Paris: Champion, 1985), pp. 83–104.
Morrison, Elizabeth, 'Illuminations of the *Roman de Troie* and French royal dynastic ambition (1260–1340)' (unpublished PhD thesis, Cornell University, 2002).
Morrison, Elizabeth, 'Linking ancient Troy and medieval France: illuminations of an early copy of the *Roman de Troie*', in Henry Ansgar Kelly and Christopher Baswell (eds), *Medieval Manuscripts: Their Makers and Users. A Special Issue of Viator in Honor of Richard and Mary Rouse* (Turnhout: Brepols, 2011), pp. 77–102.
Murray, Alan V., 'Sex, death and the problem of single women on the First Crusade', in Ruthy Gertwagen and Elizabeth Jeffreys (eds), *Shipping, Trade and Crusade in the Medieval Mediterranean: Studies in Honour of John Pryor* (Farnham: Ashgate, 2012), pp. 255–70.
Murray, Alan V., 'Women in the royal succession of the Latin Kingdom of Jerusalem (1099–1291)', in *Mächtige Frauen? Königinnen und Fürstinnen im Europäischen Mittelalter (11. –14. Jahrhundert)* (Ostfildern: J. Thorbecke, 2015), pp. 131–62.
Niall, Christie and Maya Yazigi, *Noble Ideals and Bloody Realities* (Leiden: Brill, 2006).
Nicholson, Helen J., 'Women on the Third Crusade', *Journal of Medieval History* 23 (1997), pp. 335–49.
Nicholson, Helen J., *Medieval Warfare: Theory and Practice of War in Europe, 300–1500* (Basingstoke: Palgrave Macmillan, 2003).
Nicholson, Helen J., 'Women's involvement in the crusades', in Adrian J. Boas (ed), *The Crusader World* (Abingdon: Routledge, 2016), pp. 54–67.

Nolan, Barbara, 'The Judgement of Paris in the *Roman d'Enéas*: a new look at sources and significance', *Classical Bulletin* 56 (1980), pp. 52–56.
Nolan, Barbara, 'Ovid's *Heroides* contextualized: foolish love and legitimate marriage in the *Roman d'Enéas*', *Mediaevalia* 13 (1989), pp. 157–87.
North, Sally Burch, 'The role of advice in Marie de France's *Eliduc*', in Sally Burch North (ed), *Studies in Medieval French Language and Literature Presented to Brian Woledge* (Geneva: Droz, 1988), pp. 111–34.
Nye, Robert A., 'Western masculinities in war and peace', *The American Historical Review* 112 (2007), pp. 417–38.
Obermeier, Anita, 'Witches and the myth of the medieval *Burning Times*', in Stephen Harris and Bryon L. Grigsby (eds), *Misconceptions about the Middle Ages* (New York: Routledge, 2008), pp. 218–29.
O'Callaghan, Tamara F., 'Love imagery in Benoît de Sainte-Maure's *Roman de Troie*, John Gower's *Confessio Amantis* and Geoffrey Chaucer's *Troilus and Criseyde*' (unpublished PhD thesis, University of Toronto, 1995).
O'Callaghan, Tamara F., 'Tempering scandal: Eleanor of Aquitaine and Benoît de Sainte-Maure's *Roman de Troie*', in Bonnie Wheeler and John Carmi Parsons (eds), *Eleanor of Aquitaine: Lord and Lady* (New York: Palgrave Macmillan, 2003), pp. 301–17.
Ogée, Jean, *Dictionnaire Historique et Géographique de la Province de Bretagne*, 2 vols (Rennes: Molliex, 1843–53).
Parsons, John Carmi, 'Mothers, daughters, marriage, power: some Plantagenet evidence, 1150–1500', in John Carmi Parsons (ed), *Medieval Queenship* (New York: St. Martin's Press, 1998), pp. 63–78.
Parsons, John Carmi, 'Damned if she didn't and damned when she did: bodies, babies and bastards in the lives of two queens of France', in Bonnie Wheeler and John Carmi Parsons (eds), *Eleanor of Aquitaine: Lord and Lady* (New York: Palgrave Macmillan, 2003), pp. 265–99.
Pascua, Esther, 'Peace among equals: war and treaties in twelfth-century Europe', in Philip de Souza and John France (eds), *War and Peace in Ancient and Medieval History* (Cambridge: Cambridge University Press, 2008), pp. 193–210.
Peek, Wendy Chapman, 'King by day, Queen by night: the virgin Camille in the *Roman d'Enéas*', in Kathleen Coyne Kelly and Marina Leslie (eds), *Menacing Virgins: Representing Virginity in the Middle Ages and Renaissance* (Newark, NJ: University of Delaware Press, 1999), pp. 71–82.
Petit, Aimé, 'Aspects de l'influence d'Ovide sur les romans antiques du XIIe siècle', in R. Chevallier (ed), *Présence d'Ovide. Actes du Colloque d'Azay-le-Ferron (26–28 Sept. 1980)* (Paris: Les Belles Lettres, 1982), pp. 219–40.
Petit, Aimé, 'La reine Camille dans le *Roman d'Enéas*', *Les Lettres Romanes* 36 (1982), pp. 5–40.
Petit, Aimé, 'Le traitement courtois du thème des Amazones d'après trois romans antiques: *Enéas, Troie* et *Alexandre*', *Le Moyen Âge* 89 (1983), pp. 63–84.
Petit, Aimé, *Naissances du Roman. Les Techniques Littéraires dans les Romans Antiques du XIIe Siècle* (Paris: Champion-Slatkine, 1985).
Petit, Aimé, 'La réception de la *Thébaïde* à travers la tradition manuscrite du *Roman de Thèbes*', in Dominique Boutet and others (eds), *'Plaist vos Oïr Bone Cançon Vallant?' Mélanges de Langue et de Littérature Médiévales offerts à François Suard* (Lille: Université Charles-de-Gaulle Lille 3, 1999), pp. 703–12.
Petit, Aimé, *L'Anachronisme dans les Romans Antiques du XIIe Siècle: le Roman de Thèbes, le Roman d'Enéas, le Roman de Troie, le Roman d'Alexandre* (Paris: Champion, 2002).

Petit, Aimé, 'La chevalerie au prisme de l'Antiquité', *Revue des Langues Romanes* 110 (2006), pp. 17–34.
Petit, Aimé, 'De l'épopée antique au roman médiéval', in Michèle Guéret-Laferté and Daniel Mortier (eds), *D'un Genre Littéraire à l'Autre* (Mont-Saint-Aignan: Publications des Universités de Rouen et du Havre, 2008), pp. 41–50.
Petit, Aimé, 'A commentary on some singular aspects of Manuscript A (BnF 375) of the *Roman de Thèbes*', *Le Moyen Âge* 119 (2013), pp. 597–620.
Phillips, Joanna, 'The experience of sickness and health during crusader campaigns to the eastern Mediterranean, 1095–1274' (unpublished PhD thesis, University of Leeds, 2017).
Phillips, Kim M., 'Written on the body: reading rape from the twelfth to fifteenth centuries', in Noël James Menuge (ed), *Medieval Women and Law* (Woodbridge: Boydell Press, 2000), pp. 125–44.
Phillips, William D., *Slavery in Medieval and Early Modern Iberia* (Philadelphia: University of Pennsylvania Press, 2014).
Poirion, Daniel, 'De l'*Enéide* à l'*Enéas*: mythologie et moralisation', *Cahiers de Civilisation Médiévale* 19 (1976), pp. 213–29.
Poole, Reginald L., 'The masters of the schools at Paris and Chartres in John of Salisbury's time', *The English Historical Review* 35 (1920), pp. 321–42.
Pope, Nancy P., 'The *Aeneid* and the *Roman d'Enéas*: a medieval translator at work', *Papers on Language and Literature* 16 (1980), pp. 243–49.
Porter, L. C., 'The "Cantilène de Sainte Eulalie": phonology and graphemics', *Studies in Philology* 57 (1960), pp. 587–96.
Post, J. B., 'Ravishment of women and the statutes of Westminster', in J. H. Baker (ed), *Legal Records and the Historian* (London: Royal Historical Society, 1978), pp. 150–64.
Powell, James M., 'The role of women in the Fifth Crusade', in Benjamin Z. Kedar (ed), *The Horns of Hattin* (Jerusalem: Yad Izhak-Ben-Zvi, Israel Exploration Society, 1992), pp. 294–301.
Power, Daniel, 'The stripping of a queen: Eleanor of Aquitaine in the thirteenth-century Norman tradition', in Marcus Bull and Catherine Léglu (eds), *The World of Eleanor of Aquitaine: Literature and Society in South France between the Eleventh and Thirteenth Centuries* (Woodbridge: Boydell Press, 2005), pp. 115–36.
Pratt, Karen, 'The image of the queen in Old French literature', in Anne Duggan (ed), *Queens and Queenship in Medieval Europe* (Woodbridge: Boydell Press, 2002), pp. 235–62.
Prawer, Joshua, *A History of the Latin Kingdom of Jerusalem* (London: Weidenfeld and Nicolson, 1972).
Pryor, John H., *Logistics of Warfare in the Age of the Crusades* (Aldershot: Ashgate, 2006).
Purcell, Maureen, 'Women crusaders: a temporary canonical aberration', in L. O. Frappell (ed), *Principalities, Powers and Estates* (Adelaide: Adelaide University Union Press, 1979), pp. 57–67.
Putter, Ad, 'Transvestite knights in medieval life and history', in Jeffrey Jerome Cohen and Bonnie Wheeler (eds), *Becoming Male in the Middle Ages* (New York: Garland Publishing, 1997), pp. 279–302.
Reno, Christine, 'Virginity as an ideal in Christine de Pizan's *Cité des Dames*', in Diane Bornstein (ed), *Ideals for Women in the Works of Christine de Pizan* (Detroit: Michigan Consortium for Medieval and Early Modern Studies, 1981), pp. 69–90.
Ridoux, Charles, 'Trois exemples d'une approche symbolique: le tombeau de Camille, le nain Frocin, le lion', in *Et c'est la Fin pour quoy Sommes Ensemble: Hommage à Jean Dufournet* (Paris: Champion, 1993), pp. 1217–21.

Robbert, Louise Buenger, 'Venice and the crusades', in Norman P. Zacour and Harry W. Hazard (eds), *A History of the Crusades: The Impact of the Crusades on the Near East* (Madison: University of Wisconsin Press, 1985), pp. 379–451.

Robertson, Elizabeth and Christine M. Rose (eds), *Representing Rape in Medieval and Early Modern Literature* (New York: Palgrave Macmillan, 2001).

Roques, Mario, 'Le manuscrit fr. 794 de la Bibliothèque nationale et le scribe Guyot', *Romania* 73 (1952), pp. 177–99.

Rouse, Mary and Richard Rouse, 'The crusade as context: the manuscripts of *Athis et Prophilias*', in Keith Busby and Christopher Kleinhenz (eds), *Courtly Arts and the Art of Courtliness: Selected Papers from the Eleventh Triennial Congress of the International Courtly Literature Society, University of Wisconsin-Madison, 29 July–4 August 2004* (Cambridge: D. S. Brewer, 2006), pp. 49–103.

Royer, Katherine, 'The body in parts: reading the execution ritual in late medieval England', *Historical Reflections* 29 (2003), pp. 319–39.

Rubin, Miri, *Mother of God: A History of the Virgin Mary* (New Haven: Yale University Press, 2009).

Rudy, Kathryn M., 'Kissing images, unfurling rolls, measuring wounds, sewing badges and carrying talismans: considering some Harley manuscripts through the physical rituals they reveal', *Electronic British Library Journal* (2011), pp. 1–56.

Russell, Delbert W., 'The cultural context of the French prose *remaniement* of the *Life of Edward the Confessor by a Nun of Barking Abbey*', in Jocelyn Wogan-Browne (ed), *Language and Culture in Medieval Britain: The French of England c. 1100–c. 1500* (York: Boydell and Brewer, 2009), pp. 290–302.

Ruys, Juanita Feros, '"He who kills himself liberates a wretch": Abelard on suicide', in Babette S. Hellemans (ed), *Rethinking Abelard: A Collection of Critical Essays* (Leiden: Brill, 2014), pp. 230–50.

Salih, Sarah, *Versions of Virginity in Late Medieval England* (Cambridge: D. S. Brewer, 2001).

Salverda de Grave, J. J., 'Recherches sur les sources du *Roman de Thèbes*', in *Mélanges de Philologie Romane et d'Histoire Littéraire offerts à M. Maurice Wilmotte, Professeur à l'Université de Liège, à l'Occasion de son 25ᵉ Anniversaire d'Enseignement, Accompagné de Facsimilés et d'un Portrait* (Paris: H. Champion, 1910), pp. 595–618.

Saunders, Corinne J., 'A matter of consent: Middle English Romance and the law of *raptus*', in Noël James Menuge (ed), *Medieval Women and the Law* (Woodbridge: Boydell Press, 2000), pp. 105–24.

Saunders, Corinne J., *Rape and Ravishment in the Literature of Medieval England* (Cambridge: Cambridge University Press, 2001).

Saunders, Corinne J., 'Women and warfare in medieval English writing', in Corinne Saunders, Françoise Le Saux and Neil Thomas (eds), *Writing War: Medieval Literary Responses to Warfare* (Cambridge: D. S. Brewer, 2004), pp. 187–212.

Saunders, Corinne J., 'Sexual violence in wars: the Middle Ages', in Hans-Henning Kortüm (ed), *Transcultural Wars from the Middle Ages to the Twenty-First Century* (Berlin: Akademie Verlag, 2006), pp. 151–64.

Sayers, William, 'The Wyvern', *Neuphilologische Mitteilungen* 109 (2008), pp. 457–65.

Scaffai, Marco, *Baebii Italici* Ilias Latina: *Introduzione, Edizione Critica, Traduzione Italiana e Commento* (Bologna: Pàtron Editore, 1982).

Scalini, Mario, 'Armi e Armature', in Enrico Castelnuovo and Giuseppe Sergi (eds), *Arti e Storia nel Medioevo, 2: Del Costruire. Tecniche, Artisti, Artigiani, Committenti* (Turin: Einaudi, 2003), pp. 441–53.

Scheller, Robert, 'The *Lit de Justice* or how to sit on a bed of estate', in *Annus Quadriga Mundi: Opstellen over Misseleeuwse Kunst Opgedragen aan Prof. de. Anna C. Esmeijer* (Utrecht: De Walburg Pers, 1989), pp. 193-202.
Schroeder, Horst, *Der Topos der Nine Worthies in Literatur und bildender Kunst* (Göttingen: Vandenhoeck & Ruprecht, 1971).
Shahar, Shulamith, *The Fourth Estate: A History of Women in the Middle Ages* (London: Methuen, 1983).
Sharrock, Alison, 'Warrior women in Roman epic', in Jacqueline Fabre-Serris and Alison Keith (eds), *Women and War in Antiquity* (Baltimore: Johns Hopkins University Press, 2015), pp. 157-78.
Shirt, David J., 'The Dido episode in *Enéas*: the reshaping of tragedy and its stylistic consequences', *Medium Ævum* 51 (1982), pp. 3-17.
Short, Ian, 'Patrons and polyglots: French literature in twelfth-century England', in Marjorie Chibnall (ed), *Anglo-Norman Studies XIV: Proceedings of the Battle Conference 1991* (Woodbridge: Boydell Press, 1992), pp. 229-49.
Siberry, Elizabeth, *Criticism of Crusading 1095-1274* (Oxford: Clarendon, 1985).
Singerman, Jerome, *Under Clouds of Poesy: Poetry and Truth in French and English Reworkings of the Aeneid, 1160-1513* (New York: Garland, 1986).
Smeets, Jean Robert, *La Bible de Jehan Malkaraume (Ms. Paris, Bibl. Nat. f.fr. 903) (XIIIe/ XIVe siècle)*, 2 vols (Amsterdam: Van Gorcum, 1978).
Smeets, Jean Robert, 'La Bible de Jehan Malkaraume', in W. Lourdaux and D. Verhelst (eds), *The Bible and Medieval Culture* (Leuven: Leuven University Press, 1979), pp. 220-35.
Solterer, Helen, 'Figures of female militancy in medieval France', *Signs* 16 (1991), pp. 522-49.
Stafford, Pauline, 'The portrayal of royal women in England, mid-tenth to mid-twelfth centuries', in John Carmi Parsons (ed), *Medieval Queenship* (Stroud: Alan Sutton, 1994), pp. 143-67.
Stahuljak, Zrinka, *Bloodless Genealogies of the French Middle Ages: Translatio, Kinship and Metaphor* (Gainesville: University Press of Florida, 2005).
Stahuljak, Zrinka, 'Sexuality, shame and the genesis of Romance', in William Burgwinkle, Nicholas Hammond and Emma Wilson (eds), *The Cambridge History of French Literature* (Cambridge: Cambridge University Press, 2011), pp. 57-66.
Stock, Lorraine Kochanske, '"Arms and the (wo)man" in medieval Romance: the gendered arming of female warriors in the *Roman d'Enéas* and Heldris's *Roman de Silence*', *Arthuriana* 5 (1995), pp. 56-83.
Strickland, Matthew, *War and Chivalry: The Conduct and Perception of War in England and Normandy, 1066-1217* (Cambridge: Cambridge University Press, 1996).
Stringer, Keith J., *The Reign of Stephen: Kingship, Warfare and Government in Twelfth-Century England* (London: Routledge, 1993).
Stuard, Susan Mosher, 'Ancillary evidence for the decline of medieval slavery', *Past and Present* 149 (1995), pp. 3-28.
Swanson, R. N., *The Twelfth-Century Renaissance* (Manchester: Manchester University Press, 1999).
Swift, Helen J., *Gender, Writing and Performance: Men Defending Women in Late Medieval France (1440-1538)* (Oxford: Clarendon Press, 2008).
Tanner, Heather J. (ed), *Medieval Elite Women and the Exercise of Power, 1100-1400: Moving Beyond the Exceptionalist Debate* (Cham: Palgrave Macmillan, 2019).

Taylor, Craig, 'The Salic Law, French queenship, and the defense of women in the late Middle Ages', *French Historical Studies* 29 (2006), pp. 543–64.
Taylor, Craig, *Chivalry and the Ideals of Knighthood in France during the Hundred Years War* (Cambridge: Cambridge University Press, 2013).
Thoss, Dagmar, *Benoît de Sainte-Maure: Roman de Troie (Österreichische Nationalbibliothek, Wien, Codex 2571)* (Munich: Lengenfelder, 1989).
Tolhurst, Fiona, 'What ever happened to Eleanor? Reflections of Eleanor of Aquitaine in Wace's *Roman de Brut* and Lawman's *Brut*', in Bonnie Wheeler and John Carmi Parsons (eds), *Eleanor of Aquitaine: Lord and Lady* (New York: Palgrave Macmillan, 2003), pp. 319–36.
Truax, Jean A., 'Anglo-Norman women at war: valiant soldiers, prudent strategists or charismatic leaders?', in Donald J. Kagay and L. J. Andrew Villalon (eds), *The Circle of War in the Middle Ages* (Woodbridge: Boydell Press, 1999), pp. 111–25.
Turner, Ralph V., 'Eleanor of Aquitaine and her children: an inquiry into medieval family attachment', *Journal of Medieval History* 14 (1988), pp. 321–35.
Turner, Ralph V., *Eleanor of Aquitaine: Queen of France, Queen of England* (London: Yale University Press, 2011).
Van Wyhe, Cordula (ed), *Female Monasticism in Early Modern Europe: An Interdisciplinary View* (Aldershot: Ashgate, 2008).
Varty, Kenneth, 'The giving and withholding of consent in late twelfth-century French literature', *Reading Medieval Studies* 12 (1986), pp. 27–49.
Venarde, Bruce L., *Women's Monasticism and Medieval Society: Nunneries in France and England, 890–1215* (Ithaca: Cornell University Press, 1997).
Verbruggen, J. F., 'Women in medieval armies', *Journal of Medieval Military History* 4 (2006), pp. 119–36.
Verdon, Timothy, *Mary in Western Art* (Washington, DC: Pope John Paul II Cultural Center, 2006).
Viejo, Jesús Rodríguez, 'Royal manuscript patronage in late Ducal Normandy: a context for the female patron portrait of the Fécamp Psalter (*c.* 1180)', *Cerae* 3 (2016), pp. 1–35.
Vines, Amy N., 'Invisible woman: rape as a chivalric necessity in medieval Romance', in Amanda Hopkins and others (eds), *Sexual Culture in the Literature of Medieval Britain* (Cambridge: D. S. Brewer, 2014), pp. 161–80.
Walker, Sue Sheridan, 'Punishing convicted ravishers: statutory strictures and actual practice in thirteenth and fourteenth-century England', *Journal of Medieval History* 13 (1987), pp. 237–50.
Warren, F. M., 'On the Latin sources of *Thèbes* and *Enéas*', *Publications of the Modern Language Association of America* 16 (1901), pp. 375–87.
Waswo, Richard, 'Our ancestors, the Trojans: inventing cultural identity in the Middle Ages', *Exemplaria: A Journal of Theory in Medieval and Renaissance Studies* 7 (1995), pp. 269–90.
Weikert, Katherine, 'The princesses who might have been hostages: the custody and marriages of Margaret and Isabella of Scotland, 1209–1220s', in Matthew Bennett and Katherine Weikert (eds), *Medieval Hostageship c. 700–1500* (New York: Routledge, 2016), pp. 237–71.
Wheeler, Bonnie and John Carmi Parsons (eds), *Eleanor of Aquitaine: Lord and Lady* (New York: Palgrave Macmillan, 2003).
White, Graeme J., *King Stephen's Reign (1135–54)* (Woodbridge: Boydell Press, 2008).

Wijsman, Hanno, *Luxury Bound: Illustrated Manuscript Production and Noble and Princely Book Ownership in the Burgundian Netherlands (1400–1550)* (Turnhout: Brepols, 2010).
Willard, Charity Cannon, 'Early images of the female warrior: Minerva, the Amazons, Joan of Arc', *Minerva* 3 (1988), pp. 1–11.
Wilmotte, Maurice, *L'Évolution du Roman Français aux Environs de 1150* (Paris, 1903).
Wogan-Browne, Jocelyn (ed), *Saints' Lives and Women's Literary Culture, 1150–1300: Virginity and Its Authorizations* (Oxford: Oxford University Press, 2001).
Wogan-Browne, Jocelyn, *Language and Culture in Medieval Britain: The French of England c. 1100–c.1500* (York: Boydell and Brewer, 2009).
Wolfthal, Diane, *Images of Rape: The 'Heroic' Tradition and Its Alternatives* (Cambridge: Cambridge University Press, 1999).
Wright, Monica L., *Weaving Narrative: Clothing in Twelfth-Century French Romance* (Philadelphia: Pennsylvania State University Press, 2009).
Wyatt, David, *Slaves and Warriors in Medieval Britain and Ireland, 800–1200* (Leiden: Brill, 2009).

Index

abduction 23–8, 49–51
Adela of Blois 138
Adela of Normandy 119
advisors and advice-giving 121–30, 137–8
Aethicus Hieronymus, *Cosmographia* 97
Albert of Aachen, *Historia Ierosolimitana* 87–8
Albert the Great 94
Alice de Montmorency 138
Alice of Antioch 120
Amazons 19–20, 104, 107
Anarchy, The, civil war in England and Normandy 6, 96
Andromache, wife of Hector
  as an advisor 125–8
  after the fall of Troy 48
  blocking Hector from battle 18, 37–8, 90
  caring for Hector 79–80, 83
  descriptions of 107
  grieving 54
  illustrations of (*see* illustrations)
Antigone, daughter of Jocasta and Oedipus 6, 30, 53, 55–6, 131–2
Argia, daughter of King Adrastus and *amie* of Polynices 6, 9, 37, 53, 142
Aristotle, *Politics* 94
armour (*see* military equipment)
Aucassin et Nicolette 49, 82

Baldwin III of Jerusalem 120
Baldwin IV of Hainaut 96
Béatrice de Gavre 16–18, 93
Beatrice I of Burgundy 17
Beaufort, Margaret 143
Beaujeu, Renaut de, *Le Bel Inconnu* 89
Benoît de Sainte-Maure 5–9
  Chronique des Ducs de Normandie 9–11
  Roman de Troie (*see Roman de Troie*)
Bernard of Clairvaux 110
Béroul, *Le Roman de Tristan* 82

Bertrade of Montfort 54
Bertram, John of Thorp Kilton 16
Biblical *topoi* 41–2, 44, 50–1, 97, 121, 125
Biket, Robert, *Lai du Cor* 109
Black Agnes 143
Blanche of Castile 142
Boccaccio, Giovanni, *De Mulieribus Claris* 142
Bodel, Jean 2
Boni, Lucas of Florence 16
booty (*see* prizes and prize-giving)
Borromeo, Cardinal Federico 16–17
Bourdelot, Pierre 17
Bridget of Sweden 109
Briseide, Greek *amie* of Troilus and Diomedes 30–2, 46–8, 87, 91
burial of the dead (*see also* tombs) 78, 83–5, 87, 141

Camille, queen of the Volsci
  as a warrior 93–4, 97–106
  as one of the *Neuf Preuses* 142
  death of 83, 112–16
  illustrations of 20, 133
  in other literary texts 142
  virginity of 106–8
Cantilène de Sainte Eulalie 43
Cassandra, daughter of Priam and Hecuba
  as advisor 122–5, 128–9, 137
  as peacemaker 37
  after the fall of Troy 48
  caring for Hector 81
  grieving 54
  in other literary texts 142
chansons de geste 3, 37, 39, 110, 137–8
  Aymeri de Narbonne 121
  Chanson d'Antioche 15, 77, 88
  Chanson d'Aspremont 15
  Chanson de Floovant 37
  Chanson de Guillaume 121, 138
  Chanson de Jérusalem 78

Chanson de la Croisade Albigeoise 33, 88, 138
Chanson de Roland 47
Garin le Loherenc 121, 138
Girart de Vienne 39, 121
Charles V, Holy Roman emperor 16–17
Charles VII of France 16
chastity (*see* virginity)
Chaucer, Geoffrey, *Canterbury Tales* 97
chivalric orders 95
chivalry 14, 34, 97–106, 109–17, 142, 183 n.43
Christina of Markygate, *Vita* 97
Clemence of Barking 109
clothes and clothing 32, 79, 88–90, 101, 131
Continuations, of the Grail narrative 14, 109
Cretensis, Dictys, *Ephemeridos belli Trojani*
  representation of Cassandra 122
  representation of Hecuba 44, 134
  representation of Helen of Troy 24, 26–7
  representation of Hesione 50
  representation of hostages 47
  representation of Medea 129
  representation of Penthesilea 101–5
  representation of Polyxena 41–2
  source for the *Roman de Troie* 4–6, 97
Crusades
  Albigensian Crusade 138
  Fifth Crusade 82
  First Crusade 5, 15, 40–1, 49, 77–8, 87–8, 95
  Fourth Crusade 8, 21
  Second Crusade 5, 87, 95–7, 120
  Third Crusade 48–9
Curthose, Robert 5, 119

d'Armagnac, Jacques, duke of Nemours 16
d'Arras, Gautier, *Ille et Galeron* 14–15, 17
d'Arras, Jean, *Roman de Mélusine* 78, 90, 133
d'Averton, Jean, lord of Couldreau 16
de Bourbon, Jacques II 15–16, 133
de Bourbon, Jean 15–16, 133
de Champagne, Marie 8–v9, 17
de Charny, Geoffrey, *Livre de Chevalerie* 34
de Croÿ, Charles, count of Chimay 16
de Fougères, Etienne, *Livre des Manières* 34

de France, Marie 15, 17, 28
Deiphyle, daughter of King Adrastus 6, 9, 53, 142
de Mazarin, Cardinal 17
de Pizan, Christine 23, 94, 109, 137, 142
  Cité des Dames 45, 94, 97, 108, 142
  Ditié de Jeanne d'Arc 97
  Epistre Othea 128–29, 142
  Livre des Trois Vertus 23, 37, 137–9
Despenser, Henry, the 'fighting' bishop of Norwich 16–17, 133
de Troyes, Chrétien 9, 14, 20, 51, 98
  Cligès 14
  Erec et Enide 14, 28, 82
  Lancelot, ou le Chevalier de la Charrette 23, 78, 89
  Perceval, ou le conte du Graal 14, 109
  Yvain 14, 28, 53, 78, 82
Dido, queen of Carthage 4, 6, 13, 18, 44–5, 142
d'Oisy, Huon, *Tournoiement des Dames* 93

Eleanor of Aquitaine 7–10, 51, 54, 87, 96–7, 133
Eleanor of Castile 7, 142
Eleanor of Provence 142
enslavement (*see* slavery)
espionage (*see* spying)
euhemerism 90
execution 39, 42–7, 57

fabliaux 13, 15
Fantosme, Jordan, *Chronique de la Guerre entre les Anglais et les Écossais en 1173 et 1174* 88, 138
Fille du Comte de Ponthieu, La 51
Fontevraud Abbey 54
food (*see* logistics)
Fredegar, *Chronicle* 12
Fulcher of Chartre, *Historia Hierosolymitana* 41, 88

gender and gendering (*see also* masculinity) 35–8, 57, 90, 99–100, 110, 141
Geoffrey of Anjou 51
Geoffrey of Monmouth, *Historia Regum Britanniae* 12
Geoffrey of Villehardouin 8–9, 16–17, 21
Gesta Francorum 41, 77

Gesta Stephani 57
gifts and gift-giving 28, 30–2, 86–9, 129
Giles of Rome 94
Gonzaga, Francesco I 16
Gonzaga, Guido 16
Goyon-Matignon family 15–16
Grandes Chroniques de France 3, 11
Gratian, *Concordantia Discordantium Canonum* 33–4
Gregory VII, Pope 95
Guibert of Nogent 77

hagiography 43–4, 109, 113, 139
Harley, Edward, earl of Oxford 17
healing (*see* health care)
health care 79–87, 91, 129, 141
Hector et Hercule 15
Hecuba, queen consort of Troy
  blocking Hector from battle 126–8
  caring for Hector and others 79–81, 86
  death of 44
  grieving 52–4
  illustrations of (*see* illustrations)
  negotiating with Achilles 36–7, 134–7
  in other literary texts 142
  retaliation against the Greeks 44
Heldris of Cornwall, *Le Roman de Silence* 15, 93, 108–9
Helen of Troy, *amie* of Paris
  abduction of 23–8, 33–5, 51
  as an *amie* 53
  blocking Hector from battle 126–7
  caring for the Trojan men 81, 86–7
  descriptions of 107
  grieving 54
  illustrations of (*see* illustrations)
  in other literary texts 142
Henry I of England 5, 95, 120
Henry II of England 6–10, 15, 20, 54, 96, 119–20
Henry IV, Holy Roman emperor 95
Henry V, Holy Roman emperor 95
heraldry 102, 132
Hesione, sister of Priam 23–4, 27–8, 33–4, 48–51
Hipsipyle, a noblewoman of *Thèbes* 77, 142
Histoire ancienne jusqu'à César 15, 23
Histoire de Guillaume le Maréchal 33

Historia Brittonum 12
History of William Marshal 29
Holy Grail narratives and *topoi* (*see also* Continuations of the Grail narrative and de Troyes, Chrétien) 14, 106, 109–10
homosocialism 36, 100
hostageship 46–7, 55–6
Houdenc, Raoul de, *Vengeance Raguidel* 15
Hundred Years War 16, 84–5, 88

iconophilia 18–19
illustrations of the *Romans d'Antiquité* 11–13, 143, 155–63
  of Achilles abstaining from battle 36–7
  of Andromache 127–9, 155–63
  of armour-making 89
  of Briseide 31–32, 156–8, 160–3
  of Camille 20, 133
  of Cassandra 124–5, 157–60, 162–3
  damage to 18–19, 133
  of Dido 45–6, 156
  of Hecuba 44, 134–6, 155–63
  of Helen 18–19, 25, 133, 155–60, 162
  of Hesione 24, 157–8, 162
  of Lavine 32, 156
  of Medea 130, 156–8, 160, 162
  of MS Nt in general 15
  omissions of 20, 133
  of Penthesilea and the Amazons 19–20, 102–4, 113–15, 155–7, 159, 161–3
  of Polyxena 44, 155–63
  of *Thèbes* in general 13
  of *Troie* in general 11, 13
  of unnamed women 32
  of women as booty 48
  of women grieving 54, 57
  of women handling military equipment 90–1
  of women in general 18–19
  of women providing comfort to men 86–7
  of women providing health care 79–81
Imād ad-Din al-Isfahani 48–9
Innocent III, pope 125
Investiture Controversy 95, 120
Isabella of Aragon 142
Isabella of Castile 142

Isabella of France 133, 143
Isidore of Seville, *Etymologiae* 97, 108
Ismene, daughter of Jocasta and Oedipus 6, 53–4

Joan of Arc 108, 117, 125, 141, 143, 174 n.17
Joan of Navarre 143
Joanna of Flanders 143
Jocasta, queen consort of Thebes 13, 18, 55–6, 121–2, 130–3, 142
John of Joinville 82
John of Salisbury 97
Johnson, Maurice 17
John II of France 16–17
Judith, anonymous Old English poem 97
Julian of Norwich 109
Just War doctrine 39

La Curne de Sainte-Palaye, Jean-Baptiste 17
Lai du Cort Mantel 109
la Mare, Philibert de 17
Laval family 16
Lavine, noblewoman of Latium and future wife of Aeneas 6, 18, 28–9, 32–3, 133, 142
Le Fèvre, Jean, *Livre de Leësce* 13, 94
le Franc, Martin, *Champion des Dames* 142
Lichtenstein, Ulrich von 116
Livre de Caradoc 109
logistics 77–8
Louis VII of France 7, 87
Louis IX of France 82
Louis XIV of France 17, 133
Lull, Ramon, *Libre del Ordre de Cavayleria* 34

MacDuff, Isabelle 143
Malory, Thomas, *Morte d'Arthur* 109–10
Marbod, bishop of Rennes 94
Margaret of Anjou 143
masculinity (*see also* gender and gendering) 23, 30, 33–6, 38
Matilda, Holy Roman empress 6, 95–6, 119–20
Matilda of Anjou 54

Matilda of Boulogne 96, 119
Matilda of Canossa 95, 114, 119
Matilda of Carinthia 54
Matilda of Flanders 119
Matilda (or Edith) of Scotland 120
Medea, daughter of King Aeëtes and *amie* of Jason 18–19, 107, 129–30, 142
medical care (*see* health care)
Melisende of Jerusalem 120
military equipment 84, 88–91, 102, 126
military orders 95
Milon of Brabant 16–17, 21
Minstrel of Reims 97
Montfort, Simon de 88
Moro, Cristoforo 16
Mort Artu 78

negotiators and negotiation 96, 130–5, 137
Neuf Preux and *Neuf Preuses* 13, 94, 106–10, 116–17, 142

Oliver of Paderborn, *Historia Damiatina* 78, 88
Ordène de Chevalerie 15, 20, 34
Ovid 5–6, 24, 38, 97
Ovide moralisé 78

peace agreements and negotiations 34, 37–8, 48, 112–16, 121, 132–9
Peace of God movement 37
Penthesilea, queen of the Amazons 5, 13, 18–20, 94–108, 111–17, 142
Peter the Venerable, abbot of Cluny 94
Philip I of France 54
Phillips, Thomas 17
Phrygius, Dares, *Excidio Trojae historia*
    representation of Cassandra 122–3
    representation of Hecuba 134–5
    representation of Helen of Troy 26
    representation of Hesione 50
    representation of hostages 47
    representation of Medea 129
    representation of Penthesilea 101, 103–5
    representation of Polyxena 41–2
    source for the *Roman de Troie* 4–6, 26, 97
Pinelli, Gian Vincenzo 16

Plato, *Republic* 94
Polyxena, daughter of Priam and Hecuba
   as an *amie* 53
   during the fall of Troy 52
   execution of 42–5, 106
   grieving 54
   in illustrations 19–20, 125
   and interaction with Trojan men 81, 86, 126–7
   in other medieval texts 142
   relationship with Achilles 36–7, 134–6
   and virginity 106
prizes and prize-giving 23, 28, 48, 55–6
prostitution 86–8, 107
Ptolemy of Luca 94

rape 46, 48–51, 57, 109
Raymond of Aguilers, *Historia Francorum qui ceperunt Iherusalem* 40
Raymond of Poitiers 97
Robert of Anjou 16–17
Robert the Monk, *Historia Hierosolymitana* 87
Roman d'Alexandre 14–15, 23
Roman de Dolopathos 14
Roman d'Enéas
   manuscript tradition of 10–20
   and military equipment 89–90
   and scenes of grief 53–4
   and scenes of health care 82–3
   patronage of 7–10
   the text and its sources 4–6
   and women as reasons for war 28–9
   and women as victims of war 44–6, 56–7
   and women warriors 93, 98–108, 112–16, 142
Roman de Renart le Contrefait 109
Roman de Thèbes
   and hostages 55–6
   and logistics of warfare 77–8
   manuscript tradition of 10–20
   patronage of 7–10
   and peacemaking 37
   and scenes of grief 53–4
   and scenes of health care 80, 83–6
   the text and its sources 4–6, 41, 96
   and women as diplomats in war 121–2, 130–3
   and women as reasons for war 30–3
Roman de Troie
   and hostages 46–9
   and logistics of warfare 78
   manuscript tradition of 10–20
   patronage of 7–10
   and scenes of health care 79–86
   the text and its sources 4–6
   and women as companions 86–7
   and women as diplomats in war 122–30, 134–7
   and women as reasons for war 23–8, 30–8
   and women as victims of war 39–44, 49–55
   and women warriors 93, 98–116
romances (*see* entries under names of author or text)
Rufus, William 5

Saladin, Sultan of Egypt, Syria, Yemen and Palestine 48, 97
Salamander, daughter of Darius in *Thèbes* 55–6
Salic law 114
Saluces, Richarde de 143
sexual assault (*see* rape)
Sibylla of Anjou 96
sickness (*see* health care)
sieges 33, 77–8, 87–8, 91, 131, 134
slavery 49–50
Speculum Virginis 97
spying 88–9
Statius, *Thebaid* 4–6, 37, 53, 56, 84, 130–3
Stephen of England 6, 96
suicide 44–6, 57
Sylvia, a noblewoman of *Enéas* 56–7

Tabourot, Étienne, lord of the Accords 16
Talbot, John, earl of Shrewsbury 16–17
Theobald V of Blois 51
Thibaut IV of Blois 54
tombs (*see also* burial of the dead) 44–5, 83, 86, 114
tournaments 28, 32, 89, 93, 116
treasure (*see* prizes and prize-giving)
Tristan, prose version 109
Trivulzio, Cardinal Agostino 16–17

Trojan origin stories
    of the Anglo-Normans 12, 20
    of the Britons 12
    of the Capetian dynasty 11
    of the Franks 12
    of the French 12

Virgil, *Aeneid* 4–6, 45, 56, 101, 103
Virgin Mary 8, 97, 106, 128
virginity 43, 106–10, 113
Vitalis, Orderic 57
Vulgate cycle (of the Grail narrative) 109

Wace, Robert
    Roman de Brut 9–10, 14, 23
    Roman de Rou 9–10, 14
washing and cleanliness (*see* logistics)
water (for drinking) (*see* logistics)
weaponry (*see* military equipment)
White Ship disaster 54
William of Tyre, *Historia rerum in partibus Transmarinis Gestarum* 78, 97, 120
William the Atheling 54

www.ingramcontent.com/pod-product-compliance
Lightning Source LLC
Chambersburg PA
CBHW072232290426
44111CB00012B/2060